POOR RELIEF AND THE CHURCH IN SCOTLAND, 1560–1650

Scottish Religious Cultures *Historical Perspectives*

Series Editors: Scott R. Spurlock and Crawford Gribben

Religion has played a key formational role in the development of Scottish society shaping cultural norms, defining individual and corporate identities, and underpinning legal and political institutions. This series presents the very best scholarship on the role of religion as a formative and yet divisive force in Scottish society and highlights its positive and negative functions in the development of the nation's culture. The impact of the Scots diaspora on the wider world means that the subject has major significance far outwith Scotland.

Available titles

George Mackay Brown and the Scottish Catholic Imagination
Linden Bicket

Poor Relief and the Church in Scotland, 1560–1650
John McCallum

Forthcoming titles

The Catholic Church in Scotland: Financial Development, 1772–1930
Darren Tierney

Miracles of Healing: Psychotherapy and Religion in Twentieth-century Scotland
Gavin Miller

Presbyterianism Re-established: The Presbyteries of Dunblane and Stirling after the Williamite Revolution
Andrew Muirhead

edinburghuniversitypress.com/series/src

POOR RELIEF AND THE CHURCH IN SCOTLAND, 1560–1650

JOHN McCALLUM

EDINBURGH
University Press

For Hannah

Edinburgh University Press is one of the leading university presses in the UK. We publish academic books and journals in our selected subject areas across the humanities and social sciences, combining cutting-edge scholarship with high editorial and production values to produce academic works of lasting importance. For more information visit our website: edinburghuniversitypress.com

Edinburgh University Press Ltd
The Tun – Holyrood Road
12 (2f) Jackson's Entry
Edinburgh EH8 8PJ

First published in hardback by Edinburgh University Press 2018

Typeset in 10/12 ITC New Baskerville by
Servis Filmsetting Ltd, Stockport, Cheshire

A CIP record for this book is available from the British Library

ISBN 978 1 4744 2727 2 (hardback)
ISBN 978 1 4744 7478 8 (paperback)
ISBN 978 1 4744 2728 9 (webready PDF)
ISBN 978 1 4744 2729 6 (epub)

Contents

Tables

Acknowledgements

This book really had its origins in the research for its predecessor. When working on the kirk session minutes of Fife, I became intrigued by the collections and relief payments sitting alongside the cases of fornication, slander and adultery. Realising that they raised questions which could not be satisfactorily dealt with in a short sub-section of a doctoral thesis, or the book which it became, the subject morphed into one which would occupy me for not far short of a decade. As a result, I have amassed many years of debts to individuals and institutions, which are rather inadequately repaid here. The ideas for the project were first properly aired at the St Andrews Reformation Studies Institute's reading weekend in 2010, and the incredibly stimulating response from those present in the form of encouragement, specific suggestions, and pertinent questions was formative. As the project developed further feedback and stimulation was provided by audiences in Durham, Glasgow, the Institute of Historical Research, Stirling and Warwick, and in the closing stages of research at Edinburgh, Newman University Birmingham, and Oxford. Colleagues have been generous in conversation and correspondence ranging from points of detail and commenting on drafts, to general comparisons, principles, and encouragement, including Martyn Bennett, Jane Dawson, Helen Gair, Kevin Gould, Nick Hayes, Alan MacDonald, Roger Mason, Andrew Pettegree, Steven Reid, Jamie Reid-Baxter, Bess Rhodes, and Alec Ryrie. Particular thanks go to Chris Langley for constant encouragement, advice, references and feedback: I'm looking forward to his book coming out almost as much as I've been looking forward to this one being published.

Part way through the research for this book, I was lucky enough to join the History team at Nottingham Trent University (NTU), and I could not imagine a more fantastic group of colleagues and students to work alongside while finishing it. Special shout-outs go to Amy Fuller, Kevin Gould, Carl Kilcourse, Sergio Lussana and Jenny Woodley, and in particular to Lizbeth Powell not just for her friendship, or for all the beer, but also for putting up with limitless amounts of poor relief chat, asking the right questions, and through her own work inspiring what I hope will be my next major project. The PhD students I have had the pleasure of co-supervising have collectively taught me more about the research process than I suspect they realise. More practically I am immensely grateful to the School of Arts and Humanities at NTU for supporting my archival research and conference travel, and most importantly providing a sabbatical (or 'gap-year', or 'holiday', according to some of the aforenamed), which provided the space in which to complete the book. I also gratefully acknowledge financial assistance from the Strathmartine Trust which facilitated some of the early archival research. In the early stages I also benefitted hugely from working with Alan MacDonald on a Leverhulme-funded project on early modern climate, which enabled me to look at the church court records and the economic context in new ways (and to spend more of my time reading kirk session and presbytery minutes!). Very useful feedback and suggestions came from Edinburgh University Press's anonymous peer reviewers (as well as from referees of previous articles relating to this subject). Archivists and staff at the institutions listed in the Bibliography, especially the National Records of Scotland, have never failed to be helpful and friendly, and equal thanks must go to the extraordinarily effective Inter-Library Loan team at NTU's library. These institutions provided materials, but Nottingham's Bromley House Library provided something just as important: an incredibly conducive environment in which to write, peacefully. Although the people mentioned above (anonymously or otherwise) have made the book better than it would otherwise have been, they should not be held accountable for its flaws, which are my responsibility alone.

Closer to home, my parents continue to be supportive, reading drafts and taking an impressive interest in a subject which they are unlikely ever to have chosen for themselves. The book's dedication expresses my greatest debt. Hannah deserves to have a far cooler book than this one dedicated to her, but I am unlikely to write one, so this will have to do.

Conventions

All sums of money are expressed in pounds Scots, except on a few occasions where noted otherwise. The pound Scots was worth 1/12th of a pound Sterling as of 1603. A merk was 13s 4d, and other units or coins are explained where mentioned in the text. Throughout the text, dates are given in post-1600 style, that is assuming the year to begin on 1 January (the change is made silently where required). The original spelling has been maintained when quoting from manuscripts but the spelling and transliteration of printed primary source editions has been retained even where the editorial presentation would now be considered unconventional. Contractions (such as qlk > quhilk) have been silently expanded from both manuscripts and printed primary sources however. Spellings of names have generally been standardised (except in quotations), and place names are also normally given in their modern form although where this is not entirely obvious (for example within some quotations) the original spelling is left intact. Parish names have generally been given using the format used in the catalogues of the National Records of Scotland (NRS) for ease of identification. All manuscript church court records (CH2-prefixed) have been accessed and cited via the NRS Virtual Volumes system where they can be accessed, even though some of the originals are now located in other Scottish archives. Therefore any reference prefixed CH2 is in the NRS; other manuscript references give the archival location at the first citation. Where multiple paginations or foliations are found within a volume, the version used by the Virtual Volumes navigation system has been cited in the interests of accessibility to future researchers.

Abbreviations

ABA – Pryde, G. S. (ed.), *Ayr Burgh Accounts 1534–1624* (Edinburgh: SHS, 1937)

BUK – *Acts and Proceedings of the General Assemblies of the Kirk of Scotland, From the Year MDLX,* 3 vols (Edinburgh, 1839–45)

C&C – *Continuity and Change*

Canagait – Calderwood, A. B. (ed.), *The Buik of the Kirk of the Canagait, 1564–1567* (Edinburgh: SRS, 1961)

COP – Todd, M., *The Culture of Protestantism in Early Modern Scotland* (New Haven: Yale University Press, 2002)

CSP – *Calendar of State Papers*

DSL – *Dictionary of the Scots Language,* <www.dsl.ac.uk> (all references last accessed 2 May 2017)

DUA – Dundee University Archives

Dundonald – *Dundonald Parish Records: The Session Book of Dundonald, 1602–1731,* transcribed by Paton, H. (Edinburgh[?]: privately published, 1936)

EcHR – *Economic History Review*

ECRBA 1398–1570 – *Extracts from the Council Register of the Burgh of Aberdeen, 1398–1570* (Aberdeen: Spalding Club, 1844)

ECRBA 1570–1625 – *Extracts from the Council Register of the Burgh of Aberdeen, 1570–1625* (Aberdeen: Spalding Club, 1848)

ECRBA 1625–42 – *Extracts from the Council Register of the Burgh of Aberdeen, 1625–42* (Scottish Burgh Records Society, 1871)

ERBE 1589–1603 – *Extracts from the Records of the Burgh of Edinburgh,* A.D. *1589 to 1603* (Edinburgh: Scottish Burgh Records Society, 1927)

ERBE 1604–1626 – *Extracts from the Records of the Burgh of Edinburgh,* A.D. *1604 to 1626* (Edinburgh: Scottish Burgh Records Society, 1931)

ERBE 1626–41 – *Extracts from the Records of the Burgh of Edinburgh,* A.D. *1626 to 1641* (Edinburgh: Scottish Burgh Records Society, 1936)

ERBG – *Extracts from the Records of the Burgh of Glasgow,* A.D. *1573–1642* (Glasgow: Scottish Burgh Records Society, 1876)

ERRBS 1519–1666 – *Extracts from the Records of the Royal Burgh of Stirling,* A.D. *1519–1666* (Glasgow: Scottish Burgh Records Society, 1887)

ERRBS 1667–1752 – *Extracts from the Records of the Royal Burgh of Stirling* A.D. *1667–1752, with Appendix,* A.D. *1471–1752* (Glasgow: Scottish Burgh Records Society, 1889)

FBD – Cameron, J. K. (ed.), *The First Book of Discipline* (Edinburgh: Saint Andrew Press, 1972)

FES – Scott, H. (ed.), *Fasti Ecclesiae Scoticanae: the succession of ministers in the Church of Scotland from the Reformation*, 8 vols (Edinburgh: Oliver and Boyd, 1915–50)

GRO – General Register Office for Scotland, Edinburgh

Inverness Recs I – Mackay, W. and H. C. Boyd (eds), *Records of Inverness. Volume I, Burgh Court Books 1556–86* (Aberdeen: New Spalding Club, 1911)

Inverness Recs II – Mackay, W. and G. S. Laing (eds), *Records of Inverness. Volume II, Burgh Court Books 1602–37; Minutes of Town Council, 1637–88* (Aberdeen: New Spalding Club, 1924)

JMD – *The Autobiography and Diary of James Melville* (Edinburgh: Wodrow Society, 1842)

Knox, *Works* – Laing, D. (ed.), *The Works of John Knox*, Volumes 1–4, 6 (Edinburgh: Wodrow Society, 1895)

NRS – National Records of Scotland, Edinburgh

ODNB – *Oxford Dictionary of National Biography* (Oxford: Oxford University Press, 2004)

OPL – Mitchison, R., *The Old Poor Law in Scotland: The Experience of Poverty 1574–1845* (Edinburgh: Edinburgh University Press, 2000)

OTP –Hindle, S., *On the Parish? The Micro-Politics of Poor Relief in Rural England c. 1550–1750* (Oxford: Oxford University Press, 2004)

P&P – *Past and Present*

PKSB – Todd, M. (ed.), *The Perth Kirk Session Books* (Woodbridge: SHS, 2012 for 2008)

RPC – *Register of the Privy Council of Scotland*, eds Burton, J. H. *et al.* (Edinburgh, 1877–)

RPS – *The Records of the Parliaments of Scotland to 1707*, eds Brown, K. M. *et al.* (St Andrews, 2007–17), <http://www.rps.ac.uk> (all references last accessed 2 May 2017)

RSCHS – *Records of the Scottish Church History Society*

RStAKS – Hay Fleming, D. (ed.), *Register of the Minister, Elders and Deacons of the Christian Congregation of St Andrews, 1559–1600*, 2 vols (Edinburgh: SHS, 1889–90)

SHR – *Scottish Historical Review*

SHS – Scottish History Society

SRS – Scottish Record Society

STS – Scottish Text Society

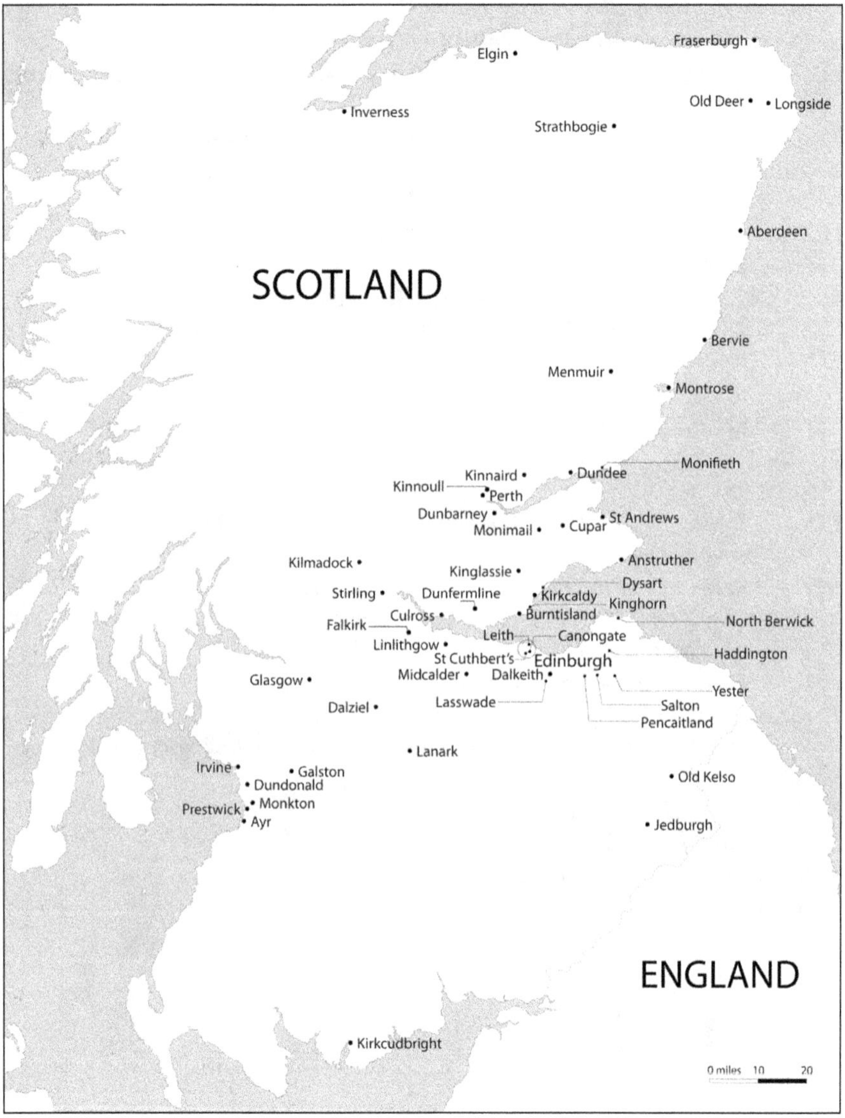

Map of Key Locations Mentioned

Introduction

The church that emerged from the Protestant Reformation of 1559–60 influenced the lives of Scots in countless ways. One of the most striking and novel ways in which it made its presence felt was through its kirk sessions. These new parish courts came to represent the local face and authority of the church, and we have come to learn a great deal about their impact on ordinary people's religion and personal lives – not least through their punishment of 'ungodly' behaviour, and the inculcation and mediation of new religious ideology. This book is about an aspect of the church's role in Scottish communities which is much less familiar. The kirk sessions were also the principal providers of poor relief. This mission reflected some of the foundational aspirations and rhetoric of the Reformation's leaders, but more than that, it became a duty which they undertook over the long term with much consistency, effort, and resilience. This relief has not been studied in any depth, especially for the first phase after the official and legal establishment of Protestantism in 1560 up until the mid-seventeenth century.

This book seeks to address this gap, and to argue that the poor relief undertaken by the kirk sessions was more effective, substantial, and wide-ranging than has been assumed. Moreover, it suggests that kirk sessions were uniquely suited to administer welfare in the context of sixteenth- and seventeenth-century Scotland, primarily, though not solely, through public collections. They were also well-placed to know (and judge) the local poor and to operate relief with some flexibility and responsiveness. This work – deeply integrated with other elements of their reforming agenda – is an important and neglected strand in the story of the Scottish Reformation, as well as the longer term history of Scottish welfare. On a wider scale, poor relief in pre-industrial Europe, and especially the reforms and developments of the sixteenth century, have received a great deal of attention from historians. Scotland is normally present as an afterthought (at best) in wider or comparative studies, but the health, durability and resilience of this local, voluntary and ecclesiastical relief system offers a new perspective on wider developments in sixteenth- and seventeenth-century poor relief.

This study therefore stands at an intersecton between various historiographies, especially of Scottish, British and European poor relief and Scottish religious and social life. This Introduction's first section situates the study within these historiographies. The next section sets out more of the context for the book's main analysis of local poor relief, introducing the policy blueprints and legislative background, economic contexts and the ecclesiastical framework for relief. Sources and methodologies are then introduced, together with the parameters and structure of the study.

Debates

Scottish Historiography

What little study there has been of Scottish poor relief prior to the late seventeenth century has been particularly concerned with national policy, legislation and the failure of schemes for funding relief through compulsory taxation. Very little serious investigation of the practice and provision of poor relief has been undertaken.[1] The main monograph on the subject, Rosalind Mitchison's *The Old Poor Law in Scotland*, ranges from the initial legislation of 1574 through to the start of the New Poor Law in 1845. The vast majority of its material relates to the later part of that period. This is understandable, because the author's main research expertise was in the later period and, as the name suggests, it is a study concerned with the poor law. The coverage prior to 1649, when implementation of the statutes was still very limited, comprises a short chapter entitled 'Getting Started', and is based on, at most, anecdotal reference to local provision. More concerned with the background and development of policy and legislation, this chapter presents a fairly bleak view of the situation in the late sixteenth and early seventeenth centuries, because of the minimal local implementation of statutory relief.[2] Provision by the church's parochial kirk sessions is briefly acknowledged, but as in Mitchison's previous articles and chapters on the topic, not taken very seriously, and not directly analysed.[3] Discussion of the later seventeenth century is slightly fuller, and by the eighteenth-century heart of the book there is some fuller consideration of local provision.[4] Justifiably, in a book covering three centuries of national history, Mitchison refers to 'untapped' primary source material in parish registers and states that she hopes that further studies will follow.[5]

This book is one such further study, and the first to explore the parochial evidence on relief across the lowlands prior to 1650. However it is

[1] This contrasts with flourishing literature on other parts of Europe; this is discussed below but useful surveys include Fideler, 'Study of the Early Modern Poor'; Olson, 'Continuity or Radical Change?'; and, for what remains, the best single-volume overview, Jutte, *Poverty*.

[2] *OPL*, pp. 6–19.

[3] *OPL*, pp. 8–12; Mitchison, 'Poor Relief and Health Care'; Mitchison, 'Making', pp. 62–3; Mitchison, 'North and South', pp. 204–5. Writing earlier on a European scale, Mitchison made clear her sense that secular systems inherently worked better than ecclesiastical relief: Mitchison, *Coping*, pp. 33–4, 36, 48–9.

[4] *OPL*, Chapters 2, 4–5. Local coverage also picks up from the later seventeenth century in Mitchison, 'Making', pp. 69–73; Mitchison, 'North and South', pp. 208–20.

[5] *OPL*, p. 2.

motivated not just by a desire to tap the neglected parish material, but also to reconsider the way that we think about the provision of poor relief in Scotland after the Reformation. This is because Mitchison's approach to this period is representative of a wider consensus in discussion of the topic, and indeed has served to reinforce it. This consensus is that in the absence of the welfare provision envisioned by parliamentary legislation of the 1570s (and of the reformed church's unsuccessful bid to reclaim ecclesiastical revenues to fund the ministry, schools and the poor), Scottish relief was weak, erratic, inadequate and ineffective.[6] Smout refers to relief provision as 'weak and mean', with only insubstantial sums paid, and emphasises the resistance to introducing compulsory rates.[7] Indeed the presence or absence of compulsory rates, as mandated by statute, is one of the key yardsticks by which Scottish relief was deemed a failure.[8] It is clear that rating was rarely implemented during this period; however it is less apparent why it should be assumed, without testing of the evidence, that the primarily voluntary relief which did take place was necessarily a failure.[9] Another characteristic of Scottish poor relief on the ground that has contributed to its neglect by historians is its ecclesiastical status. Mitchison notes that when sessions relieved the poor they did so as a Christian obligation, rather than 'as servants of the state'.[10] Whyte refers to this relief as 'simple Christian charity' rather than a 'standardised poor law system', and it is often emphasised that the church was left to provide relief as a stop-gap in the absence of statutory welfare and secular enforcement.[11] The 'lack of an effective lay system of relief' in Scotland has naturally been translated into the (very limited) commentary on Scotland in European surveys of the subject.[12] One of the aims of this book is to challenge this conflation of effectiveness with secularity, as well as the related assumption that because grand legislative visions failed, 'little or nothing was done' for the Scottish poor.[13]

Some of this suggestion of a weak, haphazard and insubstantial relief system is based on assumptions about ecclesiastical relief which follow from the failure of proposed national schemes for relief, rather than on direct

6 *OPL*, pp. 11–12; Mitchison, 'Poor Relief and Health Care', pp. 221–2, 229.

7 Smout, *History*, pp. 86–7.

8 See, for example, Mitchison, 'Poor Relief and Health Care', p. 220 (where the chapter's subject is defined as 'the failure of social legislation'); Symonds, 'Death, Birth and Marriage', pp. 97–8. The failure to raise taxation and implement legislation was also the focus of older studies, such as Cormack, *Poor Relief*, pp. 39, 41; Hamilton, *Poor Relief in South Ayrshire*, pp. 14–19; Ferguson, *Dawn of Scottish Social Welfare*, pp. 170, 175–6.

9 Mitchison, 'Poor Relief and Health Care', p. 224, revises upwards her previous estimates of the extent of rating in Scottish towns, but it was still very limited before 1649.

10 Mitchison, 'Making', pp. 62–3.

11 Whyte, *Scotland Before the Industrial Revolution*, p. 168; Mitchison, 'North and South', p. 205; Cowan, *Scottish Reformation*, p. 195; Wilbraham and Lodge, 'Responses to Poverty', p. 58; Cormack, *Poor Relief*, p. 39.

12 Jutte, *Poverty*, p. 124, apparently quoting Mitchison, 'Making', p. 64.

13 Mitchison, 'Poor Relief and Health Care', p. 220.

study, and often, inevitably, from the reading of Mitchison's work by historians writing on wider canvases. There have been some studies that have looked at relief more directly, although these still amount to a very small and imbalanced coverage overall. The richest study to follow Mitchison's book is Laura Stewart's article on Edinburgh's responses to the famine of the early 1620s, which questions the common assumption of 'little or nothing' being done, and finds strength in Edinburgh's provision of relief, even during the dearth.[14] Its wider reflection on the national picture is more pessimistic, deferring to Mitchison's emphasis on weakness in rural relief although it is striking that Stewart's analysis of Edinburgh is far more detailed and thorough than anything offered in Mitchison's work on any area prior to the later seventeenth century, whether in a time of crisis or a time of normality.[15] Also dealing with a time of famine, Karen Cullen finds that relief responses to the 'ill years' of the 1690s were more substantial than had been appreciated, although still struggling enormously with the severity of the crisis. Again, when commenting on relief beyond her own material on the 1690s, Cullen defers to Smout's assessment: 'weak and mean'.[16]

In these and other studies which engage more directly with early modern Scottish poor relief, the emphasis on the issue of compulsory rating (or lack of) remains very strong. Julian Goodare's doctoral thesis contains one of the more sensitive readings of sixteenth-century relief, and as a study of state and government focuses on the failure to impose taxation as the key narrative. 'Poor relief' and 'poor law' are sometimes treated as more-or-less synonymous, as in other studies.[17] However Goodare also draws attention to the significance of local practices of relief by kirk sessions and notes that their relief was 'making all the running' and ultimately more lasting than secular experiments.[18] Other historians have also briefly noticed the provision of relief by kirk sessions, often as part of wider studies of ecclesiastical administration. Di Folco discusses collections and distributions in a few seventeenth-century Fife parishes, while Bardgett notes varying collection totals as part of his evidence on church attendance in Monifieth from the 1560s to the 1580s.[19] Cowan's book on the Scottish Reformation mentions the relief work of some later sixteenth-century kirk sessions, while Foster

[14] Stewart, 'Poor Relief in Edinburgh', pp. 6–7.

[15] Stewart, 'Poor Relief in Edinburgh', p. 6+n.

[16] Cullen, *Famine*, pp. 98, 188.

[17] Goodare, 'Parliament and Society', pp. 405–44, especially p. 427; see also Goodare, *Government*, p. 195; Stewart, 'Poor Relief in Edinburgh', p. 6. In Mitchison, 'A parish and its poor', p. 15, 'social welfare' and 'the poor law' are treated as synonymous, and Yester from 1650 to 1700 is selected as particularly worthy of study because of two attempts to raise compulsory assessments in 1650 and 1698.

[18] Goodare, 'Parliament and Society', pp. 418, 420, 430–3, 436.

[19] di Folco, 'Discipline and Welfare', pp. 177–80; Bardgett, *Scotland Reformed*, pp. 102, 158–60. Lynch, *Edinburgh*, p. 20 touches on relief; Verschuur, *Politics or Religion?* concludes its coverage before kirk session records survive; however see *PKSB*, pp. 56–60.

offers counts of collection totals and comments briefly on distributions for a few years in three parishes.[20] These studies are not concerned with relief itself, and do not develop wider arguments on its significance, but they do identify that routine relief was taking place. More recently there has been some appreciation of the significance of the church's work in poor relief, with one study of the civil war period noting the 'incredible adeptness' of fundraising mechanisms for various causes, including relief.[21] Moreover, the existence of relief provided by kirk sessions has been invoked (though not explored) in wider arguments about sessions as local drivers of the successful bedding down of the Scottish Reformation and providers of valued social services.[22] Significantly, then, the handful of more focused assessments of relief provision, and wider studies in religious history which utilise parochial records extensively for other purposes, have tended to offer, or at least to imply, slightly more generous verdicts on local relief.[23]

As well as outlining the limited extent of studies, the previous discussion implicitly points to areas of particular focus in the literature, especially Edinburgh, and periods of dearth. Alongside Stewart's work on the famine of the early 1620s as experienced in Edinburgh, Dingwall's demographic research identified some strength in the town's relief in the 1680s and 1690s, while Houston's work on Edinburgh's social history in the century after 1660 includes some sensitive analysis of the poor.[24] The limitations on our understanding of poor relief are therefore most serious beyond Scotland's (very atypical) capital city. The two big seventeenth century famines also recur disproportionately frequently in discussions of poor relief in the wider early modern period.[25] It is essential to probe the relief system over a longer timeframe: not excluding times of famine, but not privileging them as the relief system's defining test.[26] There is also a chronological imbalance in the existing literature. In addition to studies such as Dingwall's and Cullen's, and the bulk of the analysis in Mitchison's *Old Poor Law*, later periods (including the later seventeenth century but especially the period after 1700) are much better-studied, although perhaps still not richly covered in comparative terms.[27] The normal operation of poor relief across Scottish towns and countryside during the first century

[20] Cowan, *Scottish Reformation*, pp. 194–7; Foster, *The Church Before the Covenants*, pp. 81–3.

[21] Langley, *Worship*, p. 149; see also Langley, 'Caring for soldiers'. For an urban case-study during the civil war period see McCallum, 'Charity and Conflict'.

[22] *COP*, pp. 107, 305–10; Goodare, *Government*, pp. 255–6.

[23] See also a preliminary survey in McCallum, '"Fatheris"'.

[24] Dingwall, *Late 17th-Century Edinburgh*, pp. 247–71; Houston, *Social Change*.

[25] For example *OPL*, pp. 15–17, 33–42; Mitchison, *Coping*, pp. 29, 37, 41; Smout, *History*, p. 86; Mitchison, 'North and South', pp. 208–14.

[26] *OPL*, p. 42.

[27] DesBrisay, 'Authority and Discipline'; Tyson, 'Poverty and Poor Relief'; Mitchison, 'A parish and its poor'; Mitchison, 'North and South', pp. 215–20; Houston, 'Poor Relief and the Dangerous and Criminal Insane'; Cage, *Scottish Poor Law 1745–1845*; Blaikie, 'Nuclear hardship or variant dependency?'.

or so after 1560 seems, therefore, to be one of the most urgent gaps in the literature.

Why is it worth filling this gap? This book proposes that unpicking the church's welfare provision during this period offers the potential to advance our understanding of the Reformation as well as the wider development of poor relief in early modern Europe. Scottish reformation studies have expanded in depth and in range since the 1990s, and this has included a shift towards engaging with people and localities as well as ecclesiology and church politics.[28] There remains a need for studies addressing grassroots religion, religion 'in the pew'.[29] But debate has grown on the success and impact of the reformed church during the decades after 1560, leading to more nuanced understandings of the ways in which the church achieved (or failed to achieve) its ambitions in moral discipline and education, for example.[30] Yet its other key social reform goal, improved care for the poor, has not been evaluated.[31] Indeed despite a general awareness that the church undertook poor relief, it has been an oddly marginal element in local reformation studies to date.[32] This leaves us with only a partial assessment of the new church's success in living up to its stated goals, and of the impact it had on its parishioners' lives across the social scale.

By far the most important contribution to debates around this aspect of Scottish reformation history and the lived, social history of religion from 1560 to 1640 is Margo Todd's magisterial *The Culture of Protestantism in Early Modern Scotland*. This moved beyond an emphasis on discipline to consider ways in which reformed religious culture developed and accommodated itself in Scottish communities. Amongst its innovative features was an emphasis on the more appealing features of kirk session activity: providing conflict resolution and other forms of 'social services' – such as poor relief – that might be particularly valued by congregations.[33] But although the existence of poor relief provided by kirk sessions is mentioned at various points, including in the service of this wider argument about the popular engagement achieved by kirk sessions, its extent, effectiveness and character is not subjected to direct analysis, and it is more often touched upon in relation to other issues.[34] This is very understandable: *The Culture of*

[28] McCallum, 'Introduction', in *Scotland's Long Reformation*, pp. 6–8, 10–12.

[29] *PKSB*, pp. 1n, 2, 63.

[30] Graham, *Uses of Reform*; McCallum, *Reforming*, chapters. 2, 7; Durkan, *Scottish Schools and Schoolmasters*, pp. 45–74.

[31] *FBD*, pp. 158, 160.

[32] Bardgett, *Scotland Reformed*, p. 158; Lynch, *Edinburgh*, p. 20; cf. for example Fehler, *Poor Relief and Protestantism*; Parker, *The Reformation of Community;* Wandel, *Always Among Us*.

[33] *COP*, especially. pp. 22–3, 265–314, 410; cf. Wormald, 'Reformed and Godly Scotland?', pp. 207–9.

[34] See, for example, *COP*, pp. 111, 198–9, 210, 383; by contrast, social harmony and the family receive extended treatment throughout chapters 5 and 6.

Protestantism was an anthropologically-informed cultural study of religion, and one which was hesitant about any quantification.[35] But the argument about the positive services provided by local churches is so important – and already influential[36] – that the full range of kirk session provision needs to be properly understood. Scottish historians, then, have started to become more aware of the relief work of kirk sessions, and even to ascribe some significance to it in explaining religious and cultural transformations.[37] This book proposes that it is time to look at it directly.

In doing this, there are key lessons to be considered from the terms of recent debate. Most obvious is the sessions' central role in directing local religious practice and scrutinising congregations, and as key intermediaries between parishioners and the higher authorities of the church. Their significance as important 'new and effective' agencies of local government has also been stressed, as has their systematic and accountable record-keeping practice.[38] As the twenty-first century has progressed, it has therefore become more plausible to engage seriously with kirk sessions as potentially organised and competent relief administrators. Equally, it has become apparent that the process of establishing kirk sessions across lowland parishes was not always swift, and could be a question of decades rather than years.[39] Such conclusions insist that we avoid assuming that kirk session practices were developed swiftly overnight or that early record survivals from the 1560s to the 1590s are representative of common practice in other parishes. Chapters 2 and 3 of this book therefore offer a chronological and geographical assessment of the development of kirk session practices of poor relief.

Poor relief is important for Scottish reformation studies, but it was also a process which connected local elites with some of the poorest inhabitants of sixteenth- and seventeenth-century Scotland. As Keith Brown has noted, most of the advances in early modern Scottish social history that have been concerned with the mass of the population have taken place for the period after 1660, and especially after 1700.[40] More needs to be known about ordinary Scots' lives during the earlier part of the early modern period.[41] It has often been observed, quite correctly, that studies of pre-modern poor relief tend to reveal far more about the wealthy providers of relief than

[35] *COP*, pp. 16–18.

[36] Cornell, 'Gender, Sex and Social Control', pp. 179–80, 265; Glaze, 'Women and Kirk Discipline', p. 134n.

[37] See also Stewart, *Rethinking the Scottish Revolution*, p. 19.

[38] Goodare, *Government*, pp. 201–2; Mutch, *Religion and National Identity*, especially chapters 4 and 5; Mutch, 'Data mining'; cf. Mitchison, 'North and South', p. 201.

[39] McCallum, *Reforming*, pp. 4, 37–72; Wormald, 'Reformed and Godly Scotland?', p. 206.

[40] Brown, 'Early Modern Scottish History', pp. 15–16, 19n.

[41] Signs that this is starting to be redressed include Spence, *Women, Credit and Debt*; Falconer, *Crime and Community*.

about the poor themselves.[42] This observation is inescapably true of much of this book, because it is an attempt to open up the study of poor relief practices in sixteenth- and seventeenth-century Scotland.[43] Yet even though the glimpses of ordinary poor people and their lives are fleeting and always heavily mediated by the kirk session, their records offer potential insight into the experiences of poor people which could not otherwise be available for this period. Moreover, the kirk session system was not simply funded by the wealthiest, being based on church collections among other sources, and those needing and receiving relief were not simply the poorest, as a whole range of causes could combine to push early modern Scots into states of necessity which the church might help to relieve.[44] The social relations presented in the relief records were therefore more complex than a top-down transfer of resources from the wealthy to the conventionally poor. Direct study of kirk session relief offers another potential pathway into the difficult terrain of the social history of non-elite Scots in the sixteenth and seventeenth centuries.

Wider Contexts

At this point it is worth stepping back to place the Scottish material in the context of the much larger and more diverse historiography of early modern European poor relief. In particular, important developments in thinking on English and mainland European relief need to be outlined because they suggest ways in which the current Scottish situation needs to be reconsidered, and because they point to areas where the Scottish experience has something distinctive to contribute to existing debates. These developments are overlapping, and they centre around growing challenges to teleological, binary-led, and Anglo-exceptionalist interpretations of sixteenth- and seventeenth-century European poor relief schemes.

Historians have now decisively moved away from the idea of a clean and simple transition from medieval charity to rational early modern welfare in the sixteenth century.[45] There has also been growing scepticism about teleological approaches which privilege forms of welfare that more closely resemble, or seem to offer progress towards, the modern welfare state. This approach was perhaps best exemplified by Olwen Hufton's work on

42 Dyer, 'The Experience of Being Poor', p. 19.

43 Progress in understanding experiences of poverty in other historical settings has similarly tended to follow after expanding knowledge of elite ideas about and treatment of the poor: Scott, 'Experiences of Poverty', p. 1. Scott's follow-up collection emphasises the importance of revisiting the study of relief and charity with the perspectives gained from the recent focus on the poor themselves: Scott, 'Experiences of Charity', pp. 1–2.

44 Jutte, *Poverty*, pp. 21–44; see also Chapters 6 and 7 of this book.

45 See, for example, Pullan, 'Support and redeem', p. 180; Olson, 'Continuity or Radical Change?'; Slack, *Poverty and Policy*, p. 168; Scott, 'Experiences of Poverty', p. 5; Davis, 'Social and Religious Meanings of Charity'.

France, where a broad European narrative of progress is suggested, from 'a religiously based voluntary charity, as expounded by the evangelists, to the complete assumption by the state of responsibility for the neediest members of society'.[46] Relief provision before the modern welfare state or without the enforcement of compulsory poor laws has often been assumed to be 'erratic', and, by implication, systems (like Scotland's) which did not make progress or point towards this goal were backwards, or dead-ends in the history of welfare.[47] The limitations of such a narrative are increasingly stressed by later twentieth and early twenty-first-century studies, although this has yet to inform thinking on Scotland.[48]

There has also been a growing critique of several linked binary distinctions which have often been applied to relief systems as they developed in the early modern period.[49] Particularly significant for this study are the supposed contrasts between ecclesiastical and secular schemes, and between voluntary and compulsory provision. Because the state and alleged processes of secularisation were associated with many sixteenth-century developments in poor relief, ecclesiastical systems tended to be treated as inherently inferior and backwards – an assumption that historians of Catholic Europe took the lead in challenging.[50] There have also been moves to reinsert religion more sensitively into the debate, following what Grell called a process of throwing out 'the baby with the bath-water', when excessively confessional Protestant-centric explanations of relief reforms were revised to place more emphasis on socio-economic explanations.[51] The importance of religious motivation for relief in diverse forms and settings has now been re-emphasised, among other factors.[52] Of course, assuming too great a separation between religious and secular impulses and structures in the sixteenth and seventeenth centuries is always problematic, but the traditional dichotomy poses particular problems for understanding Scottish relief. In Scotland, local ecclesiastical institutions were staffed primarily by lay elders and deacons, and perhaps more importantly they were institutions with unique reach and authority – especially in the rural areas where most Scots lived. Considering this in the context of wider

46 Hufton, *Poor of Eighteenth Century France*, p. 131.

47 van Leeuwen et al, 'Provisions for the elderly', pp. 2–3; Davis, 'Social and Religious Meanings of Charity', p. 937.

48 Frohman, *Poor Relief and Welfare*, p. 1; van Leeuwen, 'Giving in early modern history', p. 303; Goose, 'The English almshouse', p. 17.

49 McIntosh, 'Local Responses', p. 212; McIntosh, *Poor Relief in England*, p. 296; Houston, 'Poor Relief and the Dangerous and Criminal Insane', pp. 453, 467; Davis, 'Social and Religious Meanings of Charity', p. 944.

50 Jutte, *Poverty*, pp. 101–2; Mitchison, *Coping*, p. 36; Pullan, 'Catholics and the Poor'; Davis, *Society and Culture*, pp. 17–20.

51 Grell, 'Religious Duty of Care', p. 258; Pullan, 'Catholics and the Poor', p. 33; Fehler, 'Burden of Benevolence', pp. 232–6.

52 Grell, 'Protestant Imperative', pp. 57–8; Broomhall, 'Politics of Charitable Men', pp. 155–6; McIntosh, *Hadleigh*, pp. 141–7.

challenges to the ecclesiastical-secular dichotomy, the fact that the church was left to provide poor relief in Scotland now looks much less like an inherent weakness of the system.

Another traditional binary in the literature on trends in early modern poor relief is the distinction between schemes based on compulsory contribution and voluntary contribution. As already discussed, the failure to implement compulsory rates on a widespread basis is one of the key reasons why Scottish relief has been viewed as weak and insignificant. Yet a great deal of recent work has undermined the centrality of the distinction between compulsion and voluntarism.[53] This has included research emphasising the strength and durability of (non-compulsory) giving in the Dutch Republic, as well as McIntosh's studies of English relief which critique the categorisation of relief in 'dichotomous terms', and notes that 'apparently contradictory types were intertwined in practice'.[54] As Horden has said of the late medieval period: 'In the collection of revenue, statutory taxes are not everything. Customary mechanisms may be no easier to evade'.[55] The fact that other forms of relief, assistance, and charity survived, co-existed with and even flourished alongside the famous Poor Laws in seventeenth-century England further undermines any sense of a sharp opposition between the two.[56] This does not mean that there were no differences between compulsory and voluntary mechanisms, or that compulsion might not have had advantages, but it does suggest a need to focus on actual practice rather than the overall legal status of the system: on poor relief holistically, not just on poor laws.[57] Scotland provides an important example of a relief system where the national law on taxation was not widely implemented, and contributions were mainly voluntary but relief was run by a well-organised, local ecclesiastical institution.

Building on the trend to look beyond legal frameworks and policies to local practice, historians have also developed more balanced understandings of the role of formal relief payments in the survival of the poor. It has become increasingly apparent that relief payments, whether statutory or otherwise, were generally only partial contributions to the needs of poor people. They were supplementary payments, not full pensions which met

[53] Jones, 'Some recent trends in the history of charity', in Daunton (ed.), *Charity, Self-Interest and Welfare*, pp. 52–3.

[54] Meerkerk and Teeuwen, 'Stability of voluntarism'; van Bavel and Rijpma, 'How important were formalized charity and social spending before the rise of the welfare state?', pp. 181–2; Goose and Looijesteijn, 'Almshouses'; McIntosh, *Poor Relief in England*, pp. 12–13, 296; see also McIntosh, *Hadleigh*, p. 6 and passim; Ben-Amos, *Culture of Giving*, pp. 10, 12, 111.

[55] Horden, 'Small Beer?', p. 343.

[56] *OTP*; Ben-Amos, *Culture of Giving*, pp. 2–4, 379.

[57] See also King, 'Poor Relief and English Economic Development Reappraised', p. 362; McIntosh, *Poor Relief in England*, pp. 8, 142–3, 295; Houston, 'Poor Relief and the Dangerous and Criminal Insane', p. 456; Daunton, 'Introduction', in Daunton (ed.), *Charity, Self-Interest and Welfare*, p. 9.

living expenses.[58] This has led to fascinating research on the other sources of income and survival strategies of the poor but it also necessitates more careful analysis of relief payments themselves.[59] Given that normal practice elsewhere in Europe was to make relief payments that were generally supplementary, and as it is widely accepted that 'as a percentage of wages or of the minimum cost of living, most social assistance before the welfare state was indeed modest', then to ask whether relief payments in Scotland were meeting the full needs of poor people is to use a wholly unrealistic yardstick.[60] The fact that the most influential descriptions of the relief provided by kirk sessions as modest and weak tend to predate the widespread emphasis on this point in other national historiographies may help to explain some of the negative framing of such descriptions – although because Scottish relief payments have not been analysed directly it seems to be a question of a lack of research as much as of problematic benchmarking.

Indeed, current thinking on Scottish poor relief prior to the eighteenth century does not take into account (or predates) many of these key developments in the European historiography.[61] The distinctive nature of Scotland's relief programme means that it suffers disproportionately when viewed through the conventional lens of ecclesiastical-secular and voluntary-compulsory binaries.[62] Taking this historiography into account repositions the narrative of the failure of compulsory taxation under national poor laws as, at most, half the story. It is equally important to note that current understanding of the Scottish experience in the wider literature on early modern poor relief is minimal. Wider studies of the period prior to the late seventeenth century have had to rely mainly on Mitchison's brief discussion of the legislation and its failure to translate into compulsory exactions. Mitchison's interpretation of voluntary and ecclesiastical poor relief in principle – not just Scotland's – was very negative, and her

[58] van Leeuwen, 'Giving', p. 303; McIntosh, 'Local Responses', p. 211; Wales, 'Poverty, poor relief and the life-cycle', pp. 352, 388; Meerkerk and Teeuwen, 'Stability of Voluntarism', p. 86.

[59] For example *OTP*; Scott (ed.), *Experiences of Poverty* (especially Part I); Healey, *First Century of Welfare*, especially chapter 5.

[60] van Leeuwen et al, 'Provisions for the elderly', p. 2; cf. for example Goodare, 'Parliament and Society', p. 430; Mitchison, 'Poor Relief and Health Care', p. 224. The fact that typical Scottish wages have often been found to fall short of estimated living expenses further emphasises the problematic nature of 'meeting the needs' as a measure of relief: Spence, *Women, credit and debt*, p. 6; Gibson and Smout, *Prices*, pp. 349–50.

[61] Cf. studies of later periods, e.g. Houston, 'Poor Relief and the Dangerous and Criminal Insane'; Blaikie, 'Nuclear hardship or variant dependency?'.

[62] Scotland's relief also sits awkwardly with the binary tendency to classify systems into centralised and decentralised: the system was led by local church courts at their own initiative (albeit linked together through the hierarchy of presbytery and synod), but is sometimes listed within a 'centralised' grouping by virtue of the little-implemented English-style Poor Laws – a categorisation that prompts and reinforces narratives of failure: Jutte, *Poverty*, pp. 105, 124.

conclusion that little was done for the Scottish poor prior to the later seventeenth century has formed the basis for Scotland's place in the literature.[63] According to conventional thinking, there was actually little reason to pay attention to Scotland because nearly all relief there was merely ecclesiastical, and merely voluntary.[64] But as historians move beyond these assumptions, and towards an emphasis on local practices and their flexibilities rather than legal and national frameworks, Scotland's distinctive relief provision and source material offers opportunities for fresh perspectives on the nature of early modern poor relief.

It follows from much of the foregoing discussion that one of the most pressing issues to be addressed is the contrast between poor relief in England and in Scotland. England has traditionally been seen as exceptional in early modern European relief studies: through its Poor Laws a uniquely strong, dominant and effective welfare system was put in place involving statutory contributions and secular authority. This has been questioned and challenged on various fronts, including in research on other countries and especially the Dutch Republic which has sought to question English exceptionalism.[65] Work on England itself has also raised questions both about the centrality of statutory Poor Law relief to the survival of the poor, and in the wider range of charitable spending,[66] and even about the extent and uniformity of its implementation across England.[67] The English Poor Law now appears more of a mosaic than a monolith.[68]

Scotland's poor relief, on the other hand, has appeared as the weaker and unsuccessful cousin of the English achievement. They tried to be like England and failed. One revealing statement of this contrast is the claim that 'efforts to build up an English-style system of poor relief failed

[63] Mitchison, *Coping*, pp. 33–6; Mitchison, 'Poor Relief and Health Care', pp. 220, 229. The introductory chapter to the volume in which the latter was published draws on Mitchison's chapter to emphasise the near-total failure of compulsory rates, although it had earlier softened distinctions between 'voluntary' and 'compulsory': Grell and Cunningham, 'Reformation and changes in welfare provision', pp. 30, 34–5.

[64] This approach is particularly apparent in work informed by Marxist theory: Patriquin, *Agrarian Capitalism*, pp. 152–3; Lis and Soly, *Poverty and Capitalism in Pre-Industrial Europe*, pp. 88, 95.

[65] Meerkerk and Teeuwen, 'Stability of Voluntarism', pp. 98–100; Goose and Looijesteijn, 'Almshouses'; for continuing emphasis on English uniqueness in other studies see Patriquin, *Agrarian Capitalism*; Solar, 'Poor Relief and English Economic Development', p. 3; Healey, *First Century of Welfare*, p. 4.

[66] Wales, 'Poverty'; *OTP*; King, 'Poor Relief'; Ben-Amos, *Culture of Giving*.

[67] Slack, *Poverty and Policy*, pp. 171–3; Hindle, *State and Social Change*, pp. 153–62; *OTP*, pp. 229–56; King, 'Poor Relief and English Economic Development Reappraised', pp. 362–3.

[68] The specific nature of the diversity in English poor law practice is more contested however: see, for example, *OTP*, p. 282–3 (referring to 'mosaics' at local level rather than wider regional divides); cf. King, "Poor Relief and English Economic Development Reappraised', p. 366; King, 'Welfare Regimes and Welfare Regions'.

because of the different structures of power at the local level'.[69] Judged by the implementation of central legislation, the Scottish system inevitably appears as an underdeveloped and weak version of the English ideal, and any relief that did take place appears simply as a fall-back option.[70] In fairness, this is not simply a result of the familiar process of Scottish actions being subjected to misleading Anglo-centric perspectives.[71] There were acts of the Scottish Parliament aiming at a specific set of outcomes which failed to be widely achieved. But, especially given the growing questioning of the overarching strength and centrality of the English Poor Laws in favour of more fine-grained reading of local practices, and the well-established significance of Scotland's kirk sessions as distinctive organs for religious change and local governance, it is necessary to evaluate the Scottish system as it developed in practice (whatever the theory) without a presumption of failure.[72] Naturally, such an evaluation should not ignore important contrasts between English and Scottish processes of relief, nor assume that the Scottish system was just as strong as the English. Indeed one of the few passing references to Scotland in Hindle's ground-breaking *On the Parish?* is probably – in contrast to most wider commentary – overly generous to the Scottish system in suggesting that the ability to raise funds through fines for offences under the disciplinary system meant that rating was not even necessary.[73] Indeed Scotland has a somewhat awkward situation in current categorisations of European relief systems – not quite England, but with too many legislative (and other) affinities with England to be considered within the range of ecclesiastical and voluntary systems of Catholic and Protestant mainland Europe.[74]

Looking beyond this immediate British context, three comparative surveys have reflected on criteria for success and reasons for giving and fundraising in preindustrial European charity and welfare. Olson suggests four conditions on which successful schemes drew, only one of which the Scottish system addressed here could convincingly boast: organisational skills and wide soliciting of funds (but less of an exile community, sizeable medieval endowment, or prosperous population).[75] This might help to explain the effort and organisation that went into fundraising by kirk

[69] Ellis, *Making of the British Isles*, p. 209.

[70] Wilbraham and Lodge, 'Responses', p. 58; Whyte, *Scotland Before the Industrial Revolution*, pp. 167–8. The workings of Scotland's poor relief during a later period are revealingly described by an otherwise deeply nuanced article as having 'little such complexity', in contrast to the English system: King, 'Welfare Regimes', pp. 50–1.

[71] Stewart, 'Power and Faith', p. 37+n.

[72] For a valuable questioning of severe Anglo-Scottish contrasts for the later eighteenth and nineteenth centuries, see Houston, 'Poor Relief and the Dangerous and Criminal Insane', pp. 453–4, 456.

[73] *OTP*, p. 375n. On fines, see below, pp. 141–3.

[74] Jutte, *Poverty*, p. 124; for examples of the mainland literature see Pullan, 'Catholics and the Poor'; Fehler, *Poor Relief and Protestantism*; Safley (ed.), *Reformation of Charity*.

[75] Olson, 'Continuity or Radical Change?', p. 172.

sessions. Instructively, a recent large-scale analysis of charity and social spending as a percentage of Gross Domestic Product, although dealing in statistics that are simply unavailable for Scotland at this time, identifies two routes to high social spending, not just one. The predictable route is centralised and mandatory enforcement of relief, broadly on the traditional English model, but the second, less familiar hypothesised route is that 'in a situation of decentralized organization and voluntary funding of poor relief, the presence of strong associations and corporations could lead to high levels'.[76] The areas involved in the latter model were parts of England, the Italian Alps and the eastern Netherlands, so the social context, prosperity levels and the associations themselves were very different from Scotland and its kirk sessions, and the spending levels were also unlikely to be similar. But the findings do suggest the possibility for decentralised and voluntary systems of poor relief to perform effectively within their societies. Focusing on motivations for giving, van Leeuwen suggests a range of reasons why elites might consider it in their interests to give (beyond either religious impulses or legal compulsion). Most of these have the potential to apply to the giving solicited by kirk sessions: maintaining social order and hierarchy; keeping public order and avoiding discontent; maintaining moral order and improving the behaviour of poorer sorts, although medical imperatives (reducing risk of infection) and labour-reserve theory are less obviously relevant in the context of kirk session relief.[77] The Scottish material has the potential to contribute to the further development of all three of these hypotheses, just as understanding Scottish relief requires us to consider these theoretical perspectives and the range of potential routes to poor relief, alongside the familiar narrative of legislative failure.

A related final lesson from the historiographical developments of the late twentieth and early twenty-first centuries concerns the historian's overall range and scale of vision when assessing relief. As we have seen, it is problematic to ask whether early modern relief payments 'met the needs' of poor people. Moreover, the limitations on focusing relief studies on lists of payments and distributions have been emphasised, and scholars have also stressed how difficult relief fundraising was in early modern societies where so much was spent on subsistence, and urged more realistic assessments of what could have been raised in most settings (and Scotland was not, of course, a prosperous country in any comparative terms).[78] Of course, evaluating the extent of fundraising, and how much poor people were paid still

[76] van Bavel and Rijpma, 'How important were formalized charity and social spending before the rise of the welfare state?', pp. 181–2.

[77] van Leeuwen, 'Logic of Charity', pp. 592–5.

[78] *OTP*, p. 451; van Leeuwen et al, 'Provisions for the elderly', p. 3; van Bavel and Rijpma, 'How important were formalized charity and social spending before the rise of the welfare state?', p. 183; Mitchison, 'Poor Relief and Health Care', p. 231; Houston and Whyte, 'Introduction: Scottish Society in Perspective', p. 13.

remains vital, especially for an area as under-researched as Scotland, and it is this issue that is often the focus in the chapters that follow.[79] However, as well as counting sums raised and paid, recent studies have emphasised the value of asking wider sets of questions such as how funds were raised and managed, and whether relief provision was organised on a predictable and durable basis; what range of people received relief; what processes determined who received relief and how did different welfare providers relate to each other.[80] This book attempts to draw on these developments and questions to offer a more holistic assessment of Scottish relief processes and cultures than has been possible previously.

Contexts

Welfare Policy Visions in Post-Reformation Scotland

Scottish poor relief did not begin in 1560. Although late medieval relief has yet to be studied in its own right or evaluated in any detail, it is clear that some took place. Evidence is fragmentary, and indeed provision must often have been patchy and unsystematic, but a range of individuals and institutions provided assistance to the needy in various forms, and the importance of caring for the poor was recognised.[81] Because much was informal and unrecorded, it is not clear how much disruption the coming of the Protestant Reformation in 1559–60 caused; although hospitals were clearly affected in the short-term, they went on to function in the post-reformation period, too.[82] Protestant doctrine meant that good works like almsgiving were no longer seen as helping to attain salvation, although this did not necessarily undermine religious impulses to giving or prompt immediate changes in attitudes to charity.[83] Something must have been lost with the passing of the old church, although fuller study of the pre-1560 period in Scotland would be needed to establish how much was lost. More importantly for our purposes, the 1560s and 1570s witnessed two grand manifestos for a transformed approach to welfare.

Firstly, the Protestant reformers had lofty ambitions for social policy. In 1560 the *First Book of Discipline* set out to claim the 'entire patrimony of the old Church' for the new one.[84] The old ecclesiastical revenues (teinds, or

[79] See especially Chapters 2–4 of this book.

[80] McIntosh, *Poor Relief in England*, p. 96; Meerkerk and Teeuwen, 'Stability of Voluntarism', p. 83; McIntosh, 'Poor relief in Elizabethan English communities'; McIntosh, *Hadleigh*, p. 3; King, 'Welfare Regimes and Welfare Regions'. For these areas see especially Chapters 4–5, 6, 7 and 8 respectively.

[81] Cowan, *Death, Life and Religious Change*, pp. 23, 104, 113–14; Durkan, 'Care of the Poor'; below pp. 29–32.

[82] McCallum, '"Nurseries of the Poore"', p. 432.

[83] See below, pp. 42–8.

[84] Dawson, *Knox*, p. 203.

tithes) should be used to fund the preaching ministry, as well as education and poor relief.[85] But famously this bid for resources was unsuccessful, and the compromise whereby the Kirk shared just a third of the revenues with the crown paved the way for ongoing difficulties funding ministerial stipends, let alone a wider social reform programme.[86] The failure of this ambitious vision has set the tone for commentary on the church's actual poor relief, often presented as, at best, a way to 'compensate' for the failure to acquire teind revenue for the poor.[87] It was much bemoaned by the church's national leadership, too, in subsequent years and decades.[88] It certainly was a failure on its own terms, but it is not clear why this should obscure what local churches went on to do instead in subsequent years and decades. Kirk sessions developed and implemented collection-based parochial relief with a focus and intensity which suggests that the failure was not considered the final word at local level, or as definitive in the eyes of local religious leadership as in those of historians.

A second failure of a grand welfare scheme – and one that has been even more prominent in perceptions of Scottish poor relief – is that of the Poor Laws of the 1570s.[89] Based on the English Act of 1572, the 1574 Poor Law laid out a system based on compulsory contribution by local taxation (or 'stenting'), meaning that those in each parish who were judged capable of paying for poor relief would be compelled to do so. It also foregrounded the punishment of idle beggars and other undesirables.[90] Unlike English legislation, it was not based on existing experience of this form of poor relief, or indeed a strong precedent for comparable regular taxation.[91] The Act is quite detailed but execution of its stipulated compulsory taxation to fund pensions for the deserving poor was very limited and intermittent, even in urban Scotland. Edinburgh made some progress later in the sixteenth century and after, and some stenting took place in various seventeenth century burghs.[92] But implementation was sparse. Subsequent

85 *FBD*, pp. 108–14, 156–64.

86 *FBD*, pp. 29, 74; Donaldson, *Scottish Reformation*, pp. 68–72; Cowan, *Scottish Reformation*, p. 194; Whyte, *Scotland Before the Industrial Revolution*, pp. 99–100.

87 Cowan, *Scottish Reformation*, p. 197; Smout, *History*, p. 85.

88 See, for example, Dawson, *Knox*, pp. 209, 222; *BUK*, i, pp. 146, 339, ii, p. 425; *JMD*, p. 188.

89 The origins and details of these laws are comparatively well-understood: Mitchison, 'Making', pp. 59–67; *OPL*, pp. 6–8, 16–19; Goodare, 'Parliament and Society', pp. 425–9.

90 *RPS*, A1575/3/5 (the Act was passed on 5 March 1574–5, but is often referred to as an Act of 1574). Although temporary, it was renewed in 1579: Mitchison, 'Making', p. 59; *RPS*, 1579/10/27. This was not the first Scottish legislation concerning the poor, but pre-1560 acts relating to poverty and charity had mostly focused on the problem of idle beggars and vagabonds, and the organisation of hospitals: *RPS*, 1425/3/3; 1425/3/22; 1450/1/20; 1458/3/13; 1466/42; A1552/2/16. An Act of 1535 made rather more reference to the provision of alms (*RPS*, 1535/38) but the 1570s legislation was of a different order.

91 *OPL*, pp. 7–8. The other main difference was the omission of work materials provided for the unemployed, in contrast to English legislation: Mitchison, 'Making', p. 60; *OPL*, p. 7.

92 *OPL*, p. 10; Mitchison, 'Poor Relief and Health Care', p. 224.

legislation recognised this, with kirk sessions' responsibility for undertaking and overseeing relief – already a long-established fact on the ground – formalised by acts in the 1590s.[93] Legislation by the covenanting parliament in 1649 paved the way for a more explicit responsibility to undertake stenting, and according to Mitchison limited the extent to which elites could ignore the duty to provide relief.[94] Overall then, from the 1570s to at least the middle of the seventeenth century, the legislation broadly failed: compulsory stents to fund relief were not generally implemented, and a system of national welfare backed by statutory exaction was not created. The fact that it was left to the kirk sessions to undertake relief based on primarily voluntary funding is one of the principle reasons for negative assessments of early modern Scottish poor relief. One of this book's aims is to flip this assumption and suggest that the kirk session relief system was ideally suited to relief administration in the context of sixteenth- and seventeenth-century Scottish parishes, and that the failure of the statutory approach should not be taken to define the subject.[95] Instead, parochial practice is the book's focus.

Economic Patterns and Contours of Poverty

Contemporary discussion of welfare did not take place in an economic vacuum. The economic backdrop to this period can be painted only in relatively broad brushstrokes, but some general patterns are fairly clear. Although it is important to avoid excessively pessimistic assumptions about the early modern Scottish economy, it was clearly one which faced great challenges.[96] The later sixteenth century in particular was a difficult time for Scotland's economy.[97] This was a time of inflation (with baskets of non-elite goods particularly badly hit from the 1560s), as well as significant population pressures by the later sixteenth and early seventeenth centuries.[98] This was a time of increased poverty for many, and vagrancy was observed to be on the increase, as in England.[99] The economic fortunes

[93] *OPL*, p. 11; *RPS*, 1592/4/91, 1597/11/46. Developments in a later Act of 1617, making more thorough provision for work materials and destitute children, were essentially abortive: *RPS*, 1617/5/24; Goodare, *Government*, pp. 266–7.

[94] *RPS*, 1649/1/192; *OPL*, p. 19.

[95] This is not to suggest that attempts to raise taxation should be ignored, and they are addressed where relevant in chs 2, 8 below. See Stewart, 'Poor Relief in Edinburgh', for detailed analysis of compulsory taxation for relief in the town where it was most convincingly implemented.

[96] Devine, 'Reappraising the Early Modern Economy', pp. 236–9.

[97] Wormald, *Court, Kirk, and Community*, pp. 166–8; Lythe, *Economy of Scotland*, pp. 16–21.

[98] Blakeway, 'The sixteenth-century price rise', pp. 175, 183; Houston, *Population History*, pp. 17–18.

[99] Dawson, *Scotland Re-Formed*, pp. 286–7; Goodare, *Government*, pp. 268–9; Whyte, *Scotland's Society and Economy*, pp. 129–30, 132; Wrightson, *Earthly Necessities*, p. 148; Beier, *Masterless Men*, pp. 14–22.

of rural Scotland, especially between the earlier sixteenth century and the later seventeenth century, are notoriously hazy, although one thing that is apparent is their chronological and regional complexity – a 'jigsaw', as Whyte puts it.[100] It has also been noted that the late sixteenth century was 'a bad time to be a small tenant farmer', while things may have been rather better for larger farmers.[101] So the overall picture is still far from clear, but it is apparent that many rural dwellers were facing significant and growing economic strain. And in the rapidly growing urban centres too, the later sixteenth century saw 'growing problems of poverty', although there are also suggestions that the situation was not nearly as severe as in England.[102] As the seventeenth century progressed, economic fortunes seem to have improved somewhat, with the very significant exceptions of major crisis in the early 1620s, ongoing localised food shortages, and further crises including warfare in the 1640s.[103] Albeit with more confidence than precision, it is possible to conclude that the period as a whole was one of growing economic pressure and an expanding poverty problem. This had the potential both to enhance the need for poor relief mechanisms, and to place greater strain on them, by increasing demand for relief and squeezing the purses of some of those who would fund it.

One economic fact is simple and clear, however. For large numbers of Scots, and for most at the humbler levels of society, 'just getting by was intensely difficult, with most surviving just beyond the margins of subsistence'.[104] Indeed, understandings of poverty developed for other parts of Europe suggest numerous reasons why large swathes of the Scottish population could potentially find their situation dipping into serious poverty. The life-cycle is an important factor, and young people, parents of young children and the elderly are frequently apparent in the records of kirk session relief. Accidental causes of poverty were not lacking either, ranging from personal or local disaster to the wider ravages of famine, disease and war. Downward trends in the economy are less frequently and overtly visible in relief records, although they must have been a leading factor in some cases, and a contributing factor in many more.[105] The poverty which kirk sessions sought to relieve certainly existed against a backdrop of economic pressure (sometimes intense, even if imperfectly understood), but

[100] Whyte, 'Poverty or Prosperity?', pp. 19, 23.

[101] Goodare, 'In Search of the Scottish Agrarian Problem', p. 113. Complexity in patterns of rural wealth and prosperity – even in a single community – also emerges in Whyte and Whyte, 'Debt and Credit, Poverty and Prosperity', pp. 77–8.

[102] Whyte, *Scotland Before the Industrial Revolution*, pp. 172–3, 202; Whyte, 'Occupation Structure of Scottish Burghs', pp. 228–9.

[103] Whyte, 'Poverty or Prosperity?', pp. 21, 29–30.

[104] E. Foyster and C. A. Whatley, 'Introduction: Recovering the Everyday in Early Modern Scotland', in Foyster and Whatley (eds), *Everyday Life in Scotland*, p. 9; Whyte, *Scotland's Society and Economy*, pp. 42–3.

[105] Jutte, *Poverty*, pp. 21–42; see especially Chapters 4, 6 and 7 of this book.

it should be appreciated as complex and multi-faceted rather than a direct offshoot of economic trends.

Moreover, the study of poor relief demands relative rather than absolute understandings of poverty. Beyond the imprecise understanding of overall economic trends and diverse and overlapping causes of poverty, and even beyond more practical problems of identifying useful measures of incomes, prices and standards of living, the subject is necessarily defined not by an external reference point for poverty, but by the decision of institutions or individuals to provide (or refuse) assistance.[106] This book therefore has little to contribute to discussions about overall levels of poverty and prosperity as mentioned above, and also cannot be considered a study of underlying economic structures and inequalities. The defining feature of the 'poor' people studied here was not their actual income or resources, nor was it the difference in wealth and status between them and those richer than them, but their need for relief by others, whether it was forthcoming or not.[107] This was obviously not unrelated to their resources or their position in the social hierarchy, but it also depended on other factors. The complexity of the relationship between these factors and people's need for assistance requires that we keep in mind a fluid understanding of 'poverty' and 'poor', rather than ever considering the terms as concrete descriptors.

The Parish and the Kirk Session

The kirk session is an increasingly familiar and central figure in analysis of religion and culture in the early modern Scottish parish. From its origins in the establishment of Scotland's reformed church (and, in turn, the influence of the Calvinist consistory), after 1560 it grew into a significant instrument of local authority and a defining religious influence on people's lives.[108] Kirk sessions comprised parish ministers plus lay elders and deacons, forming a male parochial council which met weekly to undertake ecclesiastical administration and, amongst a range of spiritual functions, imposed discipline on the congregation. They were the most junior in Scotland's hierarchy of church courts, below the local presbyteries (once established from the 1580s), regional synods, and the national General Assembly.[109] But although sessions were monitored by presbyteries, and higher courts might become involved with session affairs such as difficult disciplinary cases or matters relating to the clergy, for most aspects of parish life they acted relatively independently and undertook the bulk of

[106] Scott, 'Experiences of Poverty', pp. 3–4.

[107] Scott, 'Experiences of Charity', p. 9.

[108] Graham, *Uses of Reform*, pp. 4–27, 36–8, 73–5

[109] Graham, *Uses of Reform*, pp. 64–72, 130–46; Foster, *Church Before the Covenants*, pp. 111–32.

local business themselves.[110] Normal poor relief was naturally the preserve of the kirk session as the parochial court.

The way in which kirk sessions organised and administered poor relief is of course one of the central themes of the book, but it is worth introducing some of the basic features and processes of their relief. Kirk sessions arranged dedicated collections for poor relief at public worship, as well as receiving income from fines, voluntary bequests and donations, and more minor miscellaneous sources. The money raised for relief – the majority of which was from collections – was held and overseen for the kirk session by one or more of its officials. When the session decided to make relief payments, whether as a one-off or as an ongoing pension, they would be passed to the recipients by a session member, typically a deacon. At the same time, the session had dealings with recipients, other poor folk and the wider congregation through the work of discipline, overseeing catechism, baptisms, marriages and other business discussed at their routine meetings. Although this book is focused directly and fairly exclusively on poor relief practices, these were part of a wider framework of responsibilities which sessions would not have seen as hermetically sealed from each other. Indeed these other interventions in parishioners' lives sometimes interacted with poor relief and thus make appearances in this study.[111] But the kirk sessions took the relief work seriously in its own right.

Approaches

Sources and Methodologies

As the significance of kirk sessions as historical actors has been increasingly appreciated, so has awareness of the richness of their records as sources on religious and social life. For the subject of poor relief, they contain unrealised potential. This varies in depth and detail, from separate books of accounts and full lists of payments and distributions, through to briefer and more scattered noting of collections or individual payments amongst the considerable bulk of business undertaken by sessions.[112] This bulk, and the absence in many session books of distinct sections to record relief, may help to explain the lack of attention from historians. Theoretical categorisations of poor relief also played a part, however. Revealingly, Michael Lynch suggests the difficulty of studying the early modern urban poor because of the lack of the compulsory rate-based relief which would have created 'adequate' records. [113] Compulsory relief might have created better

[110] McCallum, *Reforming*, pp. 171–7.

[111] See especially Chapter 7 of this book.

[112] Mutch, 'Data-Mining'; see (for example) discussion of St Cuthbert's, Galston, and Elgin below.

[113] Lynch, 'Introduction: Scottish Towns, 1500–1700', pp. 26–7.

records, perhaps, but this does not seem a compelling reason to bypass the records of voluntary relief, especially as they are hardly slapdash. Indeed for the eighteenth century, but reflecting practices developed earlier, Alistair Mutch has demonstrated the importance of paying attention not just to the contents but the format, organisation, and even the very existence, of kirk session books and accounts. The systematic and accountable record-keeping was, he argues, influential on the development of Scottish culture and identity, but this argument aside, for our purposes it is also an indication of the importance of poor relief to kirk sessions.[114]

The limitations of the kirk session source material are not to be denied. As with other institutional welfare records, they allow us to view the poor only through the lens of the session's attitudes and prejudices. Only occasional and heavily mediated fragments of the words and lives of the poor can be glimpsed. Even for the study of relief itself, they tend to record outcomes rather than deliberations and negotiations, and they provide less information about the recipients' backgrounds than we would like – often only a name. And where collections are recorded there is naturally no way of knowing who had contributed or how much. But there is enough material to permit cautious assessments of relief provision and its extent, nature, and impact, and to gain insight into some aspects of life for poor Scots.[115]

This book ranges across the Scottish lowlands, but focuses much of its analysis on a group of 25 parishes and their records.[116] This enables intensive discussion of the scope and character of relief in a series of communities, especially for the assessment of the expansion and development of poor relief in Chapters 2 and 3. To balance the emphasis on these kirk sessions, their records were supplemented by session minutes from a wider range of parishes, especially to provide a more extensive coverage of sources for specific periods (such as the dearth of the 1620s) or for thematic

114 Mutch, *Religion and National Identity*, pp. xii, 15, 19–22.

115 This is an area which promises to be developed much more comprehensively by C. R. Langley's forthcoming study of informal care networks in the seventeenth century, *Cultures of Care* (Leiden: Brill).

116 These are Aberdeen, Anstruther, Ayr, Canongate, Dunbarney, Dundonald, Edinburgh, Elgin, Galston, Glasgow, Haddington, Kilmadock, Kinnaird, Lasswade, Midcalder, Monifieth, Monimail, Montrose, Old Deer, Perth, Salton, South Leith, St Andrews, St Cuthbert's, Stirling (see Bibliography for full details). Many of these survive only for limited runs; others are primarily utilised in this study for specific periods or themes. The Edinburgh records are mainly discussed for the early experience of relief in the 1570s (see Chapter 2), for fuller coverage of the capital see Stewart, 'Poor Relief in Edinburgh'; Dundee has excellent records surviving from 1640, of which some use is made, but for full discussion see McCallum, 'Charity and Conflict'. The selection targeted as full a coverage as possible for the much patchier source survival before *c.* 1600, and a variety of types of parish and regions for the increasingly well-evidenced seventeenth century half of the period. By the 1630s and 1640s, inevitably, a smaller proportion of the total surviving material has been discussed at length. The geographical coverage roughly reflects the overall spread of kirk session survival for this period.

questions which necessitated broader surveys of further session records.[117] Broad similarities in the fundamentals of the system were identified, even between rural and urban parishes and between different regions, as well as some local variations on individual issues. The chapters therefore contain both direct analysis of individual parishes in turn, and wider-ranging arguments, and strive to balance the goal of establishing the first broad assessment of Scottish relief in the period, with maintaining the local specificity so vital to any discussion of kirk session activity and parish religion.[118]

The methodology employed also attempts a balance: between quantification and more qualitative readings of poor relief. Scepticism has rightly been expressed about quantitative approaches to kirk session minutes, especially concerning discipline where attempts to assess misbehaviour and its punishment are hampered by unrecorded variations in disciplinary enthusiasm, scribal diligence and comprehensiveness, as well as more universal problems with record damage and survival.[119] Foster is particularly pessimistic about quantifying poor relief from session records because of incomplete record coverage, although this surely rules out definitive and precise overall totals or indices of sums raised for relief, rather than more fine-grained and contextual statistics which can allow for gaps, missing totals, or variations in detail between parishes.[120] It will certainly never be possible to point to an accurate total raised for poor relief in a specific region of Scotland for a given period of time, and even parish totals would have to be approximate and highly qualified. Some parish records provide very limited quantitative information. But with caution, and in the service of qualitative interpretations rather than as definitive findings in themselves, it is sometimes possible to produce estimates of (for example) collection totals, amounts distributed to the poor, numbers of poor helped on one occasion or over a period of time, typical sums received, or gender patterns in the numbers and payment sizes of the named poor. The figures produced are often approximate and normally minimums, but they are utilised as part of the evidence-base at various points.

Beyond imperfections in the session records themselves, there are more fundamental challenges to quantifying the poor relief discussed here, and in particular these caution against amalgamating the data. While the out-

[117] Chapters 1 and 8 focus on themes requiring more diverse source types, from literary treatises to testaments and burgh records: these sources are discussed where relevant in the chapters. Higher church courts were rarely concerned with routine relief, so presbytery and synod records are mainly utilised when considering responses to extra-parochial emergencies in Chapter 4.

[118] Goodare, 'Review of *The Culture of Protestantism in Early Modern Scotland*', p. 376.

[119] *COP*, pp. 16–18; Pollman, 'Off the Record'; cf. Graham, *Uses of Reform*, pp. 74, 83–7 and passim; McCallum, *Reforming*, pp. 39+n, 190–1; *PKSB*, pp. 45–7. Off-the-record payments might occasionally have been made, and some recipients were anonymous, but unlike discipline there would generally be little reason (and obvious practical disadvantages) to keep normal poor relief business off the record.

[120] Foster, *Church Before The Covenants*, p. 83.

lines of each parish's relief, including data on collection or distribution patterns, can be compared and form the basis for an interpretive synthesis, the dangers of producing wider comparisons of totals and averages are immense. This is partly because of the uncertainty of population estimates. Demographers emphasise the 'relative darkness' of seventeenth-century population figures, especially in rural areas, and even by the eighteenth century there is still much circumspection and uncertainty about the reliability and scope of sources.[121] Rough population estimates or ranges for parishes can be taken into account to provide a broad sense of context, at best. Beyond population, there is also a lack of reliable information on poverty levels and trends in wealth and productivity in and between parishes (including change over time), not to mention that data on prices and wages during this period are patchy and regionally varied.[122] Family and household structure would have been a vital factor in the demand for relief as well.[123] Detailed parish case-studies and reconstructions considering relief alongside demographic sources and local economic records might have the potential to address this problem in future.[124] But the uncertainties all make overall numerical comparisons, averages or indices potentially misleading, and only approximate, qualified judgements on these areas are offered in what follows.

Beyond these challenges, the lessons of the literature on European welfare in this period discussed earlier place further qualifications on the statistics utilised in this book – even within single parishes or years. Even if we had fuller information on parish economies and populations, poverty levels, costs of living and socio-economic structures, as we have seen relief payments were also rarely likely to have been intended as meeting the full survival needs of recipients. It is more appropriate, therefore, to offer rough estimates for wages and prices as a means of establishing and conveying an approximate sense of the value of the collections and payments made by kirk sessions. This requires a great deal of caution and the comparisons with relief payments which it produces should by no means be considered as precise. This contextual information is explained fully in the Appendix, and drawn on where possible in the analysis, especially in Chapters 2 and 3.[125] But different recipients likely received different proportions of their income in relief, and as McIntosh has noted, lower relief payments indicate

[121] Flinn (ed.), *Scottish Population History*, pp. 109–16 (quotation at p. 111); Houston, *Population History*, pp. 4–15; Whyte, 'Urbanization in Early Modern Scotland', pp. 23–5; Mitchison, 'A Parish and its Poor', p. 16. Studies of better-evidenced larger burghs have offered some consideration of relief in relation to population: Stewart, 'Poor Relief in Edinburgh', pp. 7, 11; McCallum, 'Charity and Conflict', pp. 33–4, 49–51.

[122] Whyte, 'Poverty or Prosperity?'; Gibson and Smout, *Prices*, especially chapters 2, 3, 8.

[123] Wales, 'Poverty', pp. 352–4, 360, 384; Jutte, *Poverty*, p. 40; *OPL*, pp. 92–3.

[124] Wrightson and Levine, *Poverty and Piety*; McIntosh, *Hadleigh*; Houston (ed.), *Records of a Scottish Village*; Dingwall, *Late C17th Edinburgh*.

[125] This material is all derived from Gibson and Smout, *Prices*.

the existence of other (almost always unknowable) forms of income.[126] The question of 'how much they needed to survive' is contingent on too many unknown variables to answer with simple figures.[127] Most strikingly, Gibson and Smout noted when discussing those in paid employment (rather than on poor relief) and the relationship between apparent wages and living costs that 'the puzzle is how they managed'.[128] Equally, Slack has suggested that historians should double the number of listed recipients of relief to calculate the real number helped including dependents; this has not been included as an automatic multiplier in any statistics in this book, but it should serve as an important reminder that those named next to sums of money in the session minutes were not the only parishioners to benefit.[129] There is, then, no objective measure of 'need'; nor is there any remotely satisfactory formula for calculating what proportion of a parish's relief needs were being met – and this would be true even if the kirk session records were comprehensive and uniform in the level of financial detail provided. Quantification is used in this study to support certain elements of the analysis but mostly, for this subject matter, period and source material, the dangers of attempting any sort of statistical precision outweigh the advantages.

Parameters and Contents of the Volume

As this book is concerned with the relief provided by the Protestant Church in Scotland and its kirk sessions, its starting-point of 1560 is relatively straightforward. Recent scholarship has rightly problematised the use of 1560 as a sharp dividing line in Scottish history, and indeed Chapters 1 and 8 identify some continuities in thinking about poverty and in other forms of charity and welfare.[130] However, in institutional terms, the kirk session was a creation of the official Protestant Reformation, and one which had the potential to organise poor relief across Scottish parishes, and to create records, in ways which were not possible previously. The terminal date of 1650 (with occasional exceptions) is partly dictated by the manageability of primary evidence as well as the increasing coverage in the secondary literature as the second half of the seventeenth century progresses, including in the principal survey by Mitchison. Importantly, 1649 also witnessed the passing of a major Act on poor relief as part of a wider reform programme by the covenanting parliament.[131] This serves as a dividing line for Mitchison, who emphasised that this 'thorough piece of legislation'

126 McIntosh, *Hadleigh*, p. 69; McIntosh, 'Poor Relief in Elizabethan Communities', pp. 345, 352n; *OTP*, pp. 451–2.

127 McIntosh, *Poor Relief in England*, p. 35.

128 Gibson and Smout, *Prices*, p. 349.

129 Slack, *Poverty and Policy*, p. 174.

130 Holmes, *Sacred Signs*, pp. 208–9; Cowan, 'In the Borderlands of Periodization', pp. 145–9.

131 Stevenson, *Revolution and Counter-Revolution*, p. 117; Stewart, *Rethinking*, pp. 254–5.

placed a great deal of responsibility on landowners to provide support.[132] Although not immediately enforced (and rescinded at the Restoration), the Act was discussed by church courts at the time, and has been considered as a turning-point in the development of the Poor Law.[133] Although it did not transform practice overnight, it marked the tone for a new phase in the development of Scottish poor relief and therefore serves as an additional reason to conclude this study around the halfway-point of the seventeenth century.

The book's geographical remit is lowland mainland Scotland. The conventional excuse of the limitations of the primary source material and especially kirk session coverage and activity for the pre-1650 highlands and islands might be offered for this, although for this book's subject it is also worth noting differences in the socio-economic structures and experience of Calvinist religious culture of the Gaidhealtachd.[134] Beyond the church and its institutions, differing patterns of poverty, economic activity and kin structure reinforce the sense that these regions deserve dedicated studies.[135] For the lowland communities that are its focus, it should also be acknowledged that this book covers a relatively wide sweep of rural and urban settlements and regions, in an attempt to open up the subject for further study and to identify broad patterns in relief provision. There is potentially much more still to be learned through intensive case-studies.

Before looking at practice, we need to consider theory – and aims and intentions. Therefore Chapter 1 explores ideas about poverty and charity in early modern Scotland, outlining the importance of improving the treatment of the poor in the thought of Protestant reformers and others. With the ideological framework considered, Part I turns to the establishment and development of poor relief itself. Chapters 2 and 3 trace the origins, expansion and development of kirk session relief chronologically and geographically. Chapter 2 focuses on the urban experience for the first 50 years after 1560, as most of the evidence (and kirk session functioning) for this period comes from towns and especially the country's leading burghs. Chapter 3 covers a wider range of communities (with a rural emphasis) mostly during the later half of the book's period, although some early rural examples of regular and formal relief are noted. Chapter 4 focuses on the sometimes surprisingly resilient responses of this system to specific periods of stress and crisis.

132 *OPL*, pp. 17–19.

133 See, for example, Langley (ed.), *Synod of Lothian and Tweeddale*, pp. 5, 9–10; *Ecclesiastical Records: Selections from the Registers of the Presbytery of Lanark*, pp. 70–1; Mitchison, 'North and South', p. 206; Houston, 'Poor Relief and the Dangerous and Criminal Insane', p. 460.

134 Whyte, *Scotland Before the Industrial Revolution*, pp. 252–60; Dawson, 'Calvinism and the Gaidhealtachd'; *COP*, pp. 14n–15n; Langley, *Worship*, p. 8.

135 For some initial careful commentary on charity in the late-medieval highlands, see MacDonald, 'The Church in Gaelic Scotland before the Reformation', pp. 21–3.

Part II addresses the nature of kirk session relief once it was up and running. Its more thematic approach reflects the fact that although the system took time to develop in individual communities across the lowlands, once operational it had many common features and no sharp geographical or chronological divides. Chapter 5 unpicks the mechanisms and processes through which kirk sessions raised, managed and distributed funds, identifying efficiency, vigour and flexibility in their approach. Chapters 6 and 7 turn to the recipients of relief themselves: examining in turn the range and types of people assisted, and the criteria and decisions involved in allocating funds. Finally, Chapter 8 turns to sources of relief other than the kirk session, starting with other institutions, then forms of giving ranging from formal testamentary bequests and donations through to more casual forms of assistance. Important as this wider context of relief funding and support for the needy was, the chapter – and the book as a whole – ultimately emphasises how the kirk session served at the heart of Scottish welfare.

CHAPTER 1

Ideas, Attitudes and Ambitions

Introduction

This book is primarily about what the Scottish church did for (and to) the poor. But before we can assess practice, we need to consider the ideas and attitudes of church and society towards charity, poverty and the poor. This chapter therefore asks how these topics were viewed in sixteenth- and seventeenth-century Scotland. There is naturally a particular emphasis on the approaches of Protestant reformers, in order to contextualise the relief provided by the established church after 1560, but it is important to note that there was substantial continuity from the late medieval period, and also that Protestant reforming attitudes were not unique, but instead drew on wider social attitudes and traditions. Such attitudes are not always easy to glean from the sources for the early modern period, and as is so often the case, it is particularly difficult to access orthodox and conventional views. As Mitchison has noted, charitability is such an obvious and universal value that it is 'often not specifically expressed in statements on morality'.[1] There was certainly no major body of printed debate or other qualitative writings directly addressing the subject at length in Scotland during the years covered by this book. Yet close reading of some key reforming texts, as well as a wider range of literary texts, treatises and various other prose works reveals that the subject was often discussed or utilised, and was a point of particular interest for those concerned with reform of various shades in the mid-sixteenth century. It continued to play a role in understandings of piety and morality into the seventeenth century as well.

Inevitably, in searching for evidence on how Scottish writers treated this subject, one has to be open-minded and even magpie-like in the identification and selection of texts. At the same time, there is also a need for great caution in defining the subject-matter. Poverty is here defined roughly as in the rest of the book: that is as a level of serious material deprivation which prompts a need for assistance from external sources (whether that support is necessarily forthcoming or not). Therefore, poverty in the broader though overlapping sense of the condition of the common people or lower levels of society, is not the main concern here, meaning that ideas and debates about social hierarchies and relationships between social orders (or indeed what might be termed classes and class conflict) are not generally

[1] Mitchison, *Coping*, p. 3.

included. This is partly because such debates require proper assessment on their own terms, but also because they do not have a substantial bearing on the business of poor relief itself in this historical setting. [2] Many references to the poor also have to be more-or-less disregarded because they are wholly formulaic or descriptive: phrases such as 'rich and poor alike' are normally unrelated to poverty in the sense utilised here.[3] Equally, 'charity' has to be interpreted, for these purposes, in the narrower sense specific to assisting the economically poor, although this is of course very closely related to and sometimes inseparable from the wider Christian conception of the term relating to neighbourly love and community.[4] Although these broader senses naturally impose themselves at various points, the principle aim here is to understand how Scottish opinion conceptualised the needy poor and their relief.

Medieval Attitudes

The poor were an important presence in medieval European thought, and there was no doubt about the virtue of almsgiving and charity.[5] One had a duty to help the poor, in whom the image of Christ could be seen. This may have been partly for the good of one's soul, or in exchange for prayer, perhaps, but also for a wide and overlapping range of motivations. As Carol Rawcliffe has suggested, 'any historian attempting to disentangle, let alone rank, the motives of medieval benefactors is, in the final resort, bent upon an anachronistic and essentially fruitless task'.[6] Equally, the 'caricature of medieval charity as indiscriminate' (because it involved the thoughtless dispensation of alms to beggars with little care for necessity or efficacy), or as an essentially ecclesiastical enterprise, has been greatly undermined.[7] Just as our understanding of motivations and charitable impulses has been greatly nuanced, so it is important to remain aware of the broad and flexible medieval understanding of charitable giving: as *Piers Plowman* (for example) indicated, money should be given not just to the 'poor' in the narrow sense but to a range of causes including road and bridge repair, funding to support maidens becoming nuns or scholars' expenses, or to prisoners.[8] It is therefore essential for studies of early modern poor relief to avoid caricaturing or excessively simplifying medieval thought and practice, and perhaps particularly to avoid assuming that medieval charity was

[2] For some instructive comments on contemporary ideas about this issue see Goodare, *Government*, pp. 247–51.
[3] See below, p. 31n.
[4] On the latter sense see Wooding, 'Charity, Community and Reformation Propaganda'.
[5] Amongst a wide literature see especially Mollat, *The Poor in the Middle Ages*; Rubin, *Charity and Community*, especially chapter. 2; Olson, 'Continuity or Radical Change?'.
[6] Rawcliffe, '"A word from our sponsor"', p. 188.
[7] Olson, 'Continuity or Radical Change?', pp. 151–7 (quote at p. 151).
[8] Bennett, 'Conviviality and Charity', pp. 21–2.

focused on the giver and their soul, rather than the recipient, or that thinking about the poor was solely a matter of ecclesiastical propriety.

Little study has been made of medieval Scottish attitudes or responses to poverty, partly (but not entirely) reflecting a lack of obvious source materials. It seems likely that the extent of formal poor relief was fairly limited, although there is scattered evidence of pre-Reformation provision by secular authorities (for example in Aberdeen in 1546, or in Haddington in 1558), as well as by religious orders.[9] Much monastic charity might well have been informal, and the casual references that survive may represent the tip of an iceberg, although it might be hazardous to assume that it was a particularly large iceberg.[10] The royal almoner made donations to the poor (among other causes), and Scotland also had a significant number of (mostly rather small) medieval hospitals.[11] Guilds would also provide some relief for their own brethren and perhaps some local poor people.[12] Some care for the poor was certainly taking place as a matter of course in late-medieval Scotland, even if we cannot yet confidently assess its extent and workings.[13]

Whatever the scale of the actual funding, there is no doubt that charity was highly valued in medieval Scotland, and that poverty was taken seriously. Audrey-Beth Fitch's work has shown that caring for the poor was a significant element of late medieval Scottish piety. This might include the sense that charitability was among the factors to be considered to ensure salvation (for example, when being judged at the 'justice court extreme', to quote William Dunbar's striking phrase), or a more general feeling 'that God would look well on those who showed charity to the poor'.[14] In 1532 the bishop of Aberdeen argued that it was not enough to fund the clergy; instead 'the work which is of real value is supporting the poor according to the divine command, by giving them food and clothing'.[15] The poor were also, of course, a particularly useful source of prayer, especially through obit foundations where one's posthumous generosity could be returned

[9] Cowan, *Death, Life and Religious*, pp. 113–14; Paton (ed.), 'Haddington Records', p. 57; see also below, chapter 8; Coulton, *Scottish Abbeys and Social Life*, pp. 102–4; Foggie, *Renaissance Religion*, pp. 186, 234–5.

[10] Traditionally negative estimates of English monastic provision have now been challenged to suggest a more generous picture: Rushton, 'Monastic charitable provision'; Rushton, 'Forms and Functions of Monastic Poor Relief', pp. 121–6.

[11] Brown, 'Lay Piety in Later Medieval Lothian', pp. 102–4; McCallum, '"Nurseries of the Poore"', pp. 430–1.

[12] Cowan, *Death, Life and Religious Change*, p. 104; Torrie (ed.), *Gild Court Book of Dunfermline*, pp. xxii, 42.

[13] Although the Gaedhealtachd is beyond the remit of this book, it is worth noting that current research suggests that kin-based care for the poor and sick was also being provided in the highlands, although on a similarly unquantifiable scale: MacDonald, 'The Church in Gaelic Scotland', pp. 21–2.

[14] Quoted in Fitch, 'The Search for Salvation', pp. 60–1, 67, 102.

[15] Quoted in Fitch, 'The Search for Salvation', p. 395.

through prayers for one's soul from local poor layfolk. As Fitch puts it, this was 'an inexpensive means of obtaining a substantial number of prayers', although as always with cheapness came a reduction in quality: the prayers of clergy were seen as more efficacious.[16] Inmates of hospitals would also naturally provide prayers for the souls of donors.[17]

It is worth noting, however, that the poor were not simply seen as faceless participants in an alms-prayer transaction: there was also a noticeable strain of concern in late-medieval and renaissance thought about the oppression of the poor, or a lack of care for them more generally. John Bellenden criticised those who did not care about the poor even though they were able to help, and amongst Sir David Lindsay's satirical targets were noble oppressors of their poor tenants, and pardoners who ruthlessly exploited poor men.[18] The character of the Pauper, who dominates the Interlude in the *Satire of the Thrie Estaitis,* was not naturally poor but had become impoverished through the injustice of lairds and the clerical estate.[19] Sir Richard Maitland of Lethington's poetic advice to his son William at court in 1555 included the injunction not just to profit and honour 'thy prince', but also to 'set ay fordwart the puir, baith day and nicht'. The two duties are compared again at the close of the poem: 'And syne thy prince serve, luif weill, and obey/ And, as thow may, be helpand ay the puire'.[20] William Dunbar's three linked poems on Discretion (in asking, giving, and taking) include reflections on the importance of seeking alms appropriately and of donating carefully (as well as criticising those who 'take' without discretion, oppressing the poor).[21] Dunbar also juxtaposed the wealth of Edinburgh's prosperous burgesses with their lack of charity to the poor beggars, and included the avoidance of spitefulness to the poor amongst the key generic indicators of moral rectitude in his poem on 'Rewl of anis self'.[22] Robert Henryson's satirical verse condemned oppression of the poor (sheep, or lambs) by 'fals extorteneiris and oppressouris of pure men' (wolves).[23] These themes in late medieval

16 Fitch, 'The Search for Salvation', p. 352–356 (quote at p. 355). See also Brown, 'Lay Piety in Later Medieval Lothian', pp. 228–9.

17 Cowan, *Death, Life and Religious Change,* p. 23.

18 Fitch, 'The Search for Salvation', pp. 132, 164, 222; Tapscott, 'Propaganda and Persuasion', pp. 81–2.

19 Walker, 'The Popular Voice in Sir David Lyndsay's Satire of the Thrie Estaitis', pp. 41–2.

20 Bain (ed.), *Poems of Sir Richard Maitland,* pp. 19–22.

21 Small (ed.), *Poems of William Dunbar,* ii, pp. 84–5, 87–8, 90–91. Such critiques were not confined to literary texts. When the church council of 1549 ordered clergy to avoid excessive luxury in food and drink, one of the reasons given was 'that they also succour the poor in their necessities more bountifully and generously': Patrick (ed.), *Statutes of the Scottish Church,* p. 93.

22 Meikle, *The Scottish People,* p. 62; Small (ed.), *Poems of William Dunbar,* ii, p. 98 (see i, p. clxviii for the poem's title).

23 Henryson, 'The Morall Fabillis', in Kendrick (ed.), *The Poems of Robert Henryson,* quote at line 2711–12, see also lines 1258–9, 2428–9, 2762, 2770–6.

Scottish literature – the need to care for the poor and criticisms of oppression of the poor – are of course generic (and hard for anyone to object to), and they are not always particularly related to specific real-world concerns or problems.[24] This does, however, make them revealing as windows on wider social attitudes and conventional values.[25] Charity and the state of the poor seem to have been significant issues for some late-medieval Scots at least, and poor people themselves were seen as more than simple sources of cheap salvation.

This is not to suggest that the poor were always viewed with charitable concern. The fifteenth and sixteenth centuries witnessed considerable apprehension about beggars, and the threat posed by idle and sturdy beggars in particular. This was the main subject relating to the poor found in pre-Reformation legislation. As early as 1425, it was stipulated that 'no beggar be suffered to thig or beg either in burghs or in the land between fourteen and seventy years of age, unless it is seen by the council of the town that they cannot make their living in other ways', and the following year idle men were to be investigated and put to work.[26] Similar legislation (and re-statements of existing Acts) followed regularly over the following 130 years, and the only other subject relating to poverty to receive anywhere near such attention was the state of hospitals and their foundations.[27] It was, of course, not all poor people but idle beggars, 'sorners' and the like who were thus condemned: 'lame folk, blind folk, helpless folk and weak folk' were explicitly exempted in 1504, and in 1455 the culprits included 'oppressors of the king's lieges or the poor people', since idle beggars were seen as harming the genuine poor as much as anyone else.[28] A Richard Maitland poem on the New Year addresses various groups and prays that they fulfil their proper roles: the common people should work hard, while 'ydle lounis' and 'sornars' should be put in the 'galiounis' (i.e. galleys).[29] The poor were certainly not seen as a single category, to be approached

24 Although some of the discussion of oppression of poor people, such as that by David Lindsay, relates to developments in feuing: see, for example, Goodare, 'In Search of the Scottish Agrarian Problem', pp. 110–11.

25 Of less use are references to the 'poor' where they are merely juxtaposed alongside the rich to represent the social order or simply to denote all people together, 'bayth of rich and puir' (Pinkerton (ed.), *Ancient Scottish poems, Volume II*, pp. 293, 335). This does not denote indigence or necessity so much as the common people in general. Similarly, little can be read into expressions of the idea that love is no respecter of social boundaries, for example in the poem 'Luve ane Levellar' (*Ancient Scottish Poems, Published from the MS. of George Bannatyne*, p. 192. The beggar (sometimes as the 'Gaberlunzie Man') occurs as a stock figure in popular stories, although they tend not to reveal wider attitudes to poverty itself. See, for example, Callander (ed.), *Two Ancient Scottish Poems*.

26 *RPS*, 1425/3/22; 1426/29.

27 *RPS*, 1450/1/20; 1458/3/18; 1478/6/88; A1504/3/114; 1535/38; A1552/2/16; McCallum, '"Nurseries of the Poore"', p. 430+n.

28 *RPS*, A1504/3/114; 1455/10/14.

29 Bain (ed.), *Poems of Sir Richard Maitland*, p. 4. (the poem is possibly dated to 1557, and certainly from Mary of Guise's time as regent: p. 155).

in the same way. As Michel Mollat's extensive typology of the medieval terminology used to discuss poverty suggests, a wide and nuanced range of attitudes to the poor could be accommodated.[30]

Throughout the ages, of course, the key division made in considering the poor has been the perennial distinction between deserving and undeserving. The idea that this was primarily an early modern development has now been heavily undermined, although there is still some debate over when exactly this distinction became prominent in thinking about relief during the middle ages, with estimates varying from the twelfth to fourteenth centuries.[31] Whatever the precise chronology, it is clear that by the fifteenth century there was already a strong (if not universal) emphasis on the need to discriminate between those genuinely deserving of assistance, and the undeserving.[32] This was, naturally enough, true of Scotland as well.[33] We have already encountered parliamentary condemnation of sturdy beggars, and William Dunbar urging 'discretion' in giving, and worrying that 'sum gevis to thame can ask and plenyie' or 'to thame can flatter and fenyie'.[34] Helen Brown has found discriminating attitudes in the distribution of charity in the late fifteenth and early sixteenth century, and a hospital charter from as early as the 1270s demands that its beneficiaries work as far as their abilities allow or be replaced.[35] Of course, the fact that discrimination took place and that a sense of deserving and undeserving was present does not mean that there was no difference from later periods. For example, there seems to have been some more tolerance of groups which were later considered as wholly undeserving in Ayr in 1540–1, when the burgh paid for wine for 'the Egiptianis [gypsies] quhen thai dansit to the baillies', something which would be very out-of-place in late sixteenth- or seventeenth-century records.[36] But overall the sense of distinction between different categories of poor people, and especially the deserving and undeserving, appears fully evident by the eve of the Scottish Reformation. Indeed more generally there was no fundamental shift in attitudes to poverty and charity from the medieval to the early modern, and significant continuities can be identified. Medieval Scots were concerned about poverty and about the poor, and they thought that charity was a vital part of their lives, including their religious lives. The Scottish Reformation

[30] Mollat, *The Poor in the Middle Ages*, pp. 1–5. See also Scott's discussion of the portrayal of poverty in a fourteenth-century text as a 'hateful and subversive woman' rather than as a holy figure: 'Le Chastel de Labour, la Voie de Povreté ou de Richesse and a luxury book, Widener 1, Free Library of Philadelphia', in Scott (ed.), *Experiences of Poverty*, p. 254.

[31] Harvey, *Living and Dying*, pp. 7–8, 16–20; Lepine, 'Cathedrals and Charity', pp. 1087–8.

[32] See, for example, Dyer, 'Poverty and its Relief', pp. 54, 61, 63–4; Bennett, 'Conviviality and Charity', pp. 29–30; McIntosh, *Poor Relief in England*, p. 16.

[33] Cf. Wormald, *Court, Kirk, and Community*, p. 168.

[34] Small (ed.), *Poems of William Dunbar*, ii, p. 88.

[35] Brown, 'Lay Piety in Later Medieval Lothian', pp. 229–30; Anderson (ed.), *Calendar of the Laing Charters*, no. 11.

[36] *ABA*, p. 85. For policies against 'Egyptians' see Chapter 7 of this book.

would, however, have major consequences for how these issues came to be tackled in practice.

Protestant Reformers and Charity

The significance of the poor and issues of charity to Protestant reformers of various stripes is well established. Although it has now been convincingly established that Catholic and humanist reformers were also deeply committed to reforming poor relief and revitalising care for the poor, Protestants across Europe often argued for better treatment of the poor and undertook measures to improve the provision of relief.[37] They made rhetorical use of what they presented as the old Church's lack of interest in really helping the state of the poor; they conceived of poverty as an ill to be tackled (certainly not an ideal to be venerated); and from Scandinavia to Geneva they introduced new schemes to relieve poverty.[38] In England, early Reformation polemic made great play of the miserable state of the poor in contrast to the luxury of the clergy.[39] Recent scholarship has rightly stressed that the Protestant Reformation was not a starting-point in this regard, but stimulated existing impulses and reforms.[40] But it is clear that even if it was not a uniquely Reformation concern, the poor and their care was a key theme for Protestant reformers in polemic, in theory, and in practice.

This was true of Scottish Protestants as well. The most significant early example is George Wishart, who preached and ministered to plague sufferers in Dundee, emphasising the need to care properly for the poor and sick, and not to favour the rich over the poor.[41] As John Knox would later put it in a letter to Marjorie Bowes, 'the Apostill dampneth [condemns] sic as preferis a man with a goldin chayne to the pure'.[42] Knox's account of his early mentor places much emphasis on Wishart's charity, especially during the dramatic events surrounding his trial and execution.[43] When Wishart 'entered in at the Abbay Church doore, there was a poore man lying vexed

37 Pullan, 'Catholics and the Poor'; Jutte, *Poverty*, pp. 100, 104.

38 See, for example, Lindberg, *Beyond Charity*, pp. 97, 99, 105–6; Bucer, 'De Regno Christi', pp. 256–7; Wandel, *Always Among Us*; Olson, 'Continuity or Radical Change?', pp. 158–67.

39 McIntosh, *Poor Relief in England*, pp. 119–21.

40 Olson, 'Continuity or Radical Change?', p. 171.

41 Flett, 'The conflict of the Reformation and democracy in the Geneva of Scotland', p. 27; Knox, *Works*, i, p. 130. The *First Book of Discipline* echoed this point, emphasising (on the subject of burial) that 'before God there is no respect of persons' and that therefore 'whatsoever [ministers] doe to the rich [. . .] the same they are bound to doe to the poorest under their charge': *FBD*, p. 201.

42 Knox, *Works*, iii, p. 395.

43 For Wishart's importance to Knox's development see Dawson, *Knox*, pp. 28–32. Dawson also intriguingly suggests (p. 297) that Wishart's example of ministering to the suffering of Dundee may have been in Knox's mind when deciding to stay and preach in Edinburgh during a visitation of plague over twenty years later in 1568.

with great infirmities, asking of his almouse, to whome he flang his purse'.[44] Other accounts of Wishart also stress his charity, giving his clothes to the poor as well as ministering to them, and the state of the poor seems to have been a recurring interest of his.[45] Of course, Knox's account of Wishart is effectively hagiographical and so naturally emphasises his generosity, although it does seem likely to have been an important aspect of Wishart's teachings and personality.[46] But it is certainly significant that Knox chose to foreground this aspect of Wishart's personality and teaching. Similarly, in recounting the martyrdom of Adam Wallace, Knox stressed that he looked like 'a simple poore man in appearance'.[47]

Elsewhere in his writings, Knox uses hostility to or mistreatment of the poor as a key indicator of wickedness. In one tale, when a French soldier raided a poor woman's house and she 'offered unto him such breid as sche had reddy prepared' (being a model of charity), 'he, in no wayis thairwith content, wald have the meill and a lytill salt beiff whiche the poore woman had to susteine hir awin lyfe, and the lyves of hir poore chylderein; neather could tearis, nor [pitifull] wourdis mittigat the merciles man . . .' She then attacked and killed him, 'God so punishing his crewell hairt'.[48] He said of the French in Glasgow that 'silver wald thay gif nane to the poore men', and one of them slaughtered a poor craftsmen whose pitiful state was deliberately emphasised as part of the story: he was eating a morsel of a 'gray laif' and was 'putting the rest of it in his bosome' when he was attacked.[49] Oppression of the poor more generally is emphasised and condemned in Knox's 'Letter' to Mary of Guise as regent.[50] And later, when criticising life at court in Edinburgh in the early 1560s, Knox referred to 'avarice, oppressioun of the poor, excesse, ryotouse chear, banketting, immoderat dansing, and hurdome', a clear link being drawn between bad behaviour towards the poor and the ungodly debauchery and excess which is a more familiar target of godly ire.[51] The oppression and mistreatment of the poor was part of, and evidence of, the wrongness of the Catholic forces, and the Protestants by implication are associated with the honest poor people. Not

[44] Knox, *Works*, i, p. 150 (see also p. 169 for further reference for his desire to give alms).

[45] Knox, *Works*, vi, pp. 671–2. Wishart's 'oration' dialogue recounts an encounter with a Jew, who says 'we see the poore almost perish throw hunger among yow, yitt yow ar nott moved with pitie towardis thame; butt among us Jewes, thowght we be puir, thare ar no beggares found', although it is not clear how far he intended sympathy with this statement since he was distancing himself from the Jew's other statements about the idolatry of the sacrament. However he did not deny telling the story, suggesting he had at some point found the words significant (Knox, *Works*, i, pp. 158–9).

[46] Dawson, *Knox*, p. 31.

[47] Knox, *Works*, i, p. 544.

[48] Knox, *Works*, ii, pp. 14–15.

[49] Knox, *Works*, ii, p. 57.

[50] Knox, *Works*, iv, pp. 448–50.

[51] Knox, *Works*, ii, p. 362. A similar association between 'exces', 'filthie lustis' and 'unmercifulnes to the pure' is suggested in Knox's earlier correspondence: iii, p. 383.

only did Knox himself consider this a significant point, he also presumably thought it would carry some weight with his audiences.

Knox's works also reflect the more positive desire to see better support for the poor, although the two themes are not wholly separable.[52] Amongst the exhortations to those elected as superintendents and ministers appeared the phrase 'Comfort the afflicted, support the puier, and exhort utheris to support thame'.[53] Knox's treatise on true prayer (1553) stipulated (when discussing what a 'congregation' is) that as part of the distribution of the sacrament, 'inquisitioun be maid of the poore amang thame, and support provydit, whill the tyme of thair nixt conventioun, and it suld be distributit amangis thame'.[54] In ecclesiastical practice after 1560, of course, the provision of poor relief and the Eucharist would inevitably become separated, but it is striking to see poor relief included at the heart of this discussion of the nature of the sacrament. The importance of mercifulness to the poor is also stressed in Knox's personal correspondence: he signs off one letter 'Be fervent in reiding, fervent in prayer, and mercifull to the pure'.[55] The 1560 address to parliament included among the problems with misappropriation of the 'haill patrimony of the Kirk' that the poor were 'not onlie defraudit of thair portioun, but alssua tyrannouslie oppressit'.[56] Concerns about the church's revenues at this point are very familiar to historians, but seen in the context of previous statements of concern about oppression and lack of charity, the references to the poor start to seem less purely rhetorical or formulaic, and more significant. They were also expressed by Knox well before the famous compromise of the 'thirds of benefices' came to pass: in 1556 Knox's treatise on baptism emphasised that kirk rents should chiefly benefit 'the poore, the stranger, the wydow, the fatherless'.[57]

As on so many reformation issues, Knox is the loudest Scottish voice of his period. But he was not alone in emphasising and utilising the poor. Henry Balnaves' treatise on Justification included being 'mercifull to the poore; supporting the indigent after the quantitie of your riches' amongst the good examples which should be set by householders.[58] The Catholic lack of charity (instead emphasising fruitless spiritual investments) is also attacked: 'your wicked and ungodly pastors have taught you to found a soule masse with your substance and suffer father and mother to begge their breade'.[59] In his unpublished 'Godly and Golden Booke' arguing for

[52] Greaves, 'Social Awareness of John Knox', pp. 36–7.
[53] Knox, *Works*, ii, p. 150.
[54] Knox, *Works*, iii, p. 103.
[55] Knox, *Works*, iii, p. 402.
[56] Knox, *Works*, ii, p. 91 (see also pp. 486, 538).
[57] Knox, *Works*, iv, p. 127 (see ii, p. 310 for Knox's oft-cited condemnation of two thirds of the teinds being freely gifted to the devil and the remaining third shared between the devil and the kirk; see also Dawson, *Knox*, p. 222).
[58] Knox, *Works*, iii, p. 538.
[59] Knox, *Works*, iii, p. 541.

Anglo-Scottish amity in 1548, James Henryson lamented the oppression of 'the poor labourers of the ground', and included better care of the poor including 'that every parish shall uphold their own sick and impotent' amongst his numerous proposals for pan-British political and economic reform.[60] The anticlerical verses in the *Gude and Godlie Ballatis* offered opportunities to criticise the existing church's corruption and lack of care. One song, 'God send everie preist ane wyfe' suggests that if the clergy were to do the decent thing and marry, not only would there be less whoredom through the land, but also 'nor zit sa mony beggeris pure/In Kirk and mercat stand'. Another condemns the Pope, cardinals and the like for 'schawand zour relykis and your ruddis/To pluk fra vs pure men our guddis'.[61] Another anticlerical text, George Buchanan's devastating satire of the Franciscan order, 'Franciscanus' (*c.* 1538), included reference to 'the offerings of the poor suffering people going up in smoke' while the friars enjoyed their gluttony and feasting.[62] The Franciscans were of course a particularly juicy target because of the perceived hypocrisy resulting from the idealisation of poverty and what Buchanan described elsewhere as their 'shameless beggary', and an extortionate pursuit of income by any means possible.[63]

Less overtly polemical was the discussion of charity in the earliest Protestant text in the Scots language, John Gau's *The richt vay to the kingdom of hevine* (a 1533 translation of a Lutheran treatise, closely focused on the Commandments, Creed and Lord's Prayer).[64] Those who sin against the fourth commandment are introduced as those who 'lichtlis [slights] their fader and moder and their pwir frendis for powerte or seiknes and wil notht help thayme with meit and claith and oder neidful thingis', moving swiftly from the literal parents of the original text to include not just other elders or authority figures, but those in need more generally.[65] Although not an unusual application of the commandment, the poor and sick emerge particularly prominently here (in a way which was echoed in Aberdeen Kirk Session's early statutes in 1562).[66] Interestingly the separate discussion of how the commandment should be positively honoured (as opposed to how it tends to be broken currently) focuses on the more obvious application of obedience to superior authorities, perhaps suggesting a particular concern about a lack of charity as a current social ill. The commandment on theft is also interpreted to include 'thay that wil noth help their nichtburs in their necessite', and urges being charitable and 'pwir spiritualie in thy hart',

60 *CSP: Scotland, I*, pp. 140–5 (quotations at pp. 143, 144). Although not printed at the time, the work's contents are preserved through its presentation to William Cecil.

61 Mitchell (ed.), *A compendious book of godly and spiritual songs*, pp. 189, 194.

62 McGinnis and Williamson (eds), *George Buchanan: The Political Poetry*, p. 230.

63 McGinnis and Williamson (eds), *George Buchanan: The Political Poetry*, pp. 176, 208.

64 Gau, *The richt vay to the kingdom of hevine*; *ODNB*, 'Gaw, John (d. c.1553)'.

65 Gau, *The richt vay*, p. 14.

66 CH2/448/1, p. 4; see also McCallum, '"Fatheris"', pp. 74–5.

suggesting a significant if conventional interest in the issue of generosity.[67] The metrical version of the Commandments in the *Gude and Godlie Ballatis* places slightly less direct emphasis on the treatment of the poor in the fourth Commandment (give your 'Elderis', not specifically the needy, 'supplie' and what they 'requyre').[68] Other traditional messages might be presented in the *Ballatis* in such a way as to critique a contemporary lack of charity and exhort generosity. The morality tale from Luke 16 of the rich glutton and 'pure Lazarus' which contrasts the wealthy and well-fed man with the starving beggar at his door (the latter ends up in heaven, the former in hell) is given extra bite with the additional comment of the beggar that 'nane to gif him was sa liberall'.[69] The basic narrative of the story could be taken as affirming the traditional idea that the poor may suffer on earth, but would receive amends in the afterlife, potentially gravitating against interest in the issue of welfare. But the comment about a lack of liberality suggests the importance and urgency of giving, and is echoed by the closing verse of the song (after the biblical passage). These commence by urging the reader 'unto the pure be pietifull/quhill ze ar heir schwa thame zour cheritie', rather than suggesting that the poor should await their compensation in heaven.[70]

The devotional or theological nature of much early Scottish reformist literature means that the issue of poverty and charity is often only subtly present: after all when setting out evangelical views on faith, salvation, the sacraments or scripture, the state of the poor is unlikely to be at the forefront of the discussion.[71] But when reformers turned to more directly polemical matters, the issue emerges more prominently. Much of Gau's *Richt Vay* simply expresses Lutheran ideas through exposition of the Commandments, Creed and Lord's Prayer (and in translation from the original Danish and German). However, at the end when he turns to address the Lords and Barons of Scotland, and to condemn the papacy and clergy, Gau's material is both more original, and more Scotland-specific, as he contextualises the message for his audience and makes reference to the recent martyrdom of Patrick Hamilton. Here the oppression of the poor by the existing church becomes more prominent: the 'voluptuous and flesclie liff' of the papacy and clergy is gained 'of the sweit and blwid of the puir', and Gau also refers to the 'spulze quhilk thay reiff fra the pwir'.[72] The issue of poverty may not have been central to reformation dogma itself, but it was more significant in the rhetoric of reformation.

Of course, the most famous rhetorical representation of poverty and

[67] Gau, *The richt vay*, pp. 17, 22–3.

[68] Mitchell (ed.), *A compendious book of godly and spiritual songs*, p. 8.

[69] Mitchell (ed.), *A compendious book of godly and spiritual songs*, p. 40.

[70] Mitchell (ed.), *A compendious book of godly and spiritual songs*, p. 42.

[71] See, for example, Hamilton, *Paitrikes places*; Johnson, *An confortable exhortation*; Alesius, *Of the auctorite of the word of god*.

[72] Gau, *The richt vay*, p. 104.

the poor in the Scottish Reformation is the Beggar's Summons of January 1559, which played a role in the precipitation of the crisis of 1559–60 itself. It was written, for effect, from the perspective of 'the blynd, cruked, bedrelles, wedowis, orphelingis, and all uther pure, sa viseit be the hand of God, as may not worke', and addressed to 'the flockes of all freires within this realme'. The beggars 'wische restitutioun of wranges bypast, and reformatioun in tyme cuming', asserting that 'the benignitie or almes of all Christian pepill perteynis to us allanerly', and order the friars to quit their properties in favour of those in genuine poverty.[73] And in the aftermath of the Summons, while Perth was being reformed, Knox claimed that the 'spoile' from the Blackfriars (which though less rich than the Greyfriars 'was more then becam men professing povertie') 'was permitted to the poore: for so had the preacheouris befoir threatned all men, that for covetousnes saik none shuld putt thare hand to suche a Reformatioun, that no honest man was enriched thairby the valew of a groate'.[74] Quite apart from a genuine interest in the poor, the reformers were keenly aware that distributing such resources to the needy helped to advertise that self-interest was not their motivating force. It is highly significant that this rhetorical theme became so prominent when tensions came to a head in 1559, but it should not be surprising, when we consider the importance of poverty and the need to treat the poor better in previous decades' reformist writing.

Once the Reformed Kirk was officially established, poor relief took a significant place in its agenda. Most prominently, the authors of *First Book of Discipline* set out the need to provide for the (worthy) poor, 'for feareful and horrible it is, that the poore, whom not onely God the Father in his Law, but Christ Jesus in his Evangel, and the holy Spirit speaking by S. Paul hath so earnestly commended to our care, are universally so contemned and despised'. They also distinguished these worthy poor from idle beggars, for whom they were 'not Patrones'.[75] Poor scholars were to be supported especially, and the oppression and mistreatment of poor people more generally was strongly condemned.[76] While the provision of relief is the subject of later chapters, it is noteworthy that there were local expressions of the intent to reform charity and the importance of care for the poor (and the control of unworthy beggars) in the early 1560s.[77] The General Assembly expressed concern about provision too. Some of this was linked to wider concerns about ecclesiastical revenues, but the language could be striking:

> As for the very indigent and pure, to quhom God commandes a sustentatioun to be provided off the tyndes, they are so despised, that it

[73] Knox, *Works*, i, pp. 320–1n.

[74] Knox, *Works*, i, p. 323.

[75] *FBD*, pp. 112–13.

[76] *FBD*, pp. 131, 156–7, 166.

[77] *RStAKS*, i, p. 1; CH2/448/1, pp. 4–7; see also McCallum, '"Fatheris"', pp. 72–4.

> is a wonder that the sone giveth lycht and heat unto the earth, quhare Gods name is so frequently called upoun, and no mercy (according to his comandements) schawin to his creatures.[78]

Similar intensity of feeling was shown several decades later in 1588: 'what heart touched with a spark of naturall humanity or godly charity, can unbleeding behold the miserable estate of the poor vaiging in great troups and companyes through the countrie without either law or religion'.[79] And when fasts were ordered – in 1574 for example – amongst the causes might be found 'the great hounger, famine and oppression of the pure'.[80] And in 1596 the General Assembly complained about the oppression by landlords of 'poore tennents', including 'extreame thraldome in services'.[81] The oppression of the poor was also an important theme for preachers such as Robert Bruce, who included it in an attack on the faults of the wealthy, and drew strong parallels with what he described as the 'poor and oppressed' of Psalm 76 (merely 'meek' in the King James Version).[82] At the same time, the moral state of the poor was a concern: at worst they lived in fornication, unbaptised, not attending the sacrament.[83] The leaders of the Reformed Kirk continued to consider poverty and the poor as a major problem.

As is well known, the post-Reformation years also witnessed legislative attempts to tackle problems surrounding poverty. Following English legislation, the 1570s poor laws tried to set out a plan for relief through compulsory contribution, as well as a clampdown on the undeserving poor.[84] There was perhaps greater hostility to sturdy beggars and the like, although as we have seen this sort of fear was hardly new.[85] The attitudes to the poor were – in general – not necessarily more negative however. An Act of 1581 expressed worry about the implications that nobles spending less time on their estates would have for traditional hospitality and local informal relief.[86] In 1617 an Act on finding employment for the poor was striking for including a note of understanding and perhaps even sympathy for some who would often be simply considered unworthy beggars. It noted that many had been 'poor children and orphans born of poor and indigent

78 *BUK*, i, p. 22.

79 *BUK*, ii, p. 724.

80 Knox, *Works*, vi, p. 428. See also Mears *et al.* (eds), *National Prayers: Special Worship Since the Reformation, Volume 1*, p. 153 ('universall oppressioun and contempt of the poore' in 1582). Abuse of the poor might itself be viewed as one of the causes of famine: Mullan, *Scottish Puritanism*, pp. 88–9.

81 *BUK*, iii, p. 874.

82 Cunningham (ed.), *Sermons by the Rev. Robert Bruce*, pp. 143, 316 [pagination referring to the Sermon section of the volume]. For further examples of post-reformation criticism of the oppression of poor and common people see Cranstoun (ed.), *Satirical Poems*, i, pp. 18, 56, 134; Pinkerton (ed.), *Ancient Scottish Poems, Volume II*, pp. 321–3.

83 *BUK*, ii, p. 731.

84 See above, pp. 16–17.

85 *RPS*, 1592/4/91; A1593/9/14; 1597/11/46; 1600/11/41; 1609/4/32.

86 *RPS*, 1581/10/40.

parents, who, being tolerated or neglected at their first entry to begging, do contract such a custom and habit that hardly they can be drawn thereafter to any other calling': their indigence was still their fault, essentially, but it was not without an external and original cause, and nor was it necessarily a simple choice they had made.[87] Equally the church worried about the poor losing out on doles at bridals, and wanted to take steps to relieve them from paying fees they might not be able to afford (for marriages, baptisms, burials and so on).[88] The direct impact of the Reformation on the practice of poor relief will be assessed in subsequent chapters, but for now we can note that from the emergence of explicit Protestant dissent in the 1540s through to the establishment and development of a Reformed Kirk of Scotland, reformers continued to place emphasis on the better treatment of the poor, in various senses of the word.

Unsurprisingly, given the prominence of the issue of poverty in Protestant rhetoric, the subject was a source of argument between supporters and opponents of the Reformation.[89] In his 1562 tracts against the Protestants, the Catholic controversialist Ninian Winzet criticised, among other things, 'the rigour to the pure dune on your awin landis', and how tenants are paupered and 'honeste men' removed 'fra thair native roumes, be tytle off youre new quhirlie fewis'.[90] Quintin Kennedy's 'Oratioune', warning against the Reformed leaders, similarly condemns the Reformation's impact on the poor. Among the things which could have been avoided if people had seen how dangerously the Protestants were mis-applying the gospel, was that 'than [then] had nocht sa mony pure menne deit miserably under dikes through hunger, caulde, and povertie for laik of cheritie, quhilk is waxt calde through the iniquitie of thir pestilient prechouris'.[91] Catholic opponents of the Reformation were not willing to allow the Protestant interpretation of the relationship between confession and charitability to go unopposed. This was still true two decades later, when Nicol Burne's *Disputation* of 1581 asserted that 'the pure folk ar mair naikit nor ever they var', and contrasted the true Catholic Church's 'geving of almous' with the 'deformed' church's 'dissolving of hospitallis'.[92] An associated 'Admonition to the Antichristian Ministers in the Deformit Kirk of Scotland' refers to the 'Curse of the

87 *RPS*, 1617/5/24.

88 *Dundonald*, p. 418; *RStAKS*, ii, pp. 604–5; CH2/1026/1, pp. 29, 109; CH2/448/1, p. 131; CH2/521/2, f. 80r.

89 Wooding, 'Charity, Community and Reformation Propaganda', pp. 153–7; Elliott, 'Charitable "Intent" in Late Sixteenth-Century France', pp. 163, 182.

90 Winzet, *Certain tractates*, i, p. 8. The definition of 'quhirlie' posited by *DSL* is 'Taking place with a giddy rush; ? causing sudden and confusing change', implying something similar to 'whirly' (although the sole citation for this is the quotation in question).

91 Knox, *Works*, vi, p. 161.

92 Burne, *The disputation*, 179r, 185v. On the use of hospitals in religious and confessionally charged polemic, which resurfaced around the time of Charles I's visit to Scotland in 1633, see McCallum, '"Nurseries"', pp. 436–8.

pure in number gret and smal, quhom ye have scurgit and hungerit to the deid'.[93]

Interestingly, the criticism of the Reformation's impact on charity was not limited to the Protestants' most obvious opponents. In his poetic 'New Year Gift' to Queen Mary in 1562, Alexander Scott criticises both the old church and the problematic tendencies of the new church, in what Theo van Heijnsbergen has shown to be a subtle and careful moderate call for social reform and an appeal to common ground.[94] As part of this, Scott laments that 'pure folk ar famist with thir fassionis new', and elaborating in the following verse links the idea that the 'Protestandis takis the freiris auld antetweme [theme]' with greedy lairds who seek to 'pund pure communis corne and cattell keir'.[95] So although the old order was not being defended, the Reformation had, among other things, opened the way to exploitation of the poor. Another figure who could perhaps be described as 'moderate' or centrist in his post-1560 affiliations was Richard Maitland of Lethington, who famously lamented 'Quhair is the blythness that hes bein', regretting the loss of the comfortable world which had passed away.[96] Later in the same poem (his 'Satire on the Age'), he bemoaned how 'The temporall men commitis oppressioune/ Puttand the puire from thair possessioune [. . .] And chasis charitie away'.[97] And in 'On the Miseries of the Tyme', he criticises the old church for its corruption, but then makes clear that the Protestants are hardly heroes saving the day: although they claim that 'thay will mak reformatioun', instead vices are running amock, including adultery, theft, slaughter and 'oppressioun of the puir'.[98]

Another writer approaching the subject from a more balanced perspective was William Lauder, who had written plays for the regime in the late 1540s and 1550s, and whose Catholicism during the 1550s has been described as 'Biblicist and reformist'.[99] He conformed to the Reformation after 1560, serving as minister of Forgandenny, Forteviot, and Muckarsie.[100] His poetry is noteworthy for a strong emphasis on advocating for better treatment of the poor, and serves as another example of some writers' interest in the subject of poverty.[101] Moreover it is particularly striking that his post-1560 writings attack both the Catholics, and the hypocrisy of 'gredie dissemblit fals protestantes'. Writing at a time of dearth around 1568–9, 'Ane Godlie

93 Cranstoun (ed.), *Satirical Poems*, i, p. 343.

94 van Heijnsbergen 'Advice to a Princess', pp. 107–8, 111, 121.

95 Cranstoun (ed.), *Poems of Alexander Scott*, p. 6.

96 Bain (ed.), *Poems of Sir Richard Maitland*, p. 23; Lee Jr, 'Sir Richard Maitland of Lethington', p. 120.

97 Bain (ed.), *Poems of Sir Richard Maitland*, p. 25.

98 Bain (ed.), *Poems of Sir Richard Maitland*, pp. 32–3. See also pp. 43, 112, including the list of 'Causes Which Bring Realmes To Ruin', amongst which was 'Oppressioune of the puire'.

99 Ryrie, *Origins*, p. 106.

100 *ODNB*, 'Lauder, William (c. 1520–1573)'.

101 Sondergard, 'Rediscovering William Lauder's Poetic Advocacy of the Poor'.

Tractate or Mirrour' attacks those who spend more on clothes than 'wald do cleith ane hundreth of the pure that gois nakit, begging frome dure to dure'.[102] Addressing the greedy rich who claim to be Protestants he notes 'your Cheritie, it is be-cum sa cauld', and 'thocht ye sla nocht pure men with your knyves, yit with your dearth ye tak from thame the lyves'.[103] In other works he contrasts the 'Hypocreitis' with 'godlie men, tha do support the pure, and gevis thame glaidlie of thair geir and gude', and offers a 'Lamentatioun of the Pure' during the dearth of the late 1560s.[104] During such times, calls to follow the biblical injunction to be a good steward of the poor, 'helpand the Pure in thair necessite', are perhaps fairly predictable, but the attention drawn to the hypocrisy of so-called Protestants is interesting.[105] The importance of the issue around this time is also highlighted by a 1567 Exhortation to the new Regent (the Earl of Moray) to relieve the poor and to 'let thame anis knaw the defference betwene yow and the Papistis, by your charitie'.[106] Lauder's lamentations about the state of the poor went as far as expressing the fear that the papists' charity and compassion for 'thame that beggis from dure to dure/ Sall ws accuse on Domesdaye', and that 'Papistis bearis ilke ane to uther/ More liberall luife, I am moste sure/ Nor dois sum Minister to his brother'.[107] He was clearly concerned that the Catholics might be more charitable, even if their theology was false. Writers from a range of religious perspectives, then, were critical of aspects of the Reformation's impact on the poor. It was certainly an important and sometimes sensitive topic for Reformation arguments.

Post-Reformation Attitudes

What then, was the range of attitudes towards the poor and charity held in Scottish society during the period after 1560 on which this book is focused? There are signs that charity and charitable attitudes remained highly valued and associated with piety, and that the association between the poor and the ecclesiastical sphere (rather than secular authority) remained strong. In St Andrews in 1583, the seventeen poor men granted blue gowns and purses with 17s by the royal almoner were to 'pray for his hienes dayly, and keip the prayaris ilk day and the sermone every pre[aching] day, sittand all togiddir in the parroche kirk of St. Androus, ilk persoun cled with his said blew gown': they were to be highly visible figures during worship.[108] The wider body of the poor were also closely associated with the

[102] Hall and Furnivall (eds), *The extant poetical works of William Lauder*, pp. 16–17.

[103] Hall and Furnivall (eds), *The extant poetical works of William Lauder*, pp. 17–18.

[104] Hall and Furnivall (eds), *The extant poetical works of William Lauder*, pp. 26–7, 33–4.

[105] Hall and Furnivall (eds), *The extant poetical works of William Lauder*, p. 18.

[106] Cranstoun (ed.), *Satirical Poems*, i, p. 56.

[107] Hall and Furnivall (eds), *The extant poetical works of William Lauder*, pp. 27–8.

[108] *RStAKS*, ii, pp. 503–4; and for the development of the Maundy tradition ('Skeir Furisday') of gifts of blue gowns or other items to poor recipients of the same number as the king's

church, as is revealed by phrases such as 'the puir of the kirk of kilrynnie' (describing the recipients of a bequest).[109] They were the poor of the kirk, just as the beneficiaries of a grant in Perth were 'pure memberis of Jesus Chryst', or in a 1568 medical treatise they were 'the pure of Christ'.[110] In Burntisland, in a rare dispute over welfare jurisdiction, the ministers and elders claimed that they, not the town council, should distribute relief because 'thay ar fatheris and provisoners of the puir'.[111] In theory at least there still seems to have been a strong sense that the poor had a special relationship with the church.

When it comes to what individual post-Reformation Scots thought about charity and the poor, we are constrained by evidence problems. Only a tiny proportion of very unrepresentative individuals have left us writings of qualitative value, and even they were relatively unlikely to discuss such uncontroversial (and perhaps obvious?) matters at length, in contrast to theology, ecclesiastical politics, or public affairs.[112] There are some intriguing leads, however. In his study of British Protestant piety Alec Ryrie has noticed 'a repeated emphasis on charity' in many works: charitability was a key element in a successful Protestant life (and although wealth was not a sin in itself, it was potentially a spiritual trap).[113] If you had means, you must help the poor.[114] For the preacher Robert Bruce this was almost a defining element of one's faith: he asserted that 'the third effect of faith is compassion; thou man bow thy heart, and extend thy pitie, upon the poore members of Christ's bodie, and suffer them not to lack gif thou have; for except ye have this compassion, ye have na faith'.[115] The Edinburgh minister William Struther's detailed announcement and justification for a national fast in 1628 stressed that 'to be large in devotion, & niggard in our contribution to the poore, is to prove, that we count more of our moneyes than of devotion'.[116] David Mullan has suggested that charitability, and avoiding greed, was a particularly important trait for the clergy.[117] This was perhaps reflected in the emphasis on charity as an important quality

age (hence 17 in 1583), see *RPC*, 1st Series, vol iii, p. 137. In 1579 the council had determined that rather than young boys, as previously, the gifts should now be for 'aigit and decayit personis'. It was also decided to avoid superstition by bestowing the gifts on poor people of whichever location the king was on 19 June, his birthday.

109 CC20/4/5, pp. 727–9.

110 CH2/521/3, p. 165; CH2/521/7, p. 222; Skeyne, *Ane breve descriptioun of the pest*, A1r.

111 CH2/523/1, p. 175; see also McCallum, '"Fatheris"', pp. 80–1.

112 See, for example, Mullan (ed.), *Protestant Piety*; Mullan (ed.), *Religious Controversy in Scotland*); *JMD*; Calderwood, *History of the Kirk of Scotland*.

113 Ryrie, *Being Protestant*, pp. 452–3. See also p. 455 for the observation that thinking of wealth as a 'sign of divine favour' was more of an English than a Scottish mood.

114 Welch, *Forty-Eight Select Sermons*, Sermon XXVII, pp. 340–1.

115 Cunningham (ed.), *Sermons by Robert Bruce*, p. 146 [sermon pagination].

116 Mears *et al.* (eds), *National Prayers: Special Worship Since the Reformation, Volume 1*, pp. 314, 337.

117 Mullan, *Scottish Puritanism*, pp. 69–70, 118–20.

worth recording in posthumous descriptions and memorials of deceased ministers.[118]

The most striking example of pious reflection on charity however is from a lay source: Archibald Johnston of Wariston's *Diary*. Johnston's intense emotional and spiritual turmoil in the early 1630s led him to reflect on 'hou God put in thy mynd quhat to doe with thy estait, and according to thy voue to leave the 10 pairt of it to the poore'.[119] Soon after, he recorded that

> my heart was moved going to the church, evin repeating with tears, 'Nou, Lord, weary and leaden I com unto the; releave me nou; in the day of my trouble I called and yet calleth on the; delyver me and my saule schal praise the.' And thinking thir thoughts, whil I resolved only to haive custen in ane groat, and then ane cardecu, at the last God moved my heart to cast in within the tasse ane 36 schilling peace[120]

Giving generously to the poor might be a sign of faith, of God working within you. Equally, he internalised the teaching of a sermon that when we did not use the wealth God has granted us 'charitably to the weal of uthers', we 'force God to depryve us of them' – he thought this had actually happened to him. Consequently when he went to church next, he was 'moved to cast in half ane dolor to the tasse'.[121] He referred later to God's command that we join together 'the giving of almes unto fasting and praying' – pious observance and charity were intimately linked.[122] How the poor were treated was a significant part of Johnston's spiritual journey – with its ups and its downs.

Interestingly, in later years, Johnston has less to say on charity, presumably at least partly because of the distractions of the political events surrounding the Covenant and its aftermath (which by the 1650s had in any case left him in a reduced financial state).[123] In early 1638 when he heard a sermon on Job 5:15 ('The Lord saiveth the poore') his only reflections were on some apparent biblical misinterpretations by the preacher.[124] One striking incident in 1650 does shed further light on his relationship with the poor. Although his Sunday prayer had made him feel more in control of his problems with anger,

> and yet, after sermon, I strook a poor body, becaus he sought from me after that I had given amongst them in his sight. In ryding hom it did smyte me, and my hart wished and prayed to meet him agayn, that I

[118] *FES*, i, pp. 175, 279, iii, p. 7; *Collection of Epitaphs and Monumental Inscriptions*, pp. 141, 174.

[119] *Diary of Sir Archibald Johnston*, i, pp. 31–2; see pp. 120–1 for further reflections on his voluntary tithing.

[120] *Diary of Sir Archibald Johnston*, i, p. 48.

[121] *Diary of Sir Archibald Johnston*, i, pp. 69–70.

[122] *Diary of Sir Archibald Johnston*, i, p. 146.

[123] *ODNB*, 'Johnston, Sir Archibald, Lord Wariston (bap. 1611, d. 1663)'.

[124] *Diary of Sir Archibald Johnston*, i, p. 314.

> might maik him amends, which, by Providence maiking him the first man in my waye, held good; and so I recompensed him largly for my wrong to him, for he was seaklye[125]

As well as further demonstrating the intensity of his feelings on this subject, and their close association with his spiritual journey, it also indicates that he would dispense alms not just to the poor box but to poor individuals. In subsequent years the poor were more likely to be mentioned more collectively and generically, as innocent victims of God's judgement on Scotland for its wrongs, and, more positively, as the social group which he thought was most responsive to God's word and the truth.[126] Johnston offered less personal reflection on the poor and on charity during his political and worldly struggles than he had during his youthful spiritual travails.

Johnston's writings also point to a key and perhaps under-appreciated connection: the emotional aspect of giving. While there may be rational social and economic arguments in favour of poor relief, or a clear moral or theological imperative to do so, emotions must also play a part. As Ryrie has shown us, emotional intensity was a key aspiration of Protestant lives in post-Reformation Britain.[127] And giving to the poor might be a particularly fruitful way of demonstrating – to yourself and others – that a genuine emotional connection had been made. Ryrie notes that some writers considered 'willingness to give joyfully to the poorbox at the end of the service a test of the sacrament's effectiveness', and Johnston's words testify that intense engagement with prayer and worship might lead to impulse donations.[128] More generally, giving might be encouraged at a time of fear and disaster, such as in 1621 when the people of Perth suffered 'feirfull enundatiouns of watteris', engendering 'sick feir that they loukit for nothing bot to beine distroyit'. When the town was eventually saved after much fasting, preaching, prayer and humiliation, there was 'ane voluntarie contributioun to be upliftit of the haill inhabitantis for declaratioune of thair thankfulnes to god for ther delyverance', and this was to be delivered to the poor.[129] If people felt stirred to contribute – as well they might in such circumstances – the poor were seen as the natural beneficiaries.

Another source that offers some reflection of attitudes to charity is the epitaph, since these present a window onto how people wanted to be remembered, and potentially therefore on the significance of various virtues. Although very little significance can be placed on casual use of the word 'charity' (alongside generic virtues like 'faith', 'hope' and so on), more fulsome discussion of charitability features prominently in epitaphs and memorials across the seventeenth century. Among the many examples

125 *Diary of Sir Archibald Johnston*, ii, p. 1.

126 *Diary of Sir Archibald Johnston*, ii, pp. 84, 106–7, 231–2, 314–15.

127 Ryrie, *Being Protestant*, pp. 3–4 and passim, especially section I.

128 Ryrie, *Being Protestant*, pp. 327, 348.

129 CH2/521/7, pp. 280–1.

are Andrew Gray ('a man notable for his piety and goodness, and for his good offices to the church and to the poor'), Andrew Archbald ('to the poor he did impart/ His helpful hand) and John Trotter (both free from ambition and 'guardian to the poor/ Whom to assist, by pow'r, or wealth/He labour'd ev'ry hour').[130] Alongside chastity, charity was also a key virtue in the memorialisation of women such as Margaret Ramsay, Elizabeth Paton and Esther Fleming.[131] Generosity to the poor might also be particularly emphasised for individuals without children or the clergy.[132] Intriguingly, Gavin Nisbet's epitaph closed with the couplet: 'Who give to th' poor, in heav'ns treasures have/ The which no thieves can either claim or crave'. This seems to confirm the ongoing mental association between giving and salvation, although the preceding lines had made it clear that only Christ's death actually saves, and the memorial apparently had his kirk session's approval.[133] Charity was not always mentioned, and the fact that there are some substantial discussions of the deceased's virtues which do not include it may suggest that it was not one of those most conventional qualities perceived as almost mandatory in any encomium.[134] This may also suggest that when it was emphasised, it was partly in response to the interests, wishes, or character of the person in question.

Similarly, hospital inscriptions might commemorate their patron: for example Merchant's Hospital in Glasgow included a very conventional reference to 'the kind liberality and charges of the merchants', and its rebuilding in 1659 by their 'munificence'.[135] More revealingly, Hutcheson's Hospital in the same city included the lines 'In this fair hospital, should you enquire/ Who be maintain'd? I'll answer your desire/ The poor, both old and young, live in this place/ Orphans and old men of a ghostly face'. The inscription goes on to warn the viewer 'despise not thou the buildings nor the fare' as they may, for all they know, end up in similar circumstances, and equally, 'Who knows but, from this house, men of renown/ May rise, or for the sword or for the gown?'.[136] This also suggests concern about how such institutions (and their inhabitants) were viewed by the better-off, providing a glimpse into the potential for more negative and scornful attitudes even to the deserving poor – attitudes that are understandably rarely expressed by authors.[137] Disregard for the poor was certainly a worry for Gilbert Skeyne, author of Scotland's first vernacular medical treatise, *Ane breve descriptioun of the pest*, published in 1568. While the bulk of the work is

[130] *Collection of Epitaphs and Monumental Inscriptions*, pp. 29, 86, 124.

[131] See, for example, *Collection of Epitaphs and Monumental Inscriptions*, pp. 18, 121, 173.

[132] *Collection of Epitaphs and Monumental Inscriptions*, pp. 26–7, 69.

[133] *Collection of Epitaphs and Monumental Inscriptions*, pp. 81–2.

[134] See, for example, *Collection of Epitaphs and Monumental Inscriptions*, pp. 51, 87–8, 150, 183–4.

[135] *Collection of Epitaphs and Monumental Inscriptions*, p. 179.

[136] *Collection of Epitaphs and Monumental Inscriptions*, pp. 179–80.

[137] On the stigmatisation of the poor see Jutte, *Poverty*, pp. 158–65.

purely medical, it begins by noting that during 'this present plaig', the poor people were detested and shunned by others, and concludes by lamenting that the plague makes people 'detestable' to each other, 'and speciallie the pure in sicht of the riche as gif thay var not equall with thame twichand their Creatioun, bot rather without saule or spirite as beistis degenerat fra ma[n] kynd'.[138]

Some further useful glimpses into religious attitudes to charity by the end of our period come from clerical biographies of the middle or later seventeenth century. There was little sense that old-fashioned almsgiving and charity had been replaced – as an ideal in any case – by more institutionalised or secularised welfare. John Livingstone's mini-biography of John Ker claims that he 'gave almost all that he had to the poor. He catechised all the beggars that came along, and then gave them liberally'.[139] It is highly significant that his personal generosity is presented as such an important and worthy attribute, whatever the reality. The presence in the story of giving 'liberally' to beggars suggests that what could be considered casual or even 'indiscriminate' almsgiving was still a useful marker of virtue and even piety. William Guthrie's generosity when visiting poor families was also presented as a virtue: it was emphasised that he did not 'neglect' to combine his instructions with 'works of charity'.[140] This does not mean that entirely undiscriminating giving was valued – indeed, quite the opposite because in reference to another apparently highly charitable minister, Livingstone recorded approvingly that 'he would hardly ever give any thing at all to the vagrant sturdie beggers'.[141] But mercy and pity appear to be the more important values, and it seems apparent that there was still considerable moral and spiritual value not just in contributing to formal collections (or leaving formal bequests or mortifications), but also in bestowing coins or goods on indigent and needy people.[142]

There was also still a strong association between the poor and the church. Livingstone's letter to his parish in 1663 instructed that care should be taken of the poor and sick, there being 'as much in ane ordinary way as will suffice for meat and money for a year or more': the parish's resources were intrinsically related to the poor and needy.[143] In the representation of the virtues of Ker's and Guthrie's ministries the work of catechising the

138 *ODNB*, 'Skeyne, Gilbert (c. 1522–1599)'; Skeyne, *Ane breve descriptioun of the pest*, A1r, final page.

139 Tweedie (ed.), *Select Biographies*, i, pp. 314–15

140 Tweedie (ed.), *Select Biographies*, ii, p. 37.

141 Tweedie (ed.), *Select Biographies*, i, p. 342. The phrase 'hardly ever' may however be revealing in this sentence, perhaps suggesting it was not considered outright sinful or immoral to give the occasional alms to the unworthy. Similarly Livingstone urged the parishioners of Ancrum to set aside resources for the poor: 'not the sturdy vagabounds, but poor householders, *especially* those that have any good in them' (emphasis mine) – the worthy were to be especially (but not exclusively) favoured: vol. i, p. 253.

142 See also Mullan, *Scottish Puritanism*, pp. 119–20.

143 Tweedie (ed.), *Select Biographies*, i, p. 229.

poor, and caring for them, were intimately linked as well.[144] Amongst the discussion of a dying godly man is that he was still diligent in dealing with important affairs, and 'likewise, he recommended the case of the poor to his friends'.[145] Sometimes the poor were present in descriptions of piety as recipients of prayer rather than charity, but overall it seems that caring for the poor on a parochial and individual level was still an important indicator of personal virtue.[146] As with Knox's writings, there was an association between the honest poor and godliness: Livingstone's account of Euphame McCullin presents her as a 'poor woman . . . but rich in faith': her humble standing amplifies and confirms her status as a true believer (as does the fact that when granted a dollar by a minister she spent it on bread and onions for the poor 'as they came by').[147] And in Janet Hamilton's narrative of her spiritual journey, she strikingly records that her heart had been 'proud and haughty, much disdaining the converse of the poor', and when she was converted the company of the godly poor became 'dear unto me'.[148] Just as caring for the poor was a key indicator of godliness, so the poor themselves shoud be valued and cherished. They may not have been 'Christ's poor' in the medieval sense, but in seventeenth-century Scots religiosity, the poor were still very much 'with ye'.

Conclusion

Improving charity and the treatment of the poor was an important aim for Scottish reformers. This was not a new goal, nor one which was unique to those of a Protestant persuasion, and indeed the fact that there was a wider consensus about the pressing problems of poverty made it even more essential for rhetorical purposes that they deal with it seriously. At the same time, there was a strong and lasting sense of religious and moral duty to be charitable, as well as a sense that proper provision for the poor (and restraint of the sinful poor) was necessary in order to move towards the godly society which Protestant elites wished to construct. As elsewhere, the abolition of salvation by works did not remove the 'religious imperative' for relief.[149] Although the Protestant Reformation was to prove deeply transformative for the practice of poor relief through its creation of a new set of church courts, and perhaps served to foreground problems of poverty in wider discourse, actual cultural and ideological change surrounding poverty was much more gradual. A great deal of continuity in fears, con-

[144] Tweedie (ed.), *Select Biographies*, i, pp. 314–15, ii, p. 37 (see also ii, p. 50 for Guthrie's virtues, amongst which hospitality and generosity were emphasised).

[145] Tweedie (ed.), *Select Biographies*, i, p. 407.

[146] Tweedie (ed.), *Select Biographies*, ii, pp. 282–3.

[147] Tweedie (ed.), *Select Biographies*, i, pp. 336, 339, 340.

[148] Tweedie (ed.), *Select Biographies*, i, p. 498.

[149] Grell, 'Religious Duty of Care', pp. 258–61; Looijesteijn and van Leeuwen, 'Founding Large Charities', p. 24; Scott, 'Experiences of Poverty', pp. 8–10.

cerns, and charitable values can be identified well before and well after 1560, and between different shades of religious opinion. Poverty was not being straightforwardly idealised prior to the Protestant Reformation, and charity was not simply secularised in its aftermath. The overall pattern was not one of radical changes or broad reassessments, but of continuities and changes in emphasis. Of course, this chapter has been concerned with theoretical ideas about poverty and discussion of the poor by authors who were often just as concerned with other matters. The truest reflection of a society's attitudes to the poor is not its words but its deeds, and it is to these that we now turn.

PART I

The Development of Kirk Session Poor Relief

CHAPTER 2

Urban Beginnings and Developments, *c.* 1560–*c.* 1610

Introduction

More than any ideological change, it was the creation of the kirk session that provided the potential for change in the treatment of the poor after 1560. These new parochial church courts were the leading vehicle for the development of poor relief in Scotland, alongside their more familiar activities in discipline, ecclesiastical administration and their role in negotiating religious change.[1] Although in some places they were up and running before the Reformation Parliament, they certainly had no widespread equivalent in the pre-1560 Scottish parish.[2] Their ministers, elders and deacons would shape poor relief practice in the coming decades.

This chapter examines the development of poor relief provision by kirk sessions during the fifty or so years after the Reformation.[3] Although the Reformation Parliament of 1560 transformed an officially Catholic country into an officially Protestant one, recent research has demonstrated that the establishment of reformed ecclesiastical institutions was a gradual process. It took several decades before sessions were established and fully functional in many parts of Scotland, including the central lowlands and urban parishes as well as more remote parts.[4] This has a bearing on our estimate of the early post-Reformation provision of poor relief, because it is difficult to imagine how the church could provide significant or organised relief prior to the operation of a reasonably well-managed kirk session in any given parish. It also has implications for our surviving evidence, as prior to *c.* 1600 the survival of kirk session minutes is limited. The records that we do have are predominantly from urban parishes, which reflects the geographical spread of kirk session activity as well as record survival. Thus the focus of this chapter is essentially urban, and often on the largest and more prominent burghs of the realm. It should be noted, however, that this distinction is not hard-and-fast: urban parishes, especially at the smaller

[1] Graham, *Uses of Reform*; COP.

[2] Graham, *Uses of Reform*, pp. 36–8.

[3] *OPL*, p. 9, offers a very brief discussion of early provision in some of the areas examined here.

[4] Graham, *Uses of Reform*, pp. 36–8; McCallum, *Reforming*, chapter 2.

end of the scale, normally contained significant rural hinterlands, and we should not assume too sharp a disconnect between urban and rural life.[5] So the division of material between this chapter and the next, which considers relief in rural and smaller burgh parishes during a slightly later period, is in some senses artificial, and is imposed more by the spread of evidence than any sense of two wholly separate types of community or two different systems of relief. Nevertheless, it is in urban Scotland that any analysis of the Protestant welfare system must begin.

Early Provision In and Around the Major Towns, *c.* 1560–*c.* 1580

The earliest detailed evidence of poor relief activity comes from the parish of the Canongate, immediately adjacent to Edinburgh, where the kirk session minutes survive from 1564 until 1567. Graham has provided a detailed account of the kirk session's disciplinary activities over these years, but as well as discipline they were also very concerned with the relief of poverty.[6] The session organised regular collections for the poor at the church door, and also, through the deacons, regular collections in each quarter of the parish. A list of the 'namis of the faythfull that gewis almose on to the pur' in 1564 contains 28 male names (although two of these were listed as having given only once), suggesting that these collections from each quarter were made on behalf of households; it also suggests a degree of regularity in the collections.[7] Both church-door and quarter-collections were accounted on a quarterly basis, and the totals raised were normally in the range of £10–£20, and more often towards the top end of that range.[8] In the summer of 1565 they raised £16 2s 1d, then £20 6s 5d, before a less successful collection that winter when only £10 13s 7d was raised, apparently with some difficulty as one quarter was late in contributing. In 1566 collections improved again, and by the summer of 1567, when the minutes end, quarterly collection totals were above £20.[9] More tended to come from the quarters than at the church door: for example in the account of 18 May 1566 £7 3s 4½d came from the door while £8 5s 1d was raised in

[5] Whyte, 'Urbanization', pp. 27, 32–3.

[6] Graham, *Uses of Reform*, pp. 98–105.

[7] *Canagait*, pp. 5–6.

[8] To give a very rough idea of scale for these and subsequent sums in this chapter, urban workers might earn 1s 6d-2s per day at the start of the period in the early 1560s, rising to a maximum of 5–6s by the turn of the century (although 2s 8d was still the rate in Aberdeen in 1593, pointing to the high variability). A pound of bread and a pint of ale together might have cost around 5d–10d at the start of the period, perhaps rising to 20d–24d by around 1600. Some further rough comparisons are offered in subsequent footnotes, but for explanation of these figures (all derived from Gibson and Smout, *Prices*), and a fuller consideration of approximate equivalents (and the need for caution in applying these estimates), see Appendix.

[9] *Canagait*, pp. 19, 26–7, 29–30, 39, 58, 68–9, 73. A sum of £15 might have been very roughly equivalent to 150–200 urban labourer day wages (see Appendix).

the quarters.[10] An additional source of income came from fines or sureties, both from members of the congregation for moral offences and from session members who were fined for absence from meetings.[11] The sums raised in total were not huge, but they were significant, and the session was very focused on maximising relief revenue: raising and administering funds was listed as one of the most important duties of elders and deacons in 1564 and then again in 1566.[12]

The distribution of relief was taken equally seriously, and like collections it was accounted carefully. Almsgiving by the church was certainly not to be a haphazard or casual affair: only those who had communicated were to receive help, and the poor apparently had tickets which were required for the receipt of regular alms.[13] Payments went to a wide variety of recipients, most of whom received a few shillings at a time, whether as a one-off payment or a repeat payment.[14] An exception was made from the requirement to communicate in order to receive alms for those 'in extryme seiknes and in extryme poverte', which seems to imply that the scope of relief extended beyond these most severely needy and incapacitated poor.[15] Quarterly disbursement totals sometimes dropped below £10, but were more often in the range of £14 to £20, meaning that the poor as a whole tended to receive at least £1 in relief each week.[16] There were also more irregular payments, such as the 20s given to 'daft Jonet' in 1566, and occasional medical assistance such as the 50s paid to Alexander Stewart for healing Barbara Smith's head in 1565.[17] Although many were simply named with no further details provided, other recipients included those described as crippled, a poor scholar, a woman 'liand sek with child' and a blind man, further suggesting a degree of responsiveness to particular cases of necessity.[18]

This system was based, at least superficially, on a voluntary system of charity rather than the statutory exaction of compulsory payments which is often seen as the gold standard in poor relief.[19] The session minutes are sometimes explicit about this: the duties of deacons included to 'wp take the puris solver quhilkis gewin wolintarye be faythfull men'. However, the reality was more complicated when it came to the regular contributions from households in each quarter. The same entry enjoins deacons

10 *Canagait*, p. 44.
11 *Canagait*, pp. 8–9, 18, 51, 52, 57–66 passim.
12 *Canagait*, pp. 5, 51.
13 *Canagait*, pp. 7, 13, 27.
14 See, for example, *Canagait*, pp. 52–3, 65–6.
15 *Canagait*, p. 7.
16 £1 would possibly have been roughly equivalent to 10–14 days' wages for an urban labourer, or perhaps roughly 60 loaves of wheatbread at either 1550s or 1570s Edinburgh prices: see Appendix; Gibson and Smout, *Prices*, pp. 30, 278, 299.
17 *Canagait*, pp. 19, 58.
18 *Canagait*, pp. 52–3, 69.
19 See above, Introduction.

to collect from their quarters diligently so that 'non hav na excus' or could claim ignorance about the collecting: wording which suggests a heavy atmosphere of obligation, if not of actual compulsion.[20] Elsewhere in the minutes, when some contributions appear to be 'demynisching' in December 1564 the minister is instructed to pass to each person and ask what they would give. This initial gesture was reinforced the following February when the session ordained that 'sik persons as hes abstrakit thair almose from the pure or hes nocht yit gevin, quhome God hes blissit with substance' were to be summoned and required to distribute 'as becumis thame'. If they still would not, then God was to be called on 'to oppin thair hartis to knaw the benefatis of God and quhairfor thai ar gevin thame, and that thai may sie the greit necessite of the puris within this commone weltht, nocht onlye of infantis bot also of sike and aigit persons'.[21] This measure demonstrates an attempt to hint to the uncharitable that, despite the Protestant abolition of salvation by works, there were still spiritual advantages to generosity, and also to remind them of the real human suffering in the parish.[22] A few months later the session ordered that anyone who had contributed but had now 'drawn bak thair hand agane' was to appear before the session.[23] Such people had committed no offence, and could hardly be formally punished, but the session would still exert a great deal of moral and social pressure on those who did not contribute. A binary division of relief systems into 'voluntary' and 'compulsory' fails to capture the complexity of the situation in the Canongate, and it makes more sense to think of such approaches as semi-compulsory, in that giving was a social and religious imperative upon which one was strongly expected to act.[24] As we shall see, Canongate was not exceptional in operating a system which blurred the lines between compulsory taxation and voluntary almsgiving.

Although St Andrews' Kirk Session minutes are the earliest to survive, beginning in 1559, they provide much less detail on the early operation of poor relief than those of the Canongate. One of the earliest entries in the minutes, coming a week before the Reformation Parliament of August 1560, makes reference to the 'inlayk [lack] of almos, and, multitud of misterfull to be helpit therwyth': as a consequence strangers are to be denied relief.[25] But there are few details in subsequent entries of how effectively the

[20] *Canagait*, p. 5.

[21] *Canagait*, pp. 13, 17.

[22] This was not without parallel in other Reformed territories: in the Dutch Republic 'charities, and even ministers, continued to talk about "heavenly interest" to be bestowed on those who gave to charity': Looijesteijn and van Leeuwen, 'Founding Large Charities', p. 24.

[23] *Canagait*, p. 19.

[24] Meerkerk and Teeuwen, 'Stability of Voluntarism', p. 99.

[25] *RStAKS*, i, p. 1. The desire to limit alms to parish poor was widely expressed but rarely fully implemented in practice across Scotland: see McCallum, 'Charity Doesn't Begin at Home'; and below, Chapter 7.

kirk session was able to respond to the needs of the 'misterfull'. This is not to say that there was no poor relief in early post-Reformation St Andrews. Passing references in the disciplinary business of the parish during the 1560s suggest that fines, and cautions in case of future offending, were to be 'distributit to the puyr'.[26] One of these cases, in 1565, specifically indicates that if Thomas Fury fails to submit to discipline for fornication he must 'pay fyve marcas to the box of the puyr', helpfully indicating the existence of such a box.[27] And in 1568 two offenders were warned that if they relapsed, they would pay a fine of 40s 'to the collectour of the puris of this citie'.[28] So although no accounts of collections have survived, if indeed they were kept, the basic paraphernalia and personnel of ecclesiastical relief were in place during the 1560s: we can safely assume that collections took place at church, at the very least.

In 1570 we have our first evidence of the recipients of relief: deacons were instructed to distribute alms only to those who attended church, had their children baptised and could recite the Creed, Lord's Prayer and Commandments.[29] In 1575 this was followed by a visitation of the poor designed to assess their needs.[30] As well as the regular recipients of relief, who remain nameless at this time, the session also supported victims of more temporary misfortune: in 1573 £3 4s 11d was raised in a special collection for Isobel Adeson, widow of Andrew Kemp, 'being in grevous seiknes', and she was to receive the money at the rate of 8d per day for as long as it would last.[31] After this introduction of poor relief activity in St Andrews in the 1560s and 1570s, there was some formalisation of procedure in the 1580s, with the stipulation in 1585 that a (new) box be made and that there should be eight main distributions per year, and a clarification of procedures for the collection plates in 1587.[32] Slightly more frequent details of payments and support for the poor are found in the 1580s as well, although this probably reflects more formal recording practices as well as any shift in the nature of relief activities.[33] As we shall see later, it was in the 1590s that developments in St Andrews' poor relief would accelerate to produce a more intensive and thoroughly organised system. Prior to the 1590s, references which are primarily incidental demonstrate that poor relief activity was under way in St Andrews, but also that this system may sometimes have been relatively informal and ad hoc.

Turning to Aberdeen, after initial foundation statutes of 1562 that demonstrated great concern for poverty through their interpretation of the

[26] *RStAKS*, i, pp. 64, 82, 232, 243, 317.
[27] *RStAKS*, i, pp. 247, 283.
[28] *RStAKS*, i, pp. 295, 363.
[29] *RStAKS*, i, pp. 340–1.
[30] *RStAKS*, i, p. 408.
[31] *RStAKS*, i, p. 383.
[32] *RStAKS*, ii, pp. 552, 585.
[33] *RStAKS*, i, p. 465; ii, pp. 559, 629.

fourth commandment as it related to indigent parents, and the statement that the poor should be provided for 'conforme to uder godlie Reformit townis', the session did not function until 1568.[34] During the brief window of kirk session activity in that year, it is clear that some poor relief work was being undertaken: as discipline was operational, fines were available for the poor, and as in St Andrews, it is unlikely that this would happen in isolation rather than as part of a wider framework of relief.[35] On 15 April three deacons were required to report back on the needs of the poor so that the extent of their necessity could be assessed, demonstrating on the one hand that distributions had been taking place, but also that there were concerns over the efficiency of the system.[36] When the session resumed business from 1573 to 1578, we have further hints at a proper relief system. A treasurer was appointed for 'the owkle almous grantit be the town' in 1573, and in subsequent years there are examples of distributions to individual poor people.[37] More unrecorded activity was probably also taking place.

But there are also signs of weaknesses in Aberdeen's relief. In August 1574 the regent Morton visited, and the state of welfare was key among his concerns and admonitions to the city, made in the presence of the Privy Council. These included instructions to feu the Greyfriars' properties for the profit of the poor (for which cause the church organs were also to be sold), and to take order with the leper house. Perhaps most tellingly, the poor should not be defrauded of the alms collected at the church door, but instead alms were to be distributed 'as is the custome in the uther reformit kirks of this realme', echoing the 1562 concern about Aberdeen lagging behind in other towns, and re-iterating the reputational importance of poor relief identified in the previous chapter.[38] The kirk session acted on this concern in October, stipulating that 'na thing suld be gevin out off the pur folkis silver at the kirk dur, bott delvre haill togidder to the thesorior'.[39] The concern was not over literal fraud of the alms, but over the casual handing out of cash to poor people at the time of collection or just after the service; instead the treasurer and session should formally decide which causes were neediest. Alms should go to 'honest decait personis and not to commone beggaris'.[40] There were clearly genuine concerns that Aberdeen was not operating a poor relief system befitting its status within Scotland, and there are signs that its activities may have partly resembled the stereotype of medieval ecclesiastical relief: the random dispensation of pennies to beggars at the gate, rather than bureaucratic, formally recorded and carefully organised relief.

34 CH2/448/1, pp. 4, 6–7; Graham, *Uses of Reform*, 114; McCallum, '"Fatheris"', 74–5.
35 CH2/448/1, pp. 19, 22.
36 CH2/448/1, pp. 19, 23.
37 CH2/448/1, pp. 31, 60, 62, 95.
38 CH2/448/1, pp. 67–8.
39 CH2/448/1, p. 61.
40 CH2/448/1, p. 66.

There seems to have been more formalised activity after 1574, with a growing frequency of recorded payments to specific poor people. On 11 November 1574 the treasurer was ordered to pay 10s to John Molyson, who was 'both poore and sike', while on 29 March 1576 a weekly pension of 12s was granted to a poor man.[41] By 1578, when surviving minutes cease until the early seventeenth century, the extent of one-off and weekly assistance granted seems to have increased.[42] There was also growing kirk session involvement with the newly constructed hospital, whose collectors and masters were chosen from the session.[43] The session was involved with the administration of hospital finances, including bequests, and granted it funds from fines and collections when necessary.[44] This was sometimes rather innovative: in 1577 it was enacted that skippers caught selling fish during church services would have the fish offered to the hospital, where food would have been one of the main regular expenses.[45] So the poor relief system was developing significantly when our evidence ceases in 1578, although it remains unclear precisely how far this went towards alleviating the concerns of the early to mid 1570s about the informality and small scale of the system.

Kirk session minutes from Edinburgh provide us with a brief window into early poor relief in the capital in 1574–5. This is one of the few cases where historians have commented directly, if briefly, on poor relief, as it was an issue which had a bearing on the religious politics of the capital.[46] Laura Stewart has also shown how the town later developed an effective relief system by the 1620s.[47] However, for the 1570s the focus has been on the ill-fated attempt to introduce a system of compulsory taxation for the poor in 1575, rather than on the actual system of ecclesiastical relief which supported Edinburgh's poor in the mid-1570s.[48] As Michael Graham has noted, Edinburgh's was a comparatively politicised kirk session, but this did not prevent it from carrying out its charitable responsibilities.[49]

When the minutes begin in April 1574, the session was undertaking weekly collections for the poor, carried out by a collector for each quarter. The sums raised in each area were relatively consistent, suggesting a regularised system and stable set of contributors. Normally around £11 or £12

[41] CH2/448/1, pp. 62, 95, see also p. 110. 12s weekly would have equated to a reasonable rate of pay at the lower end of the scale: Aberdeen day labourer rates were set at a maximum of 2s 8d nearly two decades later in 1593, and other day wages around this time might have been in the range of 2s–5s (Appendix).

[42] CH2/448/1, pp. 130, 136, 138, 141.

[43] *RPC*, 1st Series, ii, pp. 402–3; CH2/448/1, p. 88.

[44] CH2/448/1, pp. 101, 104, 110, 116, 125, 140.

[45] CH2/448/1, p. 122.

[46] Graham, *Uses of Reform*, pp. 112–13; Lynch, *Edinburgh*, 20–2.

[47] Stewart, 'Poor Relief in Edinburgh', pp. 6–13.

[48] *OPL*, p. 10.

[49] Graham, *Uses of Reform*, pp. 106–8.

was raised each week, although the sum was often higher, especially as 1575 progressed, with some collections of £15 or even more.[50] At communion, the collection was unsurprisingly much higher, with seven collectors gathering just over £29 on 13 May 1574.[51] This pattern continued through to early 1575, with some weekly collections above £20, and the norm closer to £15.[52] The box was opened and accounted for usually on a quarterly basis, and while the totals in the box dropped from around £200 in spring and summer to just over £50 in early 1575, it was never very close to empty.[53]

The minutes also contain some information on the recipients of regular poor relief. The total number of weekly recipients is unknown as there is no separate roll of distributions, but the session minutes record very frequent admissions to the number of the 'ordinary' poor.[54] A typical weekly pension comprised only 2s, a sum which a labourer might have earned within a day.[55] The weekly collection totals of almost always more than £10 would thus have funded at least 100 individuals receiving that amount. However, many of these admissions were on a temporary basis, sometimes with the clear stipulation that payments were to be made 'during thair secknes onlye'.[56] At other times, existing recipients might have their regular payments increased.[57] Relief was not always provided in cash: gowns were often given to poor people such as John Howy who was 'puir and hes not claytis to keip him from cauds'.[58] Although the numbers helped were relatively limited considering the size of the capital, there was a busy relief system, operated by a kirk session which was willing to expend considerable effort on assisting the poor, even at the same time as it was affected by political controversy or problems with its ministry.[59]

The poor who were thus assisted were not necessarily all long-term sick or aged impotent poor. The session was also willing to assist those with an occupation who were in need, such as a bonnet-maker, a tailor, and a wobster.[60] Later on the wobster, William Gillespie, received 20s to pay for his child to be nursed, and in response he promised 'to pas to his craft in time cuming, and not to be fund begand nather yit chargeable to the kirk heirefter', indicating that the session was willing to assist able-bodied poor as well as those physically incapable of supporting themselves, if their need

50 CH2/450/1, pp. 3–5, 14–16, 18, 21. If day labourer wages had risen to 3s by 1574 this might have been roughly equivalent to about 70 day's wages.
51 CH2/450/1, p. 10.
52 CH2/450/1, pp. 24, 71, 84, 90, 98, 104, 109.
53 CH2/450/1, pp. 4, 23, 52, 79, 84.
54 See, for example, CH2/450/1, pp. 5, 16, 24, 96.
55 See Appendix.
56 CH2/450/1, pp. 9, 18, 21, 22, 39, 81, 103.
57 CH2/450/1, pp. 25, 66, 113.
58 CH2/450/1, p. 149, see also pp. 27, 65, 100.
59 CH2/450/1, pp. 96, 108.
60 CH2/450/1, pp. 13, 16, 29.

was felt to be genuine.[61] Equally, the kirk session was active in ceasing alms payments to those no longer felt to warrant them, such as Steven Kirkwod who 'mereitis not the almus long[er?]', or Alexander Carpenter 'quha is well conwellessit'.[62] That these discharges were not simply cost-cutting measures is indicated by the fact that they sometimes took place immediately alongside new admissions to the ranks of relief recipients.[63] All-in-all, Edinburgh's session ran a careful system of relief, which was also flexible and responsive to a variety of needs. Crucially, this was all taking place before the temporary parliamentary legislation of 1574–5 that formed the origins of the Scottish Poor Law and prescribed compulsory contributions, could have taken effect.[64]

This is not to suggest that the possibility of compulsory contributions for relief was not a factor in Edinburgh. As noted above, historians have focused on Edinburgh's failed attempt to introduce taxation to pay for poor relief in the summer of 1575, following the passing of legislation a few months earlier. In late 1574 and early 1575 the session had on various occasions requested that the burgh council take order with the state of the poor, and act against begging.[65] Complaints by kirk sessions to councils about a range of matters were very common indeed, but there was clearly a very real desire by the kirk session to improve relief further. On 19 May, two elders were to pass to the council and request that they banish 'vagabundis and ydill personis', and that a general taxation or stent be raised for the sustenance of the poor.[66] The kirk session's desire for compulsory contributions should be taken seriously, but it must also be read in the context of their previous activities: what they were requesting was not the introduction of formal poor relief, but the reform and improvement of an existing system. Crucially, it was not the case that the kirk session stepped in to provide voluntarily-funded relief when the plan for compulsory contributions failed to be implemented: substantial poor relief was already taking place when compulsory contributions were first mooted as a potential improvement.

After the taxation plan had been suggested, there was a fall in the value of weekly collections in Edinburgh, although this was perhaps not quite as extreme as has been implied. Weekly totals sometimes dropped to between £6 and £8, though they were not always this low, and by November 1575

[61] CH2/450/1, p. 73. The session also arranged and helped to finance the apprenticeship of a (presumably poor) lad to a skipper, for £10 (p. 123).

[62] CH2/450/1, pp. 18, 25.

[63] CH2/450/1, pp. 18, 83.

[64] *OPL*, p. 7. The temporary act was passed by a convention on 5 March '1574' (i.e. 1575), almost a year after the evidence on Edinburgh's kirk session relief system commences. *RPS*, A1575/3/5.

[65] CH2/450/1, pp. 68, 76, 108, 109.

[66] CH2/450/1, p. 115.

they had climbed above £10 again.[67] Admissions to the poor became slightly less frequent, but they still continued to take place.[68] If anything, with the prospect of a new compulsory system being introduced, it is significant that a reasonable level of voluntary contributions and relief activity was maintained at all. When the minutes end in November 1575, the session still desired some form of compulsory contribution, although as discussed earlier, the line between compulsory payments and voluntary charity was a blurry one, as perfectly reflected in the session's phrasing when it desired that people should 'give ther almous as thai ar stentit'.[69] In any case, this ambition, and the failure to introduce compulsory contributions until the late 1580s, should not obscure what the kirk session actually undertook in its poor relief work.[70] In the final few surviving entries, in November 1575, the session recorded weekly collections of around £11, admitted a new poor person to the ranks of the ordinary poor, and augmented the regular payments to another poor individual.[71] Not much had changed. For all the debate about compulsory contributions, the real story of Edinburgh's kirk session poor relief during these years is the reasonably stable system of poor relief operating on a weekly basis.

The Second Generation, *c.* 1575–*c.* 1595

During the 1560s and 1570s, the church in at least some of Scotland's major burghs was developing substantial and increasingly formal poor relief systems. The situation beyond the towns assessed above can only be guessed at. Fortunately, by the 1580s the range of burghs with surviving evidence expands, enabling a more comprehensive analysis of the implementation of Protestant poor relief.

Perth's Kirk Session minutes survive from 1577 onwards, and the first thirteen years of records have recently been edited by Margo Todd. This edition includes a helpful appendix containing some fragments of disciplinary material which was recorded in the marriage register in 1568. There is some evidence of relief activity at this stage, with fines passing to the poor, and a payment of 15s 1d for 'the puir boy that has the stane'.[72] This suggests that we should not assume a lack of charitable activity in towns without surviving evidence of relief, an impression heightened by the fact that Perth's session minutes apparently co-existed with a now-lost poor relief book.[73] Paradoxically, the extra level of organisation which sepa-

[67] CH2/450/1, pp. 137, 140, 144, 150, 153. Cf. Graham, *Uses of Reform*, p. 113n; Lynch, *Edinburgh*, p. 20.

[68] CH2/450/1, pp. 131, 132, 154.

[69] CH2/450/1, p. 151.

[70] Lynch, *Edinburgh*, p. 20; Goodare, 'Parliament and Society', p. 429.

[71] CH2/450/1, p. 154.

[72] *PKSB*, pp. 487–8.

[73] *PKSB*, p. 29.

rate account-keeping represents can thus sometimes make poor relief less visible to historians. Nevertheless, there is direct evidence of kirk session poor relief in Perth from 1577 onwards.

As with the other parishes surveyed thus far, Perth's relief was based around kirk session collections at the church door, although the hospital was also an important source of relief in Perth, making payments for the regular poor as well as its own inmates.[74] The collections have been described by Todd as 'paltry' as an opening of the box in July 1590 recorded only 11s.[75] However, because full details of collections and distributions seem to have been recorded primarily in the separate poor register, it is impossible to know what proportion of collections was retained as a surplus in the box. In 1581 the session distributed the full outstanding sum of £11 11s 5d after accounts were given in, which may suggest that surpluses were minimal, making the amount found in the box an unreliable indicator of collection size, though it may indicate a session which felt under pressure to spend nearly all it collected.[76] The only regular record of collections in the session minutes comes during a time of economic stress as a result of plague in the winter of 1584–5, when typical weekly collections were in the range of roughly 10s–15s, although with some dips to as low as 6s or 7s in February 1585.[77] In September 1585, when a few further collections were recorded, the totals had risen to above £1.[78] Still, the collections do not seem to have been very large, and there were also some problems with laxity by the collectors.[79]

Collections were, however, supplemented by other revenues, not least the hospital rents which were worth a nominal £1906, 10s 7d per year, although difficulties with revenue collection means that actual income must have been much lower.[80] The minister contributed, as did private individuals through voluntary gifts and bequests.[81] Fines were, as elsewhere, a valuable supplement to collection revenues from the very earliest minutes onwards. Fornicators tended to pay the considerable sum of 40s, while absence from session meetings would incur a fine of 6d (12d for the minister).[82] The collectors who showed laxity also paid fines, partly compensating for the uncollected alms.[83] During the economic crisis resulting from the plague in 1584–5, the difficult decision was taken to allow offenders to pay 'ane pecunnial sowm of money' instead of performing full public

[74] *PKSB*, pp. 58–9, 73, 109–10, 397.
[75] *PKSB*, p. 59n.
[76] *PKSB*, pp. 178–9.
[77] *PKSB*, pp. 290–303.
[78] *PKSB*, p. 322.
[79] *PKSB*, pp. 264, 340, 407.
[80] *PKSB*, pp. 56–8.
[81] *PKSB*, pp. 185, 211, 320.
[82] *PKSB*, pp. 70–2, 75, 179.
[83] *PKSB*, pp. 349–50.

repentance.[84] So the church-door collections did not have to take the full strain of charitable fundraising in Perth.

Our estimate of the recipients of relief must remain a minimum, as the lost poor relief register would have contained the full roll of the poor, and the session minutes do not record all recipients.[85] Nevertheless, the session minutes record at least some decisions taken about admission to receipt of regular payments, or the awarding of irregular assistance. There was some concern in 1587 about informal alms-disbursement by the deacons, who were warned 'that thai gif na silver to na puir folk bot only to the collector to be distributit to the puir', in an echo of Aberdeen's concern about casual distributions.[86] But for the most part the system was formally organised, and made considered judgements about awarding ongoing payments.[87] The principal forms of relief granted by the kirk session were regular payments to recipients, which were typically of 12d weekly, although sometimes 6d or 2s: a minimum of 33 individuals are recorded as having received regular payments between 1577 and 1590.[88] A further 83 people received individual payments (although sometimes on more than one occasion), and this does not include recipients of regular relief who received ad hoc assistance on top of their regular sum. The one-off payments were typically of 5s–20s, although occasionally smaller or larger sums were paid.[89] There was also occasional support in kind, such as through the provision of clothes or medical care, and during the plague crisis, the provision of fuel.[90] The session also tried to help 'ane pure man callit James Quhyt' by contributing to the purchase of a horse, presumably for employment purposes.[91] So, just as the sources of income for relief in Perth were diverse, so the form that welfare spending took varied according to specific circumstances. It is impossible to quantify the full extent of Perth's relief, but the session operated a thoughtful and responsive system.

Elgin's session minutes begin in 1584, and for the first few years only demonstrate a rather limited disciplinary system, with a focus solely on sexual offences.[92] By the later 1580s and 1590s discipline was established more effectively, but there was no parallel recording of regular poor relief activity, and the minutes generally read as if the session was uninterested in

[84] *PKSB*, p. 313.

[85] For example, in 1588 Janet Forrest was granted the 8d weekly that was previously paid to Janet Gairvy (*PKSB*, p. 398): we have no previous reference to Gairvy despite her status as a regular recipient, so had this replacement not taken place at this time there would be no reference to her at all.

[86] *PKSB*, p. 365.

[87] *PKSB*, pp. 272, 356, 393, 401.

[88] All of these pensions were probably slightly below a typical urban male labourer's daily wage, very substantially so for the 6d payments (see Appendix).

[89] For example, *PKSB*, pp. 106, 144, 178, 196, 206, 229, 237.

[90] *PKSB*, pp. 171, 256, 293, 321, 397.

[91] *PKSB*, pp. 95, 116.

[92] CH2/145/1, ff. 1–10.

relieving the needs of the poor. However, a few passing references reveal that this was not the case. On 2 February 1592 some men were disciplined for failing to collect the 'puiris bred': they were ordered to pay the sum which would have been collected were it not for 'thair slewthe'.[93] This reveals that regular collections were taking place, and that while there might have been some reluctance by session members to carry out this duty, it was rigorously policed, and any lost sums replaced. In the 1590s there are also occasional references to the 'puir folkis money', and the collection of 'cheriteis' at communion.[94] The poor are also mentioned in more negative tones, through acts against begging and receiving vagabonds.[95]

Most revealing of all, on 10 November 1596 a proclamation against all strangers begging in the town was accompanied by the charge that all the poor who were on the 'puir folks roll' were to attend church, and themselves desist from begging.[96] This poor roll does not seem to have survived, but its existence explains the absence of regular poor relief records from the session minutes: regular details of collections for the poor and the names of recipients must have been recorded there instead. Thus the relief work of the session appears only when it involves an element of discipline or internal session administration which required recording in the session minutes. This may, in part, help to explain the historiographical neglect of and negative judgements about kirk session poor relief: even on a reasonably thorough reading of the 169 folios of disciplinary material surviving from 1584 to 1599 it would be very easy to overlook the occasional phrases which represent the 'tip of the iceberg' of Elgin's welfare activity.

This is not to suggest that the records that do survive cannot enable some assessment to be made of the relief system. As we have seen elsewhere, the system was not purely 'voluntary' in the modern sense of the word: on 26 August 1597 the session ordained that 'all persounes refusaris almous to the puiris bred to be su[mmon?]at agane wedinsdaye nixt': six men were named as such.[97] So not only would session members be disciplined for failure to collect: members of the congregation would be summoned to appear before the session for refusing to contribute, and even if there were no serious measures which could actually be taken against the uncharitable, the social pressure involved must have been considerable. There were also further personnel problems: on 9 December 1597 some deacons were in trouble for neglecting to visit the poor, although as with the failure to carry out collections, the session's disciplinary oversight is itself significant.[98] There was some innovation and flexibility in the session's attempt to maximise relief revenue, and to align it with the disciplinary mission: in

93 CH2/145/1, f. 32v.
94 CH2/145/1, ff. 48v, 105v.
95 CH2/145/1, ff. 32v, 111r, 142v.
96 CH2/145/1, f. 89r. The roll is referred to again, ff. 126r, 141v.
97 CH2/145/1, f. 123v.
98 CH2/145/1, f. 130r.

February 1598 it was noted that elders should have a 'purse for swearing'. They would collect fines from blasphemers and the like, and the money raised in this early version of a swear-jar would be given to the poor.[99] One elder, William Young, agreed to 'ressave ane auld puir body and ane lytill puir and sustein thame', suggesting a degree of charitable-mindedness among at least some of the kirk session, and perhaps the desire to set a good example to well-off parishioners.[100] This kirk session charity was not loose and indiscriminate, however: those on the poor roll were to be examined on church attendance and behaviour every Wednesday after the sermon.[101] We will never know who they were, or precisely how much or what form of assistance they received, but Elgin's poor were by the 1590s the beneficiaries of a poor relief system which was more serious than a glance at the kirk session minutes would suggest.

At around the same time as Elgin's relief was developing, we gain our first evidence on the situation in Glasgow. In 1583, when the session minutes begin and a new kirk session was chosen, it was ordained that the collectors were to gather the contributions at services on Fridays, Sundays and Wednesdays, and then to give in their collection to the session on Thursdays. As in Elgin, if they failed to collect they would be fined 'the silver that myt haif bein gottin', at the session's discretion; if absent on Thursday they were to pay 8s.[102] At the outset of the minutes, weekly collections typically amounted to around 30s, although sometimes closer to 40s and occasionally only around £1. For much of the rest of the decade, 40s or even 50s per week was more typical. There was more fluctuation in totals than in Edinburgh, suggesting a system which was less based around relatively fixed contributions by the same group of individuals. Comprehensive details of distributions are not provided, although surpluses were often healthier than Perth's, such as the £22 found in the box on 23 May 1588, despite the dearth experienced in 1587 and concerns about the number of beggars in the town.[103] On occasion, special collections might be held for individual causes, such as John Maxwell 'for the releiff of him and his puir mitherles barnis'.[104] There was ingenuity in acquiring resources for relief, with a 1586 act stipulating that those 'quha sal bring in coles or peits on the sonday' would have the fuel 'given to the puir creatures ather in the almoushous or spittellhous'.[105] Regular disbursements to the poor were not recorded,

[99] CH2/145/1, f. 140r.

[100] CH2/145/1, f. 99r.

[101] CH2/145/1, f. 126r.

[102] CH2/550/1, p. 4. Although not its focus, Macleod's work on sixteenth-century Glasgow has also noted the 'careful documentation' of relief business: Macleod, 'Servants to St. Mungo', p. 129.

[103] CH2/550/1, pp. 187, 190, 195, 197.

[104] CH2/550/1, p. 321. See also p. 67 for a special collection for John Smith, 'being ydropik' (i.e. suffering from dropsy: *DSL*, 'Hydropik').

[105] CH2/550/1, p. 104.

though they must have taken place because the intermittent openings of the box and subsequent one-off distributions tended to comprise much less than had been gathered in the intervening period.[106] However, there are records of mass distributions to groups such as the 12 individuals who received between 5s and 10s each on 17 April 1585.[107] There were also one-off, irregular disbursements to specific individuals, including for medical assistance.[108] By the 1580s, Glasgow was another Scottish burgh whose church had developed a regular and responsive system of poor relief.

Another set of kirk session minutes from this period offers some glimpses into poor relief in the rather smaller burgh of Anstruther, and some of the nearby parishes also served by its ministers in the late 1570s and early 1580s.[109] Until the later 1580s, much of the material is fragmentary, but as early as 1577, there is a reference to the 'collector to the puir', and on some days 8s or 10s seems to have been collected.[110] There are some early disbursements to the poor in 1578, mostly of a few shillings each to various individuals.[111] By the early 1580s, we have a roll of about twenty poor in Kilrenny, many of whom are to be assisted with clothes or shoes. Others receive weekly payments of 8s, although one woman's payment was only 4s to help with rent: perhaps she had slightly more means to draw on for other expenses than her peers.[112] The first regular recorded collections begin in 1591, when £25 was collected in the year, but there are signs of regular collection taking place during the 1580s as well, with 13s 8d collected one week in Pittenweem in 1586.[113] Funds were also derived from fines, with absent elders and deacons ordered to pay 12d to the poor, and various moral offenders contributing larger sums.[114] The rather haphazard nature of the early kirk sessions in Anstruther, Kilrenny and Pittenweem must have hindered the formal organisation of poor relief, and this is reflected in the fragmentary record-keeping. But by the 1590s, things were on rather surer footing. As well as the regular collections of normally £1 or even £2 (although sometimes dropping to around 15s) recorded in the margins of the session minutes each week, together with frequent disbursements, the poor were expected to work on their knowledge of doctrine, and the

106 CH2/550/1, pp. 34, 55.

107 CH2/550/1, p. 39 (5s possibly equating very roughly to four pounds of good bread and four pints of ale: see Appendix). See also, for example, pp. 55, 153.

108 CH2/550/1, pp. 6, 382. Another volume, which appears to be a rough version of CH2/550/1, contains more details on distributions to named individuals, such as the six men and women who received a total of 50s on 4 June 1584, and three other individuals, including a 'travellor', who got 21s 8d between them two weeks later: CH2/550/2, pp. 39, 42.

109 Graham, *Uses of Reform*, pp. 222–4.

110 GRO, OPR403/1, ff. 5r, 9r; see also McCallum, *Reforming*, pp. 52–4.

111 OPR403/1, f. 11r.

112 OPR403/1, f. 28.

113 OPR403/1, ff. 54v, 67v.

114 OPR403/1, ff. 3r, 39v, 55r–v, 59r, 61v.

session was enjoying some success in encouraging contributions by collections through the town as well as at church.[115] By the 1590s, the evidence for ecclesiastical poor relief still survives from only a small fraction of Scotland's burghs, but there are signs that the administration of substantial and formally-organised relief was spreading to smaller burghs like Elgin and Anstruther, to complement the schemes already established in and around major centres like Edinburgh, Aberdeen and Perth.

Expanding Urban Coverage and Improvements, *c.* 1590–*c.* 1610

By the turn of the century yet more evidence survives from urban parishes, both of developments and of improvements in parishes which furnished material for the early years, and from newly surviving records. Significant among the latter are the records of the parish of St Cuthbert's, which lay immediately next to Edinburgh and housed many of the capital's poorer people.[116] The minutes begin in 1586, and in their early years seem to follow a similar pattern to Elgin's, in that there are passing references to poor relief activity, but no regular record of collection totals or distributions to specific poor. As well as fines passing to the poor, and the session's involvement in administering charitable bequests, in 1589 there is reference to the accounting of the box, and indeed on that occasion the box was found to contain such a 'ressonable sowme' that the poor fund could lend £30 to the fund 'for making of ane laft on the southsyde of the kirk'.[117] There are also references to the deacons reporting the names of the poor in each quarter, the standards expected of the poor if they were to receive alms, and occasional admissions of named individuals to receive support.[118] Such intermittent references continue through the 1590s, and the kirk session was clearly pro-active in its relief efforts, but we have no clear sense of their extent or priorities. Collections regularly took place at the church door, as we learn from a 1593 order that only one deacon should collect each day, but in 1595 they were found to be 'weill slak in thair convening and in doing of thair officis', apparently referring to session meetings and business rather than the actual collections.[119] But the 1590s saw continued admissions of new recipients of relief, and the problems with deacons seem to have comprised occasional slackenings in effort, rather than persistent recalcitrance, as the verdicts on their conduct swing back and forth between negative and positive.[120]

As in Edinburgh itself, there was some desire for a stronger element of compulsion. In 1592, following a visitation of the poor and concern over

115 OPR403/1, ff. 71r, 93r, 104r–107v.

116 CH2/718/1–3; Hollander, 'The Name of the Father', p. 63n.

117 CH2/718/1, pp. 6, 9–10, 74, 76, 82 (modern pagination).

118 CH2/718/1, pp. 86, 152, 157, 163.

119 CH2/718/1, p. 207; CH2/718/2, p. 4.

120 CH2/718/1, pp. 205, 206, 232, 237, 239; CH2/718/2, pp. 77, 109, 192, 237.

how payment could be got from 'the personis haveand land within this parochin and remainis without payand thair collectioun', it was proposed to introduce a stent to the value of the money already allocated to the poor. If parishioners would not agree to contribute of their own volition, then the Act of Parliament would be invoked.[121] As in Edinburgh, compulsory contributions were therefore sought as a means of improving an existing system, rather than voluntary relief stepping in as a fall-back option once compulsion had failed. Interestingly, the stent was mooted on 8 April, two months before 5 June when parliament urged the existing legislation to be enforced in other parts of the realm, 'as it hes alreddie tane effect within the partis of the burgh of Edinburgh', so formal parliamentary pressure cannot have been the immediate impulse.[122] In fact, by June the plans for a stent do not seem to have progressed, and the issue largely disappears from the minutes. Lay elites were clearly resistant to stenting, as the laird of Inverleith demonstrated in April 1593 when he 'anserit he wald nawayis stent his bounds to that effect bot he consents that the pure of this parochin have ane signe on ther clayts to be kend be uther pure'.[123] The badging of the poor did indeed take place, but by 31 May 1593 efforts had been transferred to a stent for repair and improvement of the church building, which appears to have been more successful.[124] The kirk session was clearly keen to exact compulsory contributions, and this probably reflects some dissatisfaction with the system as it existed, but it does not indicate a gap in provision, or even that provision was weak. The kirk session was, after all, an institution whose theoretical aim in matters of discipline was to repress all vice: they were used to the concept of imperfection, and without hindsight, they would have little reason to view compulsory contributions as the definitive yardstick of success.[125] Furthermore, while it may not have been the motivating factor, the threat of stenting may well have served to encourage decent levels of charity at the church door. Most tellingly of all, the previous system of collection and distribution seems to have continued in a similar manner to previous years regardless of the failure of the stent.[126]

The next volume of minutes, beginning in 1595, records apparently similar patterns of poor relief activity, albeit with more consistent recording of new admissions to the ranks of the regular poor from 1602 onwards.[127] As before, there is income from collections, fines or consignations, legacies and voluntary donations, and efforts are made to examine the state and necessity of the poor in the parish's quarters, while collection totals or

[121] CH2/718/1, pp. 163, 182, 183–4.

[122] *RPS*, 1592/4/91.

[123] CH2/718/1, p. 209 (the manuscript's phrasing is clearly 'be uther pure', but this might be an error for 'fra' other poor, which seems a more likely meaning).

[124] CH2/718/1, pp. 213, 214–21.

[125] *The Scots Confession*, p. 44; *FBD*, pp. 165–7.

[126] CH2/718/1, pp. 190, 199, 201, 205, 207 (and fn. 120 above).

[127] CH2/718/2, pp. 154, 182, 191.

individual distributions are essentially invisible.[128] But a separate volume of accounts also survives, beginning in 1608, which for the first time reveals the detailed workings of relief in St Cuthbert's. It is impossible to judge quite how representative its contents are of earlier practice, but it demonstrates that by the end of the 1600s at least, relief was operating on a larger and more organised scale than that hinted at by the references in the session minutes.[129] During the period 1608–10, a rough average of around £13–£14 was collected each month, rising to around £18–£22 if one-off donations or annualrents owed to the session are added. A typical weekly church-door collection would raise about £3–£4.[130] The accounts list a small number of payments not relating to poor relief alongside welfare payments, and in a few cases a payment may or may not have been charitable, but in the region of £500 was dispensed to the poor between May 1608 when the accounts begin, and the end of 1610.[131] The ordinary poor of the parish's quarters are listed as receiving a single payment as a group on a roughly monthly basis, which would then have been distributed to individuals by the appropriate deacon. Varying levels of poverty presumably explain the fact that the poor of the Pleasance typically received 9s, whereas the poor of Water of Leith or the West Port normally got just under 30s. Numerous individuals, named or otherwise, received one-off payments of anything from a few shillings to a few pounds. Some individuals received multiple payments, while others were clearly recipients of single payments, including the unnamed 'strangers' who were sometimes supported, albeit in much smaller numbers than the local poor.[132] Relief payments aver-

128 CH2/718/2, pp. 44, 46, 47, 56, 58, 90, 92, 114, 223, 224, 239.

129 CH2/718/60. There may or may not have been earlier such books, though the title page makes clear that this particular volume was begun in 1608. In 1607 there were instructions that 'ane buik maid to registrat the namis in that gif in the samyn [i.e. voluntary donations] to the pure' (CH2/718/2, p. 261), but the contents of the account book extend well beyond this. There is no significant change in the kirk session minutes either side of 1608 to suggest a substantial change in normal procedures. For the wider significance of this manuscript as the first separate book of account from any Scottish parish, see Mutch, *Religion and National Identity*, p. 109.

130 CH2/718/60, pp. 3–9. The totals are minimums since some sections of the manuscript are damaged, obscuring some weeks' collection sums. £3–4 would be roughly equivalent to around 11–12 day's maximum wages for an urban labourer by this time (see Appendix).

131 Reasons for payments are normally discernible. Some marginal decisions on classification have been made, however, because where payment is made to a man without any further details it may be for relief, or it may be payment for work done (female recipients are less likely to be receiving payment for work since the main tasks related to the repair of the church or other ecclesiastical property: jobs which were more likely to be performed by men in seventeenth-century Scotland). Although relief is probably more likely to be the explanation for such payments (as details of work done or materials provided are regularly mentioned alongside other payments), given the argument being pursued here the decision has been taken to err on the side of defining payments as not relating to poor relief where there is uncertainty or ambiguity.

132 CH2/718/60, pp. 57–66. For fuller analysis of the recipients of relief, see below, Chapter 6.

aged around £16 in total per month, which demonstrates the importance of one-off contributions and fines, as this slightly exceeds the basic totals collected at the church door.[133] Extensive and carefully organised relief was provided in St Cuthbert's by around 1610, and perhaps much earlier. Although the references we do have for the 1590s are evidently the tip of the iceberg, it is not known exactly how much activity was taking place unseen below the surface.

The earliest session minutes from another parish on Edinburgh's doorstep, South Leith (from 1597 to 1610) contain fewer signs of poor relief.[134] This could be a result of the fact that the manuscript is a fair copy which may well have omitted details.[135] There is an absence of the sort of glimpses and hints at regular and sizeable relief activity found in minutes such as those of St Cuthbert's and Elgin. Fornication cases dominate the minutes, and although there are references to fines passing to the poor (for example fines for drunkenness were explicitly predicated for poor relief), and the administration of a bequest to the poor, there is no mention of actual collections or distributions.[136] In December 1606 'sume silver wes stollen out of the boxe', possibly amounting to 80s.[137] This reveals that there was a box for storing kirk funds, and that some record was kept of how much it contained, and it also hints at a reasonably large surplus in kirk funds. However, it is not certain that this fund was solely for the use of the poor, and it may have been partly for expenses relating to the repair of the church and communion. Given the experience of other parishes, and the apparent incompleteness of the register, it would be unwise to assume from this relative silence that little relief was taking place, but it cannot be stated with certainty that South Leith was operating as formal and organised a welfare operation as other parishes.

Also surviving from 1597 onwards are the minutes of Stirling's Kirk Session. One of the earliest entries, from 15 December, orders an assessment of the names and status of the various poor in the parish, and reflects concern that 'Idill vagabundis have na libertie to leive Idill on the puiris almus'.[138] As well as demonstrating concern about abuses of welfare in the parish, the entry also points to the existence of regular poor relief in previous years. Indeed Stirling's Kirk Session ran a fairly effective and clearly-organised relief system, with two deacons serving each quarter and the keeping of regular accounts.[139] These accounts have not survived, but the

133 Although on 20 April 1609 penalties were diverted to fund a loft in church: CH2/718/2, p. 349.
134 CH2/716/1.
135 *COP*, p. 18n.
136 CH2/716/1, pp. 12, 27, 29, 34, 35.
137 CH2/716/1, pp. 28–9. The currency is left blank, but 80d, £80 or 80 merks seem less probable sums.
138 CH2/1026/1, p. 6.
139 CH2/1026/1, pp. 23, 45–6, 70, 173.

minutes themselves contain annual accounts of the poor box based on an inspection of the year's transactions.[140] Money from fines was accounted at the same time, but separately from charitable collections, and it was generally spent separately as well. While this prevented money from fines from benefitting the poor, as it did in other parishes, the separation of funds also protected the poor's resources.[141] Thus in 1605 and 1606 special collections were held to fund repairs to the church, despite the existence of very large surpluses in the poor funds: these were clearly not to be raided, or even borrowed from, to pay for general ecclesiastical expenses.[142] The session was also closely involved with the administration of the hospital, further pointing towards a kirk session which paid attention to its charitable responsibilities.[143]

The first account, which took place in January 1598, recorded that since December 1595 £216 3s 9d had been collected (including the sum already in the box at that time). So somewhere in the region of £100 was collected each year. Much less was distributed: only £69 11s 5d had been dispensed to the poor.[144] The hefty unspent surplus suggests that the concern that the session had recently displayed about 'Idill vagabundis' was not rooted in a fear that relief funds might be exhausted soon. Similar patterns of collection and distribution appear to have held in subsequent years. The sums gathered each year (which include the previous year's surplus) normally steadily increased: typically between about £50 and £100 was collected each year, and in most years rather less was distributed. In the course of 1598, as little as £8 17s was distributed, despite the year having seen well over £50 added to the box from collections.[145] However, in 1600, when the amount collected afresh was around £80, the significantly larger sum of £101 2s 8d had been dispensed.[146] This was perhaps a particularly bad year (also suggested by the fact that the session had recently appeared more worried than usual about the threat of idle beggars), and the session was able to use its reserves and perhaps other sources of income to dispense more than it could collect during the year. The year 1603 saw similar patterns, with roughly £55 collected, and £100 9s 2d spent on the poor.[147] But most of the time Stirling Kirk Session operated considerably within its means, occasionally even lending out money from the poor box.[148] It may be possible to characterise Stirling's relief system as rather mean, but if so this must be

140 The box and the key to the box were kept by separate individuals: CH2/1026/1, p. 9.

141 There were some exceptions involving fines which were explicitly described as for the poor: CH2/1026/1, pp. 16, 77.

142 CH2/1026/1, pp. 161, 185.

143 See, for example, CH2/1026/1, pp. 9, 27, 141, 149.

144 CH2/1026/1, pp. 8–9.

145 CH2/1026/1, p. 27.

146 CH2/1026/1, p. 73.

147 CH2/1026/1, p. 137.

148 CH2/1026/1, pp. 107, 184.

understood as a consequence of great cautiousness, rather than a general lack of funds. This interpretation is perhaps also supported by the fact that in 1604 as much as £530 10s was raised 'for the help and support of the trublit kirk of Geneva', which would suggest a session which was able to rely on reasonably generous contributions when necessary.[149]

The records include examples of admissions of new regular relief recipients, although one-off or temporary payments appear not to be recorded. In most years a few new individuals were added to the roll of the ordinary poor: fairly typical was the decision in 1600 'to give Jonet Cossur spous to Robert Russell oulklie during the kirkis will xii D', and in 1603 to grant to Duncan Pennecuik a weekly payment of 2s which had previously been paid to Peiris Focart.[150] One or two shillings were typical weekly payments, clearly providing only a small supplementary income by this date and significantly less than most male labourers would earn in a day, but the session was willing to be flexible and Janet Bowman and her bairns were granted 6s weekly in 1605, while a few years later Alexander Robertson was granted 40d weekly 'for keiping clein the kirk round about to the dur therof' (that this was a payment relating to his poverty is confirmed by the label in the rubric 'ordinar', meaning ordinary poor).[151] The total number of regular recipients is unknown, as even if the handful of new entrants recorded per year represent the total number, there is no equivalently thorough recording of deaths or removals from the list. But the annual sums dispensed to the regular poor must normally have left surplus for significant one-off or short-term payments to other poor people, especially during years when the total dispensed rose to around £100. This would have paid for about 20 individuals to receive 2s weekly: as the number of recorded admissions would indicate rather fewer recipients, and many received 12d rather than 2s, the funds could have been much more widely spread in such difficult years.

We saw earlier that relief in St Andrews, although evident from soon after the Reformation, appeared at times to be on a relatively small scale despite some signs of greater formality in the 1580s. The early 1590s witnessed further activity, with clear division of the parish into quarters for the distribution of alms and rolls of the poor taken, and attempts to ensure collectors did their duty on collection days.[152] Charity was clearly taken seriously, as in an examination of the kirk session in 1596, one of the rare complaints against a serving elder was that 'David Murray payis na thing to the contributione of the puir'. This suggests that the failure to be charitable constituted a clear moral failing, if not a punishable offence, and indeed Murray was absent from the next election list.[153] In the following

149 CH2/1026/1, p. 146.
150 CH2/1026/1, pp. 67, 129.
151 CH2/1026/1, pp. 162, 211.
152 *RStAKS*, ii, pp. 678, 760–3, 810.
153 *RStAKS*, ii, pp. 816, 831–2.

January there came a more serious challenge to the session's relief work, as reflected in the kirk session's request for the relief of their minister David Black, who had been warded for seditious behaviour, and that 'ordour may be takin with the puir quhill he cum hame, quhilks ar now all gane lous'.[154] This suggests that without ministerial direction, charitable activity and control of the poor was liable to flounder, although some order seems to have been imposed by 2 March (and some rhetorical exaggeration seems likely).[155] But more significant was the change in minister which Black's troubles initiated: he was replaced by George Gledstanes, the future archbishop, who led his first session meeting on 19 July 1597.[156] Gledstanes' reinvigoration and expansion of discipline in St Andrews has been discussed elsewhere, but the reform of poor relief was also a key part of his mission in St Andrews.[157]

The first recorded act of the session under Gledstanes was to instruct the bailies to ensure that the town's inhabitants 'pay the haill contributioun of the puir of all byganis', with double payment imposed on those who fail to do so. The money was to be collected at the church the next Tuesday, demonstrating that even though this was a compulsory payment under the legislation passed by parliament (which had been invoked previously when attempting to take order with the poor), it was not to be divorced from the church.[158] Over the next year or so the session continued to attempt to extract and encourage payments as vigorously as possible, although by 28 June 1598, when food prices had apparently lowered a little, the size of the stent was to be diminished accordingly, and a week later collectors were appointed to gather a stent which was 'partlie be voluntar offer and pairtle be stent upon the neychtbouris'.[159] As has proved to be the case elsewhere, the lines between compulsory stenting and voluntary charity are extremely blurred, but Gledstanes' arrival certainly sparked renewed charitable efforts.

This is also reflected in increasingly frequent references to relief activity beyond the attempts to impose compulsory or semi-compulsory payments. The money collected in church 'of the puir folkis broddis' was occasionally recorded: collections of £9 15s and £9 12s were recorded on 6 and 27 November 1597, respectively (presumably for all the week's services).[160]

154 *RStAKS*, ii, p. 823; *ODNB*, 'Black, David (c. 1546–1603)'.

155 *RStAKS*, ii, pp. 824–5.

156 *RStAKS*, ii, pp. 827.

157 McCallum, *Reforming*, pp. 50–1.

158 *RStAKS*, ii, pp. 678, 828.

159 *RStAKS*, ii, pp. 829, 833, 850, 851, 859. A similar combination of voluntary and involuntary contribution was mooted on 11 July 1599, when the session noted that 'thair is ane gryt number of the inhabitantis of this citie, quha hes willingly offerit contribution to the puir, and ane great number quha hes nocht offerit the samin' and therefore ask the magistrate to nominate and choose stentors 'upon thame quha hes nocht offerit' (ii, p. 897).

160 *RStAKS*, ii, pp. 839, 845. £9 might have been the equivalent of roughly 35 day's urban wages by c. 1600 (see Appendix).

Communion collections, although not totals gathered, are discussed in 1598 and 1600, and in 1600 efforts were made to encourage possessors of altarages to demit them in favour of the poor. Patrick Guthrie, possessor of one worth £6 did so, and another voluntary contribution from James Lentroun of £32, 'pairt of the vow silver gadderit in his ship this last veyage' further bolstered the poor funds.[161] Greater collecting activity is matched by a much greater density of references to payments made to the poor than is evident prior to 1597. For example, Agnes Lokkart and her son were granted 3s weekly to support him at school; Jhon Downy got 40d weekly 'in respect of his povertie and inhabilitie', while David Peblis, who was 'puir and onhabill to wirk' was granted 30d per week.[162] By 7 March 1599 it was felt that the poor were 'sufficientlie provydit' that they could be forbidden from begging on the streets or at people's doors.[163] This could, of course, be interpreted as a purely rhetorical (and wishful) justification for the prohibition of begging. But the session would hardly have viewed begging more favourably at an earlier date, and would probably have passed the act earlier had it been deemed feasible. Viewed alongside the striking increase in payments to the poor, which continued until the minutes cease in October 1600, the feeling that the poor were now better provided for seems plausible.[164] By the close of the sixteenth century poor relief in St Andrews was operating well, but much of the development of this system occurred only in the closing years of the century.

We last encountered Aberdeen in 1578, when the session minutes ceased. The next volume of minutes begins in October 1602, and the intervening years had apparently witnessed further developments in the parish's relief system.[165] Although weekly collection totals are not provided in 1602–3, much material relating to the kirk session's now extensive relief activities is recorded. As well as the 'comoun almes collectit to the puir at the kirk durris' and fines passing to the poor, relief income came from a range of other sources, which the session was keen to cultivate.[166] Items such as meat, fish, peats, herbs and kale sold on Sundays were to be given to the hospital, and the session was also consulted on or involved with bequests and gifts to the hospital, or chasing up and administering other voluntary contributions.[167] Still, the regular collections were the principal source of funding, and they naturally tried to maximise income from this source and exert more pressure on the congregation to contribute.[168] Although their success cannot be directly quantified, a strong indication is given in the

161 *RStAKS*, ii, pp. 862, 921, 927, 932.

162 *RStAKS*, ii, 845, 849, 888. See also, for example, ii, pp. 882, 890, 894, 896, 906, 907.

163 *RStAKS*, ii, p. 883.

164 *RStAKS*, ii, pp. 926, 929, 932, 943.

165 CH2/448/2, p. 1.

166 CH2/448/2, pp. 5, 7, 24.

167 CH2/448/2, pp. 19, 33, 38, 39, 44, 46, 47.

168 CH2/448/2, p. 13; see also below, pp. 137–9.

minutes that the distribution of funds to the poor was now on a larger and more formal scale than in the 1570s. A 'Roll of the puir houshalderis To be supportit quarterlie' in December 1602 contains the names of 27 women, 15 men and one child of unspecified gender.[169] They were typically granted quarterly sums – of either 6s 8d, 13s 4d or 20s – together with a few larger payments, but none smaller. These were supplementary boosts to income for these residents, clearly set at a rate designed to take into account varying degrees of necessity. A total of £42 4s was to be distributed every quarter, or just under £170 per annum. Care was taken over efficiency in the use of funds: each was first 'particularlie censurit of thair povertie and necessitie', which may have served to allay some of the concerns prevalent in the 1570s about the overly-casual dispensation of alms. And the roll is followed by a list of ten individuals who were to be discharged from quarterly alms 'upone gude consideratioune moving the sessioun'.[170] In following months there were frequent additions to the poor roll: for example, on 5 June 1603, blind Jonet Reid was enrolled for 6s 8d quarterly, while on 31 July William Findlay, 'ane puir agit man' was to get 20s quarterly.[171] There were also numerous one-off or temporary payments to a range of individuals, many of whom were sick and/or from beyond the parish, and payments for winding-sheets for the poor. These payments were rarely smaller than 10s, and sometimes exceeded £2.[172] At the end of the first accounting year of the volume, in October 1603, the collector had resting in his possession 'undebursit' £95 3s 9d.[173] The combination of a healthy surplus with frequent and careful expenditure suggests that the session's concerns about 'the cauldnes of charitie and daylie incres of the puir' may have been exaggerated, and were certainly not the whole picture. It may also raise questions about the session's fear that the common beggars found in the town meant that 'the inhabitants ar overburdenit and the townis awin purell not so weill supportit as thay would be gif stranger beggars wer removit'.[174] Such fears should not be ignored, but neither should they be privileged over the more mundane evidence of everyday relief activity. In any case, by the early seventeenth century, Aberdeen's Kirk Session had done much to allay the concerns of the 1560s and 1570s that its welfare regime lagged behind those in 'uder godlie Reformit townis'.[175]

169 CH2/448/2, p. 11.
170 CH2/448/2, p. 11.
171 CH2/448/2, pp. 30, 37; see also pp. 12–13, 24, 42, 53.
172 CH2/448/2, pp. 16, 20, 22, 23, 24, 33, 40, 48.
173 CH2/448/2, p. 51.
174 CH2/448/2, p. 30.
175 CH2/448/1, pp. 7, 67–8.

Conclusion

Poor relief became important in urban Scotland in the post-Reformation decades. In chronological terms, the evidence on poor relief accords with the judgements of much recent scholarship on other aspects of reformed ecclesiastical institutions and practices. The process by which a regular and full-scale system of poor relief came into being in urban parishes was often a gradual one, with some variations (though not sharp regional divisions) and some hesitant progress at times. However, the first half-century or so after 1560 witnessed the emergence of very significant provision by the church. Collections were usually regular, well-organised, and raised some substantial and consistent sums of money. These funds were supplemented by a range of other sources, most notably from fines resulting from the disciplinary framework which the church was establishing during the same period. Relief payments were made on both a temporary and a permanent basis to a variety of poor people, in a manner that was sensitive to individual needs, and responsive to particular problems and misfortunes. It is possible that in some burghs the system may have been smaller in scale and less organised than this summary suggests, but the majority experience, especially by the end of the sixteenth century, was of a relief system which responded effectively to the needs of many of the urban poor.

This was not, moreover, a system of poor relief that stepped into the breach once the provision imagined by the poor laws had failed. In parishes such as Edinburgh and St Cuthbert's, where compulsion was attempted and failed, the experiment was an attempt to build on and modify an already functional system. Once the ambition to compel contribution had receded, the system continued to work as before.[176] In the majority of parishes, there does not seem to have been a strong desire to exact compulsory payments, nor any sense that compulsion was the best or only way to provide effective relief. Indeed, one of the reasons for this may be that many kirk sessions felt that existing measures were broadly fit for purpose. It is tempting, of course, to explain this attitude with reference to tight-fistedness and a desire to escape contributing, although against this should be weighed the recurrent fear that local elites had about the threat that unbridled poverty may pose to the wellbeing of the community. In any case, even if a selfish desire to avoid being forced to contribute excessively to poor relief was to blame for the failure of statutory compulsion, it does not alter the fact that kirk sessions worked very hard to provide poor relief.

Equally importantly, this chapter has shown that in fact, the division of relief systems into voluntary and compulsory may often mask a much more complicated reality. Kirk sessions did their utmost to present contributing to relief as a duty, and as a social and moral expectation, and they treated

[176] Atypically, Edinburgh did develop a regular compulsory scheme by the 1590s, as discussed in Stewart, 'Poor Relief in Edinburgh', pp. 8–9.

failure to contribute as a personal failing at best, and as a moral offence at worst. The lines between a voluntary gift and a compulsory exaction were often blurred in practice. Thus, rather than focusing on the legal or technical status of poor relief contributions, or on the extent to which legislative visions were implemented across the country, historians' attentions would be more fruitfully concentrated on the everyday practice of poor relief in Scottish towns. This practice was not uniformly in evidence from 1560 onwards, and it was variable in extent and nature, but it is worth taking seriously. Strikingly, by the start of the seventeenth century it was standard practice across urban Scotland.

CHAPTER 3

Poor Relief Beyond the Main Burghs, *c.* 1590–*c.* 1650

Introduction

It is no surprise that the earliest and most significant developments in early modern Scottish poor relief came in the leading cities of the realm, and the more substantial burghs of the east coast. But the vast majority of sixteenth- and seventeenth-century Scots did not dwell in such places. They dwelt in rural areas, either in entirely rural parishes, or in parishes containing both a small burgh and surrounding countryside. What were their experiences of poor relief? How did the church in such areas attempt to tackle problems of poverty? And how did rural relief compare with welfare provision in major urban areas? The latter question typically prompts a rather negative response from Scottish historians: rural relief is seen as the poorer cousin of more substantial and forward-looking urban experiments.[1] This perhaps partly reflects the prominence of European towns and cities in the welfare reform schemes of the sixteenth century, as well as the obviously greater sophistication and weight of governance and administration in towns.[2] Indeed a recent study of English poverty stresses the uniqueness of the English Poor Law partly on the basis that 'it covered rural as well as urban areas'.[3] The kirk session, however, was a highly distinctive institution in that it had the same basic form, structure and agenda in town and countryside. And it was these kirk sessions, rather than any specific welfare-related scheme or experiment, which offered the most novel channel for poor relief in Scotland from 1560 onwards. Therefore this chapter assesses kirk session relief in rural Scotland on its own terms, examining the evidence from a range of parishes on an individual basis, as well as some smaller burghs, a wider range of which have surviving session records by the 1620s and 1630s. Rural kirk sessions had to raise funds in a different environment to their urban counterparts, and they also had to respond to different patterns of poverty.[4] While broad

1 Stewart, 'Poor Relief in Edinburgh', pp. 6–7, 25–6; Houston, *Social Change*, p. 234.

2 Jutte, *Poverty*, pp. 105–22; Goodare, *Government*, p. 192.

3 Healey, *First Century of Welfare*, p. 4 (the other unique feature cited is the Poor Law's implementation by a state institution, the civil parish).

4 Whyte, *Scotland Before the Industrial Revolution*, pp. 164–7, 202–3. See also Whyte, 'Poverty or Prosperity?', p. 23, for the additional variability in the socio-economic conditions of poorer sorts between different rural areas.

comparisons with urban trends and policies can be made, it is essential that such an analysis focuses directly on the parishes in question in their own context.

Early Rural Poor Relief: Monifieth and Galston

Monifieth is a small Tayside settlement, not far east of Dundee. In the sixteenth century, as now, it had a relatively low profile, but it enjoys the distinction of being the rural parish with the earliest surviving kirk session records. Although these records have sustained some damage and problematic binding, and are located in the General Register Office rather than with other kirk session records in the NRS (because they also served as registers of births, marriages and deaths), they contain uniquely valuable evidence on the early reformed church.[5] This significance has not been entirely lost on historians, and Monifieth has served as the basis for some discussions of early church discipline and parochial reformation.[6] The records also, however, provide the potential for detailed analysis of the rural church's charitable efforts in the early years and decades after 1560.[7]

After a brief initial entry in 1560, the kirk session records proper begin in 1562. On 10 January 1563 the minister, reader, elders and deacons were instructed to comfort the sick, and the deacons were to advise on who this should include, suggesting that there was a group of deacons in place who could reasonably be expected to assess the situations of the parish's needy.[8] Regular collections for the poor on a weekly basis are first recorded in 1563, and raised modest amounts at this early stage, averaging around 20d per week in 1563 and 1564.[9] Poor relief, more than discipline, appears to have been the session's main activity in its early stages, and even in weeks

5 GRO, OPR310/1; Bardgett, 'Monifieth Kirk Register', p. 175.

6 Graham, *Uses of Reform*, pp. 126–9, 239–45; Bardgett, *Scotland Reformed*, pp. 96–104, 158–62.

7 There is some discussion of Monifieth poor relief in Bardgett, *Scotland Reformed*, pp. 158–60, although the focus is on what collections reveal about sermon and communion attendance. Bardgett, 'Monifieth Kirk Register', offers more detail but contains a mis-transcription: 'tha wes gatherit to the puir xxid' (p. 179) should read 'th[e]r[e] wes gatherit to the puir *xiid*' (OPR310, f. 7v). Consequently, although the following passages make some use of Bardgett's helpful discussion of the register and the parish, all sums of money and averages/totals have been calculated afresh.

8 OPR310/1, f. 3v.

9 OPR310/1, f. 5r, 6r–8v. Many of the sums discussed here are minimum figures, because some figures are illegible or uncertain, and therefore (for example) a sum of 4s plus an unclear number of pence has been treated simply as 4s. For rural areas prior to the seventeenth century there are no useful wage equivalent estimates, so the figures in this first section of the chapter are particularly difficult to contextualise. With the crucial proviso that wages were lower in rural areas, the collection of 20d in the early 1560s would be roughly equivalent to slightly more than one day's maximum wages for an urban labourer, or perhaps 5–10 pints of ale in a large burgh; however the relative value of 20d in a parish like Monifieth would have been greater than this suggests. By the later sixteenth century urban workers earned up to several shillings per day, while 1611 rural pay for relatively

where no other business took place, the collection was still normally recorded.[10] In weeks when collection details are absent it is normally as a result of manuscript damage rather than skipped meetings or meetings where collections went unrecorded.[11] By 31 October, they could record that 11s 3d had been collected since 5 September, and the sum was put in the box rather than being immediately spent. There were significant fluctuations in weekly totals at this point, reflecting a less stable system (and perhaps more variable attendance) than in early urban relief: on 19 September 1563 only 15d was collected, but on 20 February 1564 (not a communion day), 6s 1d was collected.[12] Poor attendance may be the reason for some low collections, and this was explicitly the case on 22 December 1566, when there was 'notting gatherit to the pure except iii d because off the absence of sum off the congregation'.[13] Fines for disciplinary offences provided only occasional additions to the relief funds, as the session was not yet operating a very regular disciplinary programme.[14] It is striking, however, that a rural kirk session was making even small-scale efforts at poor relief as early as 1563 onwards.

The early records contain less detail on payments to the poor, which were made periodically rather than on a weekly basis. At general distributions to the poor during the 1560s names or numbers do not tend to be recorded: the note on 1 December 1566 that 'the almes wes distributed to the pour' is fairly typical.[15] Occasionally a name is mentioned, perhaps indicating that someone in particular need was receiving a one-off payment, such as the 18d given to Bessie Pye.[16] But the collection sizes suggest that only a handful of individuals could have received regular payments of any significance during the 1560s and early 1570s.

After a period of worse than usual record survival from 1568 to 1572, regular collection totals resume in 1573. As Frank Bardgett has identified, there was an increase in the funds raised for poor relief from around 1575 onwards, coinciding with a wider expansion in the session's other activities.[17] While the late 1560s and early 1570s continued to witness averages of around 15–20d per week, or even lower, from 1575 onwards average weekly collections rose to the region of 3s per week, and even up to 4–5s at some points in the 1580s and 1590s with only occasional drops below the

lowly workers might have ranged between 5s and 20s per month. See the Appendix for fuller discussion of values.

10 For example, on 5 September 1563: OPR310/1, f. 5r.

11 OPR310/1, ff. 8v–13r.

12 OPR310/1, ff. 5r–6v.

13 OPR310/1, f. 12r.

14 OPR310/1, ff. 6v, 14v; Graham, *Uses of Reform*, p. 129.

15 OPR310/1, f. 12r.

16 OPR310/1, f. 12r.

17 Bardgett, 'Monifieth Kirk Register', pp. 186, 189–90.

3s 4d mark.[18] By now, the figures were being bolstered by some significant collections at communions (such as the 18s 8d recorded at communion in April 1576), and by some collections taking place at other important occasions: 12s 11d was collected at an aristocratic burial in 1579, and 7s 1d at a fast in 1583.[19] Of course, some of the increase in funding would have been cancelled out by the inflation of the later sixteenth century, and fundraising was still subject to the vagaries of attendance and local conditions: on 31 December 1581 'to the puir nathyng because of the sna [snow]'.[20]

As well as increased collection totals, other developments from the mid 1570s onwards suggested a more formal and comprehensive system of relief, moving beyond the early efforts of the 1560s. The deacons who gathered the alms had their names recorded, and transfers of money were properly accounted. Crucially, the distribution of funds to the poor was recorded more diligently, suggesting that increasing care was being taken over the effectiveness of support.[21] The main distributions were still made every few months, in combination with responses to particular cases, such as the payment to a man sick with 'the gravell' in 1575.[22] General distributions tended to disburse the majority of available funds, but decent-sized surpluses were normally left in the box: for example on 6 November 1575 39s 6d was disbursed and 11s left in the box, while on 24 November 1577 56s was given to the poor leaving 34s 5d in the box.[23] On 5 July 1579 they left more in the box than they spent, and by 1582 the reserves in the box amounted to £7 10s 4d.[24] As far as the session was concerned at least, the problems of poverty in the charity were not so serious as to demand spending all or nearly all of the funds raised. Prudence was possible, and so was a degree of responsiveness to certain needs: as much as 28s 2d was distributed to some poor who were lying sick in 1581, while a tiny collection of 6d (as a result of weather-induced poor attendance at church) was simply passed on to Katie Guld, who was sick, in April 1584.[25]

Bardgett's discussion of Monifieth closes in the 1580s, but it is worth noting that the increase in collection totals continued, albeit not without lapses, for the rest of the century. By the first decades of the seventeenth century, weekly averages of around 60d–80d were typical.[26] And by now a more substantial list of names tended to accompany each distribution of funds: a few dozen of Monifieth's poor men and women could now

[18] These averages are simple means of all recorded collections, rather than annual totals divided by 52, as there were some missing or illegible collections.

[19] OPR310/1, ff. 31v, 42v, 56r.

[20] OPR310/1, f. 50r.

[21] OPR310/1, ff. 27r, 29r–v.

[22] OPR310/1, ff. 29r, 30r, 32v, 35v.

[23] OPR310/1, ff. 30r, 35v.

[24] OPR310/1, ff. 42v, 53r.

[25] OPR310/1, ff. 47v, 57v.

[26] OPR310/1, ff. 115r–117v, 129v–133r, 144v–146r.

expect to receive payments of around 5s when the alms were dispensed.[27] The occasional stranger might also receive assistance.[28] This more gradual expansion of relief is not unexpected, given that recent research has tended to stress a longer timescale for developing full local reformations and the development of active kirk sessions.[29] It is interesting, however, that in the rural parish with the earliest useful evidence on the activities of the post-Reformation church, poor relief lies at the heart of the session's activities, and is developed from the outset as a core priority. Poor relief was certainly not an afterthought in Monifieth. Of course, we have little indication of how far other rural parishes may or may not have conformed to Monifieth's model, and in parishes where kirk session activity was minimal or non-existent, we can be certain that formal relief would not have been provided.[30] But it would be very odd if Monifieth was entirely unique, because it was not an unusually advanced or idiosyncratic kirk session in other respects, and it is hard to see why it would have undertaken activities which were foreign to other parishes.

Our next evidence comes from Galston, a relatively small landward Ayrshire parish, whose kirk session records include accounts from the 1590s.[31] These accounts are another obscure survival, recorded at the end of an ordinary register, and covering the years 1592–4 in detail. The accounts offer a brief snapshot of a system that seemed to have already been in place by the early 1590s. This involved regular weekly collections normally amounting to several shillings, and roughly monthly disbursements to a small group of permanent recipients. Weekly collection totals were highly variable, but monthly totals were rarely below 15s–20s, and sometimes considerably higher (Table 3.1). A monthly mean of just over £1 was collected, although a significant portion of each year's collections came from communion weeks, when around £2 was normally collected.

The three regular recipients for much of this period were Allan Wilson, the unnamed disabled son of Euphame (Effie) Muir and Janet Campbell, who was blind. They each usually received 6s 8d every month or so, meaning that the typical monthly outgoing was around £1, roughly in line with income.[32] The monthly income for these individuals, although modest, would probably not have been far below the earnings of some of their lower-paid contemporaries.[33] Janet Campbell ceases to appear in

[27] See, for example, OPR310/1, ff. 101r, 103v, 112r.

[28] OPR310/1, f. 132r.

[29] McCallum, *Reforming*; Graham, *Uses of Reform.*

[30] McCallum, *Reforming*, chapter 2.

[31] NRS, CH2/1335/1, Galston Kirk Session Records, Book of Baptisms and Accounts, pp. 55–62. Galston's population was only around 1000 as late as 1755: Kyd (ed.), *Scottish Population Statistics*, p. 26.

[32] CH2/1335/1, pp. 55–7. In 1594 Wilson is named, unusually, with his wife (p. 62), indicating that he was perhaps receiving payments on their joint behalf.

[33] Based on the Fife and Perthshire annual pay rates set by JPs (albeit a few decades later in

Table 3.1 Galston Collections by Month, April 1592–March 1594

Month	Total collected (to nearest shilling)
April 1592	21
May 1592	20
June 1592	15
July 1592	17
August 1592	49 (including 40s at communion)
September 1592	5
October 1592	21
November 1592	20
December 1592	10
January 1593	11
February 1593	9
March 1593	15
April 1593	17
May 1593	20
June 1593	30
July 1593	30
August 1593	18
September 1593	30
October 1593	57 (including 41s at communion)
November 1593	14
December 1593	14
January 1594	16
February 1594	15
March 1594	20

Note: Some collections are recorded after April 1594, into 1595, but fading of the manuscript and incomplete figures preclude inclusion in this table. Even the monthly totals included here are minimums, because there were some collections where the sum recorded is illegible or missing. Where there is doubt over a sum, the lower of the possible figures has been chosen.

the accounts in February 1593, perhaps having died.[34] She was replaced as a regular recipient that May by a James Black 'in Lusnok', although the several months which passed in between would suggest that Black was not admitted as a direct replacement to the roll of regular recipients in her stead.[35] Black often received a lower sum than the others, of between 3s and 4s. In addition to this handful of regular beneficiaries, the session offered some assistance, of more variable size, to other individuals: 13s 4d to Anne Pat[erson?] 'to by [buy] ane cott', 3s 4d to 'ane creple boye', plus

1611), monthly earnings for rural labourers might have been between 5s at the lower end (young female servants), 13s for inferior farm servants, and 20s for full farm servants (see Appendix).

[34] CH2/1335/1, pp. 57–8.

[35] CH2/1335/1, pp. 59–60.

assistance to a few strangers including one who was 'ane reidar'.[36] These payments suggest that the session was not struggling greatly to support Wilson, Muir's son and Campbell or Black, but the relative infrequency of such payments suggest a rather narrow welfare programme. This does not seem to have been simply because the funds could stretch no further: the sums resting unspent were significant, normally over £1 and often twice this amount.[37] The system was modest in scope, but stable, and clearly focused on providing relief primarily to a very small group of the most needy handful of individuals in the parish, rather than extra support to a wide body of poorer sorts.

Broad Patterns in Seventeenth-century Rural Parishes

The evidence from Monifieth and Galston, although limited, suggests that significant and stable poor relief systems operated in some rural parishes prior to 1600. However, the great improvement in record survival during the early seventeenth century broadens our horizons, and enables us to assess the situation in a wider range of country parishes.[38] This section focuses on three central-belt parishes whose records permit wider discussion of the extent and nature of parochial relief: Kilmadock, just west of Dunblane; Lasswade, one of Midlothian's more hilly landward parishes; and Midcalder, south-west of the capital on the Glasgow road.[39]

Kilmadock's Kirk Session minutes proper begin in the 1650s, but the records include a 'book of penalties and payments to the poor' beginning in 1623, which provide a basic overview of several decades of poor relief provision. Fuller accounts or working documents may well have been

36 CH2/1335/1, pp. 55–8.

37 CH2/1335/1, pp. 56–61.

38 Although many more session minutes survive from the seventeenth century, in greater quantity as the decades pass and especially by the 1630s, it should be noted that some session minutes include little detail on poor relief. As discussed in the previous chapter, this need not imply deficiencies either in relief or even in contemporary record keeping: for example, a volume of testimonials and related documents from Pencaitland parish from the 1650s onwards begins with some snippets of accounts from 1626–29, which include distributions to named poor people such as Johne Thomson who received £3 'at directione of the sessione': CH2/296/14, ff. 1r–3v, quote at f. 3v. Meanwhile Pencaitland's main session minutes, CH2/296/1, survive from 1633, and even then include little detail on either collections or distributions.

39 By the seventeenth century some rural wage values are available, although still extremely limited in extent and precision. Seventeenth century rural wages seem to have been very roughly in the range of 15s–30s a month, but with plenty of variation downwards (female servants possibly earning £3 p.a in 1611, or higher later in the century at 8s per month) and upwards (some earning a good monthly wage of 40s, especially later in the seventeenth century). By the first half of the seventeenth century, during relatively normal years, a peck of oatmeal, perhaps enough for a modest weekly supply, might possibly have cost in the region of 5s–8s. These are very rough estimates, however: again see Appendix for details.

Table 3.2 Kilmadock Annual Collections and Distributions, 1624–48

Date of Account (for preceding year)	Total Collected	Total Distributed to the Poor
24 August 1624	£32 3s 2d	£32 3s 2d
11 August 1625	£44 6s 4d	£36s 6s 4d
13 August 1626	£40 6s 8d	£40
1 September 1627	£44 19s 9d	£34
11 August 1628	£31 7s	£38 13s 4d
28 August 1629	£43 12s 6d	£38 13s 6d
30 August 1630	£32 5s 10d	£31
18 July 1631	£36 16s 2s	£34 2s
11 September 1632	£37 8s 4d	£36 8s 4d
15 July 1633	£24 18s 6d	£32 18s 6d
26 August 1634	£44 7s 10d	£38 7s
10 September 1635	£22 13s	£30 13s 10d
12 August 1636	£38 16s 4d	£38 10s
15 September 1637	£48 4s 8d	£43 11s
21 August 1638	£48 4s 10d	£43 16s 10d
7 October 1639	£25	£32 10s
16 August 1640	£16	£16
1641	No accounts	No accounts
14 April 1642 – Accounts for 2 years	£106 15s 4d	£100 15s 4d
10 September 1643	£80 15s 10d	£72 15s 10d
13 October 1644	No accounts	No accounts
28 August 1645	£79 18s 10d	£71 18s 10d
16 October 1646	£64 12s	£68 2s
1647	No accounts	No accounts
17 August 1648 – Accounts for 2 years	£142 10s 6d	£120 7s 4d

Note: The figures for totals collected here exclude monies that were left over unspent from previous years in order to avoid double-counting, although the accounts tend to include them in the headline figure for the year.

kept but are not extant. Nevertheless, the annual accounts by treasurers of their income from collections and expenditure on poor relief reveal that the session was undertaking a regular relief programme. Table 3.2 shows the totals collected and distributed, as recorded at the annual summer accounts.[40] As this indicates, there were normally collections averaging a few pounds per month, and the kirk session normally paid around £30–£40 to the poor each year. This might have amounted to the equivalent of the yearly wages of a handful of full farm servants, or 10–12 lass-servants at 1611 Fife and Perthshire rates.[41] Surpluses ranging from a few pounds up to as much as £10 might be held back, meaning that in some years, such as 1635, it was possible to spend more on poor relief than had been col-

[40] CH2/212/18, pp. 2–13.

[41] See Appendix.

lected. Margins were fairly small, however, and in Kilmadock we have an example of a parish where spending decisions must have been fairly tightly constrained by fluctuations in income.

The accounts also contain details of the income from fines for disciplinary offences, and spending on ecclesiastical expenses unrelated to the poor. In Kilmadock, unlike some parishes, these two areas were kept entirely separate, meaning that the poor were unable to benefit from fine money; equally this meant that poor expenditure was kept free from the encroaching demands of church repair or church officers' fees. For example, in 1625 £8 of poor money rested unspent in the treasurer's hands, while the £48 11s from fines was exhausted on the church officers, indicating that the poor fund's surplus was to be protected even when there was a shortfall in the church's other funds.[42] A few years later, when large surpluses accrued from fines, the extra cash was spent on a new bell, apparently a priority for the minister who was concerned about attendance at church.[43] The poor might not always have been the over-riding concern of everyone on the kirk session, but throughout the 1620s the church was raising enough to keep poor relief at a fairly consistent level. In the 1630s there were some dips in the annual collection totals, although the surpluses accrued in better years ensured that spending never dropped below £30 each year. There were some problems with poor quality coinage being given to the session by the later 1630s, and as Chapter 4 discusses, Kilmadock's relief like many others faced some major challenges in the 1640s, though it also weathered them impressively at times.[44] Overall, although the scale of relief was sometimes rather small, and there is little detailed evidence on distributions to specific poor people, Kilmadock ran a fairly stable and solid system during the 1620s and 1630s.

Lasswade's earliest surviving kirk session minutes begin in 1615, with a new book and a relatively formal title-page and codification of session statutes.[45] None of these statutes mentions poor relief, and the session's early minutes suggest a relatively closed-minded approach to the poor. Lasswade's elders seemed particularly concerned to limit relief to the native poor of the parish only, and to restrict incomers to the parish, although as I have noted elsewhere, this theoretical discrimination was not always replicated in their practice.[46] In any case, by 1615 the session seems to have developed an organised system of poor relief, as the distribution of the communion collection that August was arranged around the quarters of the parish. Sums of either 20s or 30s were paid to 22 individuals in the Pendright quarter, Melville quarter, Loanhead and North Lasswade,

[42] CH2/212/18, p. 2.
[43] CH2/212/18, pp. 3–4.
[44] CH2/212/18, pp. 7–13.
[45] CH2/471/1, ff. 1r, 2r–3v. For Lasswade's later demographic history see Houston (ed.), *Records of a Scottish Village*.
[46] CH2/471/1, ff. 3r, 6r; McCallum, 'Charity Doesn't Begin at Home', pp. 121–2, 125–6.

Prestoun barony and Rosling barony, as well as 20s each to three individuals not on the regular roll of the poor.[47] Lasswade's relief therefore took in a range of poor people, possibly approximating to very roughly 1.5%–2% of the possible population, a relatively small proportion.[48] The session had also established formal administrative procedures for dealing with them, especially compared with systems like those in Monifieth and Galston.

Detailed records of collections begin in late 1616, and show that in the late 1610s substantial sums were gathered, at a mean of around 45–55s per month, albeit with some significant fluctuations masked by the average.[49] After a gap in the records, by 1626 and 1627, almost £50 was being collected each year, and by 1633 the total was closer to £70, excluding special collections which raised several pounds for extra-parochial causes or individuals.[50] The distribution of relief continued to be carefully organised by quarter, with individual kirk session members assigned to distribute the appropriate sums to the poor in each part of the parish.[51] Rather than regular weekly or monthly payments to the ordinary poor, distributions tended to be more intermittent and involve large sums of money. For example, the summer distribution in 1618 involved payments of either 24s or 26s to 26 individuals, amounting to £32 8s in total.[52] So although the overall number of regular poor was fairly large, the system was comparatively closed and fixed at this stage: turnover among these regular poor was fairly limited. By the mid-1620s, a rather more flexible and responsive week-by-week system had developed, with more irregular payments to individuals or for special causes now accompanying the occasional mass

[47] CH2/471/1, f. 7v.

[48] Parish population figures are extremely uncertain for this period. For these rough estimates, and all others which follow below, the approach has been to extrapolate very broad possible parish population ranges from the 1755 census (themselves not necessarily fully accurate), taking into account the estimated national population changes from the sixteenth century to 1755 (estimated at around x2.5 from 1500 to 1755: Whyte, *Scotland Before the Industrial Revolution*, p. 113). This means that Lasswade's population of 2190 in 1755 (Kyd (ed.), *Scottish Population Statistics*, p. 15) has been estimated to the range of roughly 1300–1700 (similar proportions are applied to subsequent examples). This range – itself uncertain – would place the 25 recipients of 1615 (or 26 in 1618) at between 1.5% and 1.9% of the population. A more extreme range allowing both for very sharp or very minimal population growth in the parish would give a range of about 1.1% to 2.5%. It should be emphasised again how approximate and imprecise these (and subsequent) calculations are, especially considering that lists and counts of recipients themselves often represent minimums, and sometimes a variety of frequency and size of payments: they should be taken as very rough indicators only.

[49] CH2/471/1, ff. 14v–24r.

[50] CH2/471/1, ff. 28v–32r, 50r–52r

[51] CH2/471/1, ff. 18v, 22r.

[52] CH2/471/1, f. 22r. As a sum, 24s or 26s might have been roughly equivalent to a decent month's pay for a rural servant in the 1610s (see Appendix), although of course these were not monthly payments.

disbursements.[53] In 1626, £4 was paid to John Lasone in Rosling for the support of an orphan for whom he was caring, and this came shortly after collections for persecuted co-religionists overseas.[54] In the early 1630s, the concern (and impressive fundraising ability) for distressed outsiders and one-off causes continued alongside the regular business of parish relief.[55] Despite the anti-outsider rhetoric of the session minutes' opening stages, and the initial emphasis on a fixed group of poor people, the practice of relief in Lasswade as the years passed shows that rural parish relief did not necessarily have to involve an inward-looking or inflexible approache. And here, in contrast to Galston, rural relief did not involve the restriction of assistance primarily to a couple of very needy individuals.

In contrast to Kilmadock, Midcalder's Kirk Session minutes contain details, in their earliest stages, of distributions to poor people, but no details of collections until rather later. In the 1600s we have numerous references to payments made on an individual basis to various poor people, such as 10s to Jonat Sandilands in Over Alderstoun in 1604, and sums ranging from 4s to 15s to various parishioners in 1605–6.[56] The accounting is not always very well-organised, but as in Monifieth it is apparent that poor relief was one of the main activities of the kirk session at this time. Regular collections must have taken place, and communion collections played a major role in fundraising, as communions were frequently followed by major disbursements.[57] Revenue from fines was also available for poor relief, albeit not exclusively.[58] Fines were set at a fairly substantial rate, with fines of 20s fairly typical and higher penalties not unheard of at several merks, or even £10 in some cases.[59] As this might suggest, relief at this point was on a fairly respectable scale and involved a sizeable group of Midcalder's poor people: a 1612 distribution involved 19 women, seven men and one group of children, with the women typically receiving 10s to 13s 4d, while the men were more likely to receive 20s.[60] This minimum of 26 recipients possibly equates to 2.5%–3% of the parish population.[61] As well as the regular poor, one-off or extraordinary payments were very frequent, perhaps reflecting Midcalder's location on the major route between Edinburgh and Glasgow: certainly several recipients appear to be outsiders.[62] The combination of payments to outsiders and new individuals, and ad hoc payments to

[53] CH2/471/1, ff. 28r–29r, 31r.

[54] CH2/471/1, f. 30r.

[55] CH2/471/1, ff. 50r–v, 52r.

[56] CH2/266/1, pp. 4, 10.

[57] CH2/266/1, pp. 9, 13–14.

[58] Some fines were explicitly dedicated to the poor, but fine revenue might also be spent on other church expenses: CH2/266/1, pp. 6–7, 109, cf. pp. 13, 17.

[59] CH2/266/1, pp. 6, 7, 9.

[60] CH2/266/1, p. 31.

[61] Kyd (ed.), *Scottish Population Statistics*, p. 15 (1755 population of 1369, estimated to range between 800 and 1100, giving a range of around 2.3%–3.2%).

[62] CH2/266/1, pp. 11, 13, 20, 23.

individuals who had previously been helped in a regular disbursement, points to a responsive approach to selecting recipients.[63]

During a time of dearth in 1623–4 the kirk session temporarily recorded full details of collections, as well as distributions.[64] Although collections were not recorded in every week, when they did take place they typically brought in around 10s–15s (albeit with significant variation above and below this norm), while the communion collection raised £13 2s.[65] While this proved to be a short-lived improvement in recording detail, it was clearly not an operational change, because similar types of payment to poor individuals continued on a weekly basis, accompanied by the regular annual distributions on a much larger scale.[66] By the mid 1630s, the annual distribution typically involved around 20 individuals in each year, each receiving a mean of roughly 20s (although with significant variation from person to person), amounting to a total sum usually around £20.[67] In 1639–40, as another time of stress began, detailed records of collections resume, and by this point 30s–40s was being collected most weeks.[68] Collections were able to continue, albeit at a temporarily reduced rate, following the death of the minister in early 1642, and as the decade progressed typical collection sums for each week increased to more like £2 or £3. Midcalder Kirk Session operated a fairly stable and responsive relief system consistently across the first half of the seventeenth century.[69]

Assessing the Extent of Rural Relief

The records of these three parishes enabled us to survey some varying long-term trends in early seventeenth century rural relief provision. Some parochial records provide more detailed snapshots of relief distributions and recipients, including evidence on a slightly wider geographical range of parishes. For example the central Perthshire parish of Dunbarney provides some useful early and detailed accounts from the 1600s. The regular weekly collections raised a total of around £14 in 1603, at an average of around 5s–6s per week; this fundraising was augmented by just over £3 collected at communion.[70] By 1607, the annual total had risen to around £23, at an average of 8s or 9s, plus just over £5 collected at communion; 1609 saw similar levels raised with a total of just over £21 in weekly col-

[63] See, for example, CH2/266/1, pp. 19–20, 22, 31, 33, 34, 41.
[64] For the famine of the early 1620s see Chapter 4 of this book.
[65] CH2/266/1, pp. 58–62.
[66] CH2/266/1, pp. 63, 67, 75, 77.
[67] CH2/266/1, p. 94.
[68] CH2/266/1, pp. 102–4.
[69] CH2/266/1, pp. 117, 143–4, 151–2, 160, 162, 184.
[70] CH2/100/1, pp. 40–1. There was also a collection of just over 5 merks at the end of the year, which was given to a laird: if this was to support poor folk, perhaps in the laird's area, this would take the annual total to around £20.

lections plus over £5 at communion.[71] A large proportion of the year's total collection tended to be distributed at annual disbursements, but a significant amount was also spent on a weekly basis, with some week's collections passing directly to needy individuals.[72] Dunbarney's distribution lists reflect a classification of the poor: the 1607 list was divided into the 'criple and blind' and 'personis not imbuikit': that is, those not recorded in the book as regular pensioners. The 'criple and blind' comprised a list of 8 women and 4 men, all of whom received 13s 4d apart from a Thomas Smyth who received £1. The list of more irregular poor was far longer, but they all received smaller sums, ranging from just 16d to a Jhone Den to 12s for Thomas Balmannow.[73] Thus roughly similar amounts were spent on the two categories: just over £8 on the 'criple and blind', and just under £10 on the irregular poor. The kirk session was distributing quite small amounts of relief, but to a comparatively wide range of recipients: a total of 46 individuals or small groups, possibly roughly 7%–9% of the population.[74]

Dunbarney's 1611 distribution list offers further insight into the state and health of the relief system. As before, the first list is of payments to 'personis that ar imbuikit to wit criple and blind', but this time the second group is described as 'the secund rank'. This suggests a clear hierarchy, with the regular impotent poor as effectively first among the poor. However, after this first group got their payments (mostly of 30s this time), the 'secund rank' received a healthy range of payments normally in the range of 6s–20s. Fascinatingly, even after this second tier were paid, the ranking system continued as 'the rest [was] distributit to the litle puir anis'. This could refer to children who were from poor families but not the worst off who were in receipt of more regular support (although it is not certain that 'litle' necessarily refers to children in this case). Even after this more informal distribution, 10 merks remained unspent, suggesting that the relief system was well enough financed to respond to at least the most pressing local needs.[75] If there was a surplus even after distribution to an unnamed group of relatively low-priority 'puir anis', it seems unlikely that there were urgent (deserving) welfare needs that were not being reasonably well met. Dunbarney's distributions continued to apply this ranking of the poor in subsequent years: in 1614 the ranking is simply numerical with first, second and third ranks of the poor receiving funds.[76] The ranking did not simply reflect the size of relief payments, as some lower-ranked individuals actually

[71] CH2/100/1, pp. 15–16, 43–4.

[72] CH2/100/1, p. 39.

[73] CH2/100/1, p. 43. No sum was given for one irregular recipient.

[74] Kyd (ed.), *Scottish Population Statistics*, p. 43 (1755 population of 764, estimated to be in the range of 500–650, giving 7%–9.2%, although this does not allow for the fact some of the 46 entries were groups of children rather than individuals, such as 'Williame Smythis bairnis').

[75] CH2/100/1, pp. 19–20.

[76] CH2/100/1, p. 26.

received higher sums: presumably the ranking reflected urgency and priority rather than the amount of cash required.[77] The accounts tell us nothing about the assessments and negotiations by which this ranking was established. But the existence of the ranking indicates a session which was taking relief, and the efficient distribution of support, very seriously. It was certainly not casually distributing alms on a haphazard basis.

Moving further north, Old Deer's Kirk Session accounts offer a useful indication of relief provision in the 1630s. In the 1633–4 accounting period, comprising about 10 months, just over £30 was raised in regular weekly collections, plus just over £20 at communion, as well as a collection of £6 4s 9d 'in the kirk be the decones' in January 1634. Thus a monthly average of between £5 and £6 was recorded.[78] Similarly in 1634–6 £160 was raised in the 23 months covered by the accounts, amounting to more like £7 per month on average; again this total was boosted by £43 from two communion seasons and some larger individual collections.[79] The monthly average was similar, at about £6 10s, in 1636–8.[80] There was also some potential for poor relief expenditure in the 'common good' funds raised from fines: 'ane distressit Irland minister' received £5 8s under this heading, but overall Old Deer was one of those parishes where fine revenue primarily supported poor relief only by meeting other ecclesiastical expenses and sheltering collection revenues from encroachment.[81]

Old Deer's accounts offer a particularly rich level of detail on the relief recipients of the 1630s.[82] The first indication of the wide-ranging system operated by this parish was the inclusion in the 1633–4 accounts of 30s 8d to buy 46 'poore folkis takinis', at 8d each. Of course, this supply may have been intended to last for some time, but the relief payments also indicate a relief system catering for a large number of poor individuals. During the 10 months covered by the accounts, 52 individuals received payments. However, the largest number of payments any individual received was five, and there were only three such recipients: Alexander Kai (38s in total), Adam Walker (37s in total) and Christine Schewane, bedfast (24s in total). Isobel Pettendreich received 33s across four payments, while another six individuals received three payments. The rest, the vast majority, received only one or two payments over the 10 months.[83] These included some large payments in response to particular circumstances, such as 90s to

77 See, for example, CH2/100/1, p. 34.

78 CH2/1217/33, f. 89r (perhaps equivalent to what two or three 1656 Midlothian farm servants might earn in a month; or at the 1611 assessment for Fife and Perthshire, possible monthly earnings for 25–30 lass servants or 5–6 full farm servants).

79 CH2/1217/33, ff. 91r-92v. See also Foster, *Church Before the Covenants*, p. 81, for some substantial collections in Belhelvie, just north of Aberdeen.

80 CH2/1217/33, ff. 100r–101r.

81 CH2/1217/33, f. 97r.

82 In the following analysis sums have been rounded to the nearest shilling.

83 CH2/1217/33, ff. 89v–90v.

Andrew Merchant 'to cuir his daughteris heid'.[84] A total of around £47 was dispensed, at a mean of roughly 18s per individual, although larger and repeat payments naturally distort this: the typical sum was more like 6s to 12s. Therefore relief in Old Deer was based around relatively infrequent payments according to need, rather than fixed weekly or monthly pensions. A few individuals received quite a sizeable total over the year, while many simply received occasional assistance on an ad hoc basis. Given that about £55 was collected during the same period, the session's funds do not seem to have been under too much pressure, with a surplus of nearly £10.

This seems to have been a persistent policy in Old Deer. The accounts for the 23 months from the end of July 1634 reveal a similar pattern of intermittent payments even to the most regular recipients, and a long 'tail' of very infrequent recipients.[85] Kai and Pettendreich continued to receive payments every few months, and the most frequently recurring recipients were Janet Daniels (and/or her children), and the unfortunate Adam More. Some of More's entries were for his son or wife, but after a payment for his son's winding-sheet he tends to be named alone. The total paid to him or his dependents was £3 16s; although the individual to receive the most over the 23 months was William Philip, who received £5.[86] Weekly payments were not out of the question, as Andrew Fyvie was temporarily paid a substantial 9s per week for the sustenance of a poor child he had apparently taken care of, but the session clearly preferred to avoid committing to regular pensions involving fixed sums.[87] In total, payments were made to over 90 separate individuals or families, amounting to a total of about £120: again a substantial surplus was retained compared to the £160 raised over the same period.[88]

The final period of fully-accounted-disbursements, from July 1636 to March 1638 suggests an essentially similar approach, although one individual, Elspet Birnie, rather dominates the accounts. She received 22 payments, far more than any other individual, that added up to a total of £7 4s over the period.[89] Presumably, after some significant payments in the previous period and the early stages of 1636–8, she fell into great need and was granted more regular assistance than was usual.[90] Unlike the more infrequent recipients, this amounts to an income which was probably not

84 CH2/217/33, f. 90v.

85 CH2/1217/33, ff. 93r–95v.

86 This excludes a one-off payment of £9 19s to Andrew Maxwell, raised by special collection in the church: CH2/1217/33, f. 95r.

87 CH2/1217/33, f. 94v.

88 This probably amounts to somewhere around 2%–4% of the population range of perhaps 2000–2400 (based on 2813 in 1755: Kyd (ed.), *Scottish Population Statistics*, p. 52), but the widely ranging field of recipients (at least 50 in 1633–4, giving about 2%–2.5%, and over 90 in 1634–6, giving 3.75%–4.5% but over a longer period of time) makes this an even rougher estimate than usual.

89 CH2/1217/33, ff. 101v–104r.

90 CH2/1217/33, f. 103r.

Table 3.3 Kinnaird Collections, 1634–42

	Total Collected (including communion)	**Weekly Mean Collection (excluding communion)**
1634	£26 6s	8s
1635	£34 1s	10s
1636	£39 5s	12s
1637	£46 5s	15s
1638	£38 14s	11s
1639	£40	12s
1640	£46 12s	10s
1641	£34 15	10s
1642	£41 5s	9s

Note: CH2/418/1, pp. 1–61. All sums have been rounded to the nearest shilling.

too far behind many female earners.[91] Several other recipients enjoyed between 5 and 10 payments, often amounting to £3–£4 over the 20 months, but the vast majority of the 82 individuals or family groups were helped on no more than a couple of occasions, typically with 6s–10s each time. As previously, a few very large payments to fund medical care slightly inflate the mean individual payment of just under 10s. A surplus of around £20 was apparently unspent from the period's collection total of about £130. Old Deer's system was clearly able to operate stably during the 1630s, and was very responsive to changes in circumstance and to one-off necessities. Of course the disadvantage with such an approach is that some of the neediest individuals may have lacked the very predictable income which their counterparts in parishes such as Galston enjoyed.

Returning to rural Tayside, Kinnaird's records from the 1630s provide a rich level of detail on individual collections and distributions. Weekly collections were significantly boosted by large collections taking place at communion (Table 3.3). While there were substantial fluctuations from year-to-year (and indeed, on a weekly basis), £25–£50 was raised from collections in most years, and often the figure was in the upper part of that range. Communion collections were also variable, which, for example, explains the high overall total raised in 1640 despite the drop in typical weekly collection size: that year there were two communions, raising over £20 by themselves.[92] Additional revenue also came from fines, which when recorded in 1634 and 1635 brought in about £3 each year, and varying collections at marriages and burials, which could amount to another pound or two every few years. This all points to a fairly healthy and stable system.

Kinnaird Kirk Session distributed these funds in ways which seem to have been quite responsive to the changing circumstances of the parish poor.

91 See Appendix.

92 CH2/418/1, pp. 40–8.

In 1633–4, when the records begin, the vast majority of payments were to two poor women, Janet Billie and Janet Mitchell. They tended to receive 6s roughly once a month, which would probably have been equivalent to a low rural wage, though still unlikely by itself to pay for food for a month.[93] There were some payments to other poor individuals, but of the £16 8d distributed to parish poor in 1634, about three-quarters went to the two Janets.[94] At this point, the concentration of funding was very much greater than in contemporary Old Deer. By 1635, however, the Janets seem to disappear from regular distributions, and may have died or left the parish. They were replaced as the most regular recipient by Euphame Pattone, although she did not dominate spending as much as they had: in 1635 she received £2 15s 6d out of the £10 18s 10d dispensed overall, and in 1636, £3 4s of the £17 8s 6d.[95] There were various other individuals who received semi-regular assistance: Catherine Bowman received 20s 'to helpe to build [i.e. repair] hir house' in August 1635, and was helped again that winter with 14s to buy shoes.[96] Other payments went to unnamed and therefore probably one-off beneficiaries such as 'ane uther poore lasse' who received 4s at the same time as Euphame Pattone on 22 November 1635.[97] In all, during the mid-1630s there were a handful of regular people who dominated the relief spending.[98] These eight individuals, possibly 1.5%–2% of the parish, received more than £2 each over the four years, or an average of more than 10s per year. A further 40 or so individuals (perhaps another 8%–10% of the parish) received much smaller sums, rarely amounting to more than £1, and payments to unnamed men, women or children, even when grouped together, are dwarfed by the eight regular recipients.[99] About £75 was spent on relief by the kirk session in these four years, and over half, around £40, went to the regulars.

Kinnaird's elders and deacons oversaw a steady system. They maintained decent surpluses, and revealingly, spending levels seem to have been more dependent on the dynamics of parish poverty than on fundraising levels. When the two Janets were removed from the system, spending dropped, as the new regular recipient, Euphame Pattone, received a smaller typical weekly sum of 4s rather than 6s. However, the overall drop in spending in 1635, from £16 8d to £10 18s 10d came at the same time as an increase

93 See Appendix.

94 CH2/418/1, pp. 1–6.

95 CH2/418/1, pp. 6–18.

96 CH2/418/1, pp. 10, 12.

97 CH2/418/1, p. 12.

98 Those receiving over £2 from 1633 to 1637 were Euphame Patton (£9 4s 6d); Janet Billie (£6 11s 6d); Janet Mitchell (£5 14s); James Poullar (£5 3s); Catherine Bowman (£4 14s 8d); Margaret Spence (£3 17s 4d); Margaret Muir (£2 17s 10d); William Duncan (£2 7s 8d).

99 Kyd (ed.), *Scottish Population Statistics*, p. 44 (1755 population of 557, which, based on a range for the 1630s of 380–500, would give 1.6%–2% for the eight core recipients, and 9.6%–12.6% for the full total of 48 individuals, excluding those with no names given).

in the total collected, from £26 5s 7d to £34 10d. So the session was not constrained by a lack of funds, and relief decisions must have been made on the basis of need, at least as perceived by the kirk session. In 1637, patterns changed again as spending went up to £25 13s 11d, spread out across a larger number of individuals each receiving smaller sums.[100] In subsequent years, patterns continued to shift slightly within this general model: in 1642, for example, relief was once again concentrated on one regular individual, Elspeth Gairdner who received 39s over the year in monthly payments, while most other recipients were helped on a more ad hoc basis.[101] The consistent combination of healthy surpluses with variable spending patterns points to an impressively robust and adaptable system in this small rural parish.

Smaller Burghs, *c.* 1610–*c.* 1640

This chapter has so far been concerned with entirely rural parishes, in contrast to the previous chapter's focus on the development of relief in Scotland's most prominent early modern burghs. However, it would be misleading to suggest too sharp a distinction between rural and urban practice, and it is important to consider the situation in the wider range of smaller urban-centered parishes from which evidence survives by the early decades of the seventeenth century. Scotland had very numerous small towns, but just a few large ones.[102] In terms of poverty and the kirk sessions' task of collecting and distributing relief funds, if not in economic function and political status, some of these might have had little more in common with major centres like Edinburgh or Aberdeen than with Midcalder, Dunbarney or Old Deer. As the seventeenth century progressed, increasing evidence points to a well-established system.

Montrose's Kirk Session accounts survive from the mid-1630s, at which point there was already a healthy income from a range of sources, including mortcloth payments, sums raised at marriages, and some apparently voluntary offerings as well as regular collections. While income was variable, in 1634–5 monthly fundraising was normally above £20, and often very much higher, and the substance and range of relief income remained similarly strong through the late 1630s and into the early 1640s.[103] By 1641 we are able to examine some (though not all) of the beneficiaries as well as the totals gathered, through detailed lists of the regular poor. This reveals a range of individuals receiving substantial and consistent support. The 1641 list contained 24 people, indicating that the regular poor were a very small percentage of the population, possibly

100 CH2/418/1, pp. 19–25.
101 CH2/418/1, pp. 55–61.
102 Falconer, 'Surveying Scotland's Urban Past' p. 39.
103 CH2/943/1, pp. 204–5, 212–16.

below 1%.[104] They typically received 5s–6s per week, amounting to a total weekly outgoing of £6 12s 4d, just about covered by the year's collections amounting to just over £340.[105] There was some turnover in subsequent years, with the period until the final list of the volume in 1645 witnessing 5–10 additions to the list each year, plus a few deaths and removals from the roll of the poor.[106] So overall, Montrose was providing solid and very regular income for a few dozen poor people per year.

By contrast, Ayr's Kirk Session minutes for the 1610s and 1620s provide frustratingly little detail on the recipients of poor relief and patterns of regular distribution. Additionally, rather than recording collection totals, the scribe kept a note of the total sum in the 'poores purse' each week.[107] While this prevents analysis of weekly collection totals, it provides an opportunity to assess the overall health of the relief system. In 1612, the first full year of accounts, there was normally a substantial surplus in the purse: the year's high was £49 16s in January, and the low was £6 12s 4d in November, but for the majority of the year there was at least £20 in the purse, and the drop to single figures was exceptional.[108] Fluctuations continued, and in early 1613 there was enough concern about fundraising to spark an exhortation to charitability from the pulpit, but the funds were never very close to running out. When funds did run low, such as the drop to £12 in mid-1613, or as low as £5 in May 1619, recovery was normally swift, often helped by the substantial sums raised at communion.[109] Ayr's welfare system even showed some resilience during the difficulties of the early 1620s, and by 1630 the sums in the 'poores purs' tended to be at least £50–£60, and often substantially higher.[110]

Various other smaller burghs show signs of well-established poor relief fundraising and distribution. A snapshot of Haddington's minutes which survive from 1630 shows that they collected typically £3 or £4 most weeks, which was boosted by some much larger communion collections and occasional special collections to add up to a total of £236 6s 5d over the year. About £200 was distributed to poor people over the year, in the form of 150 payments to about 100 individuals, averaging about 27s per payment, or perhaps around 4 day's male labouring wages (or several weeks' supply of

[104] Kyd (ed.), *Scottish Population Statistics*, p. 48 (1755 population of 4150, placing the regular poor in the range of roughly 0.7%–0.9% based on population estimates of 2750–3500).

[105] CH2/943/1, pp. 218–19. That the sums were weekly payments is made clear by the wording of the 1645 list: p. 224. By this point typical day wage rates for urban labourers (albeit mainly based on data for larger burghs) had risen above 5s–6s (see Appendix).

[106] CH2/943/1, pp. 221–4 (list for 1644 missing). See below (Chapter 6) for more detailed analysis of the recipients themselves.

[107] CH2/751/1/2, f. 238r.

[108] CH2/751/1/2, ff. 216r–239v.

[109] CH2/751/1/2, ff. 254v, 382v, 384v.

[110] CH2/751/2, ff. 158–78; for the early 1620s in Ayr see ff. 16r, 25v, 34v, 42v, and Chapter 4, below.

oatmeal), per payment.[111] Haddington's policy was clearly to assist a wide range of individuals with significant sums (but not ongoing maintenance pensions) at points when it was deemed particularly necessary, perhaps covering 3%–4% of the population.[112] At around the same time, Culross Kirk Session kept accounts which include poor relief income clearly distinguished from funds for church repair.[113] The sums raised were fairly regular and substantial, with typical collections in 1630, for example, generally falling between 60s and 75s per week, amounting to around £180 over the year (including a communion collection of over £15).[114] As the 1630s progressed collections rarely dropped below £3 per week (and even then normally to around 55s–58s), and occasionally went above £4 or even higher, while communion collections sometimes rose above £20 on each of the two Sundays.[115] The roll of regular poor was on a similar scale to Montrose, as 26 poor seals were given out in 1632, although the fact they produced 60 seals suggests they were prepared to accommodate more poor people, as well as some turnover of recipients, if needed.[116]

In Anstruther, where some early surviving evidence was discussed in Chapter 2, from around 1610 onwards the typical weekly collection was around £2, with some fluctuation down to 30s or up to 50s occasionally.[117] Weekly collections of over £3 became increasingly common (though never exclusively so as there were dips as well) in the 1610s, and large proportions of the collection often went directly to the poor, as on 19 March 1616 when £3 15s was collected and all but the 15s went directly to the poor.[118] However, the tendency to spend the bulk of the income on the ordinary poor did not seem to undermine the session's ability or desire to respond to particular circumstances, such as on 13 January 1616 when 20s was 'givin

[111] CH2/799/1, ff. 307v–317v (see Appendix). The composition of Haddington's poor is discussed in Chapter 6.

[112] Kyd (ed.), *Scottish Population Statistics*, p. 13 (1755 population of around 4000 possibly suggesting 2500–3250 in 1630, giving proportions in the range of 3%–4%; allowing for a looser range from no population change to population doubling from 1630–1755 would expand the possible proportions to 2.5%–5%). A similar percentage of the population seems to have been assisted in total in Canongate in 1649–50, with a small group of 30 regular weekly poor (possibly just 0.6%–0.75% of the population of around 4000–5000), and an additional wide range of 140 different local individuals receiving more irregular payments, adding possibly 2.8%–3.5% of the population. These distributions are discussed fully in Chapter 6, below; population range taken from Glaze, 'Women and Kirk Discipline', p. 128. Mean weekly payments to the ordinary poor in Canongate in 1649–50 were 8s–10s, perhaps equating to roughly a day or a day and a half's wages for a 1650s urban labourer, or 8–10 loaves of wheatbread at Edinburgh 1653 prices: see Appendix; Gibson and Smout, *Prices*, pp. 30, 278, 299, 319.

[113] CH2/77/1, ff. 122r–157v.

[114] CH2/77/1, ff. 126v–129v.

[115] CH2/77/1, ff. 132v, 138r, 141v, 145r, 149r, 151r–153r.

[116] CH2/77/1, f. 13r.

[117] CH2/624/2, pp. 91–2; 103–8; 126–9.

[118] CH2/624/2, pp. 154–7, 237.

to thre strangeris upone ane testimoniall from his majestie' and 12s to 'Jon Smyth for his supporte in this his present diseas', or the Moravian minister helped with 50s in 1625.[119] The relief operated by burgh kirk sessions beyond the main urban centres in the first few decades of the seventeenth century was mostly characterised by stability in both collection and in distribution, and they continued to follow the patterns developed by urban sessions over the late sixteenth century.[120]

Conclusion

As we might expect, there was a clear chronological pattern in the provision of rural poor relief. In the rare cases where we have evidence of pre-1600 relief, in Monifieth and Galston, the scale and size of the programmes tended to be comparatively modest, especially when compared to the urban provision of that period discussed in Chapter 2. Even after 1600, there were important expansions and improvements in relief operations in many parishes. This suggests that the work of poor relief was one of ongoing development, building up over years and decades, and certainly not arriving in rural Scotland fully-formed in the wake of the Reformation. The scale of relief unsurprisingly tended to be larger in parishes centred on small burghs, reflecting likely differences in both supply and demand. But there were few fundamental differences in approaches to the work of relief, and it makes sense to conceive of the rural-urban distinction as more of a sliding-scale than a binary contrast. The evidence also points to a convergence between rural and small-town relief processes by the early decades of the seventeenth century, as kirk session practice bedded in across the lowlands.

Even once poor relief was up-and-running on a stable basis in rural and small-town Scotland, the situation was far from rosy. Some parishes operated only relatively small-scale relief systems, and many recipients were helped not through weekly or monthly pensions, but with annual or intermittent distributions. In such cases, the assistance may have provided a subsidy towards the cost of food, or perhaps made accommodation costs affordable, or paid for some other expense which was not recorded. There were some individuals in some parishes, however, who received more regular assistance which was sometimes close to a low rate of pay, and for these people the kirk sessions' activities were probably a more central means of support. Some parishes, like Galston or Kinnaird in 1633–4, focused primarily on the provision of this fuller support to just a few poor folk, while others, like Old Deer and Kinnaird in the later 1630s, combined

[119] CH2/624/2, pp. 155, 255.

[120] For similar examples see North Leith in the late 1610s and 1620s (CH2/621/1, pp. 377–94, 449–51, 496–502), and Kirkcaldy from 1614 onwards (CH2/636/34, pp. 1–6; 75, 77, 96, 104); see also Foster, *Church Before the Covenants*, p. 82.

it with less frequent payments to a much wider pool of individuals. The shift in approach identified in Kinnaird points to the flexibility that could be retained, just as the finely graded 'ranks' of the poor in Dunbarney helped to avoid a one-size-fits-all approach to welfare. The balance between regular and irregular payments, between pensioners and more occasionally needy individuals, and the precise amount of relief provided, might vary from parish to parish, or over time, but ultimately these were fairly subtle variations in a single system which could be found spread across the country.

Although estimates of the proportion of the population named in receipt of relief are extremely rough, they were often in the range of 1.5%–4% (though sometimes higher or lower), which would place them towards the bottom end of ranges estimated for England or elsewhere in Europe – although those figures themselves are highly variable, ranging from 2%–6% in some Elizabethan English parishes, and typically from 2%–10% (or sometimes even higher) in a wider selection of European studies including major cities, though with a norm perhaps closer to 5%.[121] Excessive trust should not be placed in the Scottish figures, because relief recipient counts tend to be minimums, payments varied considerably in size and frequency, and of course there is uncertainty over population and demographic structures. They suggest the possibility that a noteworthy but comparatively select group of the parish poor were assisted. If Slack's suggestion that the individuals named should be doubled to assess the real numbers of people helped is roughly applicable to Scotland, it would still typically be fewer than one in ten parishioners who benefitted from session relief payments in most parishes.[122]

Even so, and even where relief payments were relatively infrequent and small, the overall contribution to parish welfare should not be underestimated. After all, elsewhere in contemporary Europe, and even in much of England under the Poor Law, poor relief income was extremely unlikely to be the sole source of support for most recipients.[123] And, while precise quantification is impossible, the provision of even relatively small-scale payments to a range of poor people must have done much to ease the state of poverty in the parish, including by lessening the burden on informal and kin-based networks of support. From the church's point-of-view, this relief programme was a substantial achievement. While accounting practices were not uniform, it is difficult to identify a parish that did not concern itself with the needs of the poor, and the majority of records point to very carefully thought-out and effective attempts at relief. If relief was sometimes limited in quantity or reach, it was not from a lack of effort or

[121] McIntosh, 'Poor relief in Elizabethan English communities', p. 342; Jutte, *Poverty*, pp. 53–4.

[122] Slack, *Poverty and Policy*, p. 174.

[123] See, for example, McIntosh, 'Poor relief in Elizabethan English communities', pp. 345, 352n; Meerkerk and Teeuwen, 'Stability of Voluntarism', p. 86; King, 'Poor Relief and English Economic Development Reappraised', p. 365.

organisation. The kirk session was, indeed, a uniquely effective charitable institution in rural areas, offering personnel and an administrative framework which could not have otherwise been available to these ends. Had kirk sessions not existed, or had they failed to concern themselves with the state of the poor in their communities, it is difficult to see how any remotely comparable provision of support could have been developed during this period. Equally importantly, it is clear that rural parishes did not operate with a substantially different agenda or vision for Christian charity than their urban counterparts. While the scale, and sometimes the range of recipients may have differed, there is little evidence that rural kirk sessions operated predominantly closed, narrow or inflexible systems of relief. The differences in how relief was structured and distributed point, above all, to each kirk session's own attempt to engage with and respond to the needs of the poor in their parish.

CHAPTER 4

Poor Relief Under Stress

Introduction

The Reformed Kirk's poor relief system, like all other aspects of its parochial programme, unfolded gradually after 1560. Chapters 2 and 3 have stressed that it did not spring into place fully formed in all parishes. They also revealed that as kirk sessions developed relief was an integral element of their work and was very widespread by the start of the seventeenth century and often much earlier, especially in urban areas. Albeit at varying pace, it became the norm for lowland Scotland. However, having unpicked the expansion of the system, it is essential to consider how it managed during times of exceptional difficulty. How did kirk sessions cope when faced with major economic crisis, warfare and those recurring terrors facing all early modern societies, plague, fire and dearth? It would be misleading to assess relief systems primarily by their response to catastrophic circumstances, just as it would be wrong to discount such experiences as aberrations: they were facts of early modern life. But exploring their capabilities, responses and decisions at difficult times offers an opportunity to understand better the strengths and weaknesses of the system, as well as the assumptions and motivations which underpinned it.

This chapter assesses the ways in which ecclesiastical relief responded to and coped with crisis in three distinct contexts. The first is the famine which struck Scotland in the early 1620s, the second is the period of conflict including the wars of the three kingdoms in the 1640s (which included grain shortages and pestilence as well as the direct disruption of warfare), while the third section considers the system's responses to more localised emergencies and disasters. Much of the discussion is therefore focused on the seventeenth-century half of the book's period. This is not to suggest that there were no such pressures in the sixteenth century, nor that there were no other significant problems between 1600 and 1650, but the early 1620s and 1640s were by far the most severe challenges to the relief system and they were also the most widespread and genuinely national periods of crisis. They are also better evidenced than earlier periods: partly because of the obvious differences in kirk session record survival (and functioning) discussed in previous chapters, although it is also noteworthy that historians know a great deal more about the wider patterns, depth, and chronology of these times of stress, and it is therefore possible to contextualise the poor relief response more fully.[1]

[1] The later sixteenth century, and especially the 1590s, witnessed some notable dearths

The Famine of the Early 1620s

In the early 1620s Scotland suffered one of the worst famines in its early modern history, second only – if that – to the famous 'ill years' of the 1690s.[2] Whereas there were other localised times of dearth and scarcity, the famine of the 1620s, like the 1690s, was genuinely national.[3] Problems began with a wet autumn and poor harvest in 1621, but it was in 1622 that disaster struck with a second bad harvest in a row, meaning that by the start of 1623 crisis was apparent.[4] Prices shot up in 1623, having already started to move upwards the year before.[5] The famine resulted in hundreds and possibly thousands of deaths around some urban centres, and was remembered in graphic language, with John Row describing how 'many died in the streets, and on highway sydes, for verie want of food, famished'.[6] The harvest of 1623 was better, but after a bitter winter it was the spring of 1624 before the period of crisis could be considered over, with one diarist thankfully noting God's 'unexpected (and much mair undeserved) guidness' in providing ideal planting conditions that March.[7] Flinn's study noted that 'any general assessment of the depth of the crisis is difficult', but as well as the high mortality rates, including deaths from disease linked to malnutrition in addition to direct starvation, it is clear that there was a great deal of vagrancy as desperate people were drawn towards the towns, where they comprised a substantial component of the deceased.[8] There is no way to measure directly the overall impact or local contours across Scotland of the famine in terms of mortality figures, but it is very apparent that the crisis was far more widespread and severe than all other seventeenth-century dearths prior to the 1690s.

Responses to the famine have traditionally been viewed as ineffective, with a great deal of emphasis placed on the very reluctant and unconvincing replies by the shires, especially East Lothian, to the Privy Council's

and epidemic outbreaks, although not necessarily on such a national scale. Evidence on the contours of food shortages and outbreaks is much thinner for the sixteenth century: Flinn (ed.), *Scottish Population History*, p. 109; Whyte, *Scotland Before the Industrial Revolution*, pp. 121–2.

2 *OPL*, pp. 15–16; Stewart, 'Poor Relief in Edinburgh', p. 5; Flinn (ed.), *Scottish Population History*, pp. 117–26. For the famine of the 1690s, see Cullen, *Famine*.

3 Whyte, *Scotland Before the Industrial Revolution*, p. 123. Flinn (ed.), *Scottish Population History*, p. 114, suggests fairly confidently that there were no other national or very widespread crises in the seventeenth century prior to the 1640s.

4 Stewart, 'Poor Relief in Edinburgh', pp. 13–14; *OPL*, p. 15.

5 Gibson and Smout, *Prices*, pp. 51, 54–6, 59, 64, 84.

6 Stewart, 'Poor Relief in Edinburgh', pp. 23, 27; Flinn (ed.), *Scottish Population History*, pp. 117-119, 123 (quotation).

7 Stewart, 'Poor Relief in Edinburgh', p. 24; DUA, Diary of Mr James Guthrie, Minister of Arbirlot, BrMS 3/DC 46, pp. 81–3. For more detail on the weather conditions underpinning the crisis see MacDonald and McCallum, 'Evidence for Early Seventeenth-Century Climate', pp. 504–7.

8 Flinn (ed.), *Scottish Population History*, pp. 117–26 (quotation at p. 126).

1623 instruction to levy a temporary compulsory assessment to provide for the poor during the famine.[9] However Laura Stewart has argued that Edinburgh was able to cope quite well with the challenges of the early 1620s, drawing on existing mechanisms to offer a more effective relief programme than has been appreciated, in contrast to rural areas where there was a failure to respond effectively.[10] Stewart also identified a rise in harsh attitudes to outsider poor as a result of the pressure from the large numbers making their way to Edinburgh in the hope of finding the means to survive which they could not in the countryside.[11] Stewart's article is the only serious analysis of relief during the crisis; although she notes that rural areas were covered by Mitchison's work at the expense of Edinburgh, Mitchison's rural discussion actually amounts to only a brief survey of county responses to the Privy Council order rather than analysis of the experience of the early 1620s in the parishes.[12] The current reading of the experience beyond Edinburgh is therefore a fairly cursory and simplistic suggestion of failure.[13] There was undoubtedly a failure to implement emergency taxation to fund relief in other parts of Scotland, and there were certainly many thousands of deaths which were not prevented by any relief system or local authority: this was inevitable almost anywhere during a serious famine.[14] But to rest content with this assessment would be to accept a zero-sum analysis of poor relief during times of famine. Instead it is important to explore more directly how the church's local relief system responded to, and was affected by, the crisis of the early 1620s.[15]

Unsurprisingly, there is often evidence to show that the scarcity disrupted or challenged the provision of relief. In Stirling, from the summer of 1622 fears had been voiced by the session about the threat of outsider beggars undermining the alms of the local poor. Although payments to the poor continued and new individuals were sometimes added to the roll of regular recipients during 1622 and 1623, by 16 September 1623 the collectors had to be ordered to ensure they passed money to the kirk session to be processed properly rather than distributing it on the spot.[16] This suggests significant pressure on funds, and a relief system struggling to cope,

9 Smout, *History*, p. 86; *OPL*, pp. 15–16; Mitchison, 'North and South', p. 205; Goodare, *Government*, p. 205.

10 Stewart, 'Poor Relief in Edinburgh', especially pp. 6–7, 18–19.

11 Stewart, 'Poor Relief in Edinburgh', pp. 26–7.

12 Stewart, 'Poor Relief in Edinburgh', p. 6; *OPL*, pp. 15–17; Mitchison, 'Making', pp. 65–7.

13 See also Meikle, *The Scottish People*, p. 65.

14 Stewart, 'Poor Relief in Edinburgh', p. 23 (Edinburgh deaths); Frohman, *Poor Relief and Welfare*, p. 30; King, 'Poor Relief and English Economic Development Reappraised', p. 363; Mitchison, *Coping*, p. 43.

15 Mitchison, 'Making', p. 67 claims that there is 'not a big enough body of coherent kirk session registers' to assess whether local relief responses were effective (instead suggesting the widespread mortality as evidence they were not effective); although their utility is variable the following discussion aims to suggest that this is unduly pessimistic.

16 CH2/1026/2, pp. 220, 239, 244, 246, 250.

with officials facing more intense pressure to relieve the needy on the spot. In Elgin, disruption seemed to be fairly minimal for much of 1622, but on 8 November the session had to arrange 'to hald abak the beggeris from the kirk dor' during preaching, a much more extreme and direct measure than more conventional and sometimes abstract statements about removing sturdy beggars and supporting the local poor.[17] Moreover, although collections continued to take place relief funds were apparently very stretched by May 1623 when the minister was to exhort the congregation 'to incres and inlairge ther charitie at the brod to the poor in respect of the straitnes of the yeer'.[18] Monkton's session was by November 1622 so concerned about coldness in donations that they introduced a more rigorous and pressurised system for gathering and soliciting the collection.[19] In summer 1623 Ayr held fasts and for the first of these ordered preaching on Ezekiel 9, a particularly resonant passage for emphasising divine punishment for human iniquity: charity was an important response to the crisis but so was repentance.[20] Regular collections continued as well, of course.[21] In Yester, by late 1622 there seems to have been pressure on relief funds, as the lower than usual sum of £3 was disbursed on 15 December, and the following March when the poor box was accounted it was found to contain only £3 6s 9d.[22] The same day, they made a deal with an offender allowing him to pay an extra fine to avoid public repentance, 'having considerit the grit number and mister of the pur in the parrochin'.[23] The famine, by placing pressures on those who were supposed to fund it, and increasing the poverty of those who claimed it, sometimes seriously threatened the provision and extent of kirk session relief in urban and rural parishes.

An even more visible and dramatic sign of the crisis faced in many parishes comes through the session's work in assisting with emergency burial expenses, especially for the poor. Although not providing direct quantitative evidence on mortality, unlike the burial registers analysed in Flinn's demographic study, the session records testify to the severity of the dearth in a wide range of parishes.[24] In Midcalder by September 1623 an increase in burials becomes apparent, and a similar timing was suggested in Stirling both by payments for burial expenses at that point and by a reference in February 1624 to the 'the buyaris of winnein sheitis to the puir

[17] CH2/145/4, ff. 4r–9v (quotation at 9v).
[18] CH2/145/4, f. 23v.
[19] CH2/809/1, p. 85; see also below, p. 139.
[20] CH2/751/2, f. 31r.
[21] CH2/751/2, ff. 31v–34v.
[22] CH2/377/1, pp. 81, 84, 87, 89. See Appendix for guidance on broad wage and price equivalents, although the time of dearth adds further uncertainty to the already very approximate estimates therein.
[23] CH2/377/1, p. 89.
[24] Flinn (ed.), *Scottish Population History*, pp. 117–20.

this last sommer sasone'.[25] In Burntisland one grave-maker reported over 300 burials of parishioners and poor outsiders, and Perth's mortality was recorded in the Chronicle of Perth as reaching ten or twelve deaths per day at its peak 'from midsomer to mychaelmas' of 1623.[26] Even if this was exaggerated, the session records suggest pressures on burial resources even much earlier, in November 1622, when a disciplinary case was raised for 'making mort kistis on the saboth dayis'.[27] Larger burghs like Perth, and important ports like Burntisland (directly opposite Leith and Edinburgh across the Forth) might have attracted particularly high numbers of poor people seeking help, but in rural Yester a man was found dead in October 1622, and the session had to help fund increasing numbers of burials in spring and summer 1623.[28] And in the north, at Fraserburgh, there were numerous poor burials in early 1623, and as early as August 1622 the minister had admonished the congregation to attend burials in larger numbers, especially those of poor people, suggesting that they were already noticeably more frequent by then.[29] As well as requiring sessions to divert precious resources to winding-sheets and other burial costs, and in addition to the obvious psychological and emotional impact, the deaths in the parish must also have caused a degree of dislocation and additional necessities. This would have been particularly true where dependents were left behind, although the scale of this problem might have been tragically lessened by the fact that in some of the few cases where direct burial statistics are available as many as half or even more of the deceased were children.[30] It is impossible to say how many of these lives could have been saved by a stronger relief system, although as Karen Cullen has suggested in relation to the 1690s famine, where food was not available for purchase then larger or more numerous cash payments would be of limited use.[31] While evaluating the relief system by its inability to avert widespread deaths during famine would be inappropriate, the mortality of these years should not be discounted as a major challenge to poor relief in its own right, or as a cautionary note about the limits of welfare in the seventeenth century.

However, there are also some signs of health, stability, and even resilience in the relief work carried out by the church through the years of crisis. This was especially true for some or all of 1622, before the height of scarcity and mortality in 1623. Some kirk sessions continued to function and provide relief as normal for much of 1622, and in several cases they managed to raise substantial funds for the distressed French church that

[25] CH2/266/1, p. 59; CH2/1026/2, pp. 247, 260.

[26] CH2/523/1, p. 205; Flinn (ed.), *Scottish Population History*, p. 119; Maidment (ed.), *Chronicle of Perth*, p. 24.

[27] CH2/521/7, p. 373.

[28] CH2/377/1, pp. 86, 90–4.

[29] CH2/1142/1, ff. 139r, 146r, 150v, 151v.

[30] Flinn (ed.), *Scottish Population History*, pp. 119–20.

[31] Cullen, *Famine*, p. 95.

year.[32] By early 1623 the pressure tended to be greater, but kirk sessions continued to make relief payments to the poor, and to admit new entrants to poor relief.[33] Sometimes this necessitated being cautious with the funds, and Perth's session told a distressed man seeking weekly support, despite 'perceaveing his neiddie estait', that he was only 'to be helpit quhen they may have occasioun', and other claimants seemed to have to wait for a pension to become vacant (presumably through death), as well.[34] This points to a system which was surviving and continuing to operate, even if on a less generous scale than desirable given the new pressures faced. In Falkirk there was little sign of disruption even in 1623, and collection totals remained steady at around £4–£6 per month.[35] In Fraserburgh, too, collections continued to be adequate to fund ongoing routine payments to various poor people. The session was even able to make a small payment related to the repair of the windows in the kirk in March 1623, and on 30 July kept a substantial part of the collection total unspent.[36] This may have been partly born of caution, perhaps with the critical impending harvest in mind, but it also suggests a relief system that was not struggling to continue operating.

The rural kirk session of Longside was able to respond well to some of the increased demand and necessities of the time. A December 1620 account of the year's poor business reveals the pre-dearth pattern: £64 8s 4d was collected over the year, of which £26 16s 6d was disbursed to the 'haill puirall' at that point, while an additional £6 2s 4d had been handed to them 'at divers tymes according to ther severall necessityis'.[37] Collections for 1621 were almost £20 higher, and there was a similar pattern of surplus, as just under £30 was paid as a regular mass disbursement in 1621, and just under £9 as incidental payments for their 'severall necessities'.[38] However scarcity had made itself felt by August 1622 when an interim account and distribution was made, and although collections had amounted to about £35, at a reasonably similar monthly rate to 1620, the irregular payments for necessities now amounted to £12 12s, which was over half the size of

32 CH2/751/2, ff. 11v–16r; CH2/521/7, pp. 314–30 (French collection at p. 328). In Elgin, even after the second calamitous bad harvest of 1622, the collection for the French was to be put to one side and spent on other pious causes only if it was confirmed that the French Protestants no longer needed it: CH2/145/4, f. 9v.

33 CH2/1026/2, pp. 244, 246, 250, 252; CH2/266/1, pp. 58–60. As noted above, Yester's relief operations came under significant pressure by December 1622, but payments to the poor continued through 1623: CH2/377/1, pp. 90–4.

34 CH2/521/7, pp. 400, 401, 404.

35 CH2/400/1, pp. 111–26.

36 CH2/1142/1, 148v–149v; CH2/1142/2, ff. 1r–v. The gap in Fraserburgh's session minutes between 23 April–23 July 1623, and 30 July 1623–July 1624 could possibly be connected with the famine but such gaps were not exceptional, and there is no indication of a recent crisis when the minutes resume in 1624.

37 CH2/699/1, p. 16.

38 CH2/699/1, p. 31.

the mass disbursement (£21 9s), leaving only a much-reduced surplus of £5 15s 10d. That December, £11 6s was handed out as the mass disbursement, but £10 had been paid in the irregular disbursements since August, and because only £19 1s 7d had been collected they were required to draw on the previous surplus to achieve this.[39] This suggests that the unpredictable and more regular sums of money needed by the poor between major hand-outs to help them survive were much higher during the dearth. By June 1623, irregular disbursements were still almost as large as the regular distribution but, impressively under the circumstances, more had been collected so the surplus had recovered to a healthier £13 19s 9d, and funds remained steadier thereafter. In August 1624 however, incidental payments for the 'severall necessities' of the poor were still a higher proportion of spending, possibly indicating the ongoing legacy and aftermath of the dearth. Irregular payments had returned to a much lower proportion of the poor funds by September 1625.[40] Overall it seems that Longside experienced a sharp increase in the incidental expenses of the poor, which it was only just able to meet during the worst times following the second bad harvest of 1622. However the session was able to accommodate some extra demand, and although they do not seem to have undertaken any widespread extra emergency relief (if any was required), they managed to maintain the support of their poor in a stable manner.

For the most part sessions tried to continue operating their existing schemes and practices for raising and distributing charitable funds. There was certainly more stability and survival than innovation. The pressures might lead them to formalise and improve their recording practices: in Midcalder, for example, the great increase in the detailed recording of collections and distributions from May 1623 to late 1624 seems likely to have been a result of the increased time and attention being paid to poor relief as part of the session's activity.[41] Some sessions achieved modest success in raising additional contributions from elites over and above the regular relief collections, such as Yester where in 1623 donations to the box were forthcoming from 'my lord Yester' (£10) and the laird of Newhall (£6).[42] Burntisland's session arranged special collections involving the laird and a bailie, raising 40 merks on 13 July 1623, and £16 6s 8d on 17 August.[43] However, the kirk sessions did not attempt to transform their approaches to relief in the face of famine, preferring instead to try to maintain their practice by continuing to support the existing poor as best they could, and

[39] CH2/699/1, pp. 39, 44.

[40] CH2/699/1, pp. 52, 66, 72, 86.

[41] CH2/266/1, pp. 58–62. There is however a gap in the minutes from October 1623 to January 1624.

[42] CH2/377/1, pp. 92, 94.

[43] CH2/523/1, pp. 203–4. In February 1623, Kirkcaldy held a separate church door collection for 'sindrie indigent persons' that raised £36 (normal weekly collections raised around £6-£8): CH2/636/34, p. 89.

accommodating new claimants where possible, but on a similar basis to existing recipients. Whether or not a more radical, ambitious or imaginative approach to famine relief was possible or could have succeeded, the kirk sessions chose to attempt as much stability as possible, and in general they managed to keep relief going on a fairly regular basis.

Despite the better harvest of 1623, factors including a very cold winter meant that the period of crisis was not considered over until the spring of 1624. There are signs that the relief system made a relatively swift recovery from the darkest days of the famine. As noted above, during 1624 and possibly into 1625, Longside Kirk Session had increased surpluses but was continuing to make irregular payments in between its regular poor distributions, possibly because the community took time to recover and the poor still faced more unpredictable conditions. Similarly, Midcalder's session still seemed to be facing more demand than had been apparent before the shortages.[44] However, in Stirling after February 1624 onwards the flow of regular new admissions to receipt of poor relief began to dry up, suggesting that times were more stable, and in Yester by November 1623 and into early 1624 the intensity of payments for the poor or winding-sheets had diminished.[45] In Ayr, in May 1624 the session decided to borrow money from 'the poor silver' to pay debts due to some of their officers (payments to whom had possibly fallen behind during the famine), suggesting that the poor funds were back in reasonable shape.[46] Ayr was able to raise money for the fire which devastated Dunfermline in 1624, further suggesting that the kirk session relief system had returned to relative normality by the middle of 1624.[47] Sessions had generally taken a cautious if unambitious approach, and ultimately weathered the storm fairly well.

The decisions taken about who to focus support on during the crisis also suggest a conservative approach. Some payments suggest assistance to a slightly wider than usual group of people, such as the 'extraordinar' payments in Midcalder's distribution of May 1623, although the bulk of funds still went to the regular 18 poor recipients.[48] Perth distributed a £3 surplus remaining after disbursing the collection after the major flood of October 1621 to 'divers persounes', and soon after an £11 surplus left after paying the ordinary poor was passed at the vestry door to sundry poor people. Similar steps were taken with a surplus (after paying the ordinary poor) on 31 December 1622.[49] Stirling enrolled three new regular recipients to 40d weekly in July 1623 'during the brethren's will', suggesting they were temporarily in need, presumably as a result of higher prices or income

[44] CH2/266/1, p. 62.
[45] CH2/1026/2, pp. 263–70; CH2/377/1, pp. 94–8.
[46] CH2/751/2, f. 42v.
[47] CH2/1026/2, f. 46r; See below, p. 125.
[48] CH2/266/1, p. 58.
[49] CH2/521/7, pp. 282–3, 388.

problems.[50] However, such expansions in the range assisted tended to be fairly slight, and sessions often seemed more concerned with ensuring that adequate relief was being provided to the regular ranks of their own existing poor and a few deserving new cases. In Perth, when things got tighter in early 1623, as we have seen, they chose to ask new claimants to wait until alms could be made available rather than making a greater number of smaller payments.[51] The increased interim payments made in Longside for the 'severall necessities' of the poor probably included additional contributions to the survival during dearth of existing poor people, and the need to monitor the poor roll more closely may explain the planned examination of the parish's poor on 16 November 1623.[52] Similarly in Fraserburgh in March 1623 greater care was taken to name individuals receiving payments.[53] Overall, although sessions must have faced growing calls for assistance from a wider than usual body of poor and less well-off parishioners, they generally preferred to maintain a regular body of poor people at the same or increased level than to channel their funds into more ad hoc general relief handouts.

People of less conventionally poor background must also have needed more help during times of famine. Some urban kirk sessions took steps to ensure that their own officers and respectable members of the community received assistance. In Ayr, at the height of famine in September 1623, 'maister William Smythe readar upon his suite in wreat in respect of this great dearthe obtenit twentie merks fra the sessioun'. The following week it was noted that 'sindrie petitiounis of the poor continewed': although continuations of session business were not unusual, this could possibly suggest that they had relieved their reader at the expense of wider petitions from the poor.[54] In any case the payment shows that supporting church officials through the dearth was a priority, and similarly in January 1623 Falkirk's session took steps to augment their reader's stipend.[55] In May 1622 Stirling's session discovered that 'thair is ane great nummer of honest indigent persones within this congregatione that levis verie hardlie thrugh want of thair necessaris and yit ar eshamed to mein[?] thair esteat publictlie as utheris dois'. These people were to be sought out and helped, and by July it was reported that £100 had been privately disbursed to them.[56] This was a rare occurrence in the records (although by its nature it could possibly have sometimes been left unminuted), but it suggests another possible angle to some urban sessions' priorities, and accords with

50 CH2/1026/2, p. 246.

51 CH2/521/7, pp. 400, 401, 404.

52 CH2/699/1, pp. 54–5 (the examination had to be cancelled as a result of bad weather).

53 CH2/1142/1, f. 150v.

54 CH2/751/2, ff. 34r–v.

55 CH2/400/1, p. 114.

56 CH2/1026/2, pp. 213, 218. The policy was repeated in 1623, with payments totalling 200 merks (pp. 243, 245).

Stewart's identification of extraordinary payments in Edinburgh during the famine which appeared to reflect social status more than necessity.[57] What it shares with the approach to the conventional poor is a desire to support the community continuing to function as stably as possible, rather than to adopt overtly emergency-centered processes.

Another group potentially claiming the benevolence of kirk sessions during this time of famine were travelling poor from beyond the parish. These were very prominent during these years, and flocked to urban centres in particular, where it has been suggested that they were viewed and treated with increasing harshness by the authorities.[58] Hostile attitudes to non-native poor were commonly expressed in this period, although these statements were not always translated into equally harsh practice.[59] But it is apparent from session records across Scotland that there was real concern to exclude wandering vagrants and focus relief on the native parish poor. This was expressed prior to 1621–4 (for example in Ayr in 1617–18, and Elgin in 1620), but stated particularly frequently, and crucially translated into actual action, during the time of famine.[60] In Elgin, as we have seen, by November 1622 beggars had to be held out at the kirk door, and earlier that year a woman was ordered to stop lodging 'outlandische people nor uncouthe beggeris'.[61] In Ayr in March 1623 there was a particularly formal act ordering the masterful and uncouth beggars to be removed and 'thair awin poor anes' to receive marks and be relieved.[62] Elsewhere, too, although not universally, there were signs of a particular clampdown on foreign beggars.[63] Aberdeen Kirk Session fired one of its officers for being bribed by stranger beggars to allow them to beg through the town.[64] Stirling's fairly conventional payment to the town officer for removing unwelcome beggars included a note that they 'oppresis the samin and hurtis the nateive puir therein', again pointing to greater intensity and fear than usual.[65] In October 1623 Fife's Synod expressed similar fears,

57 Stewart, 'Poor Relief in Edinburgh', p. 20.

58 Mitchison, *Coping*, p. 27; Stewart, 'Poor Relief in Edinburgh', pp. 15–16, 18; Cullen, *Famine*, pp. 95, 161.

59 This is discussed fully in Chapter 7 (pp. 202–4).

60 CH2/751/1/2, ff. 341v, 357v; CH2/145/3, f. 151v; Stewart, 'Poor Relief in Edinburgh', p. 27.

61 See above, p. 105; CH2/145/3, f. 186v.

62 CH2/751/2, f. 27v.

63 Sessions such as Falkirk, Fraserburgh and Longside do not seem to have expressed particular concern or fear about outsider poor.

64 CH2/448/4, p. 147.

65 CH2/1026/2, p. 239. Further evidence of an unusually intense atmosphere around the issue is found in Kinghorn where William Allane refused to take on the office of outholding sturdy beggars, and when John Newin was appointed instead it was emphasised that he should be able to call on other officials for help if he faced resistance: CH2/472/1, pp. 118, 120.

urging parishes 'to inroll their awin *kyndlie*[66] puir, and procuir means for their intertainment during the tym of this present skaircitie and dairth'.[67] Some rural parishes as well as urban ones demonstrated these attitudes: in January 1623 Menmuir session noting 'the increas of beggaris and dali[e] repair of strangeris ordeins that the actis of parliament be put in execution . . . that strangeris may be debarrit and the puir of the parische provydit', and debarring strangers and providing tokens for the parish poor are indeed the main focus of the patchy session records for 1623.[68] The dearth, then, seemed to encourage the translation of suspicion about non-parochial poor into action, and willingness to provide support to them was more limited than during better times. Relief payments to strangers were not unheard of during this period, as shown by disbursements by Monkton Kirk Session in 1621 and early 1623, and frequent payments by St Cuthbert's Kirk Session throughout 1623 (such as the payment of 20s to 'Jeane Crawfurd stranger' on 30 January 1623).[69] Even during famine they were not universally excluded. But the period of dearth seems to have seriously and uniquely (during this book's timeframe) reduced the normally more open attitude of kirk sessions to genuinely needy folk originating from beyond their bounds. This adds to the sense that the priority was to maintain the relief system and support the existing poor, rather than responding open-mindedly and expansively to the dislocations taking place.

Overall, regular session relief sometimes coped reasonably well with the time of dearth in the early 1620s, continuing a recognisable and functioning relief system in the face of national crisis. There was some variation in how effectively relief could continue, although there was no firm geographical pattern to this beyond the fact that some of the parishes that seem to have been the least badly hit were rural (Yester, Monkton) and/or in the north (Fraserburgh, Longside). Struggles to maintain relief provision, and intense concern about outsiders were perhaps most apparent in larger central burghs like Stirling and Perth, although even these distinctions are a matter of emphasis rather than absolute. There was no concrete rural-urban divide in how kirk sessions responded. Of course, very important qualifications need to be placed on the fact that the practice of relief survived the famine. The most dramatic is probably the large numbers of people dying, including in the streets and fields: kirk sessions, probably like any other seventeenth-century institution, could not prevent this.

66 Emphasis mine. As well as primarily meaning native or local poor in this context, the word could also have connotations of an ancestral right or privilege: *DSL*, 'Kindly'.

67 CH2/154/1, p. 278.

68 CH2/264/1, pp. 2–4.

69 CH2/809/1, pp. 74–6, 92; CH2/718/60, pp 110–17 (quotation at p. 110). See also some Midcalder payments to outsiders in 1621 and 1624: CH2/266/1, pp. 54, 60–2. Cullen, *Famine*, p. 95, notes that some payments to outsiders were made even during the famine of the 1690s.

There was also a lack of adaptability and ambition in kirk session responses across Scotland: they chose to consolidate rather than innovate. Ministers, elders, and deacons seem to have preferred to continue (and augment where needed) the alms they were giving to familiar poor people, or to expand the poor roll cautiously, rather than developing more innovative strategies to help much wider sectors of the needy, especially those desperate individuals arriving from elsewhere. If rural relief (or non-Edinburgh relief) 'failed', this was its failure: not a breakdown of poor relief itself, but a failure to transform its approaches to deal with a crisis.[70] It is of course impossible to say how much could have been done to avert the enormous suffering and mortality, although given the difficulty of raising funds during a time when everyone was suffering economically, there may have been some merit in the cautious approach of maintaining the familiar and existing ranks of the local poor. The system they had developed was designed to cope with a relatively normal economic situation, not crisis, and for better or worse they chose to attempt to cope and to survive with a baseline level of relief. In some senses this exposes the limitations of the relief system. Equally, the fact that normal collections and distributions were able to continue relatively stably under the economic circumstances of the early 1620s testifies to the strength of the system and the extent to which it had become an established priority for sessions and congregations across the lowlands.

The Impact of Conflict, *c.* 1639–*c.* 1651

The last decade or so covered by this book was also the most turbulent. During the 1640s ecclesiastical relief faced considerable pressures, sometimes familiar and sometimes novel. Most dramatic and new was the increasing disruption and dislocation caused by warfare in the three kingdoms, in combination with the more traditional (though unusually severe) bursts of plague and dearth by the late 1640s. This was followed by military invasion and occupation by Cromwell's English army from 1650–1 onwards. Warfare created a large number of direct victims needing support, of course, and Langley has recently demonstrated the effectiveness of some mechanisms for caring for veterans and their families.[71] But considerable stress was inevitably placed on much wider sections of Scottish society. This section explores the experience and responses of regular parochial relief under the pressures of the conflicts and other troubles.

In the early years after the National Covenant of 1638 and the start of the Bishops' Wars in 1639, any impact on poor relief was minor and gradual, not least because despite the significance of the political events, military disturbance to the bulk of Scotland's parishes was minimal, and

[70] Stewart, 'Poor Relief in Edinburgh', p. 7.

[71] Langley, 'Caring for Soldiers'.

the wider economy does not seem to have been greatly hit.[72] Times do seem to have been tougher in Kilmadock, where collection totals and the surplus after the poor had been paid dropped sharply in 1638–9, despite the fact that attendance levels had apparently increased to the point of standing room only during Sunday services.[73] In Salton the amount disbursed to the poor rose dramatically in 1639, although there were still decent surpluses of about £10 and £17 in 1639 and 1640, suggesting that increased levels of demand for relief could still be accommodated.[74] In 1641 however the surplus was only 11s, reflecting disbursements to a wider variety of local poor plus a growing number of distressed strangers which continued in the early 1640s.[75] Collections held steady in Kinnaird over the period 1638–42, and the rolls of the regular poor in Montrose remained stable through the early 1640s both in terms of numbers supported and in payment size.[76] Midcalder continued to collect and distribute at fairly steady levels from 1639 through to the mid 1640s.[77] Monimail's weekly collection totals fell between 1642 and 1644 (though partly compensated by some large communion collections), while normal relief distributions continued albeit at a necessarily reduced level by 1644, indicating a system which was being placed under growing pressure.[78] Overall while the dramatic developments of the covenanting revolution were unfolding in the late 1630s and early 1640s, parochial poor relief continued relatively unaffected, or at worst with a tightened belt.

One of the ways in which the archipelagic conflict began to have a more notable impact on relief was in growing numbers of displaced outsiders claiming relief from kirk sessions: Salton was very typical in making payments to a more varied body of recipients in the early 1640s.[79] Many of these were distressed Irish people who had fled the Ulster rebellion of 1641.[80] In Kilmadock, before the 1643 meeting for agreeing the accounts, the distressed Irish had received £29 while 'our owne poor who in their necessitie did call for our help' got just over £10. However an additional

72 Stevenson, *Scottish Revolution, 1637–44*, especially pp. 138–50, 192–213; Flinn (ed.), *Scottish Population History*, pp. 127–30.

73 CH2/212/18, pp. 7–8. See Table 3.2 above.

74 CH2/322/1, pp. 98–100.

75 CH2/322/1, pp. 103–6.

76 CH2/418/1, pp. 26–61; CH2/943/1, pp. 219–24.

77 CH2/266/1, pp. 102–17, 143–4, 172.

78 CH2/548/1, pp. 29–46.

79 See also Di Folco, 'Discipline and Welfare', p. 177.

80 These refugees and the fundraising mechanisms to support them are discussed in Young, '"Escaping Massacre"'; see also Langley, *Worship*, pp. 133, 158. Although the scale of the Irish influx after 1641 was entirely unprecedented, Irish supplicants were not a new phenomenon in Scottish parishes (see, for example, a case in Haddington in November 1630: CH2/799/1, f. 316v), and not all of the refugees claiming aid in Scottish parishes had fled from Ireland (see, for example, the deposed minister from Yorkshire helped by Monimail Kirk Session in 1643: CH2/548/1, p. 42).

£38 13s 4d was then distributed to the poor by the kirk session leaving a surplus of £8, so the Irish contribution did not lead to a shortage for the local poor.[81] In Monimail by 1643 and 1644 outsiders had come to comprise a significant part of the parish's relief expenditure, including refugees who were likely of relatively humble status (such as 'ane poor woman come out of Ireland'), and those of higher status such as ministers or their family members, and Isobel Hamilton, daughter of Sir John Hamilton.[82] However, such expenditure does not appear to have disrupted the session from its main task of internal poor relief, and payments to local poor clearly continued even in the more straitened months of 1644, since Margaret Paterson in Leatham (Letham, in Monimail parish) received 18s, and Eupham Baxter was granted a dollor as long as she was not 'chargeable' hereafter, suggesting that she was a native of the parish.[83] So the session's relief work was affected, but refugees and displaced people were an addition to its normal operation rather than a replacement – and tougher times dented rather than undermining the collection of funds. The impact was geographically specific: areas on the west coast are known to have struggled to cope with the large numbers when they landed, and in Ayr weekly collections were placed under immense pressure in 1641–2.[84] However across much of Scotland the Irish refugees and other displaced people were generally assisted by kirk sessions without a major negative impact on local relief. Throughout the 1640s in rural and urban parishes like Dundee, Haddington, Kinnaird and Midcalder, growing payments to outsiders co-existed with generally stable ongoing relief provision, and negative impacts on the local poor, such as when Isobel Hamilton was (temporarily) prioritised over the regular poor of Midcalder in 1648, were very occasional.[85] Equally, the fact that such numbers of distressed outsiders could be accommodated within the relief programme points to its flexibility at this point.

Around the middle of the 1640s, the disruption and pressure on poor relief began to intensify, starting with the first extreme and violent disruptions of regular relief. No accounts survive for Dundee's collections and distributions in 1644–5, when the town was attacked by the earl of Montrose; although this does not mean that no relief work took place, it must have been very badly disrupted at best (albeit temporarily: normal

[81] CH2/212/18, pp 9–10.

[82] CH2/548/1, pp. 42–6.

[83] CH2/548/1, pp. 44–5.

[84] Young, '"Escaping Massacre"', pp. 221–2, 227–8; Langley, 'Sheltering under the Covenant: The National Covenant, Orthodoxy and the Irish Rebellion, 1638–1644', pp. 137–60 at pp. 145–7.

[85] McCallum, 'Charity and Conflict', pp. 47–8; CH2/799/1, ff. 85v, 120v–125r, 135v–136r; CH2/418/1, pp. 55–65; CH2/266/1, pp. 216–17; McCallum, 'Charity Doesn't Begin at Home', p. 120. This was presumably the same Isobel Hamilton as assisted in Monimail four years earlier.

business was resumed in 1645–6).[86] Monimail's minutes abruptly end with the entry for 10 November 1644, coinciding with Montrose's campaigns in central Scotland including nearby Perthshire in late 1644 and early 1645.[87] Dalziel's session minutes skip from June 1645 to May 1647; again some relief may have been ongoing but it was highly likely to have been disrupted by the interruptions to the session's proceedings.[88] In some other parishes the paperwork survives but there are clear signs that the military campaigns of 1644–5 were severely effecting relief: in Kilmadock in October 1644 it was thought best to delay the distribution as a result of the small sums collected and the 'many suplicantes who requyring our help' had already received funds.[89] Elgin's session minutes make a note of the attack and spoilation of the town in February–March 1645, which was followed by a great deal of disruption to preaching and session activity, although some collections did still take place.[90] When conflict arrived in a locality, or military forces moved through or occupied an area, the disruptive effect on ecclesiastical administration as a whole formed one of the most serious challenges to any poor relief operations, something which was repeated at the end of the decade.

Nevertheless, poor relief survived into the second half of the 1640s with some impressive resilience. As well as the relatively swift recovery of relief in Dundee, Kilmadock's session reverted to relative normality in terms of collections and distributions from 1645 to 1648, although with evidence of the tougher times in the language used: in 1646 £31 12s had been given 'on severall sabbaths at the directioune of the minister and elders to the misterfull poor in ther necessitie'.[91] Significant pressures were also evident, though ultimately managed, in Kelso where on 29 March 1646 'the pensiones exceeded the contributions', although two weeks later the situation had recovered far enough that there was 6s leftover after paying the pensions, and the shortfall seems to have been exceptional.[92] Dalziel's session records are relatively disordered from their resumption in 1647 until 1649, but when the box was accounted in 1647 it was found to contain £29 6s 8d, so some relief was able to take place once the kirk session was functional again.[93] And when Bervie's session accounts begin in 1648 there were steady collections taking place as well as regular disbursements to some

86 McCallum, 'Charity and Conflict', pp. 40–1.

87 CH2/548/1, p. 46 (this entry is followed by a page and a half of blank space); Stevenson, *Revolution and Counter-Revolution*, pp. 17–19. The next surviving minutes are from the 1680s, although it is likely that the session resumed operations far sooner.

88 CH2/462/34, pp. 2–3.

89 CH2/212/18, p. 10.

90 CH2/145/6, ff. 106r–108r.

91 CH2/212/18, pp. 11–12. See Table 3.2 above.

92 CH2/1173/1, pp. 302–3. A year earlier Kelso had suffered a fire resulting from plague-cleansing: Flinn (ed.), *Scottish Population History*, p. 140.

93 CH2/462/34, pp. 4–5, 72–3.

local poor and more incidental payments including to distressed Irish.[94] Stability was also evident in some of the other parishes discussed earlier, such as Haddington, Midcalder and Kinnaird.[95] As long as kirk sessions were able to meet and operate with some normality, relief was ongoing and subject to fluctuations and pressures rather than major disruption.

Another calamity to strike during the 1640s was plague: the years 1644–9 witnessed the worst outbreak of the early modern period, with around 20,000–30,000 deaths and perhaps 20% of the urban population wiped out.[96] The plague hit various urban centres over these years in sharp and violent bursts, although it is now clear that there was significant infection passing through rural areas as well.[97] One of the most explicit and well-known accounts of the plague and responses to it come from South Leith, where the kirk session narrated the catastrophic visitation which arrived in May 1645 and ultimately claimed 2736 lives.[98] The session's fundraising and organisational efforts were of course heavily directed towards direct plague responses such as cleaning, burials and dealing with infected individuals in collaboration with the bailies, but even during the crisis relief work was not put to one side.[99] The session tried to assist those who could not support themselves as a result of plague, and even ordered that money found in houses being cleansed should be cleaned and passed to the kirk treasurer (via the bailies), for the use of the poor.[100] Afterwards they found, unsurprisingly given the enormous disruption and mortality, that no proper record of relief had been kept, but they still accounted properly for the pre-May 1645 collections.[101] Even during the crisis itself, relief had been included within the wider work of disaster response. Plague was severe nearby in Canongate too, where the session's distributions cease being formally recorded from August 1645 until February 1646, although they recover fairly quickly afterwards.[102] The session also funded emergency relief during the visitation, as shown for example by a receipt for £9

[94] CH2/34/9, pp. 2–15.

[95] See, for example, CH2/799/1, ff. 72–3, ff. 120v–125r; CH2/266/1, pp. 169–72, 184, 220; CH2/418/1, pp. 85–109.

[96] The biological and demographic contours are examined in detail in Flinn (ed.), *Scottish Population History*, pp. 133–49; the best up-to-date survey of sixteenth and seventeenth century plague as a whole is Oram, 'Responses to Epidemic Disease'.

[97] Oram, 'Responses to Epidemic Disease', pp. 17–20. Although the present discussion is concerned with impact on relief rather than the study of plague patterns, the rural examples of Kilmadock, Midcalder, and Kinnaird/Rait below certainly add further support to Oram's argument that the spread of plague in rural environments has been underestimated.

[98] Robertson (ed.), *South Leith Records*, p. 69.

[99] For direct anti-infection measures and policies in early modern Scotland, which were led by secular authorities, see Oram, 'Responses to Epidemic Disease', pp. 23–9.

[100] Robertson (ed.), *South Leith Records*, pp. 55–7, 59, 62–3.

[101] Robertson (ed.), *South Leith Records*, p. 66.

[102] CH2/122/29, pp. 420–5, 430–3, 449.

worth of bread dispensed to 'the poore and sick people within the park and toun the tyme of the infectioun', for which the kirk session treasurer reimbursed two bakers in September 1646.[103] Kirk sessions had a long tradition of both continuing relief where possible, and organising specific responses to plague: a much earlier example had come in the mid-1580s when Perth's Kirk Session arranged special contributions and distributions to diverse needy people during a serious visitation in the town.[104]

Although the most devastating visitations tended to be urban, plague affected relief in rural areas at times as well. In Kilmadock in 1648 the session made a special distribution to those who dared not seek neighbourly assistance 'in respect the plague of pestilence wes hotly raging in the land', although there was still a decent relief surplus of £22 3s 2d.[105] The phrasing suggests an element of fear rather than a definite local presence of plague, and similarly in Midcalder in 1645 a special collection was intimated for the help of the poor who were suffering from or suspected of the pestilence and were thus 'not abill to do for them selvis': £20 was raised for them.[106] Kirk sessions were responsive not just to the immediate presence of plague but also to the knock-on economic effects for the vulnerable.[107] And disruption to normal activities by the presence or threat of infection was also sometimes a problem: on 18 April 1647 Kinnaird held no collection or session because 'the plague of pestilence wes in the nichbour congregation of Raitt'. Preaching was held in the kirkyard in subsequent weeks although ultimately the impact on Kinnaird's relief collections was minimal.[108] In Bervie on 28 May 1648 preaching was to be relocated 'for fear of the infection', but the sum collected that day was 25s, slightly higher than the parish's 1648 mean collection total of 21s.[109] The extent to which sessions could maintain relief through times of plague was naturally dependent on the severity of the local infection, and at times emergency measures were all that could be taken. Overall though, there was some ability to respond effectively and to maintain relief work through the crisis, although the high mortality levels only added to the challenges of relief as the late 1640s drew on.

By 1649 the worst of the plague had receded, but the year was a very hard one. Prices were rising sharply, with Gibson and Smout identifying a 'crisis of crops' in 1647–52, and it is clear that there was an economic

103 CH2/122/74, Item 75.

104 *PKSB*, pp. 54–5, 290–5.

105 CH2/212/18, p. 12.

106 CH2/266/1, pp. 151–2.

107 See also *Records of Old Aberdeen*, vol. ii, p. 145; *Ecclesiastical Records: Presbyteries of St Andrews and Cupar*, p. 116.

108 CH2/418/1, p. 95.

109 CH2/34/9, pp. 2–15 (quotation at p. 5). If attendance was lower, as seems plausible, it may be that greater generosity amongst those who did attend was sparked by the dangerous times.

'malaise' at the end of the 1640s, at least partly exacerbated by warfare, and possibly informing the poor relief act passed by the covenanting parliament of 1649.[110] Discussion of dearth is certainly more prominent in session records in the year 1649: Old Aberdeen explained the decision to distribute immediately an entire communion collection with reference to 'the hard stres and famine in the Land', and there was 'gryt dearth' in Elgin on 15 July 1649. Struggles with providing the usual relief in this climate continued into 1650 in both parishes.[111] On 13 February 1649 Canongate noted that as a result of 'the increase of the poore within the cannongait and the dearth of all thingis in thir hard tymes' the weekly 6s was no longer adequate for the ordinary poor and therefore arranged a special collection (and added a new entrant, a widow, to the weekly roll). A week later they duly increased the weekly pension to 10s.[112] These references appear in the context of expanding relief provision, so they confirm both the seriousness of the scarcity for the parish poor, and the ability to respond to it. In Canongate hard times continued into the summer of 1649 and early 1650, but the session continued raising and administering funds, including extra payments such as the £1 16s given to 'thrie poore women of the ordinar poore starving for necessitie'.[113] At this point there were collections of around £120 per month, and around 30 ordinary poor, each getting about 8s–10s per week. One-off payments accounted for almost as much of the expenditure, and surpluses were maintained: as will be seen, only military calamity would really undermine Canongate's system.[114] In Bervie the average weekly collection went up from about 25s to about 30s in 1649, although there were fewer fast days meaning the year's total collections of just over £64 were no higher than 1648.[115] There appeared to be some surplus possible, as on 28 January some monies were left undistributed and were available for additional or incidental relief expenses.[116] The number of ordinary poor remained reasonably stable from late 1648 through to mid-1650 (though with some turnover suggesting a willingness to accommodate new claimants), and a similar variety of irregular recipients from

110 Gibson and Smout, *Prices*, p. 168; Stewart, *Rethinking the Scottish Revolution*, pp. 309, 322–3; Young, 'Covenanters and the Scottish Parliament', p. 150.

111 *Records of Old Aberdeen*, vol. ii, p. 43, 146; Cramond (ed.), *Elgin Records*, pp. 265, 273.

112 CH2/122/3, pp. 677–8. The dearth may well also explain the steps taken a few weeks earlier to tighten up accounting practices and procedures for assessing the claims of outsider poor (pp. 672–3), as well as the keeping of fuller poor-distribution lists which was ordered on 3 July 1649 (CH2/122/4, p. 4), and which survive from August 1649 as CH2/122/48.

113 CH2/122/48, p. 26. This might have been very roughly equivalent to 20 pounds of good wheatbread; if oatbread or loose meal was purchased it would have gone considerably further (see Appendix).

114 CH2/122/48, pp. 24–43.

115 CH2/34/9, pp. 17–30.

116 CH2/34/9, p. 17.

within and beyond the parish.[117] Even in 1649 there was an impressive degree of toughness in the relief system.

It was in the summer of 1650 and the following 18 months that the poor relief system was most badly damaged by conflict, with the English invasion of Scotland, victory at Dunbar on 3 September and the progress of Cromwellian forces north through Scotland.[118] Langley has shown how the invasion and occupation had a major impact on varied aspects of parish religion, and the relief work of sessions was no exception.[119] In Haddington, where the session had been functioning normally, the session minutes cease after 7 July 1650 until 9 March 1651, and the fact there was no space left in between these entries indicates that on resumption there was no intention to insert unrecorded business: possibly relief work had dried up entirely until collections had resumed on 6 March 1651.[120] In South Leith the disruption was greater with 'no session holdine' from July 1650 to December 1651.[121] Where the dislocation of occupation prevented sessions from functioning, formal session relief could not realistically take place, although it is possible that ongoing informal collection and distribution was attempted and personal charity exhorted.

Canongate's session minutes and accounts provide a particularly detailed snapshot of the disruption to relief in the aftermath of Dunbar. On 30 July, two days after Cromwell had reached Musselburgh, there was 'no sessioun keept because of the enemies approaching towards Edinburgh and Cannongate but the poores money distribut', indicating that distributions to the poor were still to be maintained even when regular session business could hardly be a priority.[122] Poor relief outlasted discipline when danger was imminent. Then on 3 September, there was 'no sessioun keipt because of the defeat of the scottish armie at dunbar by the inglish armie the whole ministers elders and ~~whole~~ honest men in the toun being removed', and for the same day the accounts record that the treasurer, John Cokburne, was passed £466 13s 4d for the use of kirk affairs, presumably in anticipation of the impending disruption to formal proceedings.[123] The kirk session reconvened on 4 July 1651, noting that no sessions had been held in the interim: as Langley has noted the parish was therefore 'left without a session for ten months'.[124] However, while this is true of formal session

117 CH2/34/9, pp. 16, 21, 23, 28, 30, 38, 40.

118 Stevenson, *Revolution and Counter-Revolution*, pp. 143–9, 172–6.

119 Langley, *Worship*, pp. 8, 55, 174.

120 CH2/799/1, ff. 185v–186r.

121 Robertson (ed.), *South Leith Records*, p. 93; Langley, *Worship*, p. 54.

122 CH2/122/4, p. 55; Stevenson, *Revolution and Counter-Revolution*, p. 144. Similarly on 27 August only minor business was transacted and poor money dispensed but that was all 'because of the enemie marching towards dunbar and our scotts armie following after them' (p. 57). See also Langley, *Worship*, p. 141.

123 CH2/122/4, p. 57; CH2/122/48, p. 43.

124 CH2/122/4, p. 57; Langley, *Worship*, p. 54.

meetings, discipline and other business, the separate distribution lists for the Canongate record payments to the poor as early as 19 October 1650. They were on a greatly reduced scale, with payments to one or two ordinary poor (rather than the previous 30 or so), plus various irregular payments, although the individual amounts paid remained comparable to previous patterns. From dispensing an average of around £100 each month, in late 1650 the session was making far fewer individual payments and giving out only a few pounds per week at most, to a much smaller body of poor people and the odd 'hurt souldier'.[125] This must have had a major impact on the lives of the ordinary poor who depended on the payments, although it is possible that some may have fled. The scale of relief expanded slightly again in early 1651, with growing numbers of recipients and around £30–£40 dispensed each month by February to April. By 18 July, once formal session business resumed, they had returned to listing payments to the 28 ordinary poor as a single formal group rather than more sporadic payments to individuals.[126] Relief in the Canongate proved remarkably resilient, then, even while wider session business was abandoned, and the treasurer (possibly assisted by deacons) clearly continued to distribute relief as far as possible in the absence of normal collections and meetings.[127] Of course wider experiences would have been very variable, and a great many lowland parishes were further removed from the military occupation, although equally other places might not have benefitted from such deeply committed personnel.

Further north it was the summer of 1651 before the occupying armies disrupted parish religion.[128] Dundee's previously resilient relief programme was temporarily halted and then reduced in scale (though not destroyed) by the sacking of the town in September, and by December 1651 the presence of English forces was causing disruption in Elgin although some preaching was able to continue.[129] Other parishes north of the Tay were less badly affected, such as Bervie where 1651–2 collections and distributions remained stable and more damage had actually been done in 1650, prior to any direct military impact, when there had been days with no preaching, and there was no communion collection.[130] If parishes were unfortunate enough to be attacked or intimidated by English soldiers, of course, poor relief might be more directly eliminated through the pillaging of the collection box, or indirectly through the poor funds having to reimburse money spent repairing damaged churches.[131] Where there was

[125] CH2/122/48, pp. 43–6 (quotation at p. 43). £100 by c. 1650 might have been approximately 250 day's wages for an urban labourer (see Appendix).

[126] CH2/122/48, pp. 47–50, 54, 57.

[127] See also Mitchison, 'A Parish and its Poor', p. 17.

[128] Langley, *Worship*, p. 55.

[129] McCallum, 'Charity and Conflict', pp. 43–4, 47–8; CH2/145/7, ff. 105r–v.

[130] CH2/34/9, pp. 48–65, 66, 72, 79.

[131] Langley, *Worship*, pp. 100, 114. Some valuables were safely hidden, however: pp. 140–1.

a major military disruption, relief work was naturally badly hit but also sometimes surprisingly persistent. During the disruption in Scoonie, on 11 May 1651 it was recorded that nothing was done by the session 'except the takeing in of the collection and some poore ones to be supplied'.[132] A factor working in favour of poor relief during this time may be that in contrast to functions such as discipline or communion, relieving the needy was consensual (not requiring decisions about guilt and punishment, nor inclusion and exclusion if dealing with familiar poor people), self-evidently necessary and urgent, and could be provided more informally and without a congregation (or bread, wine, and repentance-stool) as a last resort and while funds lasted, as in the Canongate.[133] Overall though, the invasion and occupation represented a major blow to the formal and established system which had been developed by the kirk sessions over many decades.

The period at the very end of the timespan covered by this book was, then, one of the worst times for the kirk session relief system. But an important coda to this is that recovery was relatively swift and sometimes impressive. There was growing poverty partly as a result of the invasion itself, and this placed a further strain on the system.[134] But relief systems re-established themselves firmly, or even continued to function normally in parishes where direct impact had been minimal, such as Bervie. Dalziel's accounts are scrappy at the end of the 1640s and start of the 1650s, but from 1653 on, collections were around 14s per week on average including some large communion gatherings. From 1653 onwards more relief distributions were recorded as well.[135] Having resumed more normal practices by the summer of 1651, and perhaps benefitting from a cautious and gradual increase in the scale of relief, Canongate's operations remained healthy as well, including some solid collections of £15–£20 and sometimes more (much more on fast days). In 1652 the poor expenditure amounted to over £1000, almost at pre-invasion levels, and there were as many as 37 ordinary poor by the end of the year, indicating some ability to cope with increased poverty.[136] In September the session arranged a collection for the fire in Glasgow that year, and by 3 November had raised the sum of £187 5s 4d as confirmed by a discharge from a Glasgow burgess gathering the contributions.[137] Subsequent years saw similar patterns in parish relief, as well as a continuing responsiveness to incidental claims on their charity.[138]

[132] CH2/326/1, p. 196.

[133] For the impact on communion practice see Langley, '"A Sweet Love-Token betwixt Christ and his Church"', especially pp. 105–10.

[134] Langley, *Worship*, pp. 142–3.

[135] CH2/462/34, pp. 61–6, 72–3.

[136] CH2/122/48, pp. 64, 69–70, 81–3.

[137] CH2/122/4, p. 88; CH2/122/76, item 6. By contrast, South Leith session's recovery was more problematic as a result of the heavy presence of English troops: Robertson (ed.), *South Leith Records*, pp. 93, 95.

[138] CH2/122/48, pp. 92–4, 100, 107, 119. See also CH2/799/1, ff. 186v–187r for relatively

Dundee's relief recovered well also, albeit on a smaller overall scale that may have been related to the massive reduction in population from the attack on the town as well as the tougher economic circumstances following the invasion and during the occupation.[139] Ironically, one additional indication of the strength and reliability of the relief system after 1651 was that the English themselves gave in contributions to local kirk session poor funds, suggesting the extent to which the kirk sessions were still seen as ideal institutions for the organisation of help for the poor.[140] The wider development of poor relief during the second half of the seventeenth century is beyond the remit of the present study, but it would appear that despite intense challenges around the middle of the century, kirk session relief survived, recovered and began its next phase from a strong position where it was deeply embedded in Scottish society.

Localised Crises and Emergency Relief

The food shortages of the 1620s, and the conflict, invasion and dislocation of the middle years of the seventeenth century, were easily the most traumatic and challenging of the periods covered by this book for welfare systems across a very wide range of Scottish communities. But as well as these national periods of exceptional stress, there were also more localised and temporary pressures on relief, and in particular disasters and emergencies that hit individual communities. The church was active in providing relief to areas hit by fire, flood, and other unpredictable calamities. This was in some senses distinct from the routine work of kirk sessions providing relief to impoverished parishioners or distressed outsiders, as it generally involved the raising of a single sum of money to send to where it was needed, and this money was to assist the whole community rather than specifically poor people. It would be misleading to draw this distinction too sharply, however, because a wide range of individuals including those from prosperous and respectable backgrounds, not just the lower orders, often needed normal parish relief, and on the other hand because the sorts of catastrophes that hit early modern Scottish settlements had a disproportionately harsh impact on the poor. Certainly church courts saw such causes as part of their charitable remit. Considering their reactions gives us a further opportunity to assess the resilience and responsiveness of ecclesiastical relief and the networks and processes through which it operated, as well as offering further insight into the intentions and motivations of those involved.

swift recovery of relief work in Haddington, and CH2/266/1, pp. 240–3 for Midcalder's steady recovery of regular collection and distribution from August 1651 into 1652, after 'a long intermission of session by reason of the troubles of the lands' (p. 240).

139 McCallum, 'Charity and Conflict', pp. 41–4, 48–9. Similarly Kinnaird's relief later in the 1650s involved some smaller sums but was generally stable: CH2/418/1, pp. 39–43 (1655: second pagination, beginning two-thirds through the volume).

140 Langley, *Worship*, pp. 145, 149.

As well as the national dearth of the early 1620s, there were also times when serious food shortages affected parts of Scotland. One of the most serious regional scarcities seems to have been that which hit Caithness and Orkney in 1633–4, when it was reported that at a critical time before harvest 'tempestuous and bitter weather blew frome the ocean upoun theise pairtes', and the harvest was so ruined that 'the boll of aittis in many pairtes not gewing ane peck of meale'; many people inevitably died. On 19 June 1634 the Privy Council passed an act recommending the pitiful state of the poor people suffering from this famine to the charity of Scots elsewhere.[141] The people of Caithness and Orkney were clearly suffering before June 1634, but once the Privy Council had circulated news and recommended fundraising, responses were fairly quick from church courts across Scotland. Kirkcaldy Presbytery urged collections in its parishes a week later on 26 June (based on the Bishop of Orkney's direct letter rather than the Privy Council instructions which were read another week later on 3 July), and in the rural Perthshire parish of Kinnaird £7 4s was collected on 5 July.[142] Elgin's Kirk Session raised £40 on 17 August, while on the same day 20 merks was collected in Ellon, although a further 9 merks was added in a second collection the following week.[143] The geographical spread of collections was wide, with Falkirk collecting over 100 merks on 6 July, and the rural Ayrshire parish of Galston managing over £50 across two collections on 20 and 27 July.[144] It is also striking that some of these collections took place before the Privy Council had actually nominated an official to receive all of the contributions from across the country formally and pass them on to the Bishop of Orkney, on 17 July.[145] Some funds were perhaps raised more slowly, as in some places money was collected but not yet dispatched by late 1634 or 1635 and therefore diverted to other pious uses.[146] However this included Kinnaird where in November the minister gave in 'tua dollers collectit for the people of Orkney which wes put in the box'; as there had also been a much more immediate collection this must have represented later additional fundraising, rather than suggesting that no funds from the parish went to the distressed of the north.[147] It is unclear how much the sending of aid achieved given the severity of the shortages, but it is significant that the church in other parts of Scotland was able to organise and raise funds in response to this crisis quickly and effectively.

One of the most devastating events for an early modern town and its

[141] *RPC*, 2nd Series, vol. v, pp. 284–5; Flinn (ed.), *Scottish Population History*, p. 130.

[142] CH2/224/1, pp. 133–4; CH2/418/1, p. 3.

[143] CH2/145/5, f. 130v; CH2/147/1, p. 288.

[144] CH2/400/1, p. 258; CH2/1335/3, pp. 36–7.

[145] *RPC*, 2nd Series, vol. v., p. 320.

[146] *ERRBS 1519*–1666, p. 174; in Old Kelso funds were found unspent as late as 1639: CH2/1173/1, pp. 110, 113.

[147] CH2/418/1, p. 5.

inhabitants – rich and poor – was a fire.[148] The church was active in raising and sending funds to relieve the residents of towns that were suffering in the horrible aftermath of a conflagration.[149] This was due not only to the immediate human suffering and destruction of property, but also the ongoing disruption to trade and employment, which was stressed by the Synod of Fife's intimation of the collections for Cupar after its fire of August 1616.[150] Collections for Cupar were forthcoming beyond Fife too, from rural and urban kirk sessions such as Monkton and Perth.[151] The Canongate's collection 'for the 'distressit brethreine in couper of fyiff' was apparently still needed in May 1618, when they gathered just over £80 to be passed on via the presbytery.[152] This parish had also been raising funds for a fire much nearer to hand at the Potterrow in 1616, so it is possible that aid for Cupar was slowed (but not prevented) by the more local fire.[153] This emphasises that reconstruction, not just immediate emergency aid, was part of the reason to contribute.

Another Fife town to suffer particularly badly was Dunfermline, where on 25 May 1624 large amounts of food supplies as well as many buildings were lost to 'ane suddane and terrible fyre'.[154] News of the 'pitifull stait of Dunfermling', as it was referred to in Kinghorn's meeting of 27 June, quickly reached and impressed church courts across Scotland.[155] Monkton's session had managed to gather £37 by 20 August and Elgin's had passed on £85 3s 8d to the commissioners for the collection a week later.[156] Responses took a little longer in Midcalder where it was 9 January 1625 before 20 merks had been raised to be transferred via the presbytery.[157] The presbytery of Lanark received a letter from the bishop with instructions for fundraising on 17 June 1624, and although it was 23 September before the sums were given in from each parish, they were fairly impressive, totalling about £600 from 21 parishes.[158] There were also some delays with the collections for relief after a major fire in Glasgow in the summer of 1652, which came

148 Roberts, 'Fire in French Cities', pp. 9–10.

149 For fundraising efforts in response to major fires elsewhere in Europe see, for example, Kitching, 'Fire Disasters and Fire Relief'; Roberts, 'Fire in French Cities', pp. 18–19, 24. Kirk sessions also raised funds locally for individuals who had lost property to more self-contained house-fires: see, for example, CH2/799/1, f. 309r; CH2/1173/1, p. 106.

150 CH2/154/1, p. 222.

151 CH2/809/1, p. 17; CH2/521/6, p. 220.

152 CH2/122/1, p. 406; see also *ABA*, p. 271 for funds sent to Cupar for the fire during the accounting year 1618–19.

153 CH2/122/1, pp. 264, 268. For other collections for the Potterrow fire, see CH2/471/1, f. 12r; CH2/242/1, f. 150v.

154 Henderson (ed.), *Annals of Dunfermline*, pp. 283–5; Calderwood, *History*, vii, p. 607.

155 CH2/472/1, p. 141. In nearby Dysart, the collection was announced at the next meeting after the fire, on 1 June: CH2/390/1, p. 33.

156 CH2/809/1, p. 108; CH2/145/4, f. 53v. Jedburgh Presbytery's efforts were also under way by July: CH2/198/2, f. 17r.

157 CH2/266/1, p. 63.

158 CH2/234/1, p. 10.

at a very difficult time and immediately after much effort raising funds for the relief of Scottish prisoners captured in England.[159] Like various other courts, Dingwall Presbytery tried to raise funds, but noted on 12 October that the contribution for Glasgow was coming 'bot slowe speide', and urged diligence on their brethren through November and December as well. Their persistence paid off, as they presented their payment on 18 February 1653.[160] As with some of the Dunfermline contributions, delays were relatively slight, and given that the impoverished state of the towns and their need for reconstruction was pressing, the funds were still likely to have been just as necessary over the following months. Fundraising for towns devastated by fire was generally relatively speedy, a matter of importance on which church courts were willing to expend considerable effort and persistence, and also broadly national in its intent and scope.

A major fire was an obvious catastrophe for a town that would inevitably and undoubtedly leave its people in a pitiful state. Damage to bridges and harbours, including from flooding and bad weather, might seem like a less obvious subject for emergency relief. But church courts also raised collections for assistance with the repair of bridges and sometimes harbours. Midcalder raised £35 10s in two weeks in 1633 to pass to the minister at nearby Livingstone for the bridge over the nearby water of Almond, and Perth's session collected for the bridge at 'Gairnye', around 20 miles to the south near Kinross.[161] Naturally, sessions sometimes contributed directly (not through special collection) to the expense of routine bridge repair in their own parish or for nearby routes, and this could be seen more as a contribution to local infrastructure.[162] But there are clear indications that some collections were held with distinctly charitable intentions in mind, most explicitly when Stirling Kirk Session appointed officials 'to collect almus for reparatione of the brig of Tullibody'.[163] In 1616 the Presbytery planned collections for the same bridge, 'being credablie informit of the great decay of Tullibody brig quhilk apperis to incres mair and mair to the great hurt of the commone pepill excep the samin be amendit'.[164] This suggests an acknowledgement that poorer people might particularly

159 Langley, 'Welfare, identity and Scottish prisoners of war' (forthcoming). I am grateful to Dr Langley for allowing me to consult this piece prior to publication. See also Langley, *Worship*, pp. 146–7.

160 Mackay (ed.), *Records of the Presbyteries of Inverness and Dingwall*, pp. 246–50. The size and geography of Dingwall presbytery, which included substantial highland territory, may have been a factor: pp. vi–vii, although this should not be overplayed given that they themselves saw it as a slow pace of collection. For other collections for the Glasgow fire see CH2/122/4, p. 88; CH2/145/7, f. 122r.

161 CH2/266/1, p. 83; CH2/521/6, p. 54. Gairney Bridge's location was derived from *Scotland's Places*: <http://www.scotlandsplaces.gov.uk/record/rcahms/225113/gairney-water-gairney-bridge/rcahms> (last accessed 27 September 2016).

162 CH2/266/1, p. 41; CH2/699/1, pp. 60–1.

163 CH2/1026/1, p. 265.

164 CH2/722/4, p. 453.

suffer by the economic problems raised by transport difficulties, such as a potential increase in the price of essentials or limitations on the mobility of labour. Similarly the great storm which ruined Kinghorn harbour in 1625 apparently led to great human suffering, with 'pure widowis and fatherless childrein' listed amongst those for whom charity was sought from church courts such as Perth Presbytery and the Synod of Fife, the latter court describing itself 'moved with compassion towards them' before recommending collections.[165] And in 1659 the Synod of Lothian and Tweeddale recommended 'some charitie to be contribute for a poor sinking toun', in response to commissioners from Kirkcaldy who explained how their harbour 'is demolished and throwne downe'.[166] The economic hardship imposed by damage to infrastructure was sometimes recounted at great length, and on one occasion Perth Presbytery accepted a request since it was 'godly and reasonabill', indicating a religious and pious as well as purely practical element to the requested collection.[167] Although funding repair work on bridges and piers arguably blurs the lines between charitable relief and infrastructure investment, the willingness to collect for other parts of Scotland, the way supplicants framed their requests, and the language used by the church courts, suggests that relieving distress and suffering was the over-riding aim. The collections for bridges and harbours also further emphasise that the ecclesiastical relief network was responsive to a broad range of disasters.

This breadth of concern was also evident in efforts to raise funds for the relief and ransoming of Scots who had been taken captive overseas, especially by the Turks.[168] On 8 December 1578 Perth arranged for special encouragement from the pulpit for contributions for 'the puir prisoneris into the Turkes handes'; on 19 January it was reported that the church's collection had raised £18 18s 8d, and the bailies had also collected £9 16s 9d.[169] The collection also reached rural Monifieth, where on 11 January 1579 it was recorded that 9s 6d was collected for the prisoners 'takyn with the Turkis galayis', although this had been boosted to £4 by some lairdly contributions by the time it was passed on by the minister in April.[170] Collections for captives were fairly widespread and, like the other special collections, often followed from news and instructions conveyed by the Privy Council, bishops, and higher church courts.[171] Those taken prisoner

165 CH2/299/1, p. 131; CH2/154/1, pp. 296–7.

166 Langley (ed.), *Synod of Lothian and Tweeddale*, p. 414. For comparable English collections for harbours see McIntosh, *Poor Relief in England*, pp. 170–1.

167 Langley (ed.), *Synod of Lothian and Tweeddale*, p. 306; CH2/299/1, p. 19.

168 For the wider context of the Turks' captives and ransom collections see Matar, 'Introduction: England and Mediterranean Captivity', especially pp. 1–2, 24–9.

169 *PKSB*, pp. 107, 111.

170 OPR310/1, ff. 40v, 41v; Bardgett, 'Monifieth Kirk Register', pp. 189–90.

171 See, for example, CH2/751/1/2, ff. 303r, 304r, 411v; CH2/171/2/2, f. 171v; CH2/242/2, p. 48; *PKSB*, p. 107n.

by the Turks at Algiers were the most commonly circulated cause, but not without exception: Monimail raised £6 for 'the relieff of tua distressit personis tane be the spanzeards' in 1632.[172] Langley has also shown how at the end of our period the Scottish church was active in raising funds to try to assist the suffering Scots soldiers who had been taken prisoner by the English.[173]

The range of emergencies to which the Scottish church's fundraising networks responded was diverse. These efforts were in some senses analogous to the Scottish collections for fellow Reformed Protestants suffering persecution elsewhere in Europe, which have been discussed more directly by historians.[174] Indeed the fact that the confessionally-motivated collections for co-religionists, such as the French church in England in the 1580s, were amongst the earliest special collections organised across Scotland raises the possibility that they were formative in shaping processes and strategies for fundraising for the frequent calamities of the first half of the seventeenth century.[175] The collections were frequent and substantial, although it is not possible to assess what impact the funds raised had in relieving any given emergency. This is partly because so many church court records have not survived that any estimate of funds raised for a crisis would be a fragment of the whole, and as with any disaster, historical or contemporary, there is no single identifiable sum that would be adequate. Given the scale of some of the disasters discussed above, the funds sent would have helped to alleviate some of the suffering rather than paying for full reconstruction or a return to normality. A more fruitful way to consider the effectiveness and resilience of the system to these crises is to reflect on the efficiency of the mechanisms, the support given to the fundraising efforts, and the extent to which it had a knock-on effect on other relief work.

As we have seen there were sometimes delays in carrying out collections and passing on monies raised, although in other cases the responses were relatively swift, benefitting from the fact that kirk sessions and presbyteries met regularly. The sums raised were variable, although normally fairly substantial when viewed against the context of regular relief collections: even the relatively small sum of 9s 6d gathered for the Turks' captives in Monifieth in 1579 was more than the routine relief collections before and after it, suggesting that the cause was not viewed grudgingly.[176] There were occasions where a church court complained that it could not spare the resources, such as Dalkeith Presbytery in 1620 (for the Turks' captives),

172 CH2/548/1, p. 57.

173 'Welfare, identity and Scottish prisoners of war' (forthcoming). For other special collections for charitable and military causes which were specifically prompted by the civil wars see Langley, *Worship*, chapter 6.

174 Murdock, *Beyond Calvin*, pp. 39–40; McCallum, 'Charity Doesn't Begin at Home', pp. 112–15.

175 *RStAKS*, ii, p. 610; CH2/185/1, f. 5r; CH2/424/1, pp. 200, 202.

176 OPR310/1, ff. 40v–42r.

or Strathbogie Presbytery in 1631 where three ministers collected £10, £10 and £9 each for 'the distressed clergie of the Palatinate' but four others just gave 'ane dolour for thameselffs, becaus thai culd gate no contributione of thair parochinars'.[177] As in England, 'donor fatigue' may have been a problem at times, especially when demands came frequently.[178] Certainly Dalkeith Presbytery had already recently raised funds for the Turks' captives as well as the fire at Cupar.[179] But even these were fairly exceptional cases, and the request to contribute funds rarely seems to have been contentious; presumably partly because even on the rare occasions that contributing was not possible, few could deny the importance of the causes. The widespread extent of the contributions made for the fire at Dunfermline in 1624 are particularly significant following swiftly after a period of dearth.[180] Equally, special collections do not seem to have proved disruptive of other welfare activities: for example, Kinnaird's collections continued at a similar weekly rate of about 7s after breaking off for a week to gather the much higher sum of £7 4s for the famine in Orkney in 1634.[181] And when Haddington's special collection for a house-burnt couple raised the much higher than usual sum of £14 11s 1d, there was a slight dip in the following week's total to £2 18s, but after that collections quickly returned to the usual rate of at least £3 5s.[182] Overall, the system generally seemed able to cope with and respond to crisis and calls for assistance following localised emergencies elsewhere.

As the previous discussion shows, a number of levels of the church court hierarchy were involved with fundraising for these emergencies. Various different lines of communication transmitted the news, and the funds. The church was not the only institution to respond to these sorts of emergencies, as in urban areas burgh councils also responded to calls to raise funds for other towns in distress, sometimes, though not always, in collaboration with the local kirk session.[183] Across Scotland, though, it made very good sense for kirk sessions and parish ministers to lead the church's collections, partly for the practical reason that they were firmly based in each parish, and also because preaching could be used to advertise and to stir up generosity in the parishioners. It must have been an advantage that the collectors were soliciting donations from people they knew reasonably well, rather than,

177 CH2/424/1, p. 471; *Extracts from the Presbytery Book of Strathbogie*, p. 3.

178 McIntosh, *Poor Relief in England*, p. 171.

179 CH2/424/1, pp. 437–8, 448–9. Collections for the distressed of Argyll faced some problems gaining traction in 1646–7: *Ecclesiastical Records: Selections from the Minutes of the Presbyteries of St Andrews and Cupar*, pp. 36, 108; Langley, 'Caring for Soldiers', p. 15.

180 As well as the Dunfermline contributions cited above, see, for example, CH2/562/1, p. 22; CH2/400/1, p. 133; CH2/242/2, pp. 114, 116.

181 CH2/418/1, pp. 2–5.

182 CH2/799/1, ff. 307v–310v.

183 For examples see *ABA*, p. 271; Maxwell, *History of Old Dundee*, pp. 342–3; and for an example of a joint agreement to contribute see *ERRBS 1519–1666*, p. 172.

for example, strangers representing the cause passing through a parish to collect.[184] Above that level, presbyteries could instruct their ministers, and monitor their diligence in arranging collections, as well as transferring the funds once collected.[185] Synods played an important role in transmitting news and chasing up collections both for individuals and for communities, although their lower frequency of meeting as well as wider geographical coverage meant that kirk sessions and presbyteries were at the forefront of actual collections.[186] This made for an efficient system. In terms of trustworthiness, as well as the fact that the news was being conveyed by the parish minister, and collections undertaken by local officials, it may have helped that cases often bore Privy Council approval, confirming urgency and the genuine necessity of those requesting the assistance.[187] As in England, royal authority and the name of the monarch might be invoked to encourage contribution.[188] Local initiative was always required though, and was generally forthcoming. A further element of transparency came from the careful accounting which often accompanied the collections: funds raised were monitored and receipts provided.[189] In discussing collections for the Scots soldiers taken captive by the English at the end of our period, Langley notes that even 'areas that wholeheartedly rejected the power of the Commission of the General Assembly accepted the Commission's instructions regarding charitable collections'.[190] The fact that co-operation on the collections

184 Houston, 'Church Briefs', p. 512.

185 See, for example, CH2/122/1, p. 406.

186 For an example of a presbytery receiving instructions from synod, see CH2/89/1, f. 205v; and for an example of a synod closely monitoring the progress of collections, see Kirk (ed.), *Synod of Lothian and Tweeddale*, pp. 201–3, 207, 223; also Langley (ed.), *Synod of Lothian and Tweeddale*, pp. xv, 3, 25, 51, 56.

187 As well as the cases involving Privy Council instructions mentioned above, see for further examples CH2/523/1, p. 165; CH2/171/2/2, f. 171v. On occasion instructions or news of collections also originated from parliament: see, for example, Lanark Presbytery's 1647 promise to obey parliament's recommendation the previous year of a collection for Bothwell bridge: *Ecclesiastical Records: Presbytery of Lanark*, p. 56; *RPS*, 1646/11/451; see also *RPS*, 1645/7/24/53 (parliamentary recommendation of collections for ransoming Turkish captives).

188 McIntosh, *Poor Relief in England*, p. 171; Houston, 'Church Briefs', p. 517; and see CH2/299/1, p. 40, for a particularly overt attempt to invoke royal authority in exhorting a collection in Perth Presbytery for a captive of the Turks, not only reminding the brethren of 'his ma[jesties] le[tt]re' but also urging contribution 'as they will be answerabill to his ma[jestie] and to thair ordinar'.

189 For an example of monitoring of the progress and location of funds collected for a ransoming, see Kirk (ed.), *Synod of Lothian and Tweeddale*, pp. 121–2. Surviving receipts are relatively rare for this period, but see the bundle of discharges for special collections at CH2/122/76 (item 1 is a discharge for the collection for the 'oppressed people of Argyll' in 1647, item 3 is a discharge for monies raised 'for repairing of the colt bridg' in 1648). The discharge for collections for Dunfermline's fire of 1624 were copied into the presbytery minutes of Lanark: *Ecclesiastical Records: Presbytery of Lanark*, pp. 2–3; see also the discharge for the Argyll collection in Midcalder: CH2/266/1, p. 194.

190 Langley, 'Welfare, identity and Scottish prisoners of war' (forthcoming).

transcended bitter ecclesiastical conflicts further points to the trust that had been developed in the church's competence in organising and implementing charitable collections of diverse kinds.

The church's approach to the various and unpredictable crises that hit late sixteenth- and early seventeenth-century Scotland was responsive and effective. Special fundraising collections were frequently held for various causes, and especially for local disasters like fires or collapsed bridges. The same causes often appear in kirk session, presbytery and synod records across Scotland, suggesting that the church had established and effective mechanisms for communicating news of crises, and organising and transferring emergency relief. This may have become more developed as the period progressed, although as always record survival can obscure this issue, but the mechanisms can be identified, albeit in smaller number, as early as the late 1570s in rural and urban parishes. Certainly, by the early seventeenth century the maturity and sophistication of the ecclesiastical relief network is apparent, with responses to crisis which were familiar and routine. By the 1640s and 1650s, times when such responsiveness was particularly important, a well-established and trusted system had been developed.[191] More generally, the efforts in this area tell us something about the priorities and purpose of Scotland's ecclesiastical relief system: it was genuinely outward-looking, and demonstrated an open approach to relieving those suffering elsewhere.

Conclusion

Kirk session relief kept going during some of the most difficult times, and indeed at such times it was a priority, sometimes even when the work of moral discipline, more familiar to historians, had to be abandoned. It took quite extreme external shocks from plague or military occupation to prevent relief from taking place altogether, and when disaster struck communities in other parts of Scotland, the church's fundraising mechanisms and networks sprung into action. The kirk sessions took the initiative, and were certainly not dependent on central direction during times of crisis; while urban and rural sessions alike proved remarkably resilient. Equally however, the relief programme was part of wider social and economic systems, and so during lean times, poor relief suffered. It was harder to raise funds, and more funds were needed. There were, as this chapter has shown, times when the relief system showed its limitations and when it seriously struggled to cope. This is not hugely surprising. Arguably, the more pertinent impression to emerge from this chapter is of the strength of the kirk session's poor relief, and the continuity it demonstrated even

[191] Stewart notes with reference to military fundraising for the Bishops' Wars that town councils, kirk sessions and presbyteries 'were already practised at raising money for other purposes': Stewart, *Rethinking The Scottish Revolution*, p. 183.

during very severe economic problems and external disruption. It also, under these pressures, showed how firmly established it was in the Scottish parish. It was certainly not a fair-weather relief system that worked in good times, but then failed or melted away when times were tough. Scottish kirk sessions, and by extension their congregations, did not turn away from charitable responsibilities when things were hard.

PART II

The Nature of Kirk Session Poor Relief

CHAPTER 5

The Mechanics of Relief

Introduction

In the previous section, Chapters 2–4 assessed the development and resilience of kirk session poor relief. This chapter steps back to consider the essential character and organisation of the welfare system operated by kirk sessions as a whole. There has been a growing recognition amongst historians that ecclesiastical relief schemes in pre-modern Europe were not necessarily casual or haphazard, or inherently less efficient than secular provision.[1] There has however been little consideration in Scottish studies of the possibility that the church's own relief schemes might have been effectively and carefully administered: instead the fact that the schemes were not proper Poor Laws tends to dominate.[2] One recent study of provision during the civil wars has noted the effectiveness of kirk session fundraising, and there are some signs that historians are increasingly taking the organisational and administrative efforts of kirk sessions, not just church discipline, more seriously, especially for the eighteenth century.[3] But very little attention has been paid to the actual workings of the reformed church's poor relief as a system. In order to understand the mechanisms and processes through which relief worked, this chapter adopts a tripartite structure, following the flow of resources from contributor, through the kirk session, to poor recipient. Starting with fundraising, it assesses the significance of the various sources of income which kirk sessions could draw. Secondly, it looks at those individuals in charge of overseeing and administering parish welfare, and their varying roles in the process. Thirdly, it examines the forms in which relief was provided to the poor, and the approaches that kirk sessions took to the challenging task of assisting the needy.

For each of these, evidence is gathered from across lowland Scotland, and considered thematically rather than chronologically or geographically. One important implication of previous chapters must therefore be noted. It should not be assumed that the processes and structures analysed here were entirely applicable across Scotland from 1560 to 1650. As we saw earlier, systems of relief were often gradually developed, and there is very

[1] Olson, 'Continuity or Radical Change?', p. 151 ; see also above, pp. 9–11.

[2] See, for example, Whyte, *Scotland Before the Industrial Revolution*, p. 168; Symonds, 'Death, Birth and Marriage', pp. 97–8; see also above pp. 3–5.

[3] Langley, *Worship*, p. 149; Mutch, *Religion and National Identity*; Mutch, 'Data-Mining'.

limited evidence on rural relief prior to the seventeenth century. What follows cannot be assumed to have applied equally in, say, rural Perthshire in the 1570s. But with that proviso, which also applies to the following two chapters, Chapters 6 and 7, it is striking that there were no really significant divergences or contrasts in approach along geographical or chronological lines in the nature of relief. Different regions of lowland Scotland, or urban and rural parishes, did not adopt fundamentally distinct methodologies. There was some local variation and adaptability, but rarely on the core policies and approaches. Even during times of crisis such as the 1620s or 1640s there were severe pressures but a general stability in process. It is possible, then, to speak of a general 'kirk session system' of poor relief. How effectively was it organised and managed, and what strategies did relief administrators deploy to raise funds and to assist the poor?

Fundraising

Collections

The most important mechanism through which funds could be gathered for relief was the church's collections for the poor. This was the point at which the whole congregation could contribute as they saw fit to their kirk session's welfare schemes. Previous chapters have offered assessments of patterns in parochial collections, but what did such collections actually involve, and how would they have been experienced by the parishioners who funded relief?

As we would expect, collections took place at public worship. These were important and valued occasions, when the people of the parish were gathered together in the largest numbers, and could be asked to contribute collectively.[4] There were apparently some problems with the timing of these collections during the early years after the Reformation, as in 1573 the General Assembly had to stipulate that collections should not take place during the administering of communion or during sermons, 'bot only at the kirk doores'.[5] This concern was apparently still present in Anstruther over a decade later.[6] Presumably the fear was that collections would undermine the attention and reverence which should be paid to worship. But there are signs that collecting funds within the church remained the preferred policy in some parishes: in Old Deer in the 1630s the phrase 'in the kirk' was used in reference to some collections, and in Kinnaird and Montrose collections seem to have taken place during or immediately after psalm-singing.[7] In 1611 the Synod of Fife even instructed the kirk session

[4] Ryrie, *Being Protestant*, ch. 13, especially pp. 325–7.

[5] *BUK*, i, p. 257.

[6] OPR403/1, f. 55r.

[7] CH2/1217/33, ff. 89r, 91r–92v; CH2/418/1, p. 64; CH2/943/1, p. 17. See also *PKSB*,

of Abdie to collect alms during psalm-singing.[8] However there are numerous references from across Scotland, and across the period, to collections taking place at church doors, and this seems to have been the majority approach.[9] The collectors of the funds tended to serve on a rotating basis either for a week at a time, or sometimes for a longer period of three or four weeks in a row.[10] As well as Sunday and weekday sermons, and the more infrequent but very substantial collections at communion, further opportunities for collections came at marriages and burials. In Kinnaird, additions to the poor funds from collections at marriages were fairly frequent, and 26s was gathered 'at ane sermon preached at the ministers wyfes buriall' in May 1637.[11] St Andrews Kirk Session was keen to ensure that no funds were actually dispensed at burials; instead they should be passed to the treasurer so they could be handled formally by the session.[12] This was a policy that also applied to regular collections, which were supposed to be just that: collections not distributions. Aberdeen and Perth Kirk Sessions stipulated that funds collected should be given in rather than handed out there and then at the door.[13]

Shifting to the parishioner's point-of-view, there must have been a consciousness that donating (or not donating) was a public act, visible to those around, as well as to those doing the collecting. Whether the collection was gathered during a psalm, or while filing into or out of the church, the pressure to donate must have been felt. The precise type of equipment used to collect the money is not described in the records as a matter of course (there was little reason to do so), but we have references to the 'puir folkis broddis' in St Andrews in 1587, and these were likely collection plates or boards rather than boxes or purses.[14] In Ayr in 1612, collectors were assigned to 'the pures disch'.[15] Both of these examples seem to suggest a relatively flat or shallow collecting-plate, rather

p. 107, for a special collection (as opposed to regular weekly collecting) taking place during a psalm.

8 CH2/154/1, p. 71.

9 *PKSB*, p. 290; CH2/718/2, p. 207; CH2/448/2, p. 13; CH2/550/1, p. 128; *Canagait*, pp. 13, 44, 52; CH2/154/1, p. 52; CH2/624/2, p. 160.

10 CH2/1218/16, ff. 40r–41r; CH2/450/1, pp. 9, 10, 12, 14–15; CH2/550/1, pp. 3–4; CH2/418/1, pp. 1–5.

11 CH2/418/1, pp. 1, 9, 18, 21.

12 *RStAKS*, ii, p. 883.

13 CH2/448/1, p. 61; *PKSB*, p. 365.

14 *RStAKS*, ii, p. 585; see definition in *DSL*, 'Brod' (which also supplies further examples). There are occasional references to purses or 'the commoun purse' but these are probably figurative rather than literal: e.g. *Dundonald*, p. 118; CH2/751/1/2, f. 238r; CH2/1335/1, p. 55. An exception is the Elgin purse which functioned as a sort of swear-jar, for the collection of fines rather than donations: see above, Chapter 2, p. 66, and the '2 bagis to put in the money collecttit at the communion' acquired by the Canongate in 1650: CH2/122/48, p. 33.

15 CH2/751/1/2, f. 231v.

than a bag or box for depositing coins.[16] Where boxes are referred to, it is normally in relation to the longer-term storage of funds rather than immediate gathering.[17] So there was likely an opportunity for those doing the collecting, if not other bystanders, to gauge how much individuals were contributing, or at least for it to feel that way to the contributors.[18] An inscription from as early as 1573 in the parish church at Chirnside reads 'HELPE THE PVRVE 1573', offering a rare visualisation of the sort of exhortation that was presumably normally expressed verbally by clergy, elders and deacons.[19]

There are hints that kirk sessions were keen to utilise the social pressure to contribute, and, where necessary, to enhance it. In Aberdeen in 1603, it was 'thocht meit and expedient that the magistrattis and chefest of the counsall and towne sall stand at the kirk durris everie sonday to seik the collectiouns to the puir and kirk wark' (the ministers were also to exhort charity from the pulpit).[20] The intention was probably to reinforce the importance of the collection, and to ensure that potential contributors felt the gaze of the town's social elites. This pressure would presumably have been felt most strongly by the respectable burgesses of the town who had both the funds available and the motivation to impress their peers (or potential peers).[21] Any Aberdeen parishioner entering church on Sunday under the watchful eye of the town's ruling elite, might well have struggled to appreciate the classification of kirk session relief as a 'voluntary' enterprise. The communion collection in early seventeenth century Canongate parish might include nine collectors: three at the door, two at the steeple and four at the 'utmest'.[22] It was also felt to be essential that the session's designated collectors did the work of collecting as Alexander Ogilvie was accused of sending 'his man to gadder to the poore quhen he sould have cum himself'. His servant could hardly confer the same pressure and authority on the collection.[23] In Elgin and Perth, for example, collectors at communion services gathered alms alongside the communion tokens that were required for entry to the sacrament, which may have lent further

[16] Hay, 'Scottish Post-Reformation Church Furniture', p. 55 also refers to funds being collected in alms-basins at church doors.

[17] See, for example, CH2/147/1, pp. 3–4, 10; *Dundonald*, pp. 263, 407; CH2/450/1, pp. 39, 52; CH2/548/1, p. 31. However the Synod of Fife introduced a box for collecting donations from ministers attending its meetings: CH2/154/1, p. 23.

[18] This was similar to Dutch practice, where there was some use of 'open plates instead of bags or baskets, to utilize social pressure during the collection': Meerkerk and Teeuwen, 'Stability of Voluntarism', p. 90; however in some other Dutch collections Dutch collections bags held from long poles were used: van Leeuwen, 'Giving in early modern history', p. 319.

[19] Meikle, *The Scottish People*, p. 64.

[20] CH2/448/2/, p. 13.

[21] This policy was still in place in 1620: CH2/448/4, p. 43.

[22] CH2/122/1, pp. 10, 43.

[23] CH2/122/1, p. 12 (and p. 27 for a similar case).

symbolic significance to the act of giving.[24] In Elgin, as we saw in Chapter 2, those who did not contribute were to be summoned as 'refusaris', and in Perth in 1590 bailies and elders were to attend Tuesday prayers to gather funds for a collection for Geneva 'from thes that hes not gevin as yeit'.[25] Both of these phrases further convey the sense that contributing was an expectation, not a choice. At the most extreme end of the scale, Monkton Kirk Session stipulated in 1622 that 'the money collectit for the releiffe of the poore sall be gatherit at the incoming of the kirk doore' (presumably instead of at the end of the service), and that an elder would 'have power to debar all both men and weomen that does not bestow according to ther power'.[26] This came during a time of serious dearth in Scotland and great concern about a lack of donations, and the policy was reversed less than a year later, when funds were to be 'gathrit within the kirk after sermon'.[27] But although it was an unusually stringent policy in response to famine, the implication that one was expected to contribute according to one's ability in order to be considered a proper member of the Christian community was not so unusual.

Collecting money at church also involved various problems and challenges. As well as occasional reluctance on the part of collectors to do their duty (discussed below), services and therefore collections might also be disrupted by factors beyond the kirk session's control such as bad weather or plague.[28] And whether because of irregularities in the provision of church services, or a lack of organisation at services that did take place, in a few rural parishes like Dundonald and Midcalder there were occasional periods when collections do not seem to have taken place on a regular weekly basis.[29] Very occasionally disruption came from beggars themselves physically crowding or pressuring the collection at the church door.[30] An even more extreme though equally rare problem was assaults on the collectors of poor relief, two examples of which have been identified by Margo Todd.[31] Collecting for the poor was not always easy. But in most parishes, most of the time, serious or persistent problems were unusual, as reflected by the relative consistency of many parishes' collection levels.

One advantage of church-door collections as a means of fundraising was that money was inevitably raised in the form of ready cash, not an

24 CH2/145/1, f. 105v; *PKSB*, p. 176. For the psychological importance of communion tokens, see *COP*, pp. 96–8.

25 CH2/145/1, f. 123v; *PKSB*, p. 454. A case in the Canongate involved an offender accused of recalcitrance 'quhen his charitie wes requyred to the poore on the com[m]union day': the case is discussed in more detail below but the phrasing of 'charity' being 'required' is significant. CH2/122/1, p. 12.

26 CH2/809/1, p. 85.

27 CH2/809/1, p. 96.

28 OPR310/1, ff. 50r, 57v; CH2/418/1, p. 95.

29 *Dundonald*, p. 263; CH2/266/1, pp. 60–2.

30 CH2/751/2, f. 33r; CH2/550/1, p. 128.

31 *COP*, p. 383.

insignificant point in an economy which was not yet cash-dominated (and indeed where currency might be in short supply).[32] During the famine of 1623 special coins worth 1d and 2d were minted to encourage almsgiving.[33] However, the question of currency posed a further, albeit occasional problem with collections: bad coins. There are a few isolated examples of poor quality coinage being donated: in Stirling in November 1599 it was complained that 'ane great part of the almus gevin to the pure is fals cunzie callit tinklaris for the quhilk the puiris gaitis na thing', and consequently the minister was publicly to forbid giving false coinage, since it 'procuiris the curs of god to the gevaris therof'. However December's account revealed that this actually amounted to only £3, in contrast to £275 of good money in the poor funds.[34] The curse of God was only falling on a few of the people of Stirling. In Monifieth there were some minor problems: 'hardheids' were frequently included in collections for 1575, and in 1582 an 'evill balbie' was left in the box after a distribution.[35] The problems were slightly more substantial during the conflicts of the late 1630s onwards, when there was a shortage of currency.[36] Bad coinage was found in Kilmadock, Midcalder, and the Canongate between 1638 and 1652, for example.[37] Unsurprisingly some parishioners succumbed to the temptation to drop poor quality, false or almost worthless coinage in the collection plate, especially during times of economic difficulty. It was normally at most a minor dent in the fundraising efforts.

While the vast majority of collecting took place at church, there were occasions when the kirk session might seek to gather funds in other settings. This was often in connection with a special fundraising drive. In Aberdeen, the elders and deacons were to be divided into quarters and to 'pas throw the towne with the beidmen of St Thomas hospitall to crave support to thame of the nichtboris of the towne'.[38] The collection for the French church in 1587 was to be gathered 'within the towin' of St Andrews by the minister and bailies, as well as 'to landwart' by the 'quartermaisteris': clearly it was a very different affair to the weekly collections using

[32] Spence, *Women, Credit and Debt*, p. 2.

[33] Goodare, 'Parliament and Society', p. 442.

[34] CH2/1026/1, pp. 49–50.

[35] OPR310/1, ff. 27r–30v, 53v. A hardheid was valued at three halfpence: not entirely worthless but some of 1575's collections included 'ill' hardheids: see *DSL*, 'Hard-hede'. This was not a problem unique to poor relief: the lowest-denomination coins which inevitably ended up in the hands of the poorer sectors of society could be hard to exchange, and this was noted as a problem for the poor in the 1570s and 1580s: see Goodare, 'Parliament and Society', pp. 331–2.

[36] Parliament expressed concern about coinage in 1639: *RPS*, C1639/8/16, C1639/8/77, although coinage problems were not confined to this period: Lythe, *Economy of Scotland*, p. 101.

[37] CH2/212/18, pp. 7–8; CH2/266/1, p. 117; CH2/122/4, p. 71.

[38] CH2/448/2, p. 59.

'broddis'.[39] The 1590 Genevan collection in St Cuthbert's was also to be gathered in the quarters.[40] In Kinghorn in 1626, two men were instructed 'to go to the landwart parichionaris and crave support frome thame to the prisoneris in Dunkirke'.[41] It was unusual for what was apparently regular collection-work to take place away from church, as happened in Ayr in 1616 when it was ordained that 'he that gatheris the poores silver at the kirk duire sall await on the mercats that oulk'.[42] Naturally enough, it was generally felt that the church itself was the logical place to collect money for the regular relief work of the kirk session.

Fines

After collections, the most important source of funds for poor relief was normally fines for disciplinary offences. It has been suggested that these monies were not really available for the charitable work of the kirk session: McPherson stated that the idea that fine money went to the poor was an 'ecclesiastical fiction'.[43] There were, of course, demands on kirk session resources other than the poor, and it would be extremely unwise to rely on the phrase 'ad pios usus' as evidence that the funds were spent on welfare as opposed to church-repair, officers' fees, supplies and other ecclesiastical expenses. At the other extreme, Margo Todd's edition of the Perth Kirk Session minutes suggests that fines were 'always designated for the poor': however true of 1580s Perth, this was not always the case.[44] In fact, the situation was far more varied and fluid than any such clear-cut description of the role of fines in ecclesiastical welfare.

There are numerous examples of fine revenues passing to the poor, throughout the period. In rural Monifieth this was the case as early as the 1560s, although the fines were quite small at a shilling or two, and fairly infrequent.[45] In Aberdeen fines were explicitly predicated for poor relief from the 1560s onwards, and there are specific examples of fine money being received by the poor in practice.[46] In South Leith, similarly, the designation of fine money for the poor was more than nominal: on 6 February 1607 a fine of £6 for excessive drunkenness was passed to the poor.[47] In Perth in 1615 a fine of £6 6s 8d was immediately divided up between several individual poor people and the poor box (although soon after, a fine

39 *RStAKS*, ii, p. 610.

40 CH2/718/1, p. 97.

41 CH2/472/1, p. 179. Special collections did also take place at churches in the regular manner: see, for example, *PKSB*, p. 454.

42 CH2/751/1/2, f. 305r.

43 McPherson, *Kirk's Care of the Poor*, p. 27.

44 *PKSB*, p. 36.

45 OPR310/1, ff. 6v, 14v.

46 CH2/448/1, pp. 3–4, 22, 116; CH2/448/2, p. 23.

47 CH2/716/1, p. 29. However the kirk officer was to receive a 12d share of each fine: p. 26.

was spent solely on church repair).[48] A substantial Monimail fine had its physical resting-place described explicitly: 'his penultie being aught merkis put in the box'.[49] Further examples of fines passing specifically to poor people or the poor funds can be found, among others, in Ayr, Elgin, Ellon, Midcalder and St Andrews, right across the period.[50] Additionally, consignations, pledges and cautions – deposits or guarantees for good behaviour or similar – might also be reserved in whole or in part for the poor: for example in St Cuthbert's cautioners for re-offenders presented substantial sums to the poor box.[51] Outsiders to the parish might be forced to make a contribution, as in Old Kelso where 'a stranger who had a bastard barne baptised' paid 40s.[52] It was not only traditional moral lapses like fornication which helped to fund relief: there was also potential income from people like 'Margaret Davisone to be mariet and consignid in the hands of Johne Bell the soume of xxS in pledge that scho sall leirne the ten comandis within xx dayis and failyeing therof the xxS to be distribute to the pure'.[53] Burntisland received £6 13s 4d of consignations in 1625, and a St Andrews fornicator in 1590 pledged £10 to the poor box, which she would lose if she did not compear to make public repentance.[54] And in Midcalder the caution in a dispute was set at £40, with half of this going to the poor, the other half to the injured party.[55]

However, there are also cases where fine money was not available to assist the needy, being spent instead on the upkeep of the church building, or stipends and fees for church officials of various ranks. These include some of the places mentioned above, such as Perth, Midcalder and South Leith, where some fines went to the poor while others did not. More significantly, there were some parishes where the income from fines was essentially a separate fund, used to pay for ecclesiastical expenses. In Kilmadock, for example, the accounts are effectively divided into two: collection income, which was disbursed to the poor, and penalty income, which was spent on fees and repair.[56] Similarly, in Old Deer, income from fines was dispensed on expenses primarily unrelated to welfare.[57] In St Cuthbert's, fines generally went to the poor, but on 20 April 1609 it was

48 CH2/521/6, pp. 4, 39.

49 CH2/548/1, p. 38.

50 CH2/751/1/2, f. 217v; CH2/145/1, ff. 35v, 42r; CH2/147/1, pp. 3–4; CH2/266/1, pp. 6–7 (but cf. p. 32 where fine money is passed to the schoolmaster in Midcalder); *RStAKS*, i, pp. 232, 243; see also *COP*, pp. 198–9, 204, 210.

51 CH2/718/1, pp. 190, 199; CH2/718/2, pp. 7, 8. See also, for example, CH2/122/1, p. 8.

52 CH2/1173/1, p. 34.

53 CH2/718/2, p. 46. This task was surely easy enough that the poor might well have been cheated of their 20s.

54 CH2/523/1, p. 219; *RStAKS*, ii, p. 663.

55 CH2/266/1, p. 6.

56 CH2/212/18, pp. 1–13.

57 CH2/1217/33, ff. 96r–v.

enacted that they would be diverted to pay for a new loft in the church.[58] However, in August 1610 a foundling's payment of £6 was explicitly described as coming from 'penalties', so the loss of revenue was not total or permanent.[59] All in all, there was some variation, and change within individual parishes over how fine money was spent, and although concern was sometimes shown higher up the ecclesiastical hierarchy about money from penalties not being spent on the poor, in practice the alternatives seem to have been widely accepted.[60] And indeed, given that church-repair and officers's fees were essential expenses that could hardly be ignored, income from fines may at least have served to protect the collection funds from encroachment, even in those places where it did not directly assist the poor.

Other Sources of Funding

If collections and fines were the two primary sources of income for most kirk sessions, there was also a wide range of other fundraising opportunities that could contribute in varying proportions. Private charitable giving is examined in a later chapter, but it is worth noting that kirk sessions often received funds from legacies and lifetime gifts. These were another useful source of income, albeit one that was much less predictable than collections and fines.[61] Some revenue from rents and interest were also available to some kirk sessions. Dundee Kirk Session benefitted substantially from this in the 1640s, typically receiving £150–£200 each year from rents on properties in and near to the town.[62] The ministers of St Andrews were to encourage holders of altarages to demit them in favour of the poor in 1600, and at least one did.[63] Aberdeen Kirk Session was gifted an annualrent of ten merks, and South Leith's session received some rental income, although in one case this is apparent only because it was partly waived in return for the debtor 'keiping ane man in his house quha brake his leg for the space of half ane zeir or thairby'.[64] Annuals were a significant element in St Cuthbert's income by the time of the first full account book in 1608.[65] Revenues were also forthcoming from fees for kirk burials.[66] More unusually, Stirling Kirk Session lent money for interest, for example in 1602

58 CH2/718/1, pp. 9, 10, 13–14, 16, 227; and CH2/718/2, p. 349 for the loft act.

59 CH2/718/60, p. 65.

60 In 1613 Fife Synod ordered Kinfauns and Kilspindie 'that all penalties exacted of transgressoris be imployed to the use of the poor': CH2/154/1, p. 143.

61 CH2/448/2, p. 19; *PKSB*, p. 320; CH2/418/1, p. 8; OPR310/1, ff. 38v–39r; CH2/1026/2, p. 8; see also below, Chapter 8.

62 CH2/218/16, ff. 36r–39r, 78r–81r, 112r–113r and passim.

63 *RStAKS*, ii, p. 927.

64 CH2/448/2, p. 19; CH2/716/1, p. 47.

65 CH2/718/60, pp. 3–4.

66 *COP*, p. 334.

when they agreed to 'len furt of the puiris money out of thair box to Robert Bruce saidlar' the sum of £92 10s.[67]

Some other sources of income were highly miscellaneous. Aberdeen Kirk Session recorded that one of their deacon's sons had found 'tua peice of gold worth threttene merkis', and was unable to identify the owner; consequently the sum was to be invested for the profit of St Thomas' Hospital.[68] A similar incident in nature, if not in scale, took place in Dundee in 1641 when the kirk session received 3s 4d 'frome ane honnest man, that he did find upone the street'.[69] Charitable causes were, then as now, felt to be appropriate beneficiaries of lost property. Kirk sessions might also convert physical resources to the use of the poor: Perth Kirk Session announced that if the timber found in the church was not removed it would be applied to the use of the poor (presumably meaning it would be sold and the money received added to the poor fund).[70] And Kinnaird Kirk Session were gifted an 'oxe', which was sold for a sum which was unfortunately left blank in the minutes, though it must have been very considerably more than the 4s paid to 'ane man for keiping of the oxe'.[71] Random incidents like this were a drop in the ocean of poor relief funding from collections, fines and donations, but they suggest a degree of ingenuity on the part of the kirk session, and perhaps more importantly that the kirk session was thought to be the right means through which to channel miscellaneous resources to the poor. They could not, of course, be relied upon to support the core work of relief: for that, kirk sessions understandably spent much of their efforts focusing on the core business of regular collections.

People

Deacons and Elders

In theory, and to some extent in practice, the people at the heart of kirk session poor relief were the deacons. Deacons in Scotland, as in other Reformed churches, were assigned to activities involving poor relief and its financing.[72] In reality the distinction between the activities of deacons and their more senior (and socially superior) counterparts, the elders, was often very fluid and flexible, with a crossover of responsibilities in both directions.[73] While deacons were certainly central to the raising and dispensing of alms, elders and other church officials also had important

[67] CH2/1026/1, p. 107. See also Langley, 'Sheltering', p. 146.
[68] CH2/448/2, p. 47.
[69] CH2/1218/16, f. 47r.
[70] *PKSB*, p. 249.
[71] CH2/448/1, pp. 23, 25.
[72] McKee, *John Calvin on the Diaconate*; Parker, 'Calvinism and Poor Relief', p. 115.
[73] McCallum, *Reforming*, pp. 158–60. For the generally lower socio-economic status of deacons, see Graham, *Uses of Reform*, p. 79; *PKSB*, p. 28.

roles to play. The records do not always provide much evidence on the procedures being followed behind the scenes, but there was evidently some variation and local adaptation in the personnel structures and procedures involved in parish welfare.

In many places, naturally enough, the deacons took the lead in collecting funds. In Monifieth in 1575, for example, those collecting the alms were named in the election lists as deacons.[74] In Perth the deacons' roles were tightly focused on collecting, and the Canongate collections at the door were undertaken by the deacons.[75] As well as collecting, deacons would often be the ones to distribute alms, as in St Andrews in 1570 and Aberdeen in 1620.[76] In addition to these core functions, deacons also had an important role to play in getting to know the poor of the parish in each locality, and thereby informing the decisions that the kirk session would make about relief and other matters. One of the first acts of Monifieth's Kirk Session was for the minister, reader, elders and deacons to comfort the sick, and it was the deacons who were to find out who was sick.[77] The deacons of St Cuthbert's were to report the names of the poor to the session in 1591, and six years later a newly inducted deacon for an area was instructed to 'to haife ane ernist cair over the puir and to do dilligence in gaddering ther almous quhen ocasions servis', reflecting nicely the joint pastoral and fundraising responsibilities.[78] In Aberdeen in 1568 deacons were to provide information so that the poor could be relieved 'according to thair necessite'.[79] Although deacons sometimes fulfilled other responsibilities, including other key kirk session tasks like discipline and catechising, the welfare programme was the most significant element in their job, and they had a very important role to play.[80] They certainly did the lion's share of the manual work of collecting funds, and distributing to the needy.

However, it would be wrong to assume that deacons carried the sole burden of organising relief, or that they had the most influence over it. There are many examples of elders directly involved in poor relief. This could involve the collecting itself, such as the Kinglassie 'elders that collect the almes', or the elders involved in special collections in Aberdeen and St Andrews.[81] In some cases this may reflect the blurriness of terminology as well as the division of labour. But perhaps more significantly, elders had a key role to play in the overall administration of poor relief, the direction

74 OPR310/1, ff. 27r, 29v.

75 *PKSB*, pp. 28, 365; *Canagait*, pp. 5, 13. See also CH2/550/1, p. 320; CH2/718/1, p. 207.

76 *RStAKS*, i, pp. 340–1, ii, pp. 760–3; CH2/448/4, p. 44.

77 OPR310/1, f. 3v; see also *Canagait*, p. 5.

78 CH2/718/1, p. 152, CH2/718/2, p. 49.

79 CH2/448/1, pp. 19, 23.

80 For examples of deacons involved in catechising and discipline see *RStAKS*, ii, p. 805; CH2/718/2, p. 111.

81 GRO, OPR440/43, f. 1r; CH2/448/2, p. 59; *RStAKS*, ii, p. 610. See also CH2/550/1, p. 149.

of welfare policy, and the wider work of charity. In Aberdeen it was an elder who gave notice to the kirk session of a legacy to the hospital, and an Elgin elder agreed to shelter two poor people personally.[82] The duties of 1560s elders in the Canongate included 'to seik the puris silwer and mak compt at the quarteris', visiting sick and poor, and attending poor as well as rich folks' burials'.[83] This was still apparent nearly a century later in the parish, as in 1649 it was specifically the elders (not the 'sessioun': this word was crossed out and replaced with 'elders') who were to visit the quarters and 'take notice of the ordinars poores conditioun and report the nixt day'.[84] When St Cuthbert's deacons were instructed to assess the needs of the poor in each of the parish's quarters, an elder was to accompany each quarter's group of deacons.[85] This probably reflects the higher status of elders, and the extra authority that they would lend to proceedings. This is particularly true of special collections, and visitations of the poor that needed to command confidence in their assessment of needs in the parish. It is also worth emphasising that although deacons might collect, and then dispense alms, they were unlikely to make the decisions about how funds should be spent. Perth deacons were explicitly warned to give in the monies rather than dispensing them, and this model of centralised, whole-session decision-making seems to have been much more typical than the implied delegation of decision-making to St Andrews deacons in 1570, who were warned to distribute only to those meeting certain standards.[86] The vast majority of kirk session records suggest funds being handed in by the collectors for storage, and alms being allocated to specific poor by the kirk session at its meetings, not deacons acting independently.[87] Of course, kirk session minutes do not record the discussions that led to decisions, but we would be very unwise to assume that phrases like 'the ministeris eldairs and deaconis present thocht gude' imply an equal role for all in the decision-making.[88]

The Treasurer

This leads us to another officer with an essential but less familiar role in kirk sessions' poor relief. There was of course no formal place for the 'treasurer' in Calvin or any other theologian's theorising of the diaconate or offices of the church, but as the pragmatic kirk sessions realised, such an office was advantageous to the efficient administration of relief.[89] Many

[82] CH2/448/1, p. 101; CH2/145/1, f. 99r.
[83] *Canagait*, p. 51.
[84] CH2/122/4, p. 19.
[85] CH2/718/1, p. 163.
[86] *PKSB*, p. 365; *RStAKS*, i, pp. 340–1.
[87] See above, Chapters 2–3.
[88] CH2/718/1, p. 76.
[89] For the significance and role of treasurers in eighteenth-century practice, see Mutch, *Religion and National Identity*, pp. 121, 125–6.

parishes employed such an officer to look after and keep an account of the alms raised and dispensed, and it was generally considered to be an important job (the exception, perhaps, being the Synod of Fife's instruction to the parish of Edzell that they acquire either a poor box or a treasurer: a rather demeaning comment for any treasurers, but not a representative one).[90] Aberdeen's treasurer was appointed in 1573, and he was supposed to receive all the monies collected.[91] By 1602 what appears to be essentially the same office was referred to as the 'collector'; the role still involved receiving alms, fine-money and making accounts of the poor funds.[92] John Mathesone served as treasurer for St Cuthbert's in the 1600s, and was probably responsible for the creation of a very detailed account book beginning in 1608.[93] Kilmadock's series of treasurers from the 1620s to 1640s produced a series of thorough annual accounts of income and expenditure both for poor relief and for church repair.[94] Treasurers might simply pass the deacons defined sums of money to distribute locally, or 'throw their quarteris' as the Canongate accounts put it.[95] Robert Gourlaw, the Edinburgh treasurer in the mid-1570s, received various instructions to pay sums to individual needy people, or to the deacons for general disbursement: treasurers were not in a position to make their own decisions about who should get what, of course. But equally, they were more than mere human replacements for boxes: Gourlaw had clearly made some payments from his own pocket and had to be repaid by his replacement as treasurer.[96] It is not always clear whether the treasurer was an elder or deacon: in Montrose however, we know that John Wood was elder as well as treasurer in 1634.[97] In Perth and Ayr the treasurers or equivalent seem to have received stipends or honoraria, but this does not seem to have been standard practice.[98] The office of treasurer was certainly not particularly coveted in Dundee, where there were problems in the late 1630s getting people to serve as treasurer: however the burgh council was able to encourage diligence (and the creation of some exceptionally detailed accounts) by making the refusal to serve a barrier to senior office in the council.[99]

90 CH2/154/1, p. 6.

91 CH2/448/1, pp. 31, 61.

92 CH2/448/2, pp. 7, 19, 44, 51. Both terms were also used in St Andrews: *RStAKS*, ii, pp. 824, 882. Perth's 'collector' seems to have also been effectively a treasurer: *PKSB*, p. 365. In Salton the 'boxmaister' appeared to act as treasurer, being commanded by the kirk session to make payments: CH2/322/1, pp. 91–2.

93 CH2/718/2, pp. 250, 308; CH2/718/60.

94 CH2/212/18, pp. 1–13 (and pp. 14–17 for their rough workings out).

95 CH2/122/48, p. 29.

96 CH2/450/1, pp. 4, 13, 17, 52, 95, 99.

97 CH2/943/1, pp. 11, 204.

98 *PKSB*, p. 329n; CH2/751/1/2, f. 250r.

99 DCA, Dundee Town Council Minutes, Volume 4 (1613–53), f. 128v; McCallum, 'Charity and Conflict', pp. 35–6.

Overall the organisation of responsibilities within kirk session relief was usually logical and effective: a treasurer (or similarly named officer) would oversee the storage and accounting of funds, and control the distribution of funds at the instruction of the kirk session as a whole. Elders, the session members with the highest social and economic status, played the key strategic and administrative roles, while deacons, of rather lower social standing, were the natural choice to do the bulk of the hard work of collecting at the church door. Elders might sometimes assist with collections, and lend their status to special collections where the generosity of the town's respectable was sought. They were, however less likely to be involved with the actual dispensing of funds to poor people. After all, it was the lowlier deacons who were best suited for the task of networking with the poorer people of the parish, assessing and reporting on their needs, and handing them cash.

Ministers

One other person had a role to play in poor relief. Ministers' most unique contribution was, of course, preaching and exhorting charity from the pulpit. While session minutes almost never record the content of a week's sermon, there are times when it was recorded that the minister was to preach on charity or encourage generosity from the pulpit.[100] They might also need to announce a special collection in advance, or as noted earlier, exhort better attendance at the funerals of the poor (during a time of dearth).[101] Such references are fairly scattered, but it is highly likely that the subject of charity and the poor would be mentioned by ministers more frequently than recorded in the church's administrative documents. Preaching was certainly a prime opportunity to exhort generosity. Ministers might also contribute more directly to relief themselves, ideally acting as an exemplar. This could include straightforward donations to the poor funds, which would normally go unrecorded, of course, although larger gifts might occasionally make it into the records.[102] Ministers in a variety of parishes left charitable bequests, normally to the local parish poor.[103] Aberdeen's William Guild was well-known for his large-scale philanthropy, although of course few ministers could afford such munificence even if they were that way inclined.[104]

Another contribution by the clergy was in the organisation of welfare

[100] CH2/471/1, ff. 12r, 17r. See also CH2/122/1, p. 268; CH2/550/1, p. 320; CH2/751/1/2, f. 242v. For the 'relative success' of some English exhortations to charity see Hindle, 'Dearth, Fasting and Alms', p. 77.

[101] CH2/799/1, f. 308r; CH2/1142/1, f. 139r; see also above, p. 106.

[102] *PKSB*, p. 185.

[103] *FES*, i, pp. 200, 203, 292; v, pp. 94, 128, 160, 302.

[104] *ODNB*, 'Guild, William (1586–1657)'. For ministerial incomes, some of which were precarious and most of which were modest, see McCallum, 'Economic Fortunes of Ministers'.

itself. This is especially true of extra-parochial relief: when presbyteries or synods organised or assisted with wider fundraising drives, such as those discussed in Chapter 4, it was ministers who took the lead in co-ordinating such efforts.[105] The ministers might also be involved with collections, or looking after some or all of the monies raised.[106] More routine parish poor relief might have been less dependent on direct ministerial work, and it did seem to be possible for it to continue without close ministerial assistance such as in Kinnaird in the summer of 1644 when the minister was absent in England. Midcalder's collection totals dropped, but did not cease, after the minister's death in 1642.[107] Relief business might be affected, but it could survive ministerial absences.

While deacons carried out the day-to-day work of relief, ministers must have been directly involved in the discussion and decision-making process. Their role can sometimes be glimpsed behind the formulaic language of kirk session records and the statement that 'it was ordained that . . .' When a substantial legacy was left to the poor of old Aberdeen, it was to be distributed 'be the advyse of the ministrie of the burt and of mister Richard Irving' (a relative of the deceased). The minister sought the kirk session's advice, and they agreed that the proposed division of funds was 'verrie gude and charitable', but their role in the decision-making process was clearly secondary and advisory.[108] This may have reflected the specific circumstances of a large bequest, rather than regular collection funds. In Kilmadock, it was the minister and elders who selected the treasurer and made other decisions, although how much weighting each party's preference held is of course unknown.[109] Salton's records hint at a process by which ministers had a separate 'vote', or almost veto, when an act on the proper use of the poor funds was 'statut and ordeaned be consent both of minister and e[l]dir[s]'.[110] Interestingly, one poor man in Bervie received his 15s payment 'upon ane ticket from the minister', suggesting some informal process of ministerial intervention and approval.[111] While the dynamics of the vast majority of relief decisions made are invisible to us, it seems safe to conclude that ministers must have had an influential, if not necessarily decisive, role.

Problems

Poor relief was highly dependent on hard work and commitment by the kirk session and its individual members and officers, especially deacons

105 McCallum, 'Charity Doesn't Begin at Home', pp. 114–15.
106 See above, p. 140; CH2/418/1, p. 3.
107 CH2/418/1, pp. 72–3; CH2/266/1, p. 117.
108 CH2/448/2, p. 19.
109 CH2/212/18, pp. 5, 10–11.
110 CH2/322/1, p. 90; cf. *COP*, p. 370.
111 CH2/34/9, p. 21.

and treasurers. Was this always forthcoming, and were there other 'personnel' problems with the regular work of relief? The most common problem – though by no means a widespread one overall – was a slackening of diligence in collecting the alms. In Elgin in 1592, some collectors had to be ordered to do their duty, and if they failed they would be fined the sum that would have been collected were it not for 'thair slewthe'.[112] A similar penalty would await the slack in St Andrews in 1595, unless they had a good excuse.[113] St Cuthbert's collectors were felt to be 'sumthing negligent in collecting the almous towardis the pure' in 1598, though this apparently improved in subsequent years.[114] Perth had some similar problems in the 1580s, and also fined non-collectors, meaning that funds did not suffer as greatly from the lack of diligence as they might otherwise have done.[115] These problems were fairly infrequent, and comparatively minor in that they rarely applied to all of the collectors, were short-lived and could be circumvented through fines and/or replacing the errant indiviudal.

What about the potential problem of more nefarious failings in the personnel of relief? With large amounts of loose cash involved, the temptation to theft must sometimes have been present. Cases of theft or impropriation seem to have been rare. A couple of ministers were apparently guilty: among the reasons for William Maxwell's deprivation from the parish of Dunbar in 1639 was 'meddling with the poor's box' (although his apparent opposition to the Covenant was probably the more significant factor); Andrew Forrester of Dunfermline was another culprit.[116] Glasgow Kirk Session expressed concern about the whereabouts of some poor funds, but it seems that its threat that the collectors must present the money next Saturday or be 'accusit opinlie in pulpit as deteinaris of the puir silver' was intended as a warning for them to get their acts together, and as a statement of the seriousness of the situation, rather than as an actual accusation of embezzlement. Certainly the collectors did turn up and gave in the money as requested, presumably rather sheepishly.[117] The rarity of such incidents in church records, given the strong likelihood that they would be taken very seriously by church courts, would suggest that misappropriation of the funds was very unusual.[118] Session members were, after all, supposed to be selected for their trustworthiness among other things, and the sharing of duties. Account-keeping by the treasurer may have acted

112 CH2/145/1, f. 32v.

113 *RStAKS*, ii, p. 810.

114 CH2/718/2, pp. 77, 109, 192 (although in 1606, while conducting their offices well, they were slack in convening for session meetings: p. 237).

115 *PKSB*, pp. 264, 349–50, 407, 441. In the Canongate some collectors were accused of sending servants or others to collect in their place: CH2/122/1, pp. 12, 27.

116 *FES*, i, p. 407, v, p. 27.

117 CH2/550/1, p. 39.

118 See also Langley (ed.), *Synod of Lothian and Tweeddale*, p. 409 for an allegation of impropriety with poor money which was not upheld after the Synod's investigation.

as a further brake on impropriety.[119] There were also a few incidents possibly involving a third party: in a dispute over a disappeared poor box, the former beadle of Kilspindie told Perth Presbytery that it had been put 'in the kirk in ane Almerie that haid not ane look and it wes stollin away'.[120] South Leith took very seriously the theft of poor money from the church in 1608: they were suspicious of the kirk officer, Robert Mitchell, but ultimately made clear that his deposition from office was for his misbehaviour and anger towards the session during the investigations, not for theft.[121] Seventeenth-century security arrangements could be basic, and even when the session's personnel were entirely honest, it is unsurprising that money would occasionally go missing. But on the whole, this was not a significant drain on the relief funds.

Complaints or allegations about impropriety, incompetence or inefficiency in how the funds were spent were relatively rare. Of course private grumblings or doubts about the kirk sessions' activities in this area (or any other area) would never be recorded unless they spilled over into scandalous or slanderous words in public, but Margo Todd has identified some examples of hostility to and attacks on kirk session members.[122] Although atypical, another example from the Canongate in 1613 is particularly interesting:

> Compeirit Johne Sudderland challengit for that quhen his charitie wes requyred to the poore on the com[m]union day he not onlie refuisit the samyn bot gave ane ill anser confest the samyn and vowit in presens of the sessioun, the poores monney is ill wairit and is not imployed for sustenyng the poore as it awcht to be and sik lyke fell out in high disdanefull speiches aganes the pastor, the Baillie and haill Sessioun quhilk they all think very offensive and thairfoir commits him to waird, indureing thair will.[123]

This shows that at least one individual expressed hostility to how the poor funds were actually spent, although significantly this was in the context of being personally challenged for not contributing. Specifics are not given, and it may well be that this was an outburst of anger (possibly related to other issues not mentioned in the minutes) rather than a serious complaint about session policy. In subsequent weeks he 'declairs that he is sorie for the samyn', gave in a bill confirming this and craved forgiveness, no doubt under pressure.[124] This sort of incident seems to reflect personal grievance

119 Cf. *COP*, p. 383+n, where the alternative perspective is adopted: separate keys and signing off on accounts as evidence of a lack of trust within the sessions.

120 CH2/299/1, p. 66.

121 CH2/716/1, pp. 28–9.

122 *COP*, p. 383.

123 CH2/122/1, p. 12. I am very grateful to Dr Chris Langley for first drawing this case to my attention.

124 CH2/122/1, pp. 14, 16.

and hostility to the session than wider public disapproval of kirk session welfare. Certainly if the attitudes to poverty and charity identified from textual evidence in Chapter 1 were broadly representative of wider feelings on the subject, it would not be surprising if there was a degree of public sympathy for the poor relief system as kirk sessions chose to operate it.

Distribution

Cash

The poor received support from the kirk session in a variety of ways. The primary means through which aid would be passed to the poor was, obviously, cash. This was how the kirk session received most of its income, as we saw earlier, and it was in many ways the most logical form in which to dispense relief. The money could simply be 'distribut out of the box' in the same form that it had been deposited, and resources could be very easily and accountably divided according to the needs of the poor and the decision of the session.[125] The vast majority of payments were in cash form, and normally straightforwardly accounted with a sum of money such as 8d or 5s, although occasionally the funds as a whole were more grandly referred to with phrases like the 'almes silver'.[126] Although, as we shall see, kirk sessions did sometimes convert their cash into resources to distribute instead, alms-dispensing in cash form was so ubiquitous that there is little more to say about it.[127]

Although the cash was almost always given as a simple payment or gift, whether one-off or recurring, kirk sessions very occasionally distributed money through a loan. Mentions of loans in the records of relief are very rare, and this is one case where it is fair to assume a good deal from silence. It would be bizarre to record details of gifts of cash to the poor but not payments that were to be returned, where a record for future reference would be very handy. This is slightly surprising, in that poor relief systems elsewhere in Europe did make use of lending money as an instrument of relief.[128] Cathryn Spence has also recently demonstrated just how extensive credit and debt networks were in early modern Scotland.[129] There are some Scottish examples of relief-related loans: in Anstruther Helen Gilmour was 'ordanit to haif xxS in len till hir husband returne'.[130] During the dearth of 1623, Ayr Kirk Session recorded that 'Janet Hamilton spous

125 *Dundonald*, p. 407; see also CH2/322/1, p. 90.

126 CH2/147/1, p. 17.

127 Cash was also the primary (though similarly, not only) medium of relief in Elizabethan England: McIntosh, 'Poor relief in Elizabethan English communities'.

128 See, for example, McIntosh, *Hadleigh*, pp. 7, 102; Sprunger, 'Mennonites and Sectarian Poor', p. 152; Jutte, *Poverty*, p. 132.

129 Spence, *Women, Credit and Debt*, especially Chapter 1.

130 OPR403/1, f. 6v.

to Niniane McKolme sailler boorrowit in her desolate and miserable caice [circumstances] iii Lib', and Isobel Eglinshame received a similar loan of 24s.[131] Canongate lent £10 'to a Leiutennent . . . at Jon Caithcartis desyre' in 1650.[132] But such cases were uncommon, and reflect distinctive circumstances.[133] The sums of money were larger than most single relief payments, and in the Ayr examples went to married women. In the case of Gilmour the loan was specifically for the duration of her husband's absence. There seems to have been an attempt to provide temporary support to individuals in a short-term crisis, but who were not actually among the ranks of the long-term poor. It was obviously more practical to ask for such money to be returned when possible, although there were also cases where distressed people from substantial backgrounds would receive straight relief payments rather than loans.[134] On the other hand, long-suffering poor people would struggle to repay loans, and it would be counter-productive to ask them to.[135] The probable reason for the relatively rarity of relief-loans in Scotland was that the kirk session focused most of its efforts on the longer-term poor, and the most seriously needy, rather than on assisting respectable people going temporarily short. Most of the cash it handed out, it did not expect to see again.

Relief in Kind

Payments in kind were also a significant element in the charitable system. Clothing was a key part of this. Galston Kirk Session provided 2s for the making of a poor person's coat in 1593, and in Glasgow part of a week's collection in 1586 went straight on the purchase of a coat for David Lyon.[136] In Anstruther, many of the relief payments of the late 1570s and early 1580s were to pay for clothes, especially cloaks (a 'cassik'), and in Salton in 1639 Robert Alane was to get 12s 'to buy a plead'.[137] The type of garment was not always specified, as when Haddington Kirk Session spent £4 on clothes for Archie Weir in 1630.[138] In Perth poor people were given gowns: clearly, large and warm over-garments were one of the most useful items the kirk

131 CH2/751/2, f. 28v.

132 CH2/122/48, p. 42.

133 Stirling Kirk Session loaned out some money, but apparently as an investment rather than direct relief. For example, a notary borrowed £200, with interest, and £92 10s was lent to 'Robert Bruce saidlar' with interest. These payments may have been made to struggling and worthy individuals in the session's eyes, but do not comprise relief in most senses of the word. In 1608 the huge sum of £368 13s 4d was lent out, presumably as an investment. CH2/1026/1, pp. 107, 184, 212–13.

134 CH2/809/1, p. 12; CH2/322/1, p. 91; CH2/77/1, f. 10r.

135 On occasion existing debts owed to kirk sessions might even be waived on account of poverty: see, for example, CH2/521/6, p. 38; CH2/122/1, p. 26.

136 CH2/1335/1, p. 58; CH2/550/1, p. 86.

137 OPR403/1, ff. 4r, 8r; CH2/322/1, p. 99.

138 CH2/799/1, f. 312v.

session could assist with.[139] There was even a reference to a new recipient of relief as taking the place of 'ane of the puir gown men', suggesting a distinct group, identified by the gowns (and likely their colour) as a sort of uniform.[140] The recipients of royal doles in honour of King James' birthday were certainly to be distinguished by their blue gowns.[141] Most clothing provided to poor people across Scotland was not part of a uniform, however. Kirk sessions normally helped with clothing when they became aware of a specific shortage, rather than as a regular or symbolic event, such as when Perth Kirk Session 'being informit of the povertie and meine estait of Jhon Stanhouse son to umquhill James Stanhouse and his indigens of clothes ordains to gif him twentie schillingis to by ane coit'.[142] Perth also stepped in to provide £3 to a poor scholar for him to regain garments which he had to pawn when he fell ill.[143]

The other most common type of clothing provided was footwear: a logical choice alongside warm outer garments. Indeed, the two might sometimes be provided together, especially for poor children.[144] Thomas Ayson, a poor boy in Monimail, was bought both 'ane four tailed cott and ane pair of schoes' by the kirk session, and coat, hose, and shoes were provided to a child in Dalziel in 1644.[145] Euphame Pattone, James Pullar, and William Mitchell's wife in Kinnaird received money to pay for shoes in October 1637, perhaps as winter drew in.[146] Other beneficiaries included George Stevenson in Lasswade, and the son of Nicol Ronaldson in Perth.[147] This emphasis was a sensible one: as well as the obvious point that the Scottish poor needed substantial protection from the elements, clothing and shoes meant a one-off and expensive outlay which might be difficult to meet from a low income (whether from paid work, family, or regular payments from the kirk session itself).

Food was presumably the primary expense that kirk sessions would have expected their monetary contributions to be spent on. This means that payments in the direct form of food show up less frequently than clothing in the kirk session records. Nevertheless, such payments in kind did occur, on highly varying scales. A payment of 8s in Old Deer's relief accounts was 'to by fishe', and Salton paid as much as 16s in 1639 'for drink to James Stenhous a poor old man' (the sum suggests they were perhaps refunding

139 *PKSB*, p. 102; see also pp. 171, 414 for references to unspecified types of clothes to be bought for the poor.
140 *PKSB*, pp. 109+n.
141 *RPC*, 1st Series, vol. iii, p. 137.
142 *PKSB*, p. 429.
143 CH2/521/2, f. 167v.
144 For similar practices elsewhere see McIntosh, *Poor Relief in England*, pp. 243–4.
145 CH2/548/1, pp. 36, 37; CH2/462/34, p. 72.
146 CH2/418/1, p. 24.
147 CH2/471/1, f. 32r; *PKSB*, p. 219.

a third party's provision of drink over a period of time).[148] We have already seen how some kirk sessions sought to transfer foodstuffs, especially meat and fish, which were sinfully traded on the Sabbath to the poor.[149] On a larger scale, during times of crisis kirk sessions might arrange substantial quantities of grain to be provided to the poor, such as in Perth during the plague of the mid-1580s, where a number of respectable individuals were to be discreetly assisted with temporary weekly consignments of grain.[150] These were, however, responses to particular times of crisis, rather than flirtations with a policy of payment in kind as a regular practice.

Finally, fuel was another item that poor people would inevitably need, and kirk sessions could provide. Again, it would normally have been bought by poor people themselves with their cash handouts, but in some circumstances sessions might provide it directly, or provide payments specifically intended to provide fuel. In November 1602, Stirling Kirk Session decided 'to give Erish Cathrein iiii S ilk oulk during ther will to intertenn in the almus hous with hir self ane fund bairne besyd silver to buy ane lead of collis [load of coal] to that hous ilk oulk in this winter season'.[151] During the cold of winter, and where a foundling was involved, it was clearly thought necessary to ensure a weekly supply of coal, not just a weekly pittance. The inhabitants of Glasgow's almshouse were to receive coal or peat transported on the Sabbath, presumably as a top-up rather than the sole source of fuel, which would otherwise be worryingly dependent on the ungodliness of fuel traders.[152] And in Perth, again, the plague of the mid-1580s, and concomitant problems with trade, meant that some poor people had to be provided with coal.[153] But as with food, these switches into payments in kind through fuel were the exception, rather than the rule.

Medical Care

Poverty and illness were closely linked in early modern societies.[154] Poor nutrition and range of diet would inevitably make the poor more susceptible to illness, and on the other hand those who became ill, and lacked strong support networks, were very exposed to the risk of falling into temporary or longer-term poverty. Thus relief payments to those who were ill occur frequently in the records: sometimes they were simply described as 'sick', but there were also, unsurprisingly, many individuals labelled as 'creple' or 'blind'. Those suffering disabilities would be particularly likely to seek kirk session support. For the most part, these people received relief in similar

148 CH2/1217/33, f. 102v; CH2/322/1, p. 99.
149 See above, pp. 59, 75.
150 *PKSB*, pp. 292–3, 296; CH2/266/1, p. 8.
151 CH2/1026/1, p. 111.
152 CH2/550/1, p. 104.
153 *PKSB*, p. 293.
154 Jutte, *Poverty*, pp. 21–2.

forms to everyone else, and therefore they are considered as a category of recipients in Chapter 6. But kirk sessions also sometimes assisted with specific medical expenses, as has been noted for the eighteenth century by Mitchison.[155] In Culross 'foure dollars [were] to be givene to Robert Browne for helling of two brokene armes of the poore in Kincarne', and in Burntisland 40s went 'to nannes stewart to pay for salves to hir sair leg'.[156] Kirk sessions were also keen to support informal care arrangements, such as when South Leith Kirk Session agreed to waive £5 of the maill duty owed to them by a man who was 'keiping ane man in his house quha brake his leg for the space of half ane zeir or thairby'.[157] Assistance in procuring the treatment of broken limbs was a frequent contribution by sessions.[158] Pre-emptive support for the inevitable financial insecurity that would follow amputation was provided by Culross Kirk Session, which agreed to give 'thrie dollers to be givene to William Gray a poor man of Carnock whose arme is to be cut of'.[159] Sick children were also a cause for concern, understandably, and St Andrews Kirk Session passed a fine of 4 merks for fornication directly to William Yule 'for heling of tua puir barnis'.[160] The precise status or expertise of the men and women carrying out the treatments is rarely noted, but William Watson, who was paid by St Andrews Kirk Session for medical assistance to the injured William Ednam, was at least described as 'chirurgian'.[161] Glasgow Kirk Session made payment to a Margaret Dikson for her to provide medical treatment to poor people.[162] Kirk sessions paid considerable attention to the various health needs of their parishioners, and medical care formed a significant element in their portfolio of welfare provision.

Burials

Assistance with the costs of burial perhaps cannot be considered as poor relief in the strictest sense, but it was another important element in the kirk sessions' overall expenditure on the poor, and could be considered as charitable in broader senses of the word.[163] This was especially true if their assistance could provide more decent and respectable burials and therefore perhaps some comfort for the bereaved poor. Payments for wind-

155 *OPL*, p. 99.
156 CH2/77/1, f. 69v; CH2/523/1, p. 218.
157 CH2/717/1, p. 47.
158 CH2/450/1, p. 123; CH2/718/3, p. 32.
159 CH2/77/1, f. 72r.
160 *RStAKS*, ii, p. 734. See also CH2/718/60, p. 57.
161 *RStAKS*, ii, p. 908.
162 CH2/550/1, p. 382.
163 The poor elsewhere also received this category of non-cash assistance as well as food and clothing: McIntosh, 'Poor Relief in Elizabethan Communities', p. 350; Crossan, *Poverty and Welfare*, p. 87.

ing-sheets are very frequent in many kirk session minutes, and this form of assistance with burial costs must have been welcome to the families of the deceased who could not afford them for themselves. They were certainly not cheap: in 1608 St Cuthbert's paid 20s for the winding-sheet of Bessie Cathcart, from the Water of Leith.[164] Aberdeen Kirk Session paid for winding-sheets for poor people in 1603, including poor strangers.[165] Predictably, some winding-sheets were for previous recipients of relief: in Old Deer, William Sangster received a payment of 6s 8d on 19 December 1634, but on 8 March 1635 his wife got 8s to buy a winding-sheet.[166] Kists or coffins were less likely to be funded by kirk sessions, but occasional examples of these more costly burial paraphernalia can be found.[167] During the famine of the early 1620s, burial expenses came to be a poignantly frequent and large item within sessions' expenditure.[168]

Assistance was sometimes forthcoming with the actual making of graves: this also had to be paid for and the poor would naturally struggle. So St Cuthbert's agreed 'to gif Jon Guild [the beadle] xld out of the box and that for everie puiris grave he maks that hes nathing to gife him'.[169] Amongst others, Dunbarney Kirk Session twice passed 2s out of a week's collection total to Andrew Strachan, on each occasion for making a poor woman's grave.[170] As well as using their funds to ensure that poor people could afford a proper burial, kirk sessions were more generally keen to see that the poor were treated respectfully in death. In 1575, St Andrews Kirk Session enacted that 'the puris to be convoyit to the burial witht the inhabitantis of the town als weil as the riche', on pain of punishment; a similar requirement was placed on Canongate's elders.[171] And in 1610, South Leith's elders who were maltmen, had to agree that if their servants or recent servants died they would provide everything necessary for their burial, although they were keen not to be singled out and stipulated that the agreement was 'provyding that uther callings do the lyk'.[172] How successful such measures were is impossible to gauge; unlike the direct funding of burial expenses, this was an area in which kirk sessions had to rely upon persuasion and exhortation.

164 CH2/718/60, p. 57.

165 CH2/448/2, pp. 33, 40; see also for example CH2/34/9, p. 41; *COP*, p. 338n.

166 CH2/1217/33, f. 93v. See also CH2/462/34, p. 72; CH2/548/1, pp. 32, 37.

167 CH2/521/6, p. 218, CH2/521/7, p. 376; CH2/322/1, p. 105; CH2/266/1, p. 78; CH2/548/1, pp. 36–7.

168 See above, pp. 105–6.

169 CH2/718/2, p. 42 (referred to as beadle, p. 39).

170 CH2/100/1, p. 40. See also CH2/322/1, p. 104; CH2/523/1, p. 205.

171 *RStAKS*, i, p. 408; *Canagait*, p. 51.

172 CH2/716/1, p. 49.

The Flexibility of Relief

Ecclesiastical relief systems are sometimes seen as less flexible than secular systems.[173] But just as the kirk session drew on a diverse and sometimes imaginative range of income types, it also reacted flexibly to the varied needs of the poor. Although previous sections in this chapter have covered the main categories of distribution, it would be wrong to visualise the poor relief mission as following a schematic or narrow methodology. One of the reasons for variations was that each group of ministers, elders and deacons was developing their own responses to specific situations. This could be seen as a weakness: certainly there was no detailed 'rulebook' for how to operate a relief system. But it did allow for a certain sensitivity, which manifested itself in a number of ways.

Kirk sessions' core outgoings on relief, the cash payments to needy individuals, were not set at a fixed level either centrally or locally. It is normal to find sessions varying their payment sizes, sometimes very substantially, and this must have been based on the perceived needs of the poor people in question. A telling example of this is provided in Perth, where on 2 January 1587 two women were entered to weekly payments. There is no difference in the wording of their entries, both being described as 'ane puir woman', yet Isobel Hewat was granted 2s per week, while Maige Nory got 10s per week.[174] The decisions were made in the same meeting, so a difference in available funds cannot explain the difference. For reasons that are unrecorded, Nory was felt to need five times as much assistance as Hewat (perhaps she had dependents, or perhaps Hewat was in some form of employment but not earning quite enough to survive). Numerous examples of concurrent varying size payments to different poor individuals can be found all across Scotland, across the period.[175] As in Perth, the specific reasons why two people might need different sums are sadly normally invisible to us.

Another sign of responsiveness in the allocation of alms was the turnover of poor people. While some individuals might receive for very long periods, lists of the poor often show a fair amount of change from year-to-year, with new individuals added and old ones removed. As already noted, deacons were to ensure that the needs of the poor were carefully monitored. Reflecting this, Montrose's list of recipients for 1642 excludes several people who had been listed in 1641, such as 'Barbara Cutbuirds bearne' and Isobel Mathie. These removals were in addition to those who had died, as they were marked with an X.[176] Dundee's Kirk Session carried out visita-

173 Mitchison, *Coping*, p. 36; Goodare, 'Parliament and Society', p. 439.

174 *PKSB*, p. 356.

175 See, for example, OPR310/1, f. 101r; CH2/550/2, pp. 39, 42; CH2/1217/33, ff. 101v–104r; CH2/799/1, f. 307r; CH2/1218/16, f. 92r; CH2/448/2, p. 11; CH2/418/1, pp. 13–18.

176 CH2/943/1, pp. 219, 221.

tions of the poor in each quarter, after which the poor and their payments were altered.[177] Edinburgh's session minutes specifically emphasised that poor payments were ceasing because the recipients 'mereits not now ther almus', or words to that effect.[178] Similarly Aberdeen's session produced a list of 'theas that ar dischargit of thair quarter almes upon gude consideratioune moving the sessioun': in other words not simply through death or departure.[179] As we saw in Chapter 3, some small rural parishes had rather less turnover, with some individuals serving as the main recipients for a long time, but even in these cases there was normally some change to be found, and patterns of need there were probably less rapidly shifting than in the towns.[180]

Sessions attempted to provide aid in forms appropriate to the recipients' need, including through the payments in kind discussed earlier. An attentiveness to individual problems was shown by Edinburgh Kirk Session in their provision of a gown to John Howy 'because he is puir and hes not claytis to keip him from cauds'.[181] Catherine Bowman in Kinnaird clearly had problems with her dwelling, because in August 1635 the session granted her 20s 'to helpe to build hir house' (i.e. to repair it). That December she was further assisted with shoes.[182] In 1606 Midcalder recognised the particular shortage faced by the blind man John Brown, holding a special collection for him which raised £3, more than could have been gleaned from a week or two's collection.[183] Equally, in other cases the church assisted individuals with expenses involved in gaining employment for the future or employed them directly (cleaning the church, for example), where they were capable.[184] Kirk sessions tried to assist other poor people more indirectly, by encouraging or co-ordinating informal relief by third parties. In Kinnoull in 1633, £3 was 'collectitt for to help to nuris the berne fownd', and a Midcalder fornicator was ordered to ensure the fostering of a child until it was a year-old, at which point the mother was to do the same for the subsequent year.[185] Dundee Kirk Session paid £3 4s for board and a store of fuel to support the fostering of 'W[illia]m Swanns motherles infant'.[186] As well as assisting wounded soldiers directly with payments, Canongate Kirk Session paid £4 'to the wife that keipit a wounded soudier' in 1651, perhaps trying to show that such care might be reimbursed by the kirk session as

177 CH2/1218/16, ff. 49r–51r, 164r, 237v.
178 CH2/450/1, pp. 17, 18, 30, 33.
179 CH2/448/2, p. 11.
180 See above, pp. 83–5, 94–6.
181 CH2/450/1, p. 149.
182 CH2/418/1, pp. 10, 12.
183 CH2/266/1, p. 11.
184 CH2/521/2, ff. 155v, 167v; CH2/418/1, pp. 6–7; for English parallels to this practice see McIntosh, *Poor Relief in England*, pp. 242–3; see also below, pp. 200–2.
185 CH2/948/1, p. 3; CH2/266/1, p. 10.
186 CH2/1218/16, f. 74r.

an incentive to others in the future.[187] On the other hand, steps might be taken to discourage unkind treatment of the poor. This was seen in extreme form in Kinnaird when 'Margaret Millar wes cited for putting ane poore woman out of the house at the poynt of death'. The session probably wanted to make clear that behaviour as irresponsible as sending a seriously ill poor person out into the cold (the citation was 19 January 1645) was a matter for discipline.[188]

So while conventional cash payments, supplemented by payments in kind, were the principal channel through which the church attempted to improve the situation of the needy, we should not fall into the trap of imposing rigid categories or distinctions between discrete forms of relief. Kirk sessions chose the response they saw as most appropriate to the situation in hand, and they took a diverse range of steps to try to secure the most charitable outcomes for deserving poor people, using all the resources (including moral exhortation and discipline as well as cash) available to them. Hindle has noted that the provision of a range of forms of assistance, including 'food, clothes, shoes, fuel, rent, medical care', points to the 'extraordinary sensitivity' to need of English Poor Law practice: this phrase might be equally well applied to the work of the kirk sessions.[189]

Chargeability

It should not be assumed from this flexibility, however, that kirk sessions always sought to help each poor person as much as they possibly could in the moment, without thought for the future or any sense of the limitations of relief. Issues around eligibility and the criteria for relief are discussed fully in Chapter 7, but in assessing distribution strategies it is vital to consider what was a key concern for many sessions: 'chargeability'. Just as the decision to donate was not entirely 'voluntary', so kirk sessions' aid, as they saw it, was not entirely theirs to bestow or withhold simply at their own whim. This is reflected in their concern to avoid individual poor people becoming 'chargeable' to the kirk session in future, leading them to offer highly conditional or fixed-term relief, or to warn that future aid should not be sought.

Sessions often displayed concern about needy individuals becoming a future burden on them. This is reflected in the stipulations, discussed above, that certain payments were during a person's sickness only: they wanted to avoid an expectation of continuing long-term support. This might apply even where sickness was not apparently the problem, as for James Moreis, a former maltman in St Andrews, who received 40d weekly '*during the will of the session*, for support of him and his bairnis'.[190] The

[187] CH2/122/48, pp. 58–9.
[188] CH2/418/1, p. 76.
[189] *OTP*, p. 265.
[190] *RStAKS*, ii, p. 926 (my emphasis).

phrasing made it clear it was a fixed-term payment. Similarly, Montrose payments might be labelled 'for ane tyme' or 'for the tyme'.[191] The phrase was technically true of all payments (because no-one was entitled to receive aid forever), so the decision to write it next to some but not all payments suggests a particular concern to mark some payments as definitely temporary. Similar motives may lie behind payments such as the 40s Dundonald paid to 'John Forgushill, elder in Helie, hinderit be the present plauge fra his traffikine quhairon he leiffit and sustenit his small bairnes'.[192] Better to provide a large sum to cover his lost earnings during a short-term interruption to business, perhaps, than to risk the family falling into poverty and requiring long-term welfare.

Some parishes were very explicit about this concern. Perth's session stated that some recipients were discharged from claiming relief in future, and Nicol Ronaldson (who received a stipend for bell-ringing) was granted some shoes only 'provyding it be no preparatione to hym'.[193] This presumably meant that it was not to serve as a 'preparation' for receipt of regular relief. One St Andrews payment was followed by the insistence that 'the seat to be na forthir burdenit to mak support to the said Isobell'.[194] Some supplicants for relief were evidently alert to this concern, and framed their claims accordingly. St Cuthbert's accounts reveal payments to individuals who 'promisit never to seik na[n] agane'.[195] Edinburgh Kirk Session paid Johne Robisone 20s and Margaret Elder 40s 'sua that thai be not chargeable to the kirk in tyme cuming'; similarly Thomas Browne 'bonetmakar' got 40s, 'providing all wayis that he be not chargeable . . . heirefter'. Like the St Cuthbert's claimants, Jonet Stevinsoun 'promest that scho sall not be chargeable to the kirk heirefter'.[196] This concern was not confined to urban parishes: Longside Kirk Session paid 24s towards a 'pack' for Johne Morres, 'with this condition that he sall not charge us heirefter bot sall live honestly in ane lawfull calling'.[197] And Eupham Baxter was granted a dollar by Monimail Kirk Session in 1644, but this was 'upon condition that hereafter she sall not be chairgeable to the session'.[198]

This is an important reminder that kirk sessions' flexibility and

[191] CH2/943/1, pp. 221, 223, 224.

[192] *Dundonald*, p. 118.

[193] *PKSB*, pp. 178–9, 183.

[194] *RStAKS*, i, p. 395.

[195] CH2/718/60, pp. 99–100, 111. One of these, Isobel Straton, did not remain true to her word, although the session still made a payment, perhaps because two years had elapsed and dearth had hit by November 1622 (p. 109).

[196] CH2/450/1, pp. 4, 13, 96, further examples at pp. 29, 46, 73. A similar pledge was made in Montrose when 'Jon Smart ane poore seik boy received 46s and promised not to be chairgable to the sessioun any more': CH2/943/1, p. 63. There are exceptions: in Old Kelso 'Alexander Air gave in ane supplication for help in his sicknes ordeines to give him 24s presentlie and help also thereafter gif neid be', CH2/1173/1, p. 200.

[197] CH2/699/1, p. 56.

[198] CH2/548/1, p. 45.

responsiveness in the provision of relief did not mean that they were simply distributing resources willy-nilly. These concerns, and in particular the recurring term 'chargeable', also suggest something very interesting about the kirk sessions' own attitude to the nature of relief. Theoretically, of course, this was voluntary charity and the poor had no right to claim that relief must be given to them, or to 'charge' the kirk session for it. Even if the original Scottish Poor Law had been fully implemented, it would have placed a statutory duty to contribute on certain individuals, not conferred a statutory entitlement to permanent welfare on any individual.[199] Nevertheless, kirk sessions sometimes behaved as if there was some sort of moral right to claim relief. They felt that they needed to make clear that some payments were only temporary or conditional, and to try to minimise future supplications for assistance, even though all their payments were entirely within their own gift. To some extent this may simply reflect a practical concern about how many claims they would have to deal with. But given that saying 'No' was always an option for them, it must also reflect a sense that they had real and fundamental obligations to the poor, and that for relief to be effective they had to manage those obligations efficiently.

Non-poor Expenditure

Not all of the kirk sessions' resources ended up in the hands of the poor. We have already seen that some parishes operated separate funds for poor relief and for church repair and other ecclesiastical overheads. But in addition to this, were there problems with the diversion of alms funding away from its intended recipient? Rosalind Mitchison has suggested that there was no separate sense of poor funds, and that the poor's money might effectively mean all of a session's resources.[200] While the parishes with very distinct accounts for poor and non-poor funds like Culross and Kilmadock show that this was not always true, there were indeed some examples of general resources being spent on matters unrelated to the poor.[201] Still, even where the ledgers were not kept separate, there was a perceived distinction between the two. Concern about the problem of resources not being spent on the poor suggests that Mitchison's comment that there was 'no sense of misappropriation' may also not tell the full story.[202] Salton Kirk Session passed an act in 1638 stipulating that 'the money off the box shall not be distribut or given to ane other use quhatsoever bot the poor and their use'.[203] Burntisland's Kirk Session requested a refund from the burgh council for items paid for from the poor fund that were unrelated

199 *RPS*, A1575/3/5. See also King, 'Poor Relief and English Economic Development Reappraised', p. 362.
200 Mitchison, 'Making', p. 63.
201 See above, p. 87; CH2/77/1, ff. 134–40 and passim.
202 Mitchison, 'Making', p. 63.
203 CH2/322/1, p. 90.

to welfare: a Bible and communion paraphernalia, suggesting a perception that spending alms-money on such things was inappropriate.[204] And Kirkcaldy Presbytery's inspection of the kirk session minutes of Auchtertool revealed that 'collections for the poore were bestowit a greate part of them upon the reparation of the Kirk', the obvious implication being that this was a fault, and the matter was to be further discussed by the presbytery.[205]

So there was concern about the problem of poor funds not being spent on the poor. And it was not unjustified: Salton's minutes in the 1630s indicate that the act of 1638 was a response to a real problem, as they made payments 'for casting of divettes to the scuill' and other work on the school building, and officers' fees.[206] In Kinnaird the session paid 2s 8d to 'the smyth for mending of the bell chayne' and the clerk's fees, among other non-poor expenditure.[207] Payments for matters unrelated to welfare are also prominent in St Cuthbert's accounts, although they took up a relatively small proportion of overall spending.[208] Some blurriness occurs when we encounter spending on areas that are hard to classify: payments to refugee ministers, for the work of schools and to support students in them were certainly charitable in a sense, though not strictly part of the work of poor relief.[209] So it is clearly the case that not every penny that was raised for relief was being spent on the poor themselves.

However, deviation of funds away from welfare was not just something that the church worried about: many sessions took active steps to avoid it, and were clearly reluctant to allow subversion of the funds. Stirling Kirk Session had achieved a substantial surplus of £341 in the poor fund by January 1605, but they still chose to hold a special collection to fund church repair.[210] Elgin arranged a tax to pay for repairs to the church floor rather than raiding the poor fund, and stenting was also used for repair in Midcalder and St Cuthbert's.[211] In Monimail, the larger than usual repair sum of £20 for mending and pointing the kirk was paid from the box but it was then 'to be stentit'.[212] They might not have worried too much about minor repair expenses, but wanted to avoid large dents in the welfare fund caused by church repair. Dundee's Kirk Treasurer's Accounts contain some payments on non-poor expenditure, but much of the funding for ecclesiastical expenses came from separate sources and were accounted by

204 CH2/523/1, p. 103.

205 CH2/224/1, p. 301.

206 CH2/322/1, pp. 91–5.

207 CH2/418/1, pp. 2–3. See also Langley, *Worship*, pp. 141–4.

208 CH2/718/60, pp. 57–9, 62–3, 102–3, 137.

209 CH2/548/1, p. 42; CH2/322/1, p. 91; *PKSB*, p. 404; *Canagait*, pp. 52–3; CH2/448/2, p. 231. On a smaller scale, and at the closest intersection of repair expenses and welfare was the spending of money on a lock for the poor box: CH2/718/60, p. 60.

210 CH2/1026/1, pp. 159, 161.

211 CH2/145/1, f. 96r; CH2/266/1, p. 140; CH2/718/1, pp. 214, 221.

212 CH2/548/1, p. 33.

the Kirk Master.[213] Additionally, of course, there were the parishes where funds were kept clearly separate from each other, such as Culross with its markings for P (poor funds) and K (kirk repair).[214] In 1649, reviewing their procedures and concerned to avoid the mixing of poor and other funds, Canongate noted that the poor money should just be spent on the poor, and decided that other monies coming in 'besyde the collections', especially rents, ground annuals, pew-maills, mortcloth and burial silver were to be spent on 'uther pios usus beside the poore'. They even ordered that the poor money accounts 'sall be receavit and debursit at the sight of two deacones who sall sitt with the thesaurer at a table apairt from the sessioun table for avoiding of confusioun and that the discipline be not mard by compting of moneyis and that nothing be givin out of those collections beside the weiklie allowance of the ordinar poore [and other approved poor spending]'.[215] It was unusual for a session to record such detailed arrangements, down to the layout of furniture, but it reflects a wider concern about the intermingling of funding streams.

Another solution to the challenge of keeping the funds separate was through internal loans. For example, Old Deer's contribution to the bursaries for Divinity scholars (a persistent expense in many parishes) was 'borrowit out of the poore folkis silver': poor money could be used for this purpose if necessary, but it must be repaid.[216] St Cuthbert's poor funds loaned, rather than gave, money to the fund for the church loft, and this was permissible only because 'the lord god hes blissit the box of the pure with ane ressonable sowme'.[217] Again, the borrowing rather than transferring of money suggests that there was, in contrast to Mitchison's suggestion, a clear sense of distinct funding streams. Equally, of course, the money could be loaned in the opposite direction: Perth Kirk Session recorded in 1596 that 'the number of the pur dois dayle incres, and few be movit with naturall pitie to help them in the tyme of this great derth and necessitie'. Therefore the separate collection fund for church-repair was 'to be imployit for a certene space to the use and help of the pure quhill sum uther provisione be meid'.[218] A more stony-faced approach was taken in Kilmadock though, where there was no switching of resources from the fund for the church loft even when the poor fund was hit by the problems with coinage in 1640.[219]

The overall picture, then, is a complex one. There was both significant local variation on this aspect of relief funding, and sometimes a flexibility in

213 CH2/218/16, ff. 74r, 107r–v; DCA, Dundee Kirk Master's Account Book, 1651–1723.

214 CH2/77/1, ff. 134–40 and passim. Other examples include Kilmadock, Stirling, and Old Deer.

215 CH2/122/3, pp. 672–3.

216 CH2/1217/33, f. 93r; *COP*, p. 61n.

217 CH2/718/1, p. 76.

218 CH2/521/2, f. 146r.

219 CH2/212/18, p. 8.

how resources were divided up and managed. In some places, matters like church-repair and church officers' fees can be seen as a partial drain on the resources available to the poor. In others, there was either a careful policy of separation, or attempts to keep the subversion of money away from the poor as limited as possible. It was certainly not the case that the money was all lumped together without the strictly welfare-related spending taking any priority. And when we consider the wider aims and responsibilities of the Scottish Reformed Kirk, it would be unrealistic to expect them to neglect the state of the kirks or to leave officers unpaid. But overall, the spending of session resources on matters unrelated to the poor did not have a substantial detrimental impact on the relief programme.

Conclusion

Across lowland Scotland, kirk sessions took poor relief very seriously. They developed well-organised and bureaucratic systems for raising, managing and distributing funds, while also retaining a degree of flexibility. They did not often record policy discussions directly (rather than recording individual decisions), and the records naturally do not include theoretical or ideological debate about poverty and charity of the sort traced in Chapter 1. But there was a clear sense of responsibility and a desire to organise relief and resources effectively over the long term. If the scale and effectiveness of relief was not always consistent, as previous chapters indicated, this reflects difficulties with resources, economic problems, and the gradual development of new forms of ecclesiastical administration after 1560, rather than a lack of intent, concern or competence. Collections formed the basis of a fundraising system which went beyond the purely 'voluntary', and equally kirk session bureaucracies recognised a level of obligation to care for the genuine poor in a sensitive range of ways that catered for their varying needs.

This becomes even more apparent when we consider the Scottish experience against recent research on other poor relief systems. Brian Pullan argued that to dismiss Catholic poor relief efforts as 'essentially casual, ineffective and haphazard' is to ignore evidence of 'ingenuity and effectiveness' in church (rather than secular) relief.[220] The same could be said of kirk sessions, when the evidence of their operations is directly studied. There are also interesting parallels with McIntosh's exhaustive study of poor relief in the small town of Hadleigh in the sixteenth century.[221] It was an 'exceptionally comprehensive and expensive system', offering the 'most complex array of help' during the period, and the sums raised and

[220] Pullan, 'Catholics and the Poor', 21.

[221] McIntosh, *Hadleigh*. With a population of 2400–3300, Hadleigh is rather closer in scale to most Scottish communities than English cities such as London or Norwich.

dispensed were indeed larger than in Scottish towns.[222] But the mechanics and culture of welfare in Hadleigh are reminiscent of many of the themes identified in this chapter: fundraising included formal rates, but these were supplementary to 'voluntary charity', and contributed alongside a range of endowments, gifts and bequests.[223] Hadleigh's chief collector, and assistants (sub-collectors) administered the system, and distributed aid in the form of occasional assistance to a wide body of poor people, plus a smaller number of weekly pensioners. There was assistance with medical and other incidental expenses, and with burial costs. As well as aid in cash form, fuel and clothes might also be provided, although as in Scotland, the direct provision of food was rarer. Hadleigh was rather more active in the care of poor children, but the Scottish system made some similar attempts to encourage boarding, apprenticing, and sometimes employment of poor children and adults.[224] Hadleigh's system, which was 'unusually responsive to the needs of the poor', had many structural and procedural similarities to the Scottish norm. This predates the English Poor Laws of 1598 and 1601, of course, and the parallels should not be pushed too far. But the mechanisms of Scottish poor relief were, although operated by a distinctively Scottish institution in the kirk session, recognisable and functionally comparable within a wider international context of welfare. This may suggest that there is more to be learned by asking more comparative questions in the future. It certainly reinforces the need to take kirk sessions seriously as organisers and providers of welfare.

[222] McIntosh, *Hadleigh*, p. 1.

[223] McIntosh, *Hadleigh*, pp. 5–6. Across England, as in Scotland, fines for offences were also a 'welcome new source of income': McIntosh, *Poor Relief in England*, p. 237.

[224] McIntosh, *Hadleigh*, pp. 40–8. See also Chapter 6 of this book for comparison of the recipients of poor relief.

CHAPTER 6

Who Were the Poor? The Recipients of Relief

Introduction

Who were the beneficiaries of the poor relief devised and managed by the kirk sessions of lowland Scotland? As an inevitable consequence of the wider neglect of post-Reformation Scottish welfare, this question has scarcely been asked by historians.[1] The distributions made have received even less considered attention than kirk sessions' collections, with some ecclesiastical histories offering at least brief evaluation of collection totals but only anecdotal quoting of individual payments to recipients.[2] But it is important that we develop a proper assessment of the pool of recipients not only so that the nature and impact of the welfare itself can be better understood, but also in order to understand more fully the kirk sessions' aims and agenda. There are a number of (overlapping) issues to be considered here: gender patterns or variations in the distribution of relief, the social background or status of recipients, and also their physical and mental state, and age. It is not possible to produce a straightforward breakdown or prosopographical analysis of relief recipients, because we normally have little in the way of biographical details, or life stories behind the assistance provided. Often, all there is to go on is a series of names, meaning that, as is often the case, gender is the subject on which the evidence is clearest.[3] Nevertheless, it is possible to draw some conclusions on the key trends, and one recurring finding is that there was considerable variation between parishes rather than a uniform pattern in the distribution of relief. Both the supply and the demand for poor relief was influenced by local factors and

1 The pre-1650 discussion in *OPL*, pp. 7–19, does not attempt to analyse or break down the recipients of sessional relief (though more detailed discussion is offered for the late seventeenth and eighteenth centuries: chapter 5). Stewart, 'Poor Relief in Edinburgh', especially pp. 10–11, 23–4, offers some careful assessment of distributions although understandably given the article's focus on responses to a specific famine, the composition of the poor is not the focus. Some analysis of 1640s and 1650s Dundee recipients is offered in McCallum, 'Charity and Conflict', pp. 49–52.

2 Di Folco, 'Discipline and Welfare', pp. 177–9; Foster, *Church Before the Covenants*, pp. 81–2; Bardgett, *Scotland Reformed*, p. 116+n.

3 McIntosh, 'Poor relief in Elizabethan English communities'; Goodare, 'Parliament and Society', p. 408.

concerns. This complexity, while challenging for the historian, points to a localised and responsive ecosystem of relief. This chapter therefore offers analysis at the level of individual parishes, as to amalgamate statistics or proportions at a broader level would paper over the distinctiveness of local arrangements, and potentially offer misleading conclusions.

Most kirk sessions divided up their poor relief recipients into two types: regular and irregular, or ordinary and extraordinary. The regular or ordinary poor would receive payments at clearly defined intervals, often weekly or monthly, and there would be a formal list or roll of their names.[4] Unfortunately, these have frequently not survived, because they were kept on separate sheets of paper rather than within the main minutes.[5] In many cases what survives is a record of individual poor people being added to the body of regular poor, rather than a complete list. Extraordinary payments, as the name suggests, were made on a case-by-case basis, in response to a whole range of causes and necessities. Not all sessions followed this model explicitly, and the distinction between the two types of payment was not always sharp. In some parishes, like Kinnaird, there were simply records of payments to the poor, and only analysis of the distribution of payments can reveal who was in regular receipt of relief and who was a one-off recipient. In others, like Perth, some grants were explicitly on a weekly basis while others were one-off. In the 1640s, Dundee operated a highly classified and differentiated programme of relief, with weekly and monthly regular payments to pensioners organised by quarter, as well as extraordinary payments.[6] Even in parishes where the distinction was clearly present throughout the minutes, it was not unusual for a member of the ordinary roll of the poor to receive an extraordinary payment as well for some reason. Nevertheless, there was normally some sense of a distinction between the two, reflecting the fact that some poor people were in need of permanent or semi-permanent assistance, while others, often but not necessarily from humble or 'poor' economic backgrounds, might simply need emergency assistance. The lines between them, however, could only ever be fluid and unstable.

Gender

Studies of relief distribution across early modern Europe have indicated that there was often, though by no means always, a preponderance of

[4] For example, payments were weekly in Perth, Monifieth and Montrose, monthly in Galston, and a combination of the two in St Cuthbert's and Dundee.

[5] For references to poor rolls kept separately to the minutes and not (apparently) surviving, see, for example, CH2/450/1, p. 117; CH2/145/1, f. 89r; CH2/718/1, p. 182; CH2/1026/1, p. 347; CH2/548/1, p. 42. Examples of kirk session minutes with surviving rolls or lists include Montrose (CH2/943/1, pp. 219–24), Lasswade (CH2/47/1, f. 7v), and Aberdeen (CH2/448/2, p. 11).

[6] McCallum, 'Charity and Conflict', p. 49.

female recipients. In many cases around 60%–70% of recipients were female, or sometimes even more.[7] This may have partly reflected more hostile attitudes towards male poor and a sense that older women were more likely to be deserving in some cases, but it was also a consequence of the fact that women were often more likely to be in serious need of supplementary income.[8] This pattern also seems to have held true in Scotland during later years: addressing the later seventeenth and eighteenth centuries Mitchison notes a 'preponderance of women over men' (often with the same 2:1 split, or higher), and in 1680 60% of Aberdeen recipients were female (and the proportion was higher during crises).[9] Towns contained disproportionately large female populations as a result of domestic service, of course, and it has been suggested that in England, at least, rural women might not have been as disadvantaged economically as their urban peers.[10] But broadly speaking, there was a fairly distinct female preponderance amongst relief recipients elsewhere in Europe, and in Scotland during later years. How did the late sixteenth- and early seventeenth-century Scottish system compare?

In some parishes, there was a relatively even gender split amongst the recipients of relief: for example in Old Deer in the 1630s, where in the first accounting year for which records survive, payments were made to 23 women and 25 men, as well as three groups of children (each of which were the bairns of a named man).[11] There was no gender pattern in the frequency of payments; the four most regular recipients comprised two men and two women, and several men and women were among those who received just a single payment over the year. The mean sum received by recipients was also divided fairly evenly along gender lines: the average payment to female recipients was 15s, and to male recipients 17s, and even this small difference is largely a result of one unusually large payment to William Mair. Similarly in Canongate's early records, quarterly distributions went to reasonably large numbers of named individuals, and there was a roughly even gender split among these recipients.[12] Between 1577 and 1590, Perth Kirk Session recorded new admissions of 11 men and 9 women to the ranks of the regular poor (plus one child).[13] Although this

[7] Jutte, *Poverty*, p. 41; Martz, *Poverty and Welfare in Habsburg Spain*, pp. 202, 204; Crossan, *Poverty and Welfare*, pp. 50–1.

[8] Gowing, *Gender Relations*, pp. 55–6; Mitchison, *Coping*, pp. 20–1; *OPL*, p. 93.

[9] *OPL*, p. 92; DesBrisay, 'City Limits', p. 43; DesBrisay, 'Authority and Discipline', pp. 316–17.

[10] DesBrisay, 'City Limits', pp. 39–40; McIntosh, 'Poor relief in Elizabethan English communities', p. 343.

[11] CH2/1217/33, ff. 89v–90v. There was also an exceptional payment of 90s for medical treatment for Andrew Merchant's daughter.

[12] *Canagait*, pp. 52–3, 58, 65–6 (male-female ratios of 26:22, 18:15, and 27:26).

[13] *PKSB*. Here and elsewhere, where a married couple were listed together in the records they have been treated as one male and one female recipient, even if the sum was paid jointly.

tells us about new admissions only, and not necessarily all of them, there is no reason to suppose that this would distort the figures, as it would be odd for the minutes to consistently and deliberately omit male entrants or female entrants.[14] The typical sum granted to both sexes was 12d, but some men received 2s or 3s, while a few women received only 6d or 8d.[15] If evidence from beyond Scotland serves as a guide this may suggest that some payments to men were intended to support their wives or other dependents who remained unmentioned.[16] In any case, the majority of payments were at the typical rate of 12d per week, so the gender imbalance in payment size was fairly minimal. And Perth's irregular payments were also fairly well-balanced: 44 payments to males (including three children), 37 payments to females, plus a child of unspecified gender, and 'Saltcoittis the crepill'.[17] So in some parishes, including towns, there was no significant preponderance of either men or women amongst recipients of relief.

Some other parishes conformed to this pattern but with some variation. For example Lasswade's first recorded distribution, in August 1615, was quite evenly balanced in terms of gender, featuring 12 women and 10 men. However, as in Perth, there was a slightly higher typical payment to men than to women: all but one of the women received 20s (the other getting 30s); six of the men received 30s while only four got the smaller sum of 20s.[18] Again, the larger male-payments might reflect men appearing as the named individual where there were dependents to support. A few years later things were very different: seven men and 18 women received payments in 1617 and five men and 15 women in 1618.[19] By the time of the next lists, in 1626 and 1627, a more roughly even split had returned with eight women and five men receiving payments in both years (the poor of the district of Roslin were listed as a single entry in these years, helping to explain the drop in total numbers).[20] The variations are unexplained, but they do suggest that there was no clear policy to focus relief towards men or women in Lasswade. Similarly Monifieth's records include lists from the early 1600s, and interestingly a lengthy list from 1601 contained 21 women, nine men and three children. The gender imbalance was much less pronounced in a smaller 1604 distribution which included eight women and five men (one of whom was described as 'crippill').[21] During the 1590s Perth's Session made some mass distributions via the hospital masters in

[14] *PKSB*, pp. 102, 109–10. That not all entrants were recorded is further suggested by the fact that a list of weekly poor in 1585 includes individuals not previously referred to as new admissions: pp. 318–19 (this list included six men and eight women).

[15] *PKSB*, p. 356.

[16] McIntosh, 'Poor relief in Elizabethan English communities', p. 342.

[17] *PKSB*, p. 73.

[18] CH2/471/1, f. 7v.

[19] CH2/471/1, f. 18v, 22r.

[20] CH2/471/1, ff. 29r, 31r.

[21] OPR310/1, ff. 103v, 112r.

August: in 1593 these went to eight poor women and four poor men, however in 1595 they went to six poor men, three poor women, and a poor married couple.[22] So there were parishes where female recipients might sometimes become significantly more numerous than male, but not as a long-term pattern or deliberate policy.

Although there were sometimes larger payments to men, it was very rare for men to outnumber women significantly amongst recipients. It is no coincidence that one of the few occasions when this did happen was a time of crisis: in Perth during the plague and scarcity of the mid-1580s there was a special temporary (and secret) distribution of grain to respectable people. Men were dominant among these 'sundrie honest personis . . . quha war aschamit to be put in the roll with common beggeris and yit sustenit great peniuritie'.[23] Presumably these more respectable members of the community (including a heraldic officer, a goldsmith and a skinner), who would not normally be in receipt of any relief but were suffering from the universal shortage of food, were more likely to be heads of household, and so disproportionately male. Men also sometimes noticeably outnumbered women amongst the recipients of individually-named payments in early seventeenth-century St Cuthbert's. This probably reflects the fact that these payments were all irregular and incidental – the regular poor of each part of the parish were simply listed as a group entry rather than as individuals (e.g. the poor of the West Port, or of St Ninian's Row).[24] Male recipients here were more likely to claim extraordinary relief, as suggested by the presence of injured or shipwrecked men, as well as men from elsewhere claiming relief on behalf of their families.[25]

Bervie's account book from the latter part of our period provides one example of a parish where male recipients were consistently more numerous, albeit by a small margin. In the distributions to the ordinary poor that took place every few months from 1648 to 1652, there were always between 18 and 25 adult recipients, and on most occasions there were more male than female recipients.[26] There were a few exceptions, such as July 1651 when 10 women and eight men received, but more often men outnumbered women, occasionally by as many as 16 to eight, or 14 to 10.[27] Overall there were 119 payments to men and 100 to women, although the payment sizes at each distribution tended to be equal.[28] Reasons for poverty are not given, but as these were a group of ordinary recipients, with some new

22 CH2/521/2, ff. 82v, 129v.

23 *PKSB*, pp. 292–3.

24 CH2/718/60, pp. 57–66.

25 CH2/718/60, 57, 59, 104.

26 CH2/34/9, pp. 7–79. There were also frequent payments to a group of bairns, presumably orphans.

27 CH2/34/9, p. 7, 38, 51.

28 For example they all received 13s 4d in December 1648, and nearly all received 24s in December 1650: pp. 16, 47.

names occurring in the lists but fairly low turnover of recipients, it seems most likely that these were considered to be the neediest parishioners whose long-term incomes were considering deserving of supplement by the kirk session. The male majority was certainly not substantial enough to suggest a deliberate policy of favouring poor men as a category.

By contrast, and as in eighteenth-century Scotland, there were several parishes where women routinely and substantially outnumbered men as recipients of normal poor relief. In Montrose, where we have detailed accounts for the early 1640s, there were around 15–20 female recipients each year, 4–7 male recipients, plus a few children (whose gender was not normally mentioned).[29] So around two-thirds of all recipients were women, with only a handful of adult males receiving relief in a given year. This is a significant imbalance, although it is not large enough to indicate a conscious decision to target relief mainly towards women, or a feeling that men should not be supported. It may well have reflected local patterns of need, especially as the sizes of payments indicated a close attention to individual necessities. Most recipients got 4s, 6s or 8s, and payments were tailored to circumstances. Catring Lyell consistently received just 3s per week, less than anyone else, while Margaret Boill got 10s per week. The situation of these two women must have been very different. And of course, circumstances change: Margaret Malton got 8s in 1641 and 1642, but this was reduced to 6s in 1643, and by 1645 her name was crossed off the list (but not with the 'X' which marked the deceased). For her at least, conditions might have been improving in the mid-1640s. Montrose was a burgh, and Dundee also saw a preponderance of female recipients, but in rural parishes too women sometimes predominated.[30] In Kinnaird, a handful of women dominated the relief spending as the primary recipients of regular and substantial payments.[31] Still, James Poullar received the fourth-highest total amount in relief in the mid-1630s (behind Euphame Patton, Janet Billie and Janet Mitchell – both Janets being described as bedfast). And amongst all recipients of relief, including minor or one-off payments, as in Montrose, around two-thirds were female: a significant but not extreme imbalance. And in Dunbarney in the late 1600s, women tended to outnumber men noticeably in the list of the most needy, while the ratio was closer to being even in the wider list of poor people receiving less substantial or intermittent relief.[32] Larger burgh parishes might also focus relief disproportionately on women, for example there were female majorities (though

[29] CH2/943/1, pp. 219–24. Where there is a reference to an adult and their offspring (e.g. 'Jeales Lepper and hir daughter') the adult alone has been counted.

[30] McCallum, 'Charity and Conflict', pp. 49–51.

[31] CH2/418/1, pp. 1–25.

[32] In 1607, eight women and four men were on the 'criple and blind' list, with 11 women and eight men in the wider list; in 1609 the most needy included six women and three men, while the wider list had 13 women and 10 men: CH2/100/1, pp. 14–15, 43 (figures exclude children and a few unclear entries).

with significant numbers of men present, too) in Stirling's new admissions to the regular poor, and Aberdeen's list of quarterly poor, around the turn of the seventeenth century.[33]

Haddington's records include a brief but detailed run of minutes including relief payments from December 1629 to June 1631, enabling us to take a close snapshot of recipients in 1630, and in particular the frequency as well as size of payments. Over the year, about £200 was paid to 99 recipients, in the form of 150 payments at a mean of 27s.[34] However many of these recipients received only single payments, including both groups of outsiders (such as 'ane company of Irish people') and named local poor.[35] Overall, 70 recipients just received one payment, while only 14 received three or more payments. These more frequent recipients were fairly matched in gender terms: there were six men and eight women, each receiving roughly similar average payments. When the whole range of identifiable recipients is considered, however, a gender pattern emerges, with 53 women and 32 men receiving payments: so as in some other parishes women were around two-thirds of the total body of recipients. The mean individual payment to women was 25s, with the mean total received by women at 38s; for men the mean figures were 29s and 50s, respectively. The male mean total was higher partly because they received slightly more payments per person on average (1.7 rather than 1.5). Overall then, among the whole body of recipients in Haddington in 1630, women were more numerous but men received slightly higher payments on average. However the gender balance was more even among that select group of poor who received several payments over the year.

Monimail's records for the early 1640s offer a snapshot of rural relief payments to individuals who were not on the roll of regular poor (with a few exceptions: for the most part payments to regular recipients are not listed).[36] Again there was a gender imbalance, with twice as many female irregular recipients (22) as male irregular recipients (10), and women received slightly higher payments on average (32s as opposed to 24s). Substantial sums were also paid to distressed Irish people, and there were various payments relating to children, the disabled and the burial costs of the poor. The regular female recipients (Isobel Wishart, known as 'the blind wyff', and Margaret Allane, 'one of the poore') who did receive payments minuted by the scribe tended to get the largest sums.[37] However the biggest single category of recipient was a series of named or unnamed women who received one (or at most two) payments of anything from 10s (or occasionally even less) to a few pounds. One regular male recipient,

[33] CH2/1026/1, pp. 27, 67, 73, 107 and passim; CH2/448/2, p. 11.
[34] CH2/799/1, ff. 307r–317v.
[35] CH2/799/1, f. 316v.
[36] CH2/548/1, pp. 29–46.
[37] CH2/548/1, pp. 40, 42, 45.

William Wilson ('on[e] of our poor'), later described as a 'seik poore man' got a series of significant payments, which culminated in 44s paid for his kist.[38] Monimail's provision of relief to its own parishioners was disproportionately focused both in frequency and in payment size on the female poor.[39] But as elsewhere, men were far from absent or marginal among the ranks of the beneficiaries of relief.

In the Canongate, where some of the earliest evidence on poor relief in Scotland was discussed in Chapter 2, the closing years of our period offer unusually detailed lists of distributions to the poor. This is partly because in 1649, the kirk session became concerned about managing relief administration separately from other ecclesiastical finances, leading to the provision of a separate volume listing payments to the poor.[40] From August 1649, until military events disrupted business in September 1650, there are very detailed lists of irregular payments made individually each week, and block payments to the ordinary poor.[41] As in Haddington, there were very frequent irregular payments over the year but to a wide rotating body of recipients.[42] There were 294 payments, normally in the range of 12s to 30s, with 20s or 24s being fairly typical. 97 recipients received just a single payment over the year, while 36 received 2–4 payments, and just three men and three women received 5 or more times. The two most frequent recipients were female, Margaret Penicook and Captain Trotter's wife (perhaps

38 CH2/548/1, pp. 31, 36, 39.

39 The picture was slightly more complicated for outsiders to the parish: amongst the distressed Irish contingent there were nine women and six men (including one married couple), but four of the five outsider poor from England, Scotland, or mainland Europe were men.

40 This volume is CH2/122/48. In January 1649, it was agreed relief should be accounted separately from other expenses, and that separate and specific warrants would be needed for all payments other than the ordinary poor's weekly pensions (CH2/122/3, pp. 672–3). In July (CH2/122/4, p. 4) the deacons were asked to keep a separate book for distributions (i.e. CH2/122/48). An earlier book of accounts, CH2/122/29 contains relief payments from 1637 onwards, but these are recorded alongside payments for ecclesiastical expenses, church repair, officers' fees and the like, and many of the other non-specific payments (predominantly to male recipients) might be related to these rather than relief (see, for example, pp. 62, 64), making them much less suitable for analysis here.

41 CH2/122/48, pp. 2–43. After the disruption, the lists resume in late 1650 (CH2/122/48, pp. 44–6 and passim), but are less detailed (and busy) and reflect a kirk session recovering from a severe external shock (for more on this see Chapter 4 of this book). Therefore the analysis of recipients here focuses on August 1649 to September 1650.

42 For this analysis of recipient patterns, certain types of relief-related expenditure have been excluded in order for meaningful comparisons to be made on the key issues around gender and the demographics of relief. For example the figures exclude large payments to bursars and other students (e.g. p. 20), fees for apprenticing a poor lad (p. 39), assistance to deposed ministers (e.g. p. 37) and burial expenses for otherwise unidentified poor folk (e.g. p. 25). This also excludes strangers to the parish and recipients of unspecified or unclear gender. Stranger men and stranger women were fairly even in number, but payments to men from outside the parish tended to be noticeably larger, averaging about 100s but often up to £10, while female stranger payments averaged 50s.

widow) and her four bairns, with nine and eight payments respectively, at a mean of about 22s. However Jon Neill, Jon Cunningham and William Greinsheillis received seven, six and five payments, respectively, with Bessie Napier the only other frequent recipient with five payments over the year. Equally, among those who received only once, there was a roughly even split of 50 women and 44 men (plus three children as recipients in their own right). However among the intermediate group who received two, three or four payments over the year, women outnumbered men by 26 to 10. Overall then, women comprised nearly 60% of the individual irregular adult recipients. They received slightly more payments on average (a mean of three per person, in contrast to 1.5 per male recipient), while the mean payment size both for men and for women was 30s, although individual sums paid varied greatly because these were responses to immediate circumstances.

The ordinary poor received each week without being named individually as the deacons distributed their alms directly, and they were accounted for as a single entry. There were normally between 27 and 33 of these in 1649–50, receiving around £11 per week at a typical mean of around 8s–10s per person. Fortunately they were listed with their names in the main session minutes in October 1649.[43] There were 28 ordinary poor at this point, 21 women, five men and two children. Women typically got 6s and men 10s weekly. So unlike the roughly 60:40 female preponderance amongst irregular recipients, women more substantially dominated the ordinary poor roll, while receiving smaller average payments. These ordinary poor also sometimes received additional irregular payments in response to particular need.[44] So there was a sizeable group of poor women in the Canongate who received 6s weekly (or sometimes more), and a few men who received weekly support of more like 10s. Beyond this, there were well over a hundred other local individuals who received occasional assistance by the kirk session, in quantities that varied greatly: these individuals were more evenly balanced in gender and required assistance for various reasons at certain points in the year but not, in the kirk session's view, as a weekly supplement to income. It may well be that because irregular payments to parishioners were more dependent on circumstances and the needs of a wider group of poor or relatively humble people, there was both less focus by Canongate Kirk Session on particular demographics, and less predictable or standardised patterns of demand for support.

Overall, kirk sessions did not focus their relief narrowly on either men or women, and nor was there a standard or uniform approach. Relief was sometimes quite evenly split between men and women, while sometimes it more closely matched the systems in some other countries and later in Scotland where roughly two-thirds or more were female (although

[43] CH2/122/4, pp. 19–20.
[44] CH2/122/48, p. 26.

more detailed research on the later period would be needed to develop the comparison). Interestingly, recent research has indicated that in the earlier stages of English poor relief, especially during the sixteenth century, women did not yet 'greatly outnumber men', and in the Elizabethan countryside there were sometimes male majorities.[45] The contrast between a less consistent and less pronounced female preponderance (and sometimes an even gender balance) in late sixteenth- and early seventeenth-century Scotland, and the apparently more clear-cut and persistent female majority by the eighteenth century, suggests that a similar shift may have taken place north of the border.[46] Further research would be required to judge how far this related to socio-economic trends as opposed to kirk session decision-making, but it is clear that from 1560 to 1650 there was no general intent to exclude male recipients, or to focus relief primarily on poor women and widows as the overarching priority. It is complexity rather than a straightforward gender pattern that emerges from the session minutes and accounts. Equally, the variations between parishes do not neatly correspond with geographical boundaries, or with the distinction between urban and rural communities.[47] The patterns that do emerge may have been filtered by kirk sessions' biases and priorities, but overall they seem more of a reflection of complex local patterns of necessity in combination with the gendering of poverty whereby early modern women were generally more likely to find themselves in need, but not by consistent or predictable margins. In its range and scope, kirk session relief also reflected the fact that anyone might find themselves in need.

Occupation or Social Status

The gender of a poor relief recipient will almost always be known from their name: however it is much less straightforward to assess other issues in the demographics of relief. Where a recipient is simply listed with their name (or simply with a disability, illness or related characteristic), their social background or occupation will not be readily discernible. Of course, at the time of being granted relief these individuals were considered needy in some sense, but it would be misleading to assume that they were always therefore from a lowly socio-economic background.[48] A revealing example of this is provided by the phraseology used by Perth Kirk Session's scribe when referring to a 'pure gentillman'.[49] In fragile early modern economies, a wide range of people might find themselves in need of assistance.

In a small number of cases, we know for certain that the recipient of

45 McIntosh, *Poor Relief in England*, pp. 263–4; McIntosh, 'Poor relief in Elizabethan English communities', pp. 342–3.

46 *OPL*, p. 92.

47 Cf. McIntosh, 'Poor relief in Elizabethan English communities', p. 345.

48 Healey, *First Century of Welfare*, pp. 116–18.

49 CH2/521/6, p. 132.

relief was not from a conventionally 'poor' background. Amongst the Canongate recipients in the mid-1560s there were several individuals with trades listed, such as bonnetmaker, cordiner, plasterer ('sperginar').[50] In Perth, Thomas Sutar, a blind former fuller, was assisted, and the secret distribution of grain discussed previously included a skinner and a goldsmith among others (although equally the fact they were ashamed to be listed in the general poor roll tells us something about the likely social composition of the roll).[51] Individual payments were also made to some baxters and a cordiner.[52] Of course, as Thomas Sutar's case makes particularly explicit, men listed with a craft may often have been poor 'decayed' burgesses, no longer able to work: similarly in Aberdeen William Findlay 'fermorar' was described as 'ane puir agit man' and enrolled for 20s weekly.[53] This need not always have been the case, however, especially where a payment was temporary or one-off.[54] Edinburgh's records provide examples of craftsmen who were assisted but definitely still capable of work: a wobster named William Galespie was given 20s but instructed to return to his craft, while Thomas Browne, 'bonetmakar', was given 40s but warned not to be 'chargeable' thereafter.[55]

In many cases, however, it is not clear whether the burgess in question was decayed, or otherwise no longer able to work, or simply receiving some extra assistance. For example, 'James Nepar merchand being seik' received assistance in Bervie and was referred to as one of the ordinary poor.[56] He may have been long-term sick (and perhaps old), but this is not recorded. And Canongate recipients included an armorer and a poor bonnetmaker called Alexander Paterson who received one 20s payment, as well as a second bonnetmaker called Jon Ker who received several payments that were later followed by payments to his widow.[57] He might therefore have been rather more 'decayed' than Paterson. What is clear is that relief was not restricted to those from humble social origins: established craftsmen might be granted assistance if thought appropriate, whether because of long-term incapacity or shorter-term problems. Equally, such individuals were a minority amongst relief recipients: there is little to suggest that kirk sessions were disproportionately interested in assisting respectable burgesses and professionals who had fallen on hard times. Given that this was

50 *Canagait*, pp. 52, 58, 65; *DSL*, 'Spargenar'.

51 *PKSB*, pp. 109–10; 292–3. This would correspond with patterns elsewhere in Europe, where secret or inconspicuous assistance was given to middling sorts who had fallen on hard times: van Leeuwen, Meerkerk & van Voss, 'Provisions for the elderly', p. 11.

52 *PKSB*, pp. 155, 175, 178, 301.

53 CH2/448/2, p. 37; see also CH2/521/7, ff. 82v, 129v.

54 E.g. CH2/550/1, p. 51 (a tailor and cordiner in Glasgow); CH2/418/1, p. 58 (a merchant from Kilmarnock, assisted in Kinnaird); CH2/624/2, p. 162 (40s 'to Robert Lindsay timberman for his support' in Anstruther).

55 CH2/450/1, pp. 13, 73.

56 CH2/34/9, pp. 7, 17 (quote).

57 CH2/122/48, pp. 4, 8, 11, 25, 40.

often the focus of burgh councils' much more limited interest in relief, and considerng the overlap between council and kirk session membership, and indeed the generally high social standing of elders and deacons, this points to the kirk sessions' welfare mission as being distinct in its emphasis on poverty itself, not the respectability of their peers.[58]

Indeed, it is highly likely that in most cases the recipient of relief was from a more humble background, perhaps broadly analogous to the main group of eighteenth-century recipients identified by Mitchison as 'craftsmen, cottars and those in work with low pay', such as labourers, servants, small traders and the like.[59] Their situations were more often financially precarious, and they constituted the majority of the population. Scribes were less likely to indicate that an individual was, for example, a labourer or a servant, than, say, a merchant or a cordiner. In their recording of church discipline, kirk session minutes also tend to be more likely to take the trouble to record that an individual was a merchant, laird, goldsmith or notary, for example, than more humble (and more common) occupations. Such references are very rare: for example in Stirling there was assistance for a 'crippill sometime servant': the occupation is recorded here presumably simply to indicate that she was no longer able to work in her former occupation.[60] Poor relief was open to individuals from a range of social backgrounds, but many were from the lowlier trades and the labouring or serving classes that were most likely to fall from 'poverty' in the sense of lower socio-economic status, into 'poverty' in the sense of dependency on relief.

Disability, Incapacity and Illness

People suffering from disabilities, serious illness, or other physical incapacity were obviously particularly likely to require assistance from kirk sessions. This was often a result of an unspecified disease or physical medical condition. Various payments in Edinburgh for example, were specifically for the duration of the recipient's ill health (for example 'during thair seckness *onlye*', or 'and no ford[er]'): they were not simply poor people who happened to be sick.[61] Alexander Carpenter's payments were stopped because he was now 'well conwellessit'.[62] Similar temporary relief was provided in St Andrews, and in one case an augmentation of 2s to already-existing relief payments was provided for the duration of the illness.[63] In Old Kelso in 1646, 'Jeane Ker [was] ordained to get for hir support in tyme of hir sicknes

[58] McCallum, *Reforming*, pp. 160–5. See Chapter 8 of this book, for discussion of burgh authorities and relief.

[59] *OPL*, p. 94.

[60] CH2/1026/1, p. 193.

[61] CH2/450/1, pp. 9 (quotation, my emphasis), 15, 18, 30 (quotation).

[62] CH2/450/1, p. 25.

[63] *RStAKS*, i, p. 383, ii, p. 896.

12s and that sa long as she shall be thought misterfull of it'.[64] Early rural provision was also alert to the needs of the sick: in 1575 Monifieth made a contribution 'to Jhone Walcar beand seik with the gravell'.[65] In 1586 Glasgow arranged a special collection for a poor man 'for his present releif being ydropik' (i.e. suffering from hydropsy), and in Yester a week's collection was simply passed to a sick individual.[66] So some recipients got relief specifically because of some form of disease.

People with long-term disabilities were also prominent amongst the recipients of relief. The most common terms used in relation to what we term disability were 'blind' or 'cripple'. Blind people appear disproportionately often in the records, presumably both because blindness was such a major blow to employment prospects in the early modern period, and because many other forms of physical disability were generically covered by the catch-all term 'cripple'.[67] The latter term is rarely if ever expanded upon, and so must be assumed to cover most forms of physical disability. References to specific or named disabilities other than blindness are very infrequent, although on occasion the descriptor 'dumb' is used for recipients, perhaps to refer to mental illness of some sort rather than inability to speak.[68] More direct reference to mental illness is found in Canongate, for example, where 'a daft poore man Rolland Thomsone' (also referred to as a 'fool') was helped.[69] The assistance to 'a woman troubled in spirit in hew watts close' may also fit into this category, and there were references to a 'poore distracted woman' at various points in Canongate relief payments.[70] In Aberdeen in 1603 10s was given to Thomas Baxter 'ane puir furious boy', recommended by testimonial from the burgh of Perth.[71] Other recipients apparently suffered from some sort of long-term and/or incapacitating illness: some are described as bedfast, or 'disseased of bodie', and while the specific medical problems are generally impossible to identify, the economic consequences of these conditions in early modern Scotland are all too obvious.[72]

How prominent were such individuals amongst the recipients of kirk session relief? In some parishes, numerous recipients were designated as blind, bed-bound or otherwise incapacitated. For example, in Old Deer several of the recipients were incapable of work: a few men and women

[64] CH2/1173/1, p. 297.

[65] OPR310/1, f. 29r.

[66] CH2/550/1, p. 67; CH2/377/1, p. 29.

[67] For examples of the blind being assisted see CH2/122/48, pp. 40; CH2/296/14, f. 3v; CH2/1173/1, p. 172.

[68] CH2/418/1, p. 19; CH2/548/1, p. 44.

[69] CH2/122/48, pp. 31, 94.

[70] CH2/122/48, pp. 57–9, 80; CH2/122/29, p. 433.

[71] CH2/448/2, p. 20. This must correspond to the meaning of 'furious' as 'Of persons: Mad, insane': *DSL*.

[72] See, for example, Bervie Kirk Session, CH2/34/9, pp. 3, 10, 12 ('cripple'), 73 (bedfast); Dalziel Kirk Session: CH2/462/34, p. 19 ('disseased of bodie').

were labelled as 'bedfast', and a few others were described as sick.[73] However, the majority of men and women were listed without any reference to specific causes of poverty. While the absence of terms like 'bedfast' or 'seik' should not be taken to imply that recipients were not suffering any physical problems at all, it is most likely that the majority of Old Deer's recipients did not require assistance primarily because of major incapacity. Similarly in Perth, a few of the recipients were described as disabled, sick or injured, but the vast majority were not.[74] In Monifieth's distribution lists only the occasional recipient was described as 'crippill' or similar.[75] In Aberdeen there were several incapacitated recipients, such as Jonet Reid (who was blind), and Margaret Schand, described as 'creppill and brunit of ane of hir handis unhable to work for hir leving', and in Pencaitland 'ane impotent man'.[76] Equally such designations did not dominate, and in other cases widowhood and/or parenthood appears to be the more likely cause of poverty.[77]

In Haddington in 1630 there was a small but significant group of blind or otherwise disabled recipients. Three of the 53 female recipients were blind, two of whom received two payments over the year and there were two blind men among the 32 male recipients, each receiving a single payment. The label 'creple' was applied to six recipients, one of whom was a child, described as 'ane creple barne on ane barrow', who received 6s and was not mentioned again suggesting that he was most likely being taken through the parish seeking charity.[78] The handful of other 'creple' men and women all received single payments rather than regular support, although they were named and in one case described as 'in Byres', suggesting that they were local.[79] Thus around one in ten of Haddington's recipients was disabled, although they did not receive the largest sums or most frequent payments. However, in Montrose it is much less clear what proportion of recipients were incapacitated in some way. The fact that such characteristics were almost never mentioned (the exception being a blind boy – whose name was not given and perhaps not known) makes it probable that the scribe was not recording labels such as 'blind', 'creple', 'seik' and so on as a matter of course.[80] There could have been a large number of disabled recipients, a handful, or very few. But this is fairly unusual: in most parishes it seems clear that the incapacitated, disabled or

[73] CH2/1217/33, ff. 89v–90v.

[74] *PKSB.*

[75] OPR310/1, f. 112r.

[76] CH2/448/2, pp. 24, 30; CH2/296/14, f. 3v.

[77] CH2/448/2, pp. 11, 42 (Elspet Crombie, widow, who was continued in her previous grant of 20s weekly in the interests of her young children).

[78] CH2/799/1, f. 310r.

[79] CH2/799/1, f. 312v. For Byres' location within the parish of Haddington, see <http://canmore.org.uk/site/54869> (last accessed 14 December 2016).

[80] CH2/943/1, pp. 219–24.

long-term sick were a significant but hardly dominating presence amongst the recipients.[81]

On occasion, however, disabled people might make up a very substantial part of a parish's relief beneficiaries. In Galston during the 1590s, as we have seen, the session's funds were primarily spent on a blind woman, a 'creple' woman and a man with no stated cause of poverty.[82] In Dunbarney, when the poor were ranked in 1607, the first grouping was 'the criple and blind'. The fact that this was used synonymously with the 'maist misterfull' (most needy) or 'first rank' in subsequent years indicates a clear sense that the highest priority here amongst the poor were the most severely incapacitated and disabled.[83] Although the lower ranks tended to include more individuals, and many people who were not disabled or ill were assisted, the 'creple and blind' were clearly considered the most prominent category of poor people. And in Kinnaird there were two 'bedfast' women amongst the handful of very regular recipients of relief, and a significant number of disabled and blind people amongst the wider pool of recipients.[84] So some rural parishes, though not all as indicated by Monifieth and Old Deer, were particularly likely to focus their resources on the physically incapacitated.[85] This could well be a result of patterns of necessity in urban and rural parishes, the latter of which may have suffered fewer problems relating to the economic cycle and short- to medium-term un(der)employment, as well as fewer claimants visiting or passing through the parish. In any case, just as there were no parishes focusing exclusively or almost entirely on women or any one social group, all kirk sessions extended their relief well beyond the physically incapacitated, even if they were sometimes felt to be the foremost group amongst the needy and were often a substantial presence in alms-distribution.

Age

The specific ages of poor relief recipients were almost never recorded.[86] However from what we know about early modern poverty more generally,

81 Temporary incapacity might also be a significant factor: see, for example, the discussion of Edinburgh in Chapter 5 (p. 161) where several recipients were explicitly assisted only for the duration of their sickness.

82 See above, ch. 3.

83 CH2/100/1, pp. 14–15, 19–20, 24, 26, 28, 43.

84 CH2/418/1, pp. 1, 8, 19, 55.

85 As noted above, the more urban parish of St Cuthbert's also made many payments to people who were injured, sick or disabled, although these were irregular payments only as the regular poor in St Cuthbert's were anonymous.

86 An exception is the 'Poore Bairnes' and other mentions of poor children's ages in Aberdeen's records (CH2/448/4, pp. 8–9), although as these are children the specific ages are less helpful to the historian. A Perth recipient in 1595 was recorded to be 'thriescor ten yeiris and above': CH2/521/2, f. 129v, but this is an exceptional level of detail on age.

age and the life-cycle must have been significant factors in poverty and necessity.[87] Of course, given that some (but nowhere near all) recipients were referred to as being children or elderly, many recipients were likely adults of prime working age. This is confirmed for certain where we have references to recipients being the parents of 'bairns' (or similar wording).[88] Indeed people who were explicitly recorded as being the parents of young children were sometimes very prominent in the distribution lists.[89] But even where parenthood was not overtly recorded, a substantial number of other recipients must have been neither children nor particularly elderly, though of course the margins of old age were not fixed or precise.

Old age must have been a major factor in some people's poverty. Although the word 'agit' or similar was sometimes used in the kirk session records, beyond this elderly people are not straightforward to identify because their necessities were less likely to be simplistically linked by the kirk session to a single condition (such as blindness), and because of subjectivity and variability over the definition of the 'aged'.[90] That word and its variants were very often used to describe recipients, but it would be risky to assume that the absence of such designations by itself indicates that a recipient was young or middle-aged.[91] And of course old age – unlike, say, blindness – would not so certainly lead to poverty. In some cases old age is possibly implied by other designations, such as the 'bedfast' women of Kinnaird.[92] Where people were referred to as 'agit', however, their old age and associated physical or mental problems were likely perceived by kirk sessions as particularly significant factors in their poverty. Such recipients occasionally dominated distribution lists, such as in Perth in 1595.[93] Aberdeen Kirk Session was unusual in sometimes including 'Aged persones' as a separate category in listings of regular relief recipients.[94] Overall, older people were clearly a significant category amongst the recipients of relief, although – as with the other factors discussed in this chapter – rarely a dominant or exclusive group.

Children are rather easier to identify in the records of poor relief. Across early modern Europe, they were prominent amongst those in need of poor relief, and Scotland was no exception.[95] Children feature frequently in the

87 Houston, *Social Change*, pp. 235–6; Jutte, *Poverty*, pp. 36–7, 40; Healey, *First Century of Welfare*, pp. 174–9.

88 See, for example, CH2/448/2, pp. 11, 42, 43; CH2/1217/33, pp. 219, 224; *RStAKS*, ii, p. 926; *Dundonald*, p. 118. See also discussion of Andrew Lathangie in Chapter 7, p. 199, and the cases discussed above in this chapter where working-age was implied.

89 For example CH2/448/4, pp. 8–10.

90 Thane, 'Social Histories of Old Age and Aging', p. 98.

91 See for further examples of the many 'agit' (or similarly designated) recipients CH5/521/2, f. 82v; *PKSB*, pp. 106; CH2/718/60, p. 60; CH2/418/1, p. 19.

92 CH2/418/1, p. 1.

93 CH2/521/7, f. 129v.

94 CH2/448/4, p. 7.

95 Jutte, *Poverty*, pp. 36–9; McIntosh, *Hadleigh*, pp. 83–105; *OPL*, pp. 92–3.

distribution of ecclesiastical relief, either as recipients in their own right, or alongside their parents (normally unnamed).[96] Parents with several children, such as the woman with 'fyve bairns' helped by Perth Kirk Session, were particularly likely to need assistance.[97] Children were a significant presence in the Canongate distribution lists from 1649–50. Several recipients were listed with their children, such as Captain Patrick Trotter's wife who was described as having four bairns when first mentioned, or Margaret Leslie 'with hir small bairnes'.[98] Canongate children were also listed as recipients in their own right, both amongst the ordinary poor (Durward's bairn and William Fiddes' bairn, plus William Toures who was added to the poor roll in September 1649) and as recipients of irregular payments (such as William Lamb 'with a cancer in his arme').[99] In Haddington, however, the only mention of a child amongst the 1630 recipients was the anonymous 'creple barne on ane barrow' which may well point to many of the named poor having children who are not mentioned in the records, as it seems unlikely that none of nearly 100 poor adults assisted that year were parents.[100]

Children were probably involved more often than is recorded.[101] Poor adults may well have had children despite being listed as if they were the sole recipient of the alms payment. Certainly, children were sometimes explicitly named as a factor in someone's poverty, such as William Galespie in Edinburgh (see above), and John Forgushill, who had lost the trade through which he 'sustenit his small bairnes', and there were probably other cases where the presence of children was (silently) the reason for a recipient's poverty.[102] In other cases, payments were made to an adult and their children together, sometimes because of a deceased or absent spouse. For example, a collection was arranged in Glasgow for John Maxwell 'for the releiff of him and his puir mitherles barnis', and in Aberdeen 20s per quarter was granted to Oliver Bowes' widow for the support of her children.[103] Also in Aberdeen, 'poor bairns' was sometimes a separate category amongst the roll of the poor: those of Futtie quarter in 1620, for example, were listed and named (with their ages) as the primary recipients even though the relief was paid to their mothers.[104] In 1640s Monimail, although most of the payments went to individuals (as noted

[96] See, for example, OPR310/1, f. 103v; *PKSB*, p. 89; CH2/718/60, p. 62; CH2/943/1, pp. 219–24.
[97] CH2/521/7, f. 82v.
[98] CH2/122/48, pp. 5, 6, 40.
[99] CH2/122/4, pp. 19–20; CH2/122/48, pp. 5, 29.
[100] CH2/799/1, f. 310r.
[101] McIntosh, *Poor Relief in England*, p. 264.
[102] *Dundonald*, p. 118. See Jutte, *Poverty* p. 37 for the significance of parenthood as a factor in poverty.
[103] CH2/550/1, p. 321; CH2/448/2, p. 11.
[104] CH2/448/4, p. 8.

above, more often female than male) who were not identified as parents, two large payments were made to Agnes Wilkie 'to help to intertain hir child because the father was out in the publick service'.[105] An unnamed poor woman's bairns received £4 from St Cuthbert's Kirk Session in 1610, and Old Deer made a series of payments in the 1630s to Marjorie Innes, which are followed in the records by payments to her (presumably now orphaned) bairns.[106]

Orphans or foundlings were indeed an obvious and very prominent group of young recipients. The financial assistance provided in such cases could be very sizeable indeed, compared with regular relief payments. In St Cuthbert's £6 of income from fines was paid to a foundling, and in Old Deer Andrew Fyvie was to receive regular payments for the weekly sustenance of 'ane poore chyld' (from the phrasing, clearly not his own).[107] In 1626 Lasswade Kirk Session paid £4 to John Lasone for an orphan in his care, and Dundee stumped up £3 4s to pay for board and fuel to support the fostering out of 'William Swanns motherles infant', as well as 12s for food.[108] Large sums were often provided in St Cuthbert's, where 80s was granted on 25 August 1608 towards the support of 'the bairn castin [cast away] in the West Port', and the following year £7 was paid to 'the woman 'that hes the fund bair[n]', followed by numerous similarly large payments. A decade later, Janet Jenkinson received payments 'for the keiping of bairnes'.[109] Kirk sessions were keen to encourage existing channels of informal care and support.[110] Overall, children who found themselves in poverty or lacking care for a variety of reasons were a very significant group among the beneficiaries of relief in Scotland.

A related group of recipients were poor scholars and students.[111] While it is beyond the scope of this book to explore the kirk sessions' efforts in the educational sphere, they would not necessarily have recognised too sharp a distinction between education and charity in the Kirk's vision of a godly social order.[112] Kirk sessions were concerned with educational standards among the poor, and consequently made efforts to instruct them (such as in St Andrews, where hospital inmates were to be catechised regularly at the session's direction and expense), and to examine their religious knowledge.[113] They also provided charitable assistance to individual poor scholars, such as the shipwrecked scholar aided by St Cuthbert's Kirk Session at

[105] CH2/548/1, pp. 35, 39.

[106] CH2/718/60, p. 65; CH2/1217/33, ff. 90r–104r.

[107] CH2/718/60, p. 65; CH2/1217/33, f. 94v.

[108] CH2/471/1, f. 30r; CH2/1218/16, f. 74r.

[109] CH2/718/60, pp. 58, 60–4, 100, 12.

[110] On support for foundlings and orphans see also *COP*, pp. 309–10.

[111] On schooling in post-reformation Scotland more generally, see Durkan, *Scottish Schools and Schoolmasters*, especially pp. 45–149.

[112] *FBD*, pp. 130–2.

[113] *RStAKS*, ii, pp. 824–5; CH2/145/1, f. 126r; CH2/718/1, p. 163.

the instruction of presbytery.[114] Agnes Lokkart and her son in St Andrews were granted 3s weekly in 1597, specifically to keep him at the school.[115] In Aberdeen, a poor scholar named Andrew Stevin was passed a fornicator's fine directly because he could not afford to buy books, while Perth provided 40s to buy Aristotle's 'Logickes' for a poor student at St Andrews.[116] Perth Kirk Session also passed an act in 1588 granting 4d weekly to each of the twenty poor scholars at the school, and followed this up the next year by providing them with any books they were lacking.[117] In rural Monimail the kirk session paid the schoolmaster 30s 'for twa poor bairnes at the scoole', and later 6s 8d for 'teaching ane poor bairne at the schoole'.[118] This sort of spending was, naturally, a small minority of the church's overall welfare budget, but the maintenance and educational resource needs of Scotland's poor students were not forgotten in the provision of relief.

Conclusion

There was no uniform or textbook approach to dividing up relief among the various categories of poor people assessed here. It would be impossible to pick out the 'typical' recipient of relief, or even to sketch a representative list of recipients: many of the same types of individual would appear on such a list, but in very varying proportions, and not in all cases. Just as recent research has questioned the assumption that English relief saw a sharp narrowing of the range of recipients, or that there was a standardised and consistent approach to eligibility for relief, the Scottish evidence points to a system that supported a diverse and fluid range of individuals.[119] Of course, given the nature and causes of poverty, certain themes were relatively common: children, disability and illness often recur in the records, and more women than men were helped overall. There were some minor geographical patterns or distinctions, such as the tendency of some (though not all) small rural parishes to pay a substantial portion of relief to a small group of disabled or incapacitated men and women. But there was no overall geographical divide or predictor of how relief would be spread across parishioners.[120] There was certainly no sense that the relief should be limited to, or even mainly geared towards, specific or

114 CH2/718/60, p. 58.

115 *RStAKS*, ii, p. 845.

116 CH2/448/2, p. 23; *PKSB*, p. 135.

117 *PKSB*, pp. 404, 425.

118 CH2/548/1, pp. 29, 44.

119 McIntosh, *Poor Relief in England*, p. 295; King, 'Poor Relief and English Economic Development Reappraised', pp. 361, 366–7.

120 It is possible that more specialised local studies addressing poor relief together with the entire demographic and contextual socio-economic life of a parish over generations might offer further nuances on this subject, perhaps drawing on models such as McIntosh, *Hadleigh*, or Wales, 'Poverty, Poor Relief and the Life Cycle'.

stereotypical categories of poor aged widows, orphans, or the physically incapacitated.

A striking – if frustrating – feature of very many relief recipients is the lack of obvious explanation for their poverty. The kirk sessions knew perfectly well why they (and any dependents) needed help, and why they were considered deserving of it, but they rarely communicated this information to historians in their lists of payments. However historians can rule out the possibility that the kirk sessions set out to focus relief on fixed categories of recipient, even in individual parishes, let alone across the country. They did not see their role as providing assistance to decayed but respectable, formerly well-off people (people of similar background to them). Equally, they did not, as the *First Book of Discipline* had suggested they might, focus all their attentions on women (aged and/or widowed), and the disabled or orphaned.[121] Even where there were more women than men, there was almost always a sizeable body of men, and not apparently just old or incapacitated men either. Poverty is very obviously multi-causal, and the kirk sessions could hardly have failed to notice this obvious fact. They focused their relief efforts where they thought they were most needed, and this was in dialogue with the specific contours of poverty in individual parishes. The argument that kirk sessions were responding to (perceived) necessity is developed, and qualified, in Chapter 7, which reflects on the criteria employed by sessions in deciding who was deserving or undeserving of relief.

[121] *FBD*, p. 113.

CHAPTER 7

Who Was Deserving? Decision-making and Discrimination

Introduction

All of the poor people discussed in Chapter 6 were evidently considered by the kirk sessions to be deserving, on some level. But how were such decisions made? What sort of people did the church consider to be deserving, and who did they consider to be undeserving? In addressing these questions, one faces a good deal of historiographical baggage. It is generally emphasised by historians that the Kirk was hostile to the able-bodied, to beggars, to strangers from outside the parish, and it tends to be assumed that relief was therefore focused on the native poor of the parish, and the impotent poor incapable of work, especially the sick, elderly and disabled.[1] As Houston has noted for a later period, 'historians of Scotland have studied exclusion more than provision'.[2] Gordon Donaldson wrote that 'neither the church nor the state believed in helping the able-bodied poor, or unemployed', and Christopher Smout stated that 'it was only by entering [a house of correction] that any able-bodied pauper became entitled to any relief at all'.[3] The consensus seems to be in accord with Jenny Wormald's summation of the church's attitude as reflecting the 'condemnatory face of Calvinism'.[4] Such judgements, however, seem to have been made more on the basis of the prescriptive statements made by both the Kirk and secular authorities about the scourge of groups such as idle and sturdy beggars, rather than on the basis of the individual decisions made about relief by local kirk sessions.[5] Relief and discipline were, of course, two sides of the same coin, and relief that was provided to the deserving was accompanied by harsh treatment of the undeserving. As Frohman puts it, the emphasis

1 Dawson, *Scotland Re-Formed*, pp. 286–7; *OPL*, pp. 13-17; Jutte, *Poverty*, p. 124; Foster, *Church Before the Covenants*, pp. 82–3; Kirk (ed.), *Synod of Lothian and Tweeddale*, p. xxviii. The notion that strangers were generally excluded from kirk session relief is critiqued in McCallum, 'Charity Doesn't Begin At Home'.

2 Houston, 'Poor Relief and the Dangerous and Criminal Insane', p. 453

3 Donaldson, *Scotland*, p. 398; Smout, *History of the Scottish People*, p. 87.

4 Wormald, *Court, Kirk, and Community*, p. 168; cf. Pullan, 'Catholics and the Poor', pp. 16–17, which identifies similarly discriminating and hostile attitudes in Catholic approaches.

5 *OPL*, pp. 13–14.

on the disciplinary aspect in studies of early modern poor relief is 'not so much wrong as one-sided'.[6] But this chapter will argue that, although there was – of course – little or no sympathy for those perceived as lazy, ungodly or immoral, decisions about the worthiness for relief of others were based more on perceived necessity than on pre-conditioned assessments about the inherent worthiness or otherwise of the able-bodied poor, or other abstract groupings.

Official Statements and Hostility to the Undeserving Poor

There was, of course, a great deal of suspicion about and hostility towards sturdy, strange and idle beggars, vagabonds, gypsies, and the like. As Chapter 1 noted, discriminating attitudes and a desire to exclude and punish the idle or undeserving were not new or Protestant inventions. Hostility to these groups had been expressed in parliamentary legislation as far back as the early fifteenth century, and it continued to be a prominent theme in the pronouncements of secular and ecclesiastical authorities, especially as vagrancy problems increased.[7] The first Poor Laws of 1574 and 1579 famously emphasised 'the punisement of strang and ydle beggaris', including 'all personis being haill and stark in body and able to wirk and 'all commoun lauboraris, being personis able in body, leving ydillie and fleing laubour'.[8] The church's initial blueprint for its social policy, the *First Book of Discipline*, emphasised that its authors 'are not Patrones for stubborne and idle beggars . . . whom the Civill Magistrate ought to punish', but instead sought care for 'the widow and fatherlesse, the aged, impotent or lamed', who were unable to work for their living.[9] The implication – though no more than an implication – is that inability to work is the only or at least the defining cause of poverty. Senior church courts also expressed frequent concerns about idle beggars and vagabonds: the Synod of Fife agreed to circulate printed copies of the Privy Council's act against them in 1619, and the General Assembly itself echoed the legislation in its complaint about the 'great number of idle persons without lawfull calling'.[10] Gypsies were a particular concern for governing authorities, and in 1591 the General Assembly petitioned the crown to take order 'the colourit and vagabound Egyptians, quhilk defyles the countrey with

[6] Frohman, *Poor Relief and Welfare*, p. 2.

[7] *RPS*, 1425/3/22; 1426/29; 1450/1/20; Goodare, 'Parliament and Society', p. 412.

[8] *RPS*, A1575/3/5; 1579/10/27. For other secular authorities passing punitive acts against unworthy beggars see, for example, *ERBE 1589–1603*, pp. 18, 162, 186, 195, 379; *ERBG*, 29, 114, 174.

[9] *FBD*, pp. 112–13. Similarly, the section on the election of deacons in the 'Form of Prayers and Administration of the Sacraments etc at Geneva' urged that they should not only be charitable, but also take care that 'the charitie of godlye men be not wasted upon loytrers and ydle vagabondes': Knox, *Works*, iv, p. 176.

[10] CH2/154/1, p. 248; BUK, iii, p. 874.

all maner of abominatioun'; later that decade, Glasgow Presbytery wrote to the laird of Cathcart to banish the gypsies in 1597.[11] In 1609, parliament formally banished them.[12] It should be noted however, that apart, perhaps from gypsies and some of the other specific undesirables named in legislation (like minstrels not in the service of a master), the language is rather ambiguous. Whether someone is 'idle' or a 'vagabond' is, of course, subject to individual interpretation, and even the references to those who are 'able to wirk' directly condemn them only if they make dishonest claims about their situation.

The negative and punitive attitudes expressed by national and by regional authorities were matched in many statements by local religious elites. Numerous examples can be found of presbyteries and kirk sessions condemning the 'idill', vagabonds and stranger beggars and seeking to punish them or remove them from parishes.[13] Sturdy beggars were not to be assisted, and those who lodged or subletted to them were themselves to be punished.[14] It is often difficult to separate this from concern about receiving ungodly, sinful and disorderly characters in general: a parishioner of St Cuthbert's was ordered on pain of banishment not to receive 'beggeris lownes nor harlotts'.[15] This sort of catch-all description for undesirables, and a conflation of vagabonds with more general sinfulness and scandal, was not unusual.[16] There were, however, more statutes and statements of intent on this subject than actual examples of the punishment of sturdy beggars, although this did sometimes happen (again, often alongside a moral offence).[17] It was also common for some kirk sessions to pass orders for the forcible removal of sturdy or strange beggars from the town (or at least the churchyard), or in the case of South Leith for any of them found on a Sunday to be warded until 6pm.[18] Stirling Kirk Session, for example, ordered in the summer of 1600 that 'all uncuth puir and idill beggaris sall remove thame selfis from this congregatione and pas quhair thay war borne'; interestingly by December, possibly influenced by anti-Catholic legislation passed in November, the concern was linked to the 'resorting of uncuth straingaris to this toun

11 *BUK*, ii, p. 780; CH2/171/1/1, f. 81v.

12 *RPS*, 1609/4/32. See also Goodare, *Government*, pp. 263–5; Stewart, 'Poor Relief in Edinburgh', pp. 21–2.

13 Smith, 'Presbytery of St Andrews', pp. 230, 310, 327–8; CH2/224/1, pp. 58–9; CH2/266/1, p. 11; CH2/145/1, f. 89r; CH2/550/1, pp. 195, 197; CH2/799/1, f. 310v.

14 See, for example, *Dundonald*, pp. 312–13; CH2/145/1, f. 98r; CH2/751/1/2, f. 262v.

15 CH2/718/2, p. 362.

16 CH2/471/1, f. 3r; CH2/77/1, f. 26v; CH2/1026/1, p. 282; CH2/122/1, p. 5 ('tua wemen [who] ar Idill vagabonds out of service and scandalous personis'). A national fast in 1639 grouped together 'strong beggers, inordinat livers' (and bemoaned the lack of care for those 'whoe are poore indeed'): Mears *et al.* (eds), *National Prayers: Special Worship Since the Reformation, Volume 1*, p. 366.

17 CH2/145/1, f. 33v; CH2/1026/1, p. 77.

18 CH2/716/1, p. 44; *RStAKS*, ii, p. 652; CH2/751/1/2, ff. 269v.

quha ar suspect of religioun' (and more general fears about 'Jesuistis or seminarie preistis').[19]

There is no doubt, then, that kirk sessions, like other institutions in sixteenth- and seventeenth-century Scotland, were deeply concerned about the threats which vagabonds, sturdy beggars and the like posed to the social and religious health of their parishes. What is rather less obvious is precisely what was meant by these labels. It is significant that many of the condemnations or repressive policies towards them are tied in with their other unpleasant features, as fornicators, troublemakers, sometimes perhaps even as Catholic sympathisers. In such cases it was easy to see how to judge the beggar in question. If they were not apparently guilty of offences other than able-bodied poverty, it would be less obvious how to apply the negative messages emanating from secular and ecclesiastical authorities. The negative attitudes were certainly apparent in the words of the kirk sessions, but the blunt and negative language conceals a more complicated and ambiguous reality. As has been noted for Edinburgh in a later period, 'there was no uniform attitude towards the poor'.[20] It should also be noted that even the higher authorities were not uniformly condemnatory in their discussions of the wandering poor. In 1588, among many perennial complaints and supplications to the crown, the General Assembly lamented: 'what heart touched with a spark of naturall humanity or godly charity, can unbleeding behold the miserable estate of the poor vaiging in great troups and companyes through the countrie without either law or religion'.[21] Such sympathetic language, applied even to ungodly and disorderly wandering beggars of Scotland, should make us more alert to the complexity of ways in which the poor were judged and assessed within individual communities.

Moral and Religious Factors

How then did kirk sessions actually decide who was deserving and who was not deserving? The short answer is that we do not know. By their very nature, and despite their richness, kirk session minutes record decisions, not discussions. Essentially, the historian has to rely on their final verdicts on who should get relief, when and for how long, although as the following sections demonstrate, this can tell us a great deal. What we do know, however, is that the kirk sessions did have considerable information to draw on in making judgements. As Chapter 5 indicated, the deacons, in particular, would assess the needs and circumstances of the poor in the quarters of their parishes. Some incidental references show that poor people submitted applications (including at least some written bills) for support. For

[19] CH2/1026/1, pp. 66, 71, 73; *RPS*, 1600/11/40.

[20] Houston, *Social Change*, p. 269.

[21] *BUK*, ii, p. 724.

example, in Aberdeen in 1603, a widow was admitted to 13s 4d weekly on account of 'hir povertie gryt aige inhabilitie and seiknes as at lenth wes contenit in the said supplicatioun': the phrasing suggests a written text of some sort.[22] A written document or 'bill' is also mentioned in Ayr and Falkirk, for example.[23] Applications for relief were also sometimes supported by testimonials from other parishes.[24] On other occasions it is less clear whether supplications were written or oral, such as when St Andrews Kirk Session granted Bessy Lundy 30s 'upon hir supplicatioun' (similar wording was used in Perth), or when Monimail's scribe referred to a recipient as 'ane poor supplicant', and non-written requests were probably more common.[25] This leads one to wonder whether those with literate friends or family, or at least the more persuasive speakers, may have been at a distinct advantage in seeking relief.[26] Equally, it is hard to see the sessions being blind to this danger. There are also occasional hints at what was valued in such applications, written or otherwise. Both St Andrews and Ayr Kirk Sessions granted relief to individuals upon their 'hummill suit' and 'humble sute'.[27] The humility expressed in these applications may have reinforced the strength of the claim for assistance.[28] In Falkirk Jon Burne, a cordiner who had been 'this lang tyme bypast hevilie diseassit with seikness and is therby driven to great povertie and neccessitie', gave in 'ane bill of suplication requyring to be pitiet and helpit with sum part of the comoun collectioune', and was rewarded with £5.[29] The generous sum may have been in recognition of the fact that Burne had been struggling for some time (and possibly been too ashamed to speak up before then). On the other hand, a written Montrose supplication possibly attempts to reassure the session that the supplicant was resigned to the role of God's will in his predicament: 'desyring the sessione to consider his poore estait for the tym in respect that he and his wyff was lying bedfast ordenit that they sould have weiklie – 12. s whill it please god to restore them to health'.[30] However, in the absence of the sort of rich details that survive from some English applications for relief, we can do no more than guess at the contents of most appeals for relief.[31] The perceived necessity and extent of poverty of the supplicant must have been at the forefront of sessions' consideration.

22 CH2/448/2, p. 26.

23 CH2/751/1/2, f. 261r; CH2/400/1, p. 36.

24 CH2/448/2, pp. 20, 24; CH2/266/1, pp. 10, 13, 23; CH2/462/34, p. 73.

25 *RStAKS*, ii, p. 894; CH2/521/7, p. 64; CH2/548/1, p. 22.

26 Explicit reference to family links is rare, but Bervie Kirk Session paid 55s 'to Alexander Cant in Aberdein brother to Thomas Cant in this towne upon ane supplicatione': CH2/34/9, p. 13.

27 *RStAKS*, ii, p. 629; CH2/751/1/2, f. 305r.

28 For the importance of deference and humility in appeals for assistance, see Ben-Amos, *Culture of Giving*, pp. 202–3; *OTP*, pp. 387–90.

29 CH2/400/1, p. 36.

30 CH2/943/1, p. 186.

31 *OTP*, pp. 8, 156–63, 451; Healey, *First Century of Welfare*, pp. 82–109 and passim.

It is also important to examine the factors that seem to have made claimants eligible or ineligible for relief. A significant factor was morality and godliness. This issue is at its most obvious where people's relief payments were stopped as a result of disciplinary offences. For example, Perth Kirk Session ordered that Jonet Carnie was to be removed from the hospital for her fornication.[32] In 1613, Ayr Kirk Session decreed that 'the creple woman' was 'for her misbehaviour to be put aff the town'. It is significant that immorality here outweighed any distinction between able-bodied and impotent in determining her treatment.[33] Such cases are relatively rare in the kirk session minutes. This is partly because those who had committed offences might have been considered less favourably for relief in the first place, or having committed offences been silently removed from the ranks of the recipients of relief. Many poor and needy people may have suffered a lack of relief because of the sessions' perception of their moral and religious standing without leaving a trace in the records. But there are hints that even serious moral offences did not always permanently or automatically preclude one from consideration for relief. In Falkirk, on 18 January 1621, Alexander McGowine presented 'ane bill of suplication confessing and acknawledging in all humilitie his offence to god the minister and all utheris quhom he hes offendit', offered satisfaction, and 'requyred suport for suplement of his necessitie'. Discussion of his request was postponed 'till ane fuller meiting of the sessioun', which suggests that it was understandably felt to be a matter that required serious deliberation. He had been deposed as kirk officer for 'filthie drukines evile behavior and evile dispossit laungage gevin to the minister', but despite this on 25 January they granted him 40s monthly and assistance with clothing (albeit on strict terms not to re-offend).[34] Just as strikingly, in 1591 Glasgow Kirk Session 'ordenis Besse Vinyet as single [i.e. first-time] fornicatrix with Johnne Alderstoun cravand almous of the kirk to mak hir repentance for hir offense as becumis to begin thereto the nixt sonday, and the sondaye thaireftir, and than scho sall ressave anser to hir sute'.[35] Alderstoun was a serial offender and had refused to sustain their bairn, which may have made the session more sympathetic to her plea.[36] Although the outcome of her request for alms is not recorded, a first lapse into fornication did not apparently disbar an offender from relief automatically.

At times, the church could even be surprisingly lenient towards vagabonds: when introducing a badging policy for beggars, Dundonald Kirk Session seemed to become worried that those 'indisposed to charitie' may use the act as an excuse to withhold relief. It therefore explicitly confirmed

[32] CH2/521/3, p. 25. See also *COP*, pp. 35, 41, 68.

[33] CH2/751/1/2, f. 257v.

[34] CH2/400/1, pp. 66, 69, 70.

[35] CH2/550/1, p. 288.

[36] CH2/550/1, pp. 295, 303, 305.

that parishioners were allowed to give aid to 'any sturdie beggars, *how unwordie so ever* uther wayis of the leist help' who fell sick when passing through.[37] Although the aid should be temporary only, and proof would be required that harm would have befallen the beggar if one had failed to intervene, even an idle, villainous vagabond should be assisted if they fell ill while in the parish. There was a moral distinction drawn between the poor who behaved well and the ungodly, but it was applied with some sensitivity and flexibility.

An equally important concern for kirk sessions when assessing the status of the poor was their religious standing: their knowledge of Christian dogma, and attendance and engagement with religious services.[38] Those in receipt of relief in Aberdeen were expected to attend church and listen to the sermon (and not to sit in the kirkyard); similarly in Elgin those who begged in church or the churchyard on Sundays were to be deleted from the poor roll.[39] Elgin's recipients were also to be examined on whether they had attended sermons, morning and evening prayers, and 'behaved themselves utherwayis'.[40] Recipients of relief in St Andrews had to be catechised each Sunday in the hospital, and could collect their alms in the parish church on Monday only after prayers.[41] Poor attenders would risk forfeiting their alms in Dundonald also, where a man was told that if he missed three Sundays in a row he would be 'depryved of all benefeit that he was wont to receave of the sessioune for supplie of his necessitie and want'.[42] Canongate recipients would be stripped of alms if they failed to communicate without exceptional excuse in 1564.[43] Accurate knowledge of religious doctrine was often a requirement as well as physical presence: in St Cuthbert's in 1589 it was ruled that 'nane salbe admitit to the baptising of thair bairnes nor mariage nor repentance nor haif almos of the kirk bot thai that can say the lords prayer the belief and the commands and gif ane compt therof' (the latter requirement requiring comprehension as well as memorisation).[44] In St Andrews a 1570 act stipulated that deacons could give alms only to those who could give account of their faith and recite the Creed, Prayer, and Commandments (or at least learn them within a month).[45] The church's most significant fundamental requirement for the receipt of alms was religious observance and moral propriety.

[37] *Dundonald*, p. 399 (emphasis mine).

[38] For the similar importance of these factors in decisions about English poor relief, see *OTP*, pp. 380–1; Slack, *Poverty and Policy*, p. 168.

[39] CH2/448/2, p. 117; CH2/145/1, f. 142v.

[40] CH2/145/1, f. 126r.

[41] *RStAKS*, ii, p. 825.

[42] *Dundonald*, p. 407. See also CH2/550/1, p. 306; CH2/448/4, p. 75; *COP*, p. 35.

[43] *Canagait*, p. 7.

[44] CH2/718/1, p. 86.

[45] *RStAKS*, i, p. 340.

Beggars and Begging

The term 'beggar' is frequent in the punitive statements from secular and ecclesiastical authorities, and in Scotland and beyond considerable emphasis has been placed on fear about beggars.[46] But how did the church in the localities actually treat beggars, and begging? The first thing to note is that 'beggars' could receive poor relief; to be seen as a beggar was not automatically to be undeserving. In Kinnaird, for example, among the distributions to the poor in November 1636 was 12d to 'poore stranger beggars'. The following May, 8d was given to 'tua beggar strangers', and then 12d in July to 'thrie stranger beggaris'.[47] It was only a small sum, but it is striking to see this phrase – more reminiscent of the prescriptive statements discussed at the start of this chapter about those to be barred from relief and/or punished –appear in the records of expenditure. Indeed, the following year a payment was made for 'keiping out the stranger beggaris in tyme of sessioun'.[48] Apparently, 'stranger beggars' were not inherently unworthy: some deserved assistance, while others had to be physically restrained. The difference can only have been their (perceived) morality and behaviour. Similarly, even in Lasswade, a parish unusually suspicious about gypsies, vagabonds and foreign beggars, payments were made in the 1630s 'to the beggaris' and to 'some poor beggaris'.[49]

Urban kirk sessions were also willing to provide relief to 'beggars'. In Perth, the plague of the mid-1580s plunged some respectable people into poverty, and the session recorded 'sundrie honest personis . . . quha war aschamit to be put in the roll with common beggeris and yit sustenit great peniuritie'.[50] Of course, a contrast is being drawn here between the 'honest personis' ('honest' here conveying a sense of respectability and status more than truthfulness) and 'common beggeris'. But despite this, the 'common beggeris' are on 'the roll': in other words they are in receipt of regular poor relief. Beggar may naturally have been a word with rather dishonourable connotations, but it did not denote someone inherently unworthy of relief.[51] As in Kinnaird, the difference between the common beggars who got relief, and 'the haill puir strange and idel beggers upon the brig of Tay' who were to be 'put out at the portis' in 1587, was one of behaviour

[46] *OPL*, p. 13; Slack, *Poverty and Policy*, p. 24; Jutte, *Poverty*, p. 12.

[47] CH2/418/1, pp. 18, 22.

[48] CH2/418/1, p. 31.

[49] CH2/471/1, ff. 51v, 52r. For the parish's comparatively restrictive attitude to outsiders: CH2/471/1, f. 3r, see also McCallum, 'Charity Doesn't Begin At Home', p. 121.

[50] *PKSB*, p. 292.

[51] This is reflected in some of the more literary discussions of poverty and charity discussed in Chapter 1, such as William Lauder's critique of a lack of concern for 'the pure that gois nakit, begging frome dure to dure': Hall and Furnivall (eds), *The extant poetical works of William Lauder*, pp. 16–17, and perhaps most obviously the 'Beggars' Summonds'.

and morality, or perceived genuineness of need.[52] And Aberdeen's Kirk Session referred to the weekly alms it provided to the town's 'commoun poore' as being 'for saffing thame from begging'.[53] This is a very significant turn of phrase, because it suggests that were the alms removed, they would be forced to beg. Begging was not necessarily an idle choice made by the undeserving, rather it was something to which the deserving would have to turn were they not supported.

Indeed across Scotland there was some toleration and support for the act of begging itself: it was not ideal, and it needed to be tightly regulated, but it was not inherently unacceptable. After all, as Chapter 1 identified, willingness to give informal alms liberally could be a substantial virtue in the memorialisation of a clergyman. In Perth, regular recipients were not allowed to beg, but others were, if licensed and wearing the town's mark.[54] In Ayr, during the dearth of 1623 it was stated that

> on the sabbothe dayes in tyme of the gathering to the poore that na begger stand at the kirk doore bit remuffe thame selffes to the kirk styllis and thease that ar to giff thame sall bestowe ther almes on thame thair failyeing of onye poore within the town disobeyis theye sall want their ouklie allowance toties quoties.[55]

This suggests two significant things: firstly that begging was not permitted by the church door, but was permitted at a respectful distance (even on a Sunday); and secondly, most strikingly (and unlike Perth), even those who received a regular weekly allowance from the kirk session were permitted to beg at difficult times. In Elgin, similarly, regular recipients might beg but were prohibited from 'haunting the church and churchyard on Sunday to seek alms, on pain of being deleted from the poor roll'.[56] In much the same way, Stirling Kirk Session ruled that hospital inmates and other recipients were 'admonesit to abstein fra suting of any almus upon the sabbot', on pain of being discharged from the 'ordinar' poor.[57] So while there were subtly different approaches in Ayr, Stirling and Elgin to the monitoring of Sunday begging, in all three parishes begging was permissible at least six days per week. In 1599 St Andrews Kirk Session prohibited its poor from begging, but as discussed earlier they justified this prohibition with the statement that 'thai ar utherwayis sufficientlie provydit, partlie to the hospitall and pairtlie with ouklie almous furth of the session'.[58] Whether this

52 *PKSB*, p. 365.
53 CH2/448/4, p. 17.
54 *PKSB*, pp. 56–60, 413.
55 CH2/751/2, f. 33r.
56 CH2/145/1, f. 142v.
57 CH2/1026/1, p. 60 (the act was immediately expanded to include everyone, logically enough because it would be odd to ban existing relief recipients but not the wider body of the poor from Sabbath-begging where profanation of the Lord's Day was the problem).
58 *RStAKS*, ii, p. 883.

confidence was warranted or not, it was apparently felt that begging might have to be accepted as legitimate if welfare provision was insufficient.

Begging might be utilised as a means of raising funds rather than having to dip into the session's coffers: for example, in Elgin a man who gave in a supplication was allowed to have one of his local friends go through the town 'for gathering of support to him'.[59] Similarly in Aberdeen the elders and deacons were to 'pas throw the towne with the beidmen of St Thomas hospitall to crawe support to thame of the nichtboris of the towne': here the ostentatious public seeking of alms seems to have been a deliberate strategy for fundraising.[60] The size of the group permitted to beg could be considerable: in the rural parish of Dundonald 'the names of the poore who are permitted to beg and received markes' amounted to 43 men and 19 women, (plus one illegible).[61] There was clearly variation in the approaches that individual kirk sessions took to begging, but in general begging was tolerated and regulated rather than wholly repressed or viewed simplistically as an evil. The fact that someone was considered a 'beggar', or that they begged, did not preclude them from receiving alms. We must therefore treat with great caution the broad (and vague) statements found in legislation, statutes and ecclesiastical complaints. The vagabond and the idle beggar were all, of course, undeserving. But the beggar, in his or her own right, was mostly judged deserving or undeserving on the basis of other factors, such as morality, religion, and necessity.

The Able-bodied Poor and Work

It is an understandable assumption, based on the statements of parliament and church leaders, that relief was not primarily intended for the able-bodied poor. The emphasis (including in the *First Book of Discipline* and the 1570s Poor Laws) was generally on the lame, impotent, disabled and sick, although this was not stipulated in particularly precise or definitive terms.[62] Later developments, particularly the early nineteenth-century introduction of a tradition that the able-bodied unemployed were historically 'expressly barred from relief' (and their explicit exclusion from a right to claim relief under the New Poor Law of 1845), have perhaps reinforced a sense that Scottish poor relief was for the benefit of those who could not work.[63] The kirk session relief discussed in this book was certainly not to be provided to able-bodied poor who were felt to be idle or otherwise undeserving,

59 CH2/145/1, f. 35v.

60 CH2/448/2, p. 59.

61 *Dundonald*, p. 400.

62 *FBD*, p 113; *RPS*, A1575/3/5; Goodare, 'Parliament and Society', pp. 413–14, 425–6; Mitchison, 'Making', p. 61; Stewart, 'Poor Relief in Edinburgh', p. 12.

63 Mitchison, *Coping*, pp. 47–8. For the development of later moves to disqualify the able-bodied see Mitchison, 'Creation of the Disablement Rule'; Mitchison, 'A Parish and Its Poor', p. 22.

but that is not saying a great deal. A close reading of the operation of kirk session relief suggests that able-bodied adults of working age were often supported.

As the analysis of the recipients of relief in Chapter 6 indicated, frequent mention is made in lists of recipients, or grants of aid, of a person as 'sick', 'blind', 'agit', 'bairn', or one of a wide range of similar descriptors. This shows, unsurprisingly, that many people who were not capable of labour were helped by the system. But it also raises questions about the characteristics of other recipients, who were simply listed with their name (or in some cases anonymously as 'a puir man', rather than say 'a creple man' or a 'blind stranger'). Given that individuals without such specific designations appear in the records immediately alongside the very young and old, ill and disabled, it seems very likely that at least some of them were able-bodied: otherwise it would seem odd that their incapacity was not recorded. Kirk session scribes were normally thorough in their recording of details, and sometimes fastidiously so.[64] For example, in Galston very regular payments were made to 'Blind Janet Campbell' in 1592–3; she was designated such each time although the number of recipients in the parish was small and the scribe could have been forgiven for simply using her name. However various other recipients like Allane Wilsone and James Black were recorded simply with their names (and in Black's case his residence in Lusnok), strongly suggesting that they were lacking in obvious physical impairments.[65] St Cuthbert's accounts are thorough in their listing of disbursements, and combine frequent payments to recipients described as 'cripple', blind, injured, or foundling with payments simply to 'a poor man' or 'a poor woman', or named poor people such as Marion Bishop or Katharine Logie.[66] In Aberdeen's roll of the poor of Futtie quarter, there are separate sections for 'aged persones' then 'poore bairnes' (who received relief through their parents), followed by simply the poor who got weekly contributions. These recipients were mainly women (often widows) with young children, and were therefore of working age as well as no mentioned incapacity (although the list also included an aged woman and a man with no indication of his age or parental status).[67] Indeed, more generally, the frequent presence of men and women with 'bairns' (i.e. not grown-up children) provides further indication that working-age people were a significant element within the beneficiaries of relief.[68] The frequent variations in payment size between individuals who are not otherwise distinguished in the minutes might point to the varying degrees to which

64 McCallum, 'Charity and Conflict', pp. 37–8; see also CH2/718/60, pp. 113–17.

65 CH2/1335/1, pp. 55–9.

66 CH2/718/60, pp. 57–65. Similarly Perth Kirk Session frequently uses descriptive phrases like 'ane auld decripit and seik woman', 'lying seyk', and 'ane puir agit man', implying that these characteristics were not present in other cases: *PKSB*, pp. 106, 138, 146.

67 CH2/448/4, pp. 7–10.

68 See, for example, CH2/1217/33, ff. 89v–90v; CH2/1026/1, p. 162; CH2/1218/16, f. 58r.

recipients were able to support themselves through work, with smaller payments going to those who could partly earn their living.[69]

However, there is also more direct evidence of relief being granted to the able-bodied. Some assistance was provided to individuals with trades, such as the tailor and flesher who were among a list of recipients (alongside a man with an injured leg) in Glasgow in 1589.[70] Canongate's recipients in 1567 included people with listed occupations as well as people with disabilities, and people with children but no other cause of poverty or information given.[71] It is not possible to assume that such individuals were always of working age, because it is possible that in some cases the former trade of a recipient was being used as a descriptor even though they had retired from it. This is unlikely to apply in all, or even most cases, however, because retirement through simple old age was a luxury beyond most in early modern Scotland, and if they were also disabled or so 'aged' that work was impossible this likely would have been mentioned. On occasion we have definite evidence that the tradesperson in question was capable of work: in Salton, 'David Findlasone pauper' was granted 12s in 1635: the designation pauper, as well as the grant of aid itself, indicates that he was clearly seen as a person deserving of financial assistance as a result of poverty.[72] At other times, however, he was referred to as thatcher as well as 'poor', and indeed in 1637 was paid a fee of 5s by the kirk session 'for thiking the scholl'.[73] He was clearly capable of work, yet he was described by the session as a pauper: presumably his work was not going well, or not providing enough income to support his needs at all times. The kirk sessions reacted to individual cases rather more sensitively than the harsh and simplistic pronouncements of the higher authorities imply.

Similarly, Edinburgh Kirk Session granted a one-off payment of 40s to Thomas Browne, 'bonetmakar', but he was clearly not an elderly or 'decayed' former bonnetmaker in the ranks of the long-term impotent poor, because the payment was made 'providing all wayis that he be not chargeable . . . heirefter'.[74] These minutes were scrupulous in recording recipients' sickness (and indeed in using it as leverage when stipulating that relief should be temporary only), so its absence here strongly suggests that this man was capable of work, expected to work in the future, but still temporarily deserving of relief.[75] Edinburgh also granted William Galespie,

[69] McIntosh, 'Poor Relief in Elizabethan Communities', p. 349, refers to weekly payments by Melton Mowbray's Collectors for the Poor of 4d to 'the poor compelled to live by alms and is yet able to do some work towards their living' but 8d to those 'able to get nothing to their living'.

[70] CH2/550/1, p. 39.

[71] *Canagait*, pp. 65–6 (see also above, pp. 179–82). See also CH2/521/2, f. 102r, for a Perth distribution featuring poor craftsmen.

[72] CH2/322/1, p. 91.

[73] CH2/322/1, pp. 91, 95, 97.

[74] CH2/450/1, p. 13.

[75] See CH2/450/1, pp. 3, 9, 18, 21, 22, 25, 33, 39, for contemporary examples of recipients' sickness being recorded. See also the discussion of 'chargeability' above (pp. 160–2).

wobster, a 20s payment for his bairn to be nursed. Again he cannot have been a former wobster as he was made to promise 'to pas to his craft in time cuming, and not to be fund begand nather yit chargeable to the kirk heirefter'.[76] The forgiveness of his former begging is interesting, but most significant is the provision of a relief payment to someone with a craft, who was expected to return to it. The reference to his bairn needing nursing may point to the real reason for his necessity: he may have been widowed and left unable to work as a result of the need to care for the child. Similar parental challenges seem to have been faced by a clearly able-bodied but temporarily unemployed messenger 'John Forgushill, elder in Helie, hinderit be the present plauge fra his traffikine quhairon he leiffit and sustenit his small bairnes': in response Dundonald Kirk Session granted him 40s.[77] A recipient in Stirling was referred to as 'James Clark travellar'; given that this was an admission to a regular payment rather than a one-off payment, 'travellar' here probably refers to the occupation ('one engaged in transporting merchandise from place to place as a living') rather than simply a person who was travelling.[78] Kirk sessions seemed willing to provide recurring poor relief to workers whose incomes were apparently not meeting their necessities.

Perth Kirk Session furnishes us with another interesting example of a clearly able-bodied craftsman receiving poor relief. In August 1619, Andrew Lathangie, whose wife had been bedfast for two years, and had four young children and no resources to support them, craved assistance from the kirk session. He made his claim 'in respect that he gettis no imployment nor gayne of his craft bot that it is alluterlie decayit in this burgh'. He beseeches 'thair wisdomes' [the kirk session] for weekly alms, and to 'have compassion upone theme'. Strikingly, the kirk session granted him 6s 8d weekly; they accepted his claim.[79] He had already been in a 'pure estate' by 5 September 1616, when for this reason his arrears on an annual of 5s 4d was discharged. And we know that he was a cutler by trade from a later reference in 1622, when his widow applied (successfully) to continue receiving the relief.[80] It seems certain that if he had some physical incapacity, he would have mentioned it in what was a very carefully presented supplication for relief. Instead, he based his claim on the difficulties faced by a cutler in late 1610s Perth: unemployment or underemployment as a result of the state of trade and the local economy.[81] He must have thought the kirk session would be sympathetic to that claim, and he was proved right. Those who were able-bodied but did not have sufficient resources to

[76] CH2/450/1, p. 73. He had previously received an alms payment.

[77] *Dundonald*, p. 118.

[78] CH2/1026/1, p. 27; *DSL*, 'Travailour'.

[79] CH2/521/7, p. 64.

[80] CH2/521/6, p 100; CH2/521/7, p. 320.

[81] The reference to the state of trade, and use of words like 'compassion', is reminiscent of some English petitions for relief: *OTP*, p. 159.

support themselves and their family were not automatically considered idle and undeserving.

Such cases are the most striking, because details that demonstrate the recipients' able-bodied status happen to be mentioned explicitly. But, as argued above, there must have been many more cases where relief was simply granted to a recipient, recorded only with their name rather than any circumstances, who was an able-bodied adult. After all, craftsmen were likely to be named with their crafts: labourers, servants and the like who had fallen into poverty would more likely simply be named. Kirk sessions sometimes asked recipients to perform some work for their alms: this does not necessarily mean that they were not elderly, but it does show they were considered physically capable of at least some labour.[82] St Andrews granted relief to Nichol Cuik but also expected him 'to be reddy and obedient to serve at all tymes in soc adois as the sessioun sall charge him with': this is indeed what followed as a month later he was asked to carry out a summons as 'officiar'.[83] Dundonald Kirk Session was willing to pay Hew Wallace 23s 4d for shoes, in return 'for his careing ane beill fra the sessioun to the minister of Faill': this was rather a high fee for carrying a message, so there was clearly an element of charity as well as paid work here.[84] Alexander Robertson received 40d weekly from Stirling Kirk Session 'for keiping clein the kirk round about to the dur therof'; William Cragy in Perth received 3s weekly for similar work in 1580, as did various others later in the decade.[85] Rather like modern 'workfare' schemes, this did not comprise paid employment so much as reflecting a belief that those who receive 'handouts' should, where possible, do some work for the providing institution in return.

Sessions also sometimes provided tailored assistance in the form of investment in materials for poor people who were capable of some sort of labour, but not currently working (or earning enough). For example, in 1624, Longside Kirk Session gave 'to Johne Morres 24s to be a beginning of ane pack to him with this condition that he sall not charge us heirefter bot sall live honestly in ane lawfull calling'.[86] Clearly he was capable of work, and the session wanted to jump-start him into a new living so as not to have to pay him alms in future. Assistance with expenses incurred by employment also seems to have been the reason for Salton's decision to pay Joanet Pharies 10s 'for to helpe to buy ane forlat of salt', which was a large quantity of salt more likely to have been for baking or some other minor economic activity rather than personal supplies.[87] In 1578 Perth Kirk Session contributed silver to a poor man 'to help him by ane horse': as

[82] Thane, 'Social Histories of Old Age and Aging', p. 99.
[83] *RStAKS*, ii, pp. 629, 632.
[84] *Dundonald*, p. 118.
[85] CH2/1026/1, p. 211; *PKSB*, p. 169, 349.
[86] CH2/699/1, p. 56.
[87] CH2/322/1, p. 94.

Margo Todd has noted the intention here was probably that he could earn his own living in future.[88]

Of course, those who received assistance with external employment opportunities, or were asked to perform certain tasks in return for their alms, might not have been entirely fit and healthy. Indeed, as we know today, it is not a question of being either fully able-bodied or entirely incapable of labour. The spectrum in between the extremes was one that kirk sessions must have recognised. But they certainly did not judge that those who were capable of work, yet were in serious want, must necessarily be poor through idleness. There might well have been other individuals who the sessions did judge to be lazy, and if so they would be unrecorded because the minutes and accounts tend to record only the granting of relief, not its rejection. But if this was the case, the judgement was based on an assessment of the individual, not the blind application of pre-determined criteria or prejudices about the able-bodied. Despite this, the records do still feature substantial numbers of traditionally 'impotent' poor: 'the widow and fatherlesse, the aged, impotent or lamed' emphasised for rhetorical effect in the *First Book of Discipline*.[89] This is unsurprising because in early modern society such people would almost always be in risk of poverty. But the admittedly unquantifiable presence of relatively able-bodied adults demonstrates that kirk session poor relief in practice was not simply about helping these stereotypically 'deserving' poor people.

Some kirk sessions in towns went beyond casual financial assistance with material to assist with employment, and actually became involved with organising and financing young people's entry to trades and apprenticeships. This has been identified for the eighteenth century, and is also found in our period.[90] In 1609, St Cuthbert's Kirk Session paid £5 'to ane young boy to present him to ane craft', presumably having noted him as having some potential in this area (and also perhaps as a potential burden otherwise).[91] In Edinburgh, a lad was apprenticed to George Barbor, skipper, and his craft for seven years: for this the kirk session would pay £10 to Barbor.[92] As well as providing resources to adults to help them earn a living, Perth Kirk Session also gave 'ane pur boy callit Alexander Mertine ten merkis to help him to ane pack for winning of his living'.[93] More formally, Perth's hospital masters were requested by the session to

88 *PKSB*, p. 95n. For a similar grant to assist with the purchase of a horse see CH2/718/60, p. 106. Discussing eighteenth-century relief, *OPL*, p. 97, also argues that such payments can be read as evidence of recipients with some ability to work. See also Mutch, *Religion and National Identity*, p. 123 (including one man in 1780 to be bought an 'Anvil Bellows' to enable him to earn a living).

89 *FBD*, pp. 112–13.

90 *OPL*, pp. 94–5.

91 CH2/718/60, p. 60.

92 CH2/450/1, p. 123.

93 CH2/521/2, f. 132v.

arrange apprenticeship for a poor orphan, David Craig. He had given in a supplication 'desyring them for godis caus to give him sum support to put him to ane craft', and the session agreed, instructing the masters 'to bind this pure boy prentis to Jhone Blak talyeour and to mak ane indentour betuix them and him and to give the said Jhone ten punds to lerne him the talyeour craft'.[94] Similar intentions may have been underpinned the grant of £3 'to be bestowit upone ane pur boy callit Alexander Gibson in his woyag[?] to the east partis'.[95] The aim was presumably to fund the start-up costs of this voyage (as a deckhand or similar?), and an association with poverty is strongly suggested by their attempt to do the same for an adult, 'ane depauperit man callit Thomas Pullour', for 'support in his voyage to the eistern seas'.[96] This was not a formal apprenticeship (with binding to a master and formal contractual stipulations), but it must have been intended to serve as a leg-up into a potentially useful occupation for a poor man or boy. Such examples – whether of formal apprenticeships or informal investments – were quite rare, especially in comparative terms.[97] This may be because of the very substantial one-off outlay which was required as an investment.[98] But they further demonstrate the kirk sessions' desire to support employment and assist those capable of work, rather than simply seeking to assist the impotent.

Strangers to the Parish

The hostile statements about undeserving poor people discussed at the start of this chapter include negative references to the 'stranger' poor, and to undesirable groups and individuals from outside the parish. Gypsies and idle vagabonds were attacked in particular, and kirk sessions as well as parliament and higher church courts were capable of strong rhetoric and stated policies against outsider poor, and in favour of the native poor.[99] And historians have tended to suggest that poor relief in Protestant countries like Scotland was for the native or residential poor of the community only, and that 'wandering strangers' would not be assisted.[100] As before, this may reflect rhetorical pronouncements, approaches adopted in later years, and perhaps even the famous English policy on settlement, rather

94 CH2/521/3, p. 41.

95 CH2/521/2, f. 155v.

96 CH2/521/2, f. 167v.

97 Pullan, 'Charity and Poor Relief in Early Modern Italy', p. 48; Lane, *Apprenticeship in England*, pp. 71–8; *OTP*, pp. 202–23.

98 £10 was paid to help set up a poor boy in the weaving trade by Canongate Kirk Session in 1650: CH2/122/48, p. 39.

99 *RPS*, A1575/3/5; 1597/11/46; 1609/4/32; Goodare, 'Parliament and Society', p. 426; *RStAKS*, i, p. 1; CH2/147/1, p. 20.

100 Wandel, 'Social Welfare', p. 82; *PKSB*, p. 196n; Foster, *Church Before the Covenants*, p. 83 (quotation).

than the reality in the Scottish parish.[101] It may also in part reflect the disproportionate attention paid by historians to the famine of the early 1620s, which as discussed in Chapter 4 saw unusually restrictive approaches to the travelling poor. In general, it has been shown that kirk sessions were responsive to a wide range of charitable causes originating beyond the parish, from international confessional crises, to individual strangers and foreigners fallen on hard times.[102] The ranks of the deserving poor could easily include people from outside the parish community, and we have already encountered numerous such cases.

This was normal even in parishes where significant concern about some of the outsider poor was expressed. On 5 June 1603, Aberdeen Kirk Session passed an act against 'commoun beggers that wantis takynnis and ar not perfytlie knawin to be the townis awin purell' – they were to be warded on bread and water.[103] Nevertheless, poor outsiders had been helped earlier in the year, and a poor scholar who craved particular relief because he was 'ane native borne townis barne' did not get special treatment as a result.[104] Perth Kirk Session displayed a great deal of hostility to foreign beggars in the 1580s, and Margo Todd is right to note that in these records 'Charity to an individual of another parish is extremely unusual'.[105] But Perth seems to have been unusually restrictive in its approach to stranger poor, and even here, later unpublished minutes include references to the needy from beyond the town.[106] Assistance to non-local poor did not simply involve obviously distressed individuals who had suffered some disaster. Outsiders whose status was described as 'ane travelling man and woman' were granted 12s in Bervie, despite the implication that their mobility was more than just the result of an immediate or short-term crisis.[107] A study of rural mobility in the Angus parish of Monikie throughout the seventeenth century shows recurring payments made to stranger poor including some regularly recurring visitors, not just to one-off or to emergency claimants.[108] In fact, given that high geographical mobility was much more of a regular feature of life than was for a long time appreciated by historians, a more nuanced and tolerant (in some cases) attitude to mobile poor on the ground than in theory is perhaps not so surprising.[109]

101 Hindle, 'Exclusion Crises'; McIntosh, *Hadleigh*, pp. 101, 104.
102 McCallum, 'Charity Doesn't Begin at Home'; Mitchison, 'A Parish and its Poor', p. 19.
103 CH2/448/2, p. 30.
104 CH2/448/2, pp. 22–4.
105 *PKSB*, p. 196n, 365, 402, 412.
106 CH2/521/2, f. 80r–v, 86v, 129v. Similarly Lasswade's minutes combine particularly strong statements of hostility to outsider poor with assistance to some such people: McCallum, 'Charity Doesn't begin at Home', pp. 121–2.
107 CH2/34/9, p. 3.
108 Whyte and Whyte, 'Geographical Mobility', p. 51.
109 Houston, *Population History*, pp. 47–9. Ben-Amos, 'Good Works and Social Ties', pp. 127–30, identifies some lenient treatment and casual help for some migrant poor in English communities.

On occasion, these deserving outsiders might have been explicitly recommended by testimonial from another kirk session, such as 'ane honest puir man named walter sangster' who received 20s from Aberdeen Kirk Session thanks to a testimonial from the parish of Rayne, or 'ane pure blind man callit William King of the parochin of Kilrinnye' who received 26s from Perth Kirk Session on the basis of his testimonial from Kilrenny.[110] Or they might simply be judged as deserving, such as 'ane stranger James Quheit' given 20s by Kinnaird Kirk Session in 1636 (not the only outsider helped that year), or the unnamed stranger granted half of the week's total of 4s by Monifieth Kirk Session in 1593.[111] Assistance to deserving outsiders was particularly prominent in session expenditure during the 1640s, in contrast with parts of Europe where attitudes to outsider poor hardened during times of crisis.[112] This was also in contrast with the Scottish famine of the early 1620s when the theoretical resistance to external relief claimants was more actively (though not universally) put into practice, reflecting the difference between general economic pressures and dislocation, and specific catastrophic food shortage.[113] For the most part, even when session relief was under significant pressure, the perceived line between deserving and undeserving was not in practice coterminous with the parish boundary. And while the reasons for helping individual strangers are normally as enigmatic as for the local poor, kirk sessions showed themselves to be receptive to their necessities.

Conclusion

The Reformation may have stimulated or added to some hardening attitudes towards the able-bodied or wandering poor, but the evidence from the localities of Scotland suggests that this did not translate into a prejudicial and closed system of relief in practice. The historiographical emphasis on who was not allowed relief, and on which groups amongst the poorer sorts were victimised and punished, has arguably led to an incomplete understanding of the way in which inclusion was determined. Those who received relief were a wider and more flexibly defined range than has been suggested. Of course, the system involved harsh decisions, a high degree of moral judgement linked to the wider work of church discipline, and was in no way open-minded about the poor as a group. No-one would expect it

[110] CH2/448/2, p. 24; CH2/521/6, pp. 26–7. Presbyteries might also pass on recommendations: for example Canongate Kirk Session assisted various individuals on the Presbytery's request, or occasionally the Synod's (CH2/122/48, pp. 26–30, 119). Less typical was Anstruther's payment to 'thre strangeris upone ane testimoniall from his majestie' (presumably referring to the Privy Council): CH2/624/2, p. 155.

[111] CH2/418/1, pp. 16–17; OPR310/1, f. 83v.

[112] CH2/322/1, pp. 98–104; CH2/418/1, pp. 55–61; CH2/548/1, pp. 38–42; Cf. Henderson, 'Charity and Welfare in Early Modern Tuscany', pp. 65–6.

[113] See above, Chapter 4.

to be. But neither did it apply formal, pre-determined criteria or simplistic dividing lines between deserving and undeserving when making decisions about how to allocate relief funds. Instead they made local and individual decisions about where to prioritise spending, influenced not just by ideology, but by local practicalities and needs. This is in line with emerging understandings of the complexity and sensitivity in local decision-making in English poor relief practice, sometimes involving more leniency and compassion than legislative principles implied.[114] And in small Scottish parish communities those making the decisions were not necessarily socially disconnected from the beneficiaries and victims of the decisions. If the poor were not, as Scott puts it, a 'faceless burden' but instead 'recognisable individuals', then it perhaps becomes less surprising that kirk session decisions could be sympathetic and personalised.[115] This does not mean that we should not take into account governing ideologies and prejudices when studying early modern poor relief; but it does mean that we should recognise that they were only part of the story, and that they had to interact and negotiate with the complicated and human world of poverty.

[114] McIntosh, *Poor Relief in England*, pp. 5, 9–10, 142–5, 184; Houston, 'Church Briefs', pp. 494-5; McIntosh, *Hadleigh*, pp. 154, 295.

[115] Scott, 'Experiences of Charity', p. 2.

CHAPTER 8

Beyond the Kirk Session: Mixed Economies of Relief

Introduction

The church was the main provider of poor relief in early modern Scotland. Previous chapters in this book have explored its fundraising, distribution, and approaches to the poor in detail. However, as numerous studies in the history of pre-modern poverty and welfare have taught us, it is important to avoid focusing too narrowly on single, dominant institutional relief providers at the expense of wider and more diverse ecologies of relief.[1] This is a significant consideration in opening up the study of Scottish relief because other actors, including institutions and individuals, provided relief to the poor. The study of their activities can contextualise the kirk sessions' work and also allow us to observe how other sources and forms of relief might have worked with and alongside the church's provision. Furthermore, building on recent claims that formal institutional relief was only a part of the picture, it is essential to pay attention to the more informal help that was given, as well as attempting to flip the perspective to that of the poor themselves, in order to reflect on their survival strategies.[2] In considering the wider context of relief beyond the kirk session, this chapter focuses on three broad themes: relief and regulation of the poor by institutions (mainly urban) other than the church; private philanthropy and official charitable giving by individuals; and assistance within the community and self-help strategies employed by the poor.[3] These should certainly not be seen as mutually exclusive or independent spheres – indeed as we shall see there were important ways in which these avenues of support co-operated and overlapped.

[1] See, for example, Daunton, 'Introduction', p. 9; Goose, 'English Almshouse', pp. 6, 17; Houston, 'Poor Relief and the Dangerous and Criminal Insane', pp. 454, 467; Houston, 'Church Briefs', p. 519.

[2] *OTP*; Wales, 'Poverty, Poor relief and the life-cycle'; Hufton, *Poor of Eighteenth Century France*; Healey, *First Century of Welfare.*

[3] The urban emphasis of the discussion of institutions partly reflects record survival but also patterns of activity in the relief and regulation of the poor by bodies other than kirk sessions: as noted in Goodare, *Government*, p. 192, 'in comparison with the countryside, the towns were intensively and minutely governed'.

Other Institutions

Secular Authorities

The kirk session was not the only local authority that took an interest in the welfare and lives of the poor in early modern Scotland. Kirk sessions were the principal relief providers, and in rural parishes the only authority to organise formal relief during this period.[4] However, secular authorities in towns also had a role to play; their membership often overlapped with the kirk session, of course, but they were significant institutions in the lives of the poor in their own right as well.[5] Burgh records reveal that councils were involved in the relief and regulation of the poorer sorts and in charitable work.[6] The main business and priorities of urban secular authorities were always, inevitably, their judicial functions involving crimes and misdemeanours, and the economic regulation of the burghs: prices, craft practices, entry to burgess status and the like. Welfare was a minor element of their business. Nevertheless, throughout this period councils made some payments from their coffers or interventions that can be classified under the broad heading of welfare.

A dominant group amongst the recipients of such relief was burgesses, council officers or others associated with the urban elite who had fallen on hard times for various reasons. Typical examples came in Elgin in 1642, when 'Andro Stalker, goldsmyth' was to be paid £5 6s 8d 'to help him in his necessitie being depauperat', and Glasgow in 1574 when the entry fee

4 For other authorities in the countryside, which were not involved with the provision of formal relief, see Smout, 'Peasant and Lord in Scotland', pp. 507–13.

5 Graham, *Uses of Reform*, pp. 80, 98-99; Foster, *Church Before the Covenants*, pp. 70–1; DesBrisay, 'Authority and Discipline', p. 312. For a survey of scholarship on early modern burghs, including developments since the classic Lynch (ed.), *Early Modern Town in Scotland*, see Falconer, 'Surveying Scotland's Urban Past', pp. 38–41.

6 The following discussion is based primarily on printed burgh records, many of which are extracts or selections from the manuscripts and therefore not necessarily representative, in order to ensure adequate coverage across places and periods. Naturally no quantification, or judgement about specific absences of activity, has therefore been attempted, except where unexcerpted sources were used. It is highly unlikely that relief or poor-related activity of a qualitatively or substantially different nature to that discussed below was a significant element in the unpublished manuscripts but wholly unrepresented in the printed versions. This is a conclusion reinforced by examination of selected burgh record manuscripts, for, for example, Dundee (Dundee City Archives, Dundee Town Council Minutes, volume 4 (1613–53); Dundee City Archives, Dundee Town Treasurer's Account Book, 1646–1696), NRS, Burntisland Burgh Records, B9/11/3, B9/12/2; NRS, Dysart Council Minutes 1623–45, B21/10/1; NRS, Montrose Court Book and Council Minutes, 1603-1609, B51/10/3; St Andrews University Library, St Andrews Burgh Court Book, B65/8/1), as well as the complete and unextracted published records (see, for example, *ABA*; Beveridge (ed.), *Burgh Records of Dunfermline*; Wood (ed.), *Kirkcudbright Town Council Records*). This is not to say that specialist local studies might not be able to uncover further nuances or patterns.

of a new burgess was passed 'to George Burell merchand for his support, to releve his extreme povertie in tyneyng [losing] of his pack be the sey'.[7] A former bailie in Inverness was granted the relatively large sum of £20 per quarter 'in respect of his present necessitie and being not able to furnische and susteine himself upone his awin proper meanis'.[8] In contrast to the very wide range of individuals assisted by kirk sessions, burgh councils seem to have prioritised relief that helped maintain the respectability of people from their own socio-economic background or former officials who were no longer able to support themselves or had suffered some disaster.[9] Also particularly prominent was emergency fundraising for causes elsewhere, or contributions for distressed strangers, outsiders and foreigners. This included collections for causes such as imprisoned Scots (like those taken captive by the Turks in the 1630s), and those suffering from famine or plague in other parts of Scotland.[10] As well as raising funds to send away, burgh councils also helped victims of trouble elsewhere who arrived in their communities. Such people were particularly likely to come to towns, of course. Three Shetlanders were amongst those helped with payments by Peebles burgh council, 'poor french men' were assisted in Dundee, and in 1607 Dunfermline's bailies ordered payment of 40s to three men from Wemyss who had come 'to seik support in tyme of pest', and then 26s 8d to some shipwrecked strangers a few years later.[11] There was a distinct focus on those of elite or respectable status, external causes and distressed outsiders in the charitable contributions of urban governments.

This is not to say that burgh councils took no interest in relieving the more general ranks of the local poor. Peebles' council also made payments to various disabled and poor people, apparently from within the parish, and Irvine's recipients also included some apparently local poor and impotent people.[12] Stirling burgh ordered its quartermaster to pass coal to 'the pure folkis' during a visitation of plague in 1645.[13] Assistance with burial expenses for the poor might occasionally be forthcoming as well.[14] So it was not unheard of for urban governments to undertake

7 Cramond (ed.), *Records of Elgin*, i, p. 274; *ERBG*, p. 11.

8 *Inverness Recs II*, p. 175.

9 See also Goodare, 'Parliament and Society', p. 439; for further examples see *ERBE 1604–1626*, p. 58; *ERRBS 1519–1666*, p. 211; Shearer (ed.), *Extracts from the Burgh Records of Dunfermline*, p. 74.

10 *ECRBA 1625–42*, pp. 67, 120–1, 123; *Muniments of the Royal Burgh of Irvine*, ii, p. 69.

11 Renwick, *The Burgh of Peebles*; Dundee Town Treasurer's Account Book, 1646–1696, n.p. (second page of extraordinary discharge of 1648–9); Shearer (ed.) *Extracts from the Burgh Records of Dunfermline*, p. 43. The range of recipients and causes appears broadly comparable to those aided by authorities in English towns such as Nottingham: McIntosh, *Poor Relief in England*, p. 161.

12 Renwick, *Burgh of Peebles*, pp. 96–8, 125, 243, 251–2; *Muniments of the Royal Burgh of Irvine*, ii, pp. 239–40, 249.

13 *ERRBS 1519–1666*, p. 188.

14 *ECRBA 1398–1570*, p. 356; *ERBE 1589–1603*, pp. 360–1.

relief work of the kind generally carried out by kirk sessions, transferring resources to local poor people who were amongst the ranks of the long-term needy, rather than former burgh elites. But it appeared to be less of a priority. Additionally, during the early years after 1560 when some sessions were not yet operational, some councils played a role in supporting or even substituting for the work of kirk sessions on relief (as well as other session business).[15] More generally, burghs tried to ensure that additional income might reach poor people where possible, particularly through ordering that some of the fines imposed by the burgh be passed to the poor (sometimes via the kirk session, revealingly).[16] Most frequently, it was stipulated that ale or other products that had been sold or handled in contravention of burgh regulations would be passed to the poor: an effective and neat policy, and one that did not involve the expenditure of the burgh's own resources.[17] However, perhaps because it was the kirk sessions' main focus, routine poor relief occupied a very minor role within their charitable expenditure, which itself was a small part of their overall agenda and workload.

These trends are neatly exemplified in the very detailed accounts of burgh council expenditure in Ayr from 1534 to 1624.[18] Over this period 115 payments to individuals or groups were made that could be classified as relating to welfare; most of these were one-off payments rather than recurring and it was consistently a very small proportion of their overall business. 43 payments were to strangers to the burgh, such as shipwrecked sailors, and Scots from elsewhere or foreigners who had suffered misfortune.[19] A further 32 payments were to current or former burgesses, craftsmen or merchants, or burgh officials and servants. These included John Henderson, 'ane auld failyeit gild brother', and 'Andrew Craufurd, waulker, in support of his poverty', and the burgh also took particular steps to support its former servants and officers in hardship, ranging in status from procurator-fiscal to piper.[20] By contrast, there were only three payments to disabled recipients other than strangers or former burgh elites

[15] In Aberdeen the burgh passed acts on poor relief in 1565 and 1573, while the kirk session was in abeyance between its initial brief incarnations in 1562 and 1568, and then immediately before a proper kirk session was set up in 1574 and took over relief business: *ECRBA 1398-1570*, p. 358; *ECRBA 1570–1625*, pp. 9, 20–1; Graham, *Uses of Reform*, p. 114. In Inverness in 1562 and 1564 the provost and burgh led the way in setting up a formal kirk session, including acts on the collection and distribution of alms: *Inverness Recs I*, pp. 94–5, 113–14.

[16] *ECRBA 1625–42*, pp. 1–2, 191; Macbean (ed.), *Kirkcaldy Burgh Records*, pp. 95, 100, 114; Warden (ed.), *Burgh Laws of Dundee*, p. 33.

[17] *Inverness Recs I*, pp. 50, 58, 234; Wood (ed.), *Kirkcudbright Town Council Records*, pp. 70–1, 126, 213; *ERRBS 1519–1666*, 89, 151, 179; Warden (ed.), *Burgh Laws of Dundee*, p. 36.

[18] *ABA*.

[19] See, for example, *ABA*, pp. 143, 197, 206, 212, 249.

[20] *ABA*, pp. 109, 122, 147, 221, 229. This excludes any payments made to officials as fees for service rather than as charitable support.

and officials, plus three payments to children in need, three payments to assist with medical care, and nine payments to women without specified backgrounds. A further 22 payments went to men with little-to-no background information other than that they needed charity ('in alms', or 'of support').[21] Although some of these may have been of more humble status, it is clear that the majority of the burgh's relief efforts were concentrated on strangers in need, and those of good social standing or who worked for the council but had fallen on hard times.

A particularly prominent feature of burgh authorities' interactions with the poor was the repression of the undeserving poor. As we have seen, this was a concern for kirk sessions as well, but councils were particularly zealous in seeking the removal and punishment of idle beggars, vagabonds and the like, and it was probably the issue relating to poverty they most frequently discussed.[22] Punishments threatened for the recalcitrant could be particularly harsh, including branding or execution, as well as simple banishment.[23] Hostility to vagabonds was particularly apparent during times of plague, when towns were determined to keep out suspicious outsiders, a category that might include musicians or traders, but amongst which stranger beggars were a particular fear.[24] The perceived association between vagabonds and serious disorder or crime was also a factor, and some idle or sturdy beggars were accused of various additional offences, such as 'theft and pyikrey', drinking, quarrelling and fighting.[25] One Glasgow 'vagabund' was scourged through the town after both aggressive begging, and attacking a woman with a knife (he was to be hanged if he returned).[26] Policies against vagabonds and sturdy beggars were inevitably deeply linked to crime, plague and disorder. So as well as providing relief to a more select group of recipients, councils were particularly focused on punishing and excluding those poor who were considered a threat to the community.

One other policy that urban councils sometimes considered was raising a compulsory tax to pay for poor relief. This does not seem to have been something that the majority of burgh governments were particularly concerned with, or willing to contemplate organising and paying. But there

[21] *ABA*, pp. 145, 154, 197

[22] For examples see *ECRBA 1398–1570*, pp. 234–5; *ERRBS 1519–1666*, p. 106; *ERBE 1589–1603*, pp. 50–1; *Inverness Recs I*, pp. 289–90; *Muniments of the Royal Burgh of Irvine*, ii, p. 241; Wood (ed.), *Kirkcudbright Town Council Records*, pp. 16, 185, 222; Munro (ed.), *Records of Old Aberdeen*, pp. 63, 73.

[23] *ECRBA 1398–1570*, pp. 234–5; *Inverness Recs II*, p. 95; *ERRBS 1519-1666*, p. 119; Munro (ed.), *Records of Old Aberdeen*, pp. 60–1.

[24] *ECRBA 1398–1570*, p. 274; *ABA*, p. 211; Wood (ed.), *Kirkcudbright Town Council Records*, p. 735; *ERBG*, pp. 27–30; Munro (ed.), *Records of Old Aberdeen*, pp. 34–5. It has been suggested that Aberdeen's plague-prevention measures achieved particularly striking success from *c.* 1549–1647: Jillings, 'Preventing Plague'.

[25] *ERBG*, p. 162; *Inverness Recs II*, pp. 58–9, 110, 147–8; *ERRBS 1519–1666*, pp. 129, 162–3; Shearer (ed.), *Extracts from the Burgh Records of Dunfermline*, p. 9.

[26] *Burgh Records of the City of Glasgow*, p. 55.

were some serious attempts to raise relief funds through compulsory contributions imposed on individuals (which, as discussed, earlier have been rather prominent in the historiography).[27] Unsurprisingly, Edinburgh witnessed the most serious experiments with poor-taxation, as explored by Stewart. By the 1590s and into the seventeenth century, compulsory contributions were being exacted from Edinburgh citizens, and supplemented by the church door collections.[28] Edinburgh's experience was atypical, both in the presence and in the persistence of compulsory contribution at the heart of relief funding, and the extent of council rather than kirk session leadership in the administration of relief.[29] But other burghs did witness some attempts at or experiments with compulsion: in Dundee and St Cuthbert's, for example, there were desires amongst kirk session and burgh leaders to introduce elements of compulsion to fund relief, although when these did not come to fruition there were still effective and substantial collection-based schemes in place.[30] In the 1590s Aberdeen's council tried to stimulate an ambitious scheme whereby citizens would agree to take in orphans (or have their existing care of orphans formalised), and commit to quarterly contributions for the rest of the poor.[31] In 1619 there was some success in raising a stent for the poor, and so in 1621 the council agreed to turn what had been a temporary experiment into a longer-term policy.[32] In some urban environments, the poor might have benefited from policies to exact more compulsory contributions to their welfare, and this should not be forgotten even if it was ultimately a minor and intermittent element in the overall ecology of relief.[33]

The welfare activity undertaken by burgh governments did not take place in isolation from the kirk session. Co-operation between the two bodies was evident in, for example, the administration of legacies and gifts to the poor, the recommendation of specific individuals for assistance, removal of undeserving poor and, as discussed below, the running of hospitals.[34] They also worked collaboratively on extra-parochial causes and fundraising.[35] In Dundee the kirk treasurer, with responsibility for relief funding and distribution, was an official with close ties to both burgh and kirk session.[36]

27 *OPL*, p. 10; Mitchison, 'Poor Relief and Health Care', p. 224.

28 Stewart, 'Poor Relief in Edinburgh', pp. 8–9; Brown, 'Edinburgh merchant elite', p. 89.

29 Stewart, 'Poor Relief in Edinburgh', pp. 9–10; *ERBE 1589–1603*, p. 208.

30 See above, Chapter 2 (St Cuthbert's); McCallum, 'Charity and Conflict', p. 35; see also Goodare, 'Parliament and Society', pp. 435–6; Mitchison, 'Poor Relief and Health Care', p. 224.

31 *ECRBA 1570–1625*, pp. 124, 149.

32 *ECRBA 1570–1625*, pp. 359–61, 372–3; *OPL*, p. 10; Goodare, 'Parliament and Society', p. 437.

33 *OPL*, p. 29.

34 *ERRBS 1519–1666*, pp. 161–2; 157–8; *ABA*, p. 197.

35 For example see Maxwell, *History of Old Dundee*, p. 342; *ERRBS 1519–1666*, p. 172; *ERBE 1626–41*, pp. 88–9.

36 McCallum, 'Charity and Conflict', pp. 35–7.

Even where burgh-led taxation was central to fundraising, distribution to the poor was still more likely to be undertaken by the kirk session and its deacons.[37] And disputes between council and session over control of poor relief seem to have been exceptionally rare.[38] This may partly stem from the personnel overlap between session and council. It also reflects the fact that they had complimentary and overlapping (though as we have seen, not identical) agendas and responsibilities. Indeed, although it may not have been the overarching ambition, what emerged in towns was a diverse and mixed system, with different branches co-operating but often focusing on different aspects of charity and welfare.

Guilds

Merchant and craft guilds had a tradition of assisting their own members and their families when they fell on hard times, and this continued and perhaps expanded in the post-Reformation period.[39] This was not a contribution to the wider relief of the poorer sections of society, being even more selective and limited to 'decayit' brethren of former substance than burgh councils' relief provision. But it was a widespread practice. The Perth Guildry Book contains numerous examples of contributions – often the direct payment of a newly received entry fee – to merchants and craftsmen in need, such as James Michell, merchant 'for his support in his destitution and great need', and Alexander Chalmer 'in his need and long afflicting sickness'.[40] In Dundee in 1605, £40 was given to Henrie Cowston, 'for his support now in his sickness and decrepted age'.[41] Fines were another source of support for poor brethren: in 1567 the Edinburgh goldsmiths decreed that fines of £20 for infringing the rules concerning the melting of silver were 'to be dealt equallie be the deacone and maisteris to the pure beadmen of the craft'.[42] As pre-1560 fines had often been ordained for the altar of the craft, here the Reformation apparently helped to divert funds towards the needy.[43] As well as passing fines or fees directly to their brethren, guilds might take more active steps to ensure funds were available. The Edinburgh goldsmiths even passed an act for stenting their members 'to the support of the pouer of thair awin craft'.[44]

[37] *ERBE 1604–1626*, p. 10.

[38] One such exceptional case was a dispute over the keys to the poor box in Burntisland, on which see McCallum, '"Fatheris"', pp. 80–1.

[39] Cowan, *Death, Life and Religious Change*, p. 104; Grant, *Social and Economic Development*, p. 416; Smout, *History*, p. 163; Goodare, 'Parliament and Society', p. 439.

[40] Stavert (ed.), *Perth Guildry Book*, pp. 316, 341, 357.

[41] Warden (ed.), *Burgh Laws of Dundee*, p. 147.

[42] *Edinburgh Goldsmiths' Minutes*, pp. 221–2.

[43] *Edinburgh Goldsmiths' Minutes*, pp. 206–8, 210.

[44] *Edinburgh Goldsmiths' Minutes*, p. 220. See also Warden (ed.), *Burgh Laws of Dundee*, pp. 113, 350.

More typical was the use of a box to gather various funds for poor brethren, such as the Aberdeen merchant's box that was to include both fines and entry fees, and collections at sea for the poor and 'Goddis Pennies' (small sums put aside when deals were brokered).[45] Edinburgh's hammermen also undertook regular collections, often benefitting the widows of the craft.[46] It was generally expected that trades would have such boxes: Burntisland Kirk Session asked the tailors to set one up 'for helping the decayit pure of thair craft', and a few years later the maltmen as well, though the request also indicates that the practice was not always implemented.[47]

It was less common for guilds and crafts to assist poor people beyond their own members and dependants. As early as 1500 Dunfermline's guild court recorded payments including 2s 'in breid to the pur folk', and in 1562 they paid 10s to pay for 'ane cott to ane pwyr bairne callit Marane Barklay'. Fines were also sometimes to be paid to the poor in Dunfermline.[48] Perth's guildry provided a payment – albeit one of perhaps limited consolation – of 5 merks 'to the puyr folkis tyme of the pest put out of the toun', and during another outbreak in 1605 Stirling's guildry agreed to send 100 merks 'for support of the nychtbours of Arthe [Airth] visitit with the present plaig'.[49] Dundee's dean of guild had some discretion to make external charitable payments.[50] But the charity of guild and craft associations was generally closely focused on assisting their own. This does not mean its contribution to the wider relief system should be dismissed too lightly, partly because it reflects a mixed economy with certain institutions focusing on certain constituencies, as elsewhere in Europe.[51] Guild brethren and their dependants could receive some internal assistance and maintain some respectability, and this may also have eased pressure on other relief providers, and the kirk sessions in particular.

Hospitals

As I have argued elsewhere, hospitals and almshouses were a rather more prominent feature of early modern Scottish society than has been appreciated. They catered for a relatively small and select group of residents, but were an important feature of welfare provision, especially in towns

[45] *ECRBA 1570–1625*, pp. 215–16.
[46] Stewart, 'Poor Relief in Edinburgh', p. 11.
[47] CH2/523/1, pp. 170, 190.
[48] Torrie (ed.), *Gild Court Book of Dunfermline*, pp. 42, 102, 125–7.
[49] Stavert (ed.), *Perth Guildry Book*, p. 183; 'Extracts from the Guildry Records', in *ERRBS 1667–1752*, p. 383; see also *Hammermen of Edinburgh*, p. 142.
[50] Smith (ed.), *Guildry of Dundee*, p. 77.
[51] See, for example, Bos,'A Tradition of giving and receiving: mutual aid within the guild system'; McIntosh, *Poor Relief in England*, pp. 31–2.

where most were based.[52] Kirk sessions were often closely involved with the funding and organisation of hospital relief, and they were well placed to assist with matters relating both to hospital funding, and to the morality, behaviour and necessities of inmates and other beneficiaries.[53] Hospitals were not only associated with the church, however. Some were conceived more independently, such as George Lauder of Bass' 1595 re-foundation of the hospital at North Berwick initially founded by his ancestors in 1541. This was a pious and personal family exercise, designed to fulfil his ancestors' charitable intentions as well as to respond to 'the greit derthe that is in this cuntrie in thir dayis'.[54] And other hospitals were relatively independent from the kirk session because of a closer association with secular institutions: for example, Dundee's hospital was run by the town council separately from the wider ecclesiastical programme of relief, and Edinburgh's council managed the capital's institutional care.[55] Burghs also contributed to hospital building and repair expenses, or fuel costs, and like kirk sessions they might also be involved in the administration of private gifts and legacies to hospitals, and in regulating or confirming admissions.[56] As well as direct funding they might designate fines to be passed to the hospital, as in Stirling when feuding couples were warned that further trouble or injury to each other would result in £5 fines 'to be pait to the puir hospitale'.[57] A range of people and institutions shaped hospital provision, but town councils were often central to their administration.

Scottish hospitals varied in their demographic makeup. There were both male- and female-focused hospitals, and provision for specific groups like elderly widows or former family servants might be insisted on by a founder.[58] Lauder's North Berwick foundation was intended to benefit six or seven decrepit and loyal servants of the Bass family ('men quha hes spendit thair yeirs in the laird of Bass service'), emphasising the selective nature of some hospital foundations, both in terms of numbers of residents and in the eligibility criteria.[59] Many town hospitals, as in some other parts of Europe, were places for the relief of relatively respectable but now struggling burgesses and their ilk, rather like the beneficiaries of council and guild support.[60] Dundee's hospital residents in the mid-seventeenth century were mainly craftsmen and merchants, and Stirling's council entered a burgess

[52] McCallum, '"Nurseries of the Poore"'.

[53] McCallum, '"Nurseries of the Poore"', pp. 434–6, 440+n; see also for example *PKSB*, pp. 58, 180, 327.

[54] The re-foundation document is NRS, GD6/1223, pp. 1–2; for the earlier foundation see Hall, 'The Scottish medieval hospital', p. 102.

[55] McCallum, 'Charity and Conflict', pp. 53–5; Stewart, 'Poor Relief in Edinburgh', p. 10.

[56] *ABA*, pp. 62, 229–30, 263; *ERRBS 1519–1666*, pp. 94–5, 146, 162; *ECRBA 1570–1625*, pp. 30, 70–1, 308, 331–2; *ERBE 1589–1603*, p. 96; B51/10/3, ff. 59r, 63r.

[57] *ERRBS 1519–1666*, p. 81.

[58] McCallum, '"Nurseries of the Poore"', p. 440.

[59] GD6/1223, pp. 1–2.

[60] van Leeuwen et al, 'Provisions for the elderly', pp. 7–9.

called Andro Kirkwood to the hospital 'of thair pitie and compassioun'.[61] A dispute in Aberdeen in 1631 between merchants and craftsmen centered on the magistrates' insistence that the town hospital was for 'decayit brethren of gild of this burge' only, in other words merchants.[62] They later agreed to contribute to funding for the separate hospital for craftsmen, but the dispute highlights the exclusivity of much hospital provision.[63] The overall role of hospitals in the ecology of relief was complex: in some cases they were geared towards decayed elite figures, or another group targeted by a founder, in contrast to the wider scope of recipients of kirk session relief. Whatever their composition and management structure, though, the numbers involved were always fairly small.[64] Hospitals inevitably provided a lot of support to a select few rather than vice versa.

Institutions other than kirk sessions played some important roles in Scottish welfare. It is clear that there was sometimes significant relief work being undertaken by burgh elites. This was on a lesser scale and as a lesser priority than for the kirk sessions, and urban councils as institutions were particularly concerned with excluding idle, sturdy, or vagrant poor (as they saw them). The relief provided by councils was also focused on a more socially selective group of the needy. The same was true of much of the provision by guilds, and many of the hospitals, that tended to be based in towns. Of course, the vast majority of the Scottish population lived in the countryside, so the role of these institutions in poor relief on a national scale should not be exaggerated. The kirk session was still the most important and comprehensive provider of poor relief in nearly every Scottish town, and it was important in all. But in most towns, a range of other bodies had a role to play in welfare, especially (though not exclusively) supporting certain types of needy people.

Philanthropy and Giving

Individuals as well as institutions might provide resources for the assistance of the early modern Scottish poor. Within the broad category of private charitable giving, there was a wide variety of contributions, ranging from the formal testamentary bequest, and inter vivos donations, through to the most informal personal gift or dole. Such contributions were in some senses distinct from the regular collections made by kirk sessions – or indeed other ways of contributing, such as the involuntary fines paid to kirk sessions and councils – because they represented an individual and largely unprompted personal decision to attempt to help the needy in some way.[65]

61 McCallum, 'Charity and Conflict', pp. 53–4; *ERRBS 1519–1666*, p. 164.

62 *ECRBA 1625–42*, pp. 33–5.

63 *ECRBA 1625–42*, pp. 52–3.

64 McCallum, '"Nurseries of the Poore"', pp. 440–1.

65 This is not to suggest that the motivations for making these gifts were merely simple and straightforward impulses to give to those less fortunate. For some of the main contributions

However they were still closely connected with the other forms and providers of poor relief, with varying degrees of formality, and as was often the case in early modern charity the distinctions between different forms of philanthropy could be 'blurred'.[66] This section considers the official end of the spectrum – bequests, gifts, endowments and other formalised contributions to helping the poor, while more casual handouts or doles are considered as part of the third section's discussion of the wider ecologies of informal relief and survival strategies.

Testamentary Charity

One of the most formal ways of giving a personal donation to the poor and needy was through one's will. This was a chance to leave a charitable legacy alongside the practical business of dealing with one's estate, and before the Reformation it was also considered beneficial to one's soul. Historians have therefore paid particular attention to this form of charity in a pre-1560 setting, with Audrey-Beth Fitch noting the presence of almsgiving and other charitable bequests in some late-medieval Scottish testaments.[67] And even if one's soul could no longer be benefitted by almsgiving or prayers funded through testamentary charity, giving to the poor was still naturally an option for post-1560 testators.[68] Equally, historians are aware of the existence of some large bequests for specific schemes by high-profile individuals, although very little attention has been paid to more routine testamentary bequests.[69] We need to consider, therefore, the role that testamentary giving played in the mixed economies of relief.

In quantitative terms, the blunt answer is that it played a very small role. In samples of over 400 testaments from before and after 1560, only 24 contained explicit bequests to the poor: seven from 133 pre-1560 testaments (5%), and 17 from 300 post-1560 testaments (6%).[70] This small handful

to understanding the complex and contested nature of giving in early modern societies see Ben-Amos, *Culture of Giving*; van Leeuwen, 'Giving in Early Modern History'; Heal, *The Power of Gifts*; Davis, *The Gift in Sixteenth Century France*.

66 van Leeuwen, 'Giving in Early Modern History', p. 305.

67 Fitch, *Search for Salvation*, p. 32; Fitch, 'Search for Salvation', vol I, pp. 393–5; Rhodes, 'Property and Piety', p. 34+n.

68 Post-1560 testamentary charity is less well-studied, but see *OPL*, pp. 26, 73 for legacies and their contribution to parish resources in the period after 1650.

69 Perhaps most famously the bequest of George Heriot for the hospital and then school which bears his name: W. Steven, *History of George Heriot's Hospital*, pp. 33–5, 252–67; and also the Aberdeen philanthropist William Guild (whose testament left 7000 merks for poor orphans: *ODNB*). Bequests by wealthy women in Aberdeen are discussed in DesBrisay, 'City Limits', pp. 44–7.

70 The specific composition of each sample is discussed below when cited. All testaments were accessed through the NRS Wills and Testaments electronic search facility, that enables listing by year and by the Commissary Courts (each covering a range of parishes) with which the testament was registered. For brevity individual wills are cited by conventional manuscript references rather than name, place and date; they can still be accessed

constitutes a minimum, as it is possible that some bequests might have been made to named individuals who were known to the testator to be poor, but not described as such, although it is unlikely that this would significantly distort the picture.[71] It is also possible that generic instructions made to executors to dispose of property for the good of the testator's soul (pre-1560), as they would answer to God, or simply as they saw fit (post-1560), might have eventually included gifts to the poor. But the pious management of the estate implied in such cases could include settling debts fairly and seeing friends and family right, so it would be wrong to assume too much potential charity to the wider poor lying beneath the surface of these wills, especially given the failure by the testator to mention the poor directly.[72] Even allowing for the possibility of some unrecorded charity in these wills, this was still very much a minority practice. This is especially apparent in comparative terms because English and French wills were far more likely to include explicit charitable bequests.[73] However, it is worth probing the patterns amongst this minority in more detail.

The first sample included all 28 wills from 1514 to 1539, which included four with definite bequests to the poor.[74] There was evidence of discrimination about the recipients, as one bequest was to 'pauperibus honestis'.[75] In the 1540s there were three bequests to the poor from the 60 testaments sampled.[76] These could be very small: Peter Adam in Glasgow had a net

digitally with manuscript references alone in the NRS Virtual Volumes system. Where there was a choice – not always possible in the earlier samples – testaments dative were excluded. Where names were selected alphabetically by surname as a means of achieving a degree of randomness, direct or possible relatives or testators with other possible connections were skipped. All dates refer to the date of registration by the Commissary Court rather than date of composition or death. Additionally, all 27 wills surviving from 1559–61 were consulted but contained no information on bequests to the poor (on which see more below) and indeed offered much less detail than earlier and later wills, and so have not been included amongst the headline figures cited.

71 Horden, 'Small Beer?', p. 345.

72 Fitch, 'Search for Salvation', vol. I, p. 105, vol. II, pp. 833–4. Heal, *Power of Gifts*, p. 26, also notes that giving to family, as well as charity, was one's 'Christian duty'.

73 See, for example, Archer, 'Charity of London Widows', pp. 183–5; Archer, 'Charity of Early Modern Londoners', p. 230. The precise extent of testamentary philanthropy as a whole is hugely contested by English scholars following the extensive debunking of W. K. Jordan's figures, but regardless of the details of that controversy it is clear that testamentary giving was far more common than in the Scottish sample presented here: Archer, 'Charity of Early Modern Londoners', p. 225; Slack, *Poverty and Policy*, pp. 163–4. See also Pugh, 'Catholics, Protestants, and Testamentary Charity', pp. 482–3; van Leeuwen, 'Giving in Early Modern History', pp. 309–10.

74 These were from the Commissary Courts of Edinburgh (CC8/8/1A) and Dunblane (CC6/5/1): Edinburgh's Commissary Court included the city and its environs but also registered some testaments from elsewhere in Scotland.

75 CC/8/8/1A, pp. 7–8.

76 This sample comprised 20 from each of the three surviving Commissary Court records for this decade: Dunblane (CC6/5/1); St Andrews (1549 only, CC20/4/1) and Glasgow (1547–9 only, CC9/7/1). Because Dunblane has survivals from 1542 onwards three were

estate of £733, from which he left 26s 8d for clothing for the poor.[77] And John Franche's will, drawn up in the military camp 'aganis the Inglis army' at Musselburgh in 1547, provided an example of the blurring between charity to the poor and charity to one's (impoverished) friends: he left his goods to 'my pure freyndis to tham that misteris [needs] maist'.[78] A final pre-Reformation sample of 45 testaments from the mid-1550s threw up no further charitable bequests.[79] So before 1560, few testators chose specifically to remember the poor in their wills, although it is worth noting that many testators included no pious or spiritual bequests whatsoever (such as masses or prayers for their soul). Fitch notes that compared to the French, late-medieval Scots tended to 'make fewer bequests to religious institutions, and proportionally far more to their friends, relatives and servants'.[80] The paucity of charitable legacies may therefore partly reflect a wider absence of pious bequesting in many pre-Reformation wills rather than a deliberate spurning of assistance to the poor specifically.

Not very much seemed to change after 1560. The 27 wills surviving from 1559 to 1561 contain very limited evidence partly because many testators included only brief and formulaic legacies, more often than during other periods, simply leaving executors to deal with their goods at their discretion.[81] This may have been a response to the unstable religious situation, and it would be unwise to draw inferences about charitable giving from wills of this period. A sample of 70 testaments from the mid to late 1560s included just two charitable bequests, and there were three charitable bequests from 75 wills registered in the 1590s.[82] This represents continuity, as charitable bequesting was still a minority practice and there was not a switch from leaving money for prayers or masses to charitable purposes.

taken from each year before moving to the next year, in order to ensure a chronological spread. Although not happening to fall within the sample, Gavin Dunbar, archbishop of Glasgow, left 20 merks to the paupers of St Nicholas' Hospital: CC9/7/1, pp. 46–51, at p. 51.

77 CC9/7/1, pp. 35–6.

78 CC9/7/1, pp. 10–12.

79 This sample comprised all 45 surviving testaments from the years 1554 to 1556: Glasgow Commissary Court (CC9/7/1) and Dunblane Commissary Court (CC6/5/2).

80 Fitch, 'Search for Salvation', vol. I, p. 372.

81 These were from the Commissary Courts of Glasgow, Dunblane, and Lauder (CC15/5/1).

82 The 1560s sample comprised 50 from the Commissary Courts of Hamilton and Campsie (CC10/5/1), Glasgow (CC9/7/2) and Lauder (CC15/5/1), the only three courts with records from 1564–5. These were selected alphabetically from the 231 search results, alternating between each court in turn to ensure an even spread. An additional 20 were sampled from Edinburgh Commissary Court (CC8/8/1) which commenced in 1567 (sample spread evenly across 1567 to 1569), poor bequests at CC8/8/1, pp. 18–19, 37–8. The 1590s sample comprised 20 from Hamilton and Campsie Commissary Court (CC10/5/2), 35 from Edinburgh Commissary Court (CC8/8/21–29), and 20 from St Andrews Commissary Court (CC20/4/2–3), selected alphabetically from selected years within each Commissary Court; poor bequests at CC10/5/2, pp. 32–4; CC8/8/22, pp. 431–4; CC8/8/29, pp. 616–18.

By the seventeenth century, the pattern was similar in that a sample of 80 testaments from the 1610s includes six poor bequests, only a very marginally higher proportion and still well below 10%.[83] The 1610s donors were all from urban areas, although there was a mix of rural and urban wills in the sample, and comprised a minister (who bequeathed a poor box, rather than actual money), two Leith mealmakers, two Edinburgh merchants and an Anstruther merchant.[84] The gifts varied in size: 100 merks from the Anstruther testator's net estate of over £2000, and 40s from each of the Leith mealmakers. This suggests that among urban elites or craftsmen there was more of a tendency (as well as the means, of course), to leave gifts to the poor, but even among this demographic it was still a minority custom, and generally a small part of the bequest.[85] Another six charitable bequests, from a roughly similar profile of testators, were found in a final sample of 75 testaments from the 1630s.[86] This analysis is based on a sample, of course, and a small proportion of all surviving wills, especially by the later part of the post-Reformation period. A larger dedicated survey of wills, perhaps especially focusing on wealthier urban elites, might identify a sufficient volume of charitable bequests to undertake full analysis of this practice in its own right. But for our purposes it is very clear that, overall, very few testators specifically chose to leave anything to the poor.

Why is this? In many cases, of course, it might not have been practical to leave a legacy to the poor, especially in cases where it was already anticipated that debts would exceed the estate.[87] Occasionally estates were very small, and where the inventory amounted to only a few pounds it is most unsurprising that everything (including any debts that might be due the deceased) would be left to family and close friends.[88] The stress involved, especially for individuals like John Laing whose wife was pregnant as he made his will shortly before dying in November 1615, or Janet Reid who had five children in need of financial provision would likely reinforce the

[83] This sample included 40, selected alphabetically from Edinburgh Commissary Court 1613–15 (CC8/8/47–48); 20 selected alphabetically from St Andrews Commissary Court 1615 (CC20/4/5); and 20 from across the 1610s in Hamilton and Campsie Commissary Court (CC10/5/2–5).

[84] CC8/8/48, pp. 83–6; CC8/8/48, pp. 491–2; CC8/8/48, pp. 71–5; CC8/8/47, pp. 728–49, at 748; CC8/8/48, pp. 467–70; CC20/4/5, pp. 727–9.

[85] For some further examples of Edinburgh elites leaving bequests to the poor, see Brown, 'Edinburgh merchant elite', vol. ii, pp. 402–4.

[86] This sample comprised 20 from Hamilton and Campsie Commissary Court (CC10/5/5–6), 35 from Edinburgh Commissary Court (CC8/8/55–57), and 10 each from Glasgow Commissary Court (CC9/7/26–27) and St Andrews Commissary Court (CC20/4/9), all selected alphabetically from ranges of years within the 1630s up until 1637; poor bequests at CC8/8/55, pp. 148–50, CC8/8/56, pp. 161–3, 293–6, 303–6, 357–76, CC8/8/57, pp. 79–83 (there was also a bequest to augment a reader's stipend, but this has been classified as broadly pious than specifically charitable: CC10/5/6, pp. 142–4).

[87] See, for example, CC10/5/1, p. 38; CC10/5/4, pp. 336–8.

[88] CC20/4/5, p. 814 (£4 inventory plus debts, all left to testator's son); CC15/5/1, p. 68 (all goods and gear left to family).

prioritisation of supporting dependants and ensuring that the technicalities were all in order.[89] And of course, caring for your family (and ensuring your debts were cleared) was considered a moral duty as well as a natural human desire. We would expect the bulk of resources to be left to the deceased's kin, and especially close relatives.[90] However, the absence of small or symbolic bequests to the poor even in large, non-generic, and thorough testaments must be significant. A representative example is Michael Bartholomew, an Edinburgh merchant whose net estate was over £760, including a substantial inventory. He left a non-formulaic and piously-worded preamble: it would have not been too much trouble for him (or his survivors) to leave a small charitable bequest, but he chose not to.[91] These sorts of cases tell us that leaving money to the poor was not seen as customary, or felt to be a social or a moral expectation; it was apparently a very personal decision, relatively freely made. The fact that they were not conventional or purely customary choices might make these bequests more revealing about the testator's piety, and as biographical sources. But testamentary charity remained limited in post-Reformation Scotland, viewed from the perspective of evidence from wills themselves.

Wills are not the only source of information on this subject, however. The kirk session minutes include discussion of charitable bequests, which is significant partly as a supplement to the evidence from wills themselves, but more importantly reveals the close relationship between the testamentary charity that did occur, and the kirk sessions in their role as local welfare authorities.[92] As would be expected from the previous discussion, income from legacies was not a large and regular contribution to sessions' relief funding, and their greater visibility in the session records is simply a result of perspective: a few bequests in a few years look more prominent in session minutes that naturally never mention the dozens of local wills drawn up without charitable provisions.[93] Nevertheless it was sometimes a significant presence. In the 1640s Dundee Kirk Session's accounts included a section for legacies for the poor, and although it was only a very minor element in its overall fundraising, it could amount to several hundred pounds, although this was as a result of a few large bequests rather

[89] CC10/5/3, pp. 326–8; CC10/5/1, p. 31. John Lyon's will had to make safeguarding provisions for his daughter who was 'sumtymes Lunatik and mad': CC10/5/2, p. 438.

[90] For the dominance of immediate family in early modern English bequests, see Cressy, 'Kinship and Kin Interaction', pp. 53–9; see also van Leeuwen, 'Giving in Early Modern History', p. 317.

[91] CC8/8/47, pp. 454–9; for a similar example see CC8/8/48, pp. 101–2. For examples without such individually worded preambles, but with net estates of over £1000, specific instructions, and no poor-bequests, see CC8/8/48, pp. 151–4; CC20/4/5, pp. 830–3; CC8/8/1, pp. 58–61; CC10/5/6, pp. 123–5.

[92] Some legacies referred to in kirk session minutes do not appear to survive in the Commissary Court records, for example that left by Alexander Irving of Drum: CH2/448/2, p. 19.

[93] Cf. McCallum, '"Fatheris"', pp. 81–2.

than a steady flow of smaller legacies.[94] Parishes such as Falkirk, Ayr and Burntisland also recorded income passed to the kirk session from specific legacies to the poor.[95] Rural parishes also received legacies for the poor on various scales, ranging from £50 from a laird in Monifieth in 1578, to 40s left to the poor by Johne Lowhound's wife in Kinnaird in 1635.[96]

Indeed, there was a particularly strong psychological and practical connection between bequests to the poor and the kirk sessions, perhaps best encapsulated by the testament of John Calwart, an Anstruther merchant who left 100 merks to 'the puir *of the kirk* of kilrynnie'.[97] The phrasing suggests a firm association between the poor and the kirk, but more generally it is worth emphasising that kirk session minutes record legacies to the poor because they were often involved in administering the charity, having been passed funds by executors. There was clearly a strong feeling that they were the appropriate institution for doing this, presumably because of their wider fundraising activities and experience of distributing funds to the local poor. In rural areas, without burgh councils, they were by far the most organised and regular institution in the parish, but even in burghs this was clearly often felt to be a responsibility for the kirk session.[98] Their judgement was also clearly valued, for example by the testator who left 100 merks 'to the poore of ayre [to] be distributed be the minister and eldars of the sessioun according to the need and necessitie of the distressed within ther bounds'.[99] In 1649, the Canongate Kirk Session had to decide what should be done with 500 merks left for the use of the poor but currently invested in some properties belonging to the kirk session, and later the same year William Butter left £200 in legacy 'to the sessioun to be disposed upoun be the ministeris, elderis and deacones as they think expedient'.[100] Here the poor are not named but it is apparent that the legacy was made with pious aims in mind, and therefore the kirk session members were best placed to decide how it should be spent.[101] Kirk sessions were closely involved with the charitable process, not merely as administrators or proxy executors, but as potential sources of advice and adjudication.

Sometimes the presence of testamentary administration in kirk session records is an indication of problems. South Leith's session chased up Gilbert Lambe, who had to promise that he and his sister would pay the £100 left to the poor by their brother Archibald, in two instalments of

94 CH2/1218/16, ff. 44r, 88r and passim.
95 CH2/400/1, p. 145; CH2/751/1/2, f. 297r; CH2/523/1, p. 182.
96 OPR310/1, f. 38v; CH2/418/1, p. 8.
97 CC20/4/5, pp. 727–9 (emphasis mine). See also CH2/1218/16, f. 44r (legacy to 'the poor of the kirk of Dundie').
98 Although in Edinburgh the burgh was involved with numerous legacies to the hospital: see, for example, *ERBE 1604–1626*, pp. 101, 190, 194, 246.
99 CH2/751/2, f. 56v.
100 CH2/122/3, p. 677; CH2/122/4, p. 3.
101 See also CH2/448/2, p. 19.

£50 at the next two Witsuns.[102] And in the 1620s Ayr's session seemed to have ongoing problems actually extracting the bequests due to them, and it took several weeks of effort to bring in the £40 due from Alexander McCalmont.[103] A few years later the scribe had to scribble a note that 'legacies to be remembered that ar unpayed'.[104] Culross enacted that widows and widowers must actually pay to the poor what had been left them, suggesting that some executors saw this as a potentially easy obligation to avoid: the kirk session saw correcting this misdeed as part of its duty.[105] And perhaps unsurprisingly given the low frequency of explicit charitable bequests, sessions might exhort greater levels of testamentary charity, such as when St Andrews notaries were 'requestit be the sessioun to remember [remind] the seik, tyme of making of thair testamentis, to leif in thair legacy sum support to the puir of this citee'.[106]

Kirk sessions had a role to play, then, in co-ordinating what testamentary charity was available to the Scottish poor after 1560. They were often, if not always, administrators of bequests, and it made sense in both practical and perhaps symbolic terms for the elders and deacons to organise and distribute the funds.[107] Just as the sixteenth century in England witnessed a shift towards churchwardens administering legacies, so the advent of the Scottish kirk session provided each parish with officials who had sufficient authority to be an effective administrator of bequests, and enough knowledge of the poor to be a trusted dispenser of charity.[108] Of course, the decision to leave a bequest to the poor was a minority one, and so the actual extent of testators' contribution to the overall provision of welfare was limited, although the handful of very large bequests especially by wealthy individuals may have gone some way towards redressing this on occasion.[109] It is tempting to echo McIntosh's characterisation of relief income in England from testators as 'welcome but unpredictable': there was certainly no steady stream of income, but at certain times and places they might make a useful

102 CH2/716/1, p. 35.
103 CH2/751/1/2, ff. 413r–417r.
104 CH2/751/2, ff. 64v, 66r.
105 CH2/77/1, ff. 45r, 47v. See also *RStAKS*, ii, p. 942 where a widower agreed to pay up the 20 merks his wife had left to the poor.
106 *RStAKS*, ii, p. 776.
107 For examples where the kirk session was not apparently involved in managing the funds see CC8/8/1, pp. 18–19 (a legacy 'to be gevin to the puir hous eftir the [executor's] discretioun'); Spence, *Women, Credit and Debt*, p. 88 (surplus bequeathed to 'the poor households at the discretion of her executors').
108 McIntosh, *Poor Relief in England*, pp. 233–4.
109 See above (p. 216); see also Robert Johnstone, a Scot who moved to London and was associated with Heriot, and left large sums to various Scottish towns including £1000 Sterling for 'the poore and indigent persounes' of Dundee: Dundee Town Council Minutes volume 4, f. 148r; Maxwell, *History of Old Dundee*, pp. 467–9. Some Scots abroad also bequested large sums of money for charitable and educational causes within Scotland: Murdoch, 'Repatriation of Capital to Scotland', pp. 45–6.

contribution.[110] It was a contribution, moreover, that was often assisted by the kirk sessions, even though their regular and more mundane collection and distribution work was actually far more central to the relief of the poor in post-Reformation Scotland.

Lifetime Gifts and Donations

Many Scots chose to make formal contributions to charity and welfare before the time came to make their will, and beyond the communal collections carried out by the Kirk.[111] These were sometimes straightforward gifts passed to the kirk session for the use of the poor, such as in Haddington in 1630 when 58s was 'geven be William Smith in benevolence to the poor'.[112] A larger aristocratic donation came from the lady Wariston who gave £30 'to the support of the puir' in St Cuthbert's in 1608.[113] Sometimes the gifts would be targeted to support specific groups or schemes, such as the £100 from Captain George Wood in Ayr, 'to be imployed to the hospitall and the poore thair'.[114] Sometimes the monies presented were to be invested for the interest or profit to benefit the poor in the longer-term.[115] These were all philanthropic donations, not prompted directly by kirk session collections: at most the church had created an environment in which these individuals felt inclined to make these gifts.

Of course most people could not afford to spare such sums. But they were sometimes an apparently steady income stream for the kirk sessions: after receiving £6 given in to the kirk session via two deacons, St Cuthbert's Kirk Session concluded that 'ther be ane buik maid to registrat the namis in that gif in the samyn to the pure', suggesting a regular enough flow of gifts to make such a volume worthwhile.[116] The Dundee Treasurers' Accounts for the 1640s also contain numerous entries for voluntary gifts to the poor.[117] As some session minutes record collections and some disbursements but not full accounts, it is possible that these sorts of gifts were sometimes added to the poor box without leaving a trace in the records. And in Stirling in 1615 the session noted with concern that £20 Sterling (£240 Scots) that had been gifted to be used for the support of two poor old women in the burgh by the widow of a royal servant had not yet been

110 McIntosh, *Poor Relief in England*, p. 234.

111 There has been little study of Scottish philanthropy from 1560 to 1650, but for very useful discussion of Aberdeen's female philanthropists in the seventeenth century see DesBrisay, 'City limits', pp. 44–8. For the significance of varied forms of lifetime gifts in England see Ben-Amos, *Culture of Giving*, pp. 122–6.

112 CH2/799/1, f. 308v.

113 CH2/718/2, p. 310.

114 CH2/751/1/2, f. 295v.

115 CH2/448/2, p. 19; CH2/1173/1, pp. 207–8; CH2/718/2, p. 224.

116 CH2/718/2, p. 261.

117 CH2/1218/16, ff. 89r–90r and passim.

invested.[118] This was included in the minutes only because they decided to provide alternative temporary support to the women, so it is possible that if things had gone more smoothly we would not have direct evidence of the gift's existence.

The kirk sessions were, again, the natural choice of institution to receive these gifts: they could bolster existing funds, and the sessions were, by implication, trusted to dispense (and, where relevant, invest) the resources appropriately. It also meant one could make a large charitable donation without having to divide it up and pass it to the kirk session piecemeal, or directly to individual poor people. Motivations for actually giving in the first place are almost as hidden as they are for regular session collections. For some donors, such as the comfortably off Stirling widow leaving money for poor Stirling widows, the sense of connection with recipients was obvious, but group affinity was not the only factor as often gifts were simply for the generic poor of the area. Giving to the kirk session ensured that your minister and elders were aware of your charitability, and perhaps the desire to bolster reputation sometimes played a part. This should not be overplayed, however. Tantalising glimpses of charitability that were definitely not for public observation are provided when sessions referred to deliberately anonymous gifts: Dundee's session received £6 13s 4d, via one of their collectors, from 'ane certane person who shall nott have hir name knowine'.[119] And in Edinburgh in 1574, 'Mathow Forester eldar presentit the sowme of iiii lib delyverit to him be ane gentill man quhais name he wald not expres'.[120] Overall, the motivations for these and less anonymous gifts must remain uncertain, but it is clear that many prosperous Scots desired to make personal charitable gifts over and above any contributions to the alms-dish at church services.

Another source of voluntary donations, which could be substantial in some parishes, came from the sea. Several parishes recorded numerous contributions given in by sailors and skippers from their time at sea. Anstruther Kirk Session received several hundred pounds in routine donations from ships in the 1610s, often from voyages to Norway or England.[121] Some maritime donations followed dangerous circumstances and represented vows or pledges in response to the dangers, such as the five merks given in to St Cuthbert's session by one of its own deacons 'quhilk he promisit quhen he was in daunger upon the sie', or another parishioner who 'gaif twentie schillinges to the pures box quhilk he had appoynttit to the pure in his trubling in the sie'.[122] Two men in Perth gave 32 merks and 10 merks respectively from 'thair last wayage towardis flanderis they

[118] CH2/1026/2, p. 8.

[119] CH2/1218/44, f. 89r. Anonymity may also have been desired by 'ane charitabill person' who gave £30; f. 215v; see also Stewart, 'Poor Relief in Edinburgh', p. 22.

[120] CH2/450/1, p. 18.

[121] CH2/624/2, pp. 262–6.

[122] CH2/718/1, p. 123; CH2/718/2, p. 296.

being in great danger of ther lyffis and gudeis throw tempest and stormye wether they vowit and dedicat to the pure of this congregatioun gif it wuld pleis god to preserve them'.[123] Gifts following dangerous times were not necessarily just from men who had gone to sea: amongst the offerings listed in Dundee, mostly from voyages, was £5 6s 8d 'given be Grissell Boytter spous to Patrik Goothrie younger; when shee was delyver of hir sonne', suggesting a similar response to a rather different peril.[124] Danger was not always involved, however. Jhon Salmond of Perth, temporarily in Scotland at Dumbarton between continental voyages, sent 'to be distributit to the poore xxviiis quhilk was collectit in the schip', an impressive effort given the distance involved and the fact the kirk session would probably not have known he was present in the country.[125]

Philanthropic giving directly to kirk sessions provides further indication of the church's role in stimulating and organising relief over and above the routine work of collection and distribution. Of course, social elites in early modern Scotland also engaged in charitable endeavours that were not primarily channelled through kirk session funding streams, although the sessions, or at least ministers, did sometimes become involved with their work. Sir George Bruce's foundation of a small hospital for six poor widows in Culross was made by a charter referring to 'the zeale and affection born be me to the help and supplie of the necessities and indigencies of the decayid poor aged people' in Culross.[126] Bruce laid out detailed arrangements for the funding of the hospital, but also noted that 'I doe hereby recommend and committ the care and oversight of these poor aged people and the performance of thir presents to them in all tyme coming, to the minister and session of the kirk of Culross', and the kirk session was indeed involved in the business of the hospital in subsequent years.[127] Monimail's Kirk Session agreed that the minister should have charge of the documentation relating to the grants made by Robert, Lord Melville, for the poor (and in particular a school for the poor of the parish).[128] And the Bishop of Brechin's charter granting land to support the poor of Brechin made the grant in favour of Alexander Bisset and Charles Dempster in the name of the poor – Bisset was the minister there.[129] In larger burghs and especially Edinburgh, it might be the burgh council, or both council and kirk session, who would help to administer gifts and donations.[130] And on rare occasions

123 CH2/521/7, pp. 176–7. See *COP*, pp. 352–3 for the spiritual and theological implications of these vows.

124 CH2/1218/16, f. 46r.

125 *PKSB*, p. 211.

126 NRS, GD29/59.

127 CH2/77/1, ff. 105r, 110r, 115v.

128 CH2/548/1, p. 58.

129 DUA, BrMS 2/1/1/6; *Fasti*, v., p. 375.

130 See, for example, Maxwell, *History of Old Dundee*, p. 295; *ERBE 1589–1603*, pp. 96, 104, 198–202.

some of the realm's most powerful elites might contribute directly to local relief schemes: as part of fundraising for Perth's hospital in the 1580s, there was 'a contributioun gadderit be Mr Oliveir Colte to the pure of the burght of Perthe and ressavit be him fra the lords of our soverane lordis counsall and sessioun advocattis massris and advocattis servand'.[131] This raised £100 from the 'lordis ordinaris of the sessioun', and an itemised list of contributions mainly of a few pounds from the advocates, including a rather shameful section of the list headed 'Nihil' for those who gave nothing.

Many records of private giving reveal little about the motivations or background of the donor, especially where referred to formulaically in kirk session minutes. Occasionally some hint is offered, such as when a flesher in Kelso brought forward what had been a post-mortem bequest of 1000 merks to be endowed for the poor of the parish. The original bequest had been 'for certane causes and considerationes moving him of his awin voluntar free will and accord', and now 'for exoneration of his conscience' he paid the money immediately although he was to receive the interest on it while still alive.[132] This suggests an intriguing desire to see the money paid while still alive, and perhaps therefore to experience the positive (and conscience-salving?) feeling of giving.[133] The reference to conscience and implied moral element hints at the ongoing presence of religious motivations to give, as has been found to be significant for Protestants elsewhere in Europe.[134] Equally, George Lauder of Bass' refoundation of the hospital at North Berwick reflected a strong sense of family pride and identity, partly through the desire to care for 'poor unhabill and auld servandes to the hous of the Bass' and also through the concern that his heirs and successors maintain his 'expedient and godlie' refoundation of the hospital (located at the ancestral burial site) 'in sic Integritie as thai will answer to god thair anent'.[135] This was a philanthropic exercise that was about the past and future of his family as well as the problems of poverty. For most lifetime contributions, however, motivations remain less clear.

131 NRS, GD79/6/26. Colt was later involved in the efforts to fund the re-confirmation of the hospital charter: *PKSB*, pp. 57, 395.

132 CH2/1173/1, pp. 207–8.

133 Gratitude for divine favour might also be expressed when framing donations, such as a contribution to the Stirling poor from a Scottish colonel in the Low Countries, 'for the manifold merceis of God bestowit on him': *ERRBS 1519–1666*, p. 108.

134 van Leeuwen, 'Giving in Early Modern History', pp. 322–6; Looijesteijn and van Leeuwen, 'Founding Large Charities', p. 24. Ben-Amos, *Culture of Giving*, pp. 243–55 demonstrates how English Protestants effectively exhorted the religious imperative to give without reverting to works-salvation or implied spiritual rewards.

135 NRS, GD6/1223, p. 1. A degree of genuine religious concern here is suggested by the fact that 'as thai will answer to god thair anent' has been added in to replace the previous wording (which has been struck out but still legible): 'as thai salbe for the same', from which a word like 'answerable' is likely missing. This is one of several corrections which suggest a carefully considered choice of words.

We would likely learn more from a dedicated study of extra-ecclesiastical philanthropy and charity in sixteenth- and seventeenth-century Scotland, that could tell us more about the people who gave, and their agendas, by gathering the extensive but extremely scattered evidence from wills, charters and related foundation documents, and perhaps burgh records and family papers as well, in some cases. But from the perspective of poor relief itself, what is clear is that philanthropic giving was a useful, if minor, addition to the relief work of the kirk sessions, and also closely entwined with it in many ways. Private philanthropy by social elites was sometimes more likely than kirk sessions to target specific types of poor (like the poor old widows of Culross and Stirling), but this was by no means the case across the board. And although testamentary charity was a minority decision, the presence of lifetime grants made on an individual freewill basis suggests that this was not entirely as a result of a lack of charitable feeling. Kirk sessions' regular collections were not felt to be the limit of donors' responsibilities, nor an imposition which made the granting of additional support an undesirable or unbearable burden.

Informal Assistance and Survival Strategies

Beyond the organised relief provided by institutions and individuals, we know that there must have been a range of other mechanisms and strategies by which the poor survived. This is partly because in Scotland, as elsewhere, the formal relief provided could normally only supplement and assist, rather than provide all living expenses.[136] The seasonality and uncertainty of employment and income, in relation to necessities and the need to support dependants, also means that a fairly wide group of people would have struggled at various points in their lives. There was no straightforward cohort of paupers receiving a certain level of relief to meet specific needs across the board. Formal relief was only part of the story, perhaps even just 'the tip of the iceberg'.[137] Historians of early modern poverty in other countries have become far more alert to the informal sources of support, and the 'economy of makeshifts' that enabled the poor to survive.[138] These include casual help by other members of the community, but also, flipping the perspective to that of the poor themselves, various strategies, licit or otherwise, by which their resources could be supplemented and bolstered. This has been coupled with growing interest in the related subject of the experiences of poverty, focusing on the lives of the poor from their own

136 See above (Chapters 2 and 3); *OTP*, pp. 71, 92; McIntosh, 'Poor relief in Elizabethan English communities', pp. 345, 352+n; King, 'Poor Relief and English Economic Development Reappraised', p. 365; van Leeuwen, 'Giving in Early Modern History', p. 303; Gibson and Smout, *Prices*, pp. 349–50.

137 Ben-Amos, 'Gifts and Favors', pp. 295–6.

138 Hufton, *Poor of Eighteenth Century France*, p. 15; Jutte, *Poverty*, pp. 2–3.

perspective as opposed to studying the poor primarily as the objects of elite benevolence (or persecution).[139]

It is very challenging, but essential, to apply these concepts and questions to the poor of sixteenth- and seventeenth-century Scotland. The challenges essentially relate to sources, because some of the rich texts used to explore the worlds and narratives of the poor, and in particular their survival strategies, are not so apparent for early modern Scotland.[140] The present study revolves around kirk session relief records, which document the decisions and activities of elites more than the experiences of the poor. However, there are glimpses into the more informal, makeshift and casual world of poverty in kirk session minutes and other records, some of which are recounted in what follows.[141] Another challenge is that formal relief itself has not been explored in detail for pre-eighteenth-century Scotland as yet, whereas English and other studies of informal aid, makeshifts and experiences of poverty have followed decades of extensive study of formal and institutional welfare schemes, which have helped to open up various ways into the subject.[142] And yet, it is essential, because we have to take into account that ecclesiastical relief, while the dominant form of top-down relief, was only part of how Scotland's poor individuals actually coped. Paying attention to this issue also reveals the ways in which kirk session relief interacted with these other more informal processes.

For all that the kirk session system provided a formalised and institutionalised system of collection and distribution, direct gifts and doles of varying sizes must have still been given to poor people. Face-to face giving, and casual interactions do not create rich paper trails, but they appeared to remain persistent in England through the sixteenth and seventeenth centuries, and it is hard to imagine circumstances in which they would not have in Scotland as well.[143] Of course kirk sessions would never record a merchant handing a coin to a poor servant who had brought him a message, or a comfortably off tenant's wife giving food to some poor children. Family

139 Scott (ed.), *Experiences of Poverty*; Hitchcock *et al.* (eds), *Chronicling Poverty*, especially pp. 1–2; Healey, *First Century of Welfare*, pp. 1–3, 12. See also Stewart, 'Power and Faith', p. 31.

140 For example, the petitions for relief which Hindle used to reveal the back stories of poor folk have no Scottish equivalent for this period (the references to supplications for relief, discussed in Chapter 7, are thinner and contain far less if any reference to the poor person's previous experiences). *OTP*, pp. 156–63, 380–98; see also Gray, 'Hospitals and the Lives of the Chronically Sick', pp. 297–300. Even for England, Ben-Amos has referred to the 'patchy and sometimes invisible nature of the evidence' on informal gifts and care: *Culture of Giving*, p. 79.

141 This is not by any means exhaustive, and follows some leads prompted by the institutional activities which are this book's main focus. Chris Langley's forthcoming *Cultures of Care* promises to offer hugely significant insights into informal care networks across seventeenth-century Scotland.

142 Scott, 'Experiences of Poverty', pp. 1–2.

143 Ben-Amos, 'Gifts and Favors', p. 336.

papers offer occasional glimpses into giving by the comfortably off: some 1644 notes of expenses in the Henderson of Fordell muniments include some 12s gifts to the poor.[144] As well as reflecting spiritually on his contributions to the alms-dish in organised collections, Archibald Johnstone of Wariston apparently thought it normal to hand out alms to poor people after church, as we know from his regretful story about striking 'a poor body, becaus he sought from me after that I had given amongst them in his sight'.[145] Such handouts appeared to be a fairly unremarkable source of informal assistance to the poor. Additionally, the evidence discussed in Chapter 7 that begging was regulated rather than proscribed by many kirk sessions, and the fact that sessions had to prohibit problematic forms of begging, points to the fact that dropping some coins into the hands of a poor person was, unsurprisingly, another way in which informal assistance might manifest itself. Informal assistance with food, too, might have been neighbourly rather than just top-down, as hinted at when Kilmadock's session made payments to those who 'durst not repair to their neighbours to receive sustenance' because of the plague, indicating that neighbourly doorstep assistance would otherwise have been the likely first port-of-call.[146]

Handouts of this sort would have been only very passing contributions.[147] There is however some evidence of more substantial direct intervention in assisting the needy, and particularly the sick, by their peers or neighbours. In 1609, a South Leith man who was to pay a maill to the kirk session was allowed to keep £5 'for keiping ane man in his house qu brake his leg for the space of half ane zeir or thairby': here the kirk session was intervening to subsidise an ongoing support arrangement.[148] Culross Kirk Session also made a financial adjustment to support informal care when Besse Riddoch was 'ordined to resseave 8 merks for housmeall of a house in Kincarne apoynted for a schole and because that the elders ther declared hir to be a poor body and to have many fatherles bairns to reseave a dolar more than hir housmeall extends to'.[149] And Perth's session reimbursed George Menzies the relatively small sum of 3s for lodging a sick person who then died.[150] A George Menzies subsequently received alms on two occasions, so this was apparently an instance of a relatively poor person helping another.[151] Wounded soldiers and their dependents might also be lodged

144 NRS, GD172/2308.

145 See above, Chapter 1; *Diary of Sir Archibald Johnston*, ii, p. 1.

146 CH2/212/18, p. 12; Jutte, *Poverty*, p. 83; Healey, *First Century of Welfare*, pp. 152–4.

147 There was also no Scottish equivalent to the charity ales which, according to Judith Bennett, were such an important form of neighbourly 'self-help' for the English poor: Bennett, 'Conviviality and Charity'; for reasons behind the absence of these ales in Scotland see Houston, *Bride Ales*, pp. 50–2.

148 CH2/716/1, p. 47.

149 CH2/77/1, f. 83v.

150 *PKSB*, p. 106+n.

151 *PKSB*, pp. 219, 265; Jutte, *Poverty*, pp. 86–99.

and sheltered in individual households.[152] These sorts of examples, as well as highlighting kirk sessions' keenness to promote and subsidise existing informal care, point to wider processes of hospitality or providing shelter. At the opposite end of the social scale, hospitality was of course a desirable aristocratic character trait, and one that parliament in 1581 feared was being undermined by nobles making residence in burghs rather than their estates where they could help poor people.[153] Whether fears about declining noble hospitality were accurate, at any rate more humble Scots do seem to have taken in and cared for the needy.

Poor people would, inevitably, sometimes seek lodgings or short-term access to shelter. Evidence on this process tends to come from kirk sessions' attempts to regulate the practice of 'receiving' dubious individuals. For example, when Elgin's session ordered the removal of strange beggars it also mandated a fine of 13s 4d for 'ressavaris of thame to hospitalitie'.[154] Lasswade also forbade receiving and entertaining various undesirables, gypsies, 'sturdie idill persons' and the like.[155] Although such acts testify to sessions' concerns about the immoral and undeserving poor, the fact they were felt necessary is instructive about parishioners' propensity to accommodate travelling poor people. In doing so, the parishioners were presumably motivated by a combination (to historians, an essentially intangible one) of charity and self-interest as those 'received' presumably contributed either payment in some form to the 'receiver', or were perhaps expected to carry out tasks in return for their lodgings.[156] Sessions might not always be entirely hostile to lodging poor people temporarily, as Aberdeen stipulated that no-one was to let to any stranger poor 'longer nor [than] a nicht at fardest' (and when parishioners let to local poor for a longer period they were to be held accountable for their behaviour, as they would for their own servants).[157] So the short-term expediency of accommodating even stranger poor for one night was apparently appreciated. The evidence suggests that it was an established practice to take in and offer temporary shelter to poor people.[158] The details on which these sorts of transactions were negotiated, and the extent to which the poor people being sheltered were expected to help or pay something in return is, given the nature of the session minutes, never recorded. But it was

[152] Langley, 'Caring for Soldiers', pp. 19–20.

[153] *RPS*, 1581/10/40; Heal, *Hospitality*, pp. 13, 33–4; *OTP*, pp. 104–9.

[154] CH2/145/1, f. 98r.

[155] CH2/471/1, f. 3r. For further examples of such acts see also McCallum, *Reforming*, pp. 60, 204–6.

[156] Work on reciprocity in early modern England might suggest that it is too arbitrary to separate altruistic 'giving' from self-interested 'exchange': Ben-Amos, 'Gifts and Favors', pp. 298, 309, 315.

[157] CH2/448/2, p. 84.

[158] This seems to have been the case in England as well: Ben-Amos, *Culture of Giving*, p. 132; Healey, *First Century of Welfare*, pp. 155–6.

certainly another way in which poor people might receive some assistance within the community.

From the poor's point-of-view, which other strategies were available to provide necessities that they lacked? To what extent were the casual and informal strategies through which the English rural poor 'made shift' available to Scottish poor?[159] The opportunity to acquire small quantities of food, fuel or other materials through illicit pilfering and the like must have been present, rather like poor people in England who might gather 'thorns and bushes' from hedgerows.[160] Where this practice crossed over from picking up materials that no-one wanted (or would miss) into something closer to theft, it might leave traces in the records. In Kinnaird on 14 December 1634 a man was fined 40d for 'taking away faill [turf] from the kirkdyk', and the fact this was winter as well as the relatively small fine points to this being an attempt by someone of limited means to acquire fuel.[161] Old Aberdeen's council passed acts against the stealing of peats in 1605 and 1647, and in 1562 in Prestwick a case of theft including 'commone pykre of pettis and kayll' was investigated.[162] Of course, whether to include more general cases of theft as a potential part of the economy of makeshifts is not straightforward because of the difficulty of confirming desperation and poverty as motives.[163] But in some cases it seems most likely that they were, such as the banishment from Dunfermline of 'John Chrystie and Marane Dalgleische his spouse Alexander Chrystie thair sone with tua litle barnis with ane young hussie callit Magie Patersoun beand convict of pykrie and specialie for steilling of aittis and beir furth of the barne of Rob Sandis in Balbowgye'.[164] This was a family of several generations, stealing food from a barn: how representative their story was is impossible to say.

One resource that the Scottish poor could perhaps not draw on as readily as their English counter-parts was common land and other customary rights. The English poor could, by custom, 'glean' the scraps leftover after harvest, or enjoy access to common or waste land, including for pasturage.[165] However 'custom' had far less weight in the Scottish legal tradition, and there was no equivalent in law of the English 'common land', or the legal right to 'glean' on the basis of customary usage (Houston suggests that 'heritors simply tolerated it [gleaning] for some inhabitants in the interest of poor relief').[166] The legal situation did not necessarily mean,

159 *OTP*, especially chapter 1.

160 *OTP*, p. 43.

161 CH2/418/1, p. 5.

162 Munro (ed.), *Records of Old Aberdeen*, pp. 38, 77; *Records of the Burgh of Prestwick in the sheriffdom of Ayr*, p. 66.

163 *OTP*, pp. 81–4; Jutte, *Poverty*, pp. 151–2.

164 Shearer (ed.), *Extracts from the Burgh Records of Dunfermline*, p. 9.

165 *OTP*, pp. 28–9, 36; although for a more cautious estimate of the significance of common resources for the English poor see Healey, *First Century of Welfare*, p. 132.

166 Houston, 'Custom in Context', pp. 53–5.

in practice, that no use could be made of such resources. In burgh records there are indications that the common lands were seen as a resource that the poor (whether the most needy, or simply the poorer sorts) should be able to draw on, normally recorded when an infringement of the lands had taken place. For example, in Aberdeen in 1556 there was a complaint that the 'puir inhabitantis ar hewilie oppressit and hurt' by impediments to their being able 'to cast, win, and leid fewall, faill, and dewatt [fuel, and turf], vpoun the commounty of the towne, quhar thai had wont to cast in tymmes bigane, past memour of man'.[167] And in Kirkcudbright in 1578 an act was passed requiring those taking tacks of 'ony scair [portion] of the commone lands' to pay a fee of 13s 4d 'for ilke scairis entrie to be disponit to the puir of the town', further suggesting that the lands were felt to be associated with the poor.[168] It is impossible to say how extensively or consistently common resources were open to the poor. Much must have depended on the levels of private encroachment in towns, and in rural areas the extent of the toleration practised by landowners. Equally, tolerated or not, something close to squatting might also take place, as hinted at in Edinburgh's taxation records for the mid 1630s which refer to a property with 'dyvers poore tennants in a waiste land lyeing east of the former all payeing no maills'.[169] Overall, customary access to commons, waste land or other communal resources may have played a small role in the survival strategies of the Scottish poor.

A more direct, if still highly partial insight into the lives of some Scottish poor during this period is provided by a handful of their testaments. This requires some important provisos: the very poorest, and certainly those who wandered and scraped away at the very margins of Scottish society – such as the barn-thieves discussed above – would not have left testaments. And at a higher social level, it would be problematic to assume the extent or nature of poverty from testaments that simply have small inventories and assets at death, which could be for a number of reasons and include tenants, cottars or labourers of humble means but who were typically able to support themselves through regular work. However, a handful of testaments from this period include specific reference to the impoverished or beggarly status of the testator, and these can more safely be used to gain an insight into the world of some Scottish poor.[170]

Jonet Layng died in December 1611, without leaving a will, but her sister

[167] *ECRBA 1398–1570*, p. 295. For other references to similar infringements (either being prohibited in general or specific cases) see *ERRBS 1519–1666*, p. 40; *Inverness Recs I*, pp. 9, 191; *ERBG*, p. 38.

[168] Wood (ed.), *Kirkcudbright Town Council Records*, p. 62.

[169] Allen and Spence (eds), *Edinburgh Housemails*, p. 11.

[170] These were identified through search terms such as 'puir', 'beggar' and variants in the NRS Wills and Testaments database for the period. The ten identified are therefore not exhaustive, but the database includes fairly full descriptions of the testator (though not the contents of the will). For a larger English sample of late-medieval wills from poor

arranged for a testament dative. Jonet was referred to as 'ane puir woman begging hir meit throw the towne and countrie' and therefore had no goods or gear other than some debts owed to her.[171] As well as the fascinating description of this beggar, it is highly significant that she was apparently owed debts of £14 and £10 by two other women from Paisley (this was presumably why her sister bothered with the testament). These might have been long-term debts, but they hint at the socio-economic connections of even some of Scotland's poorest people, as well as the fact that they were not entirely disconnected from the legal system. She was not unique in this: a 'beggar' called William Lambie had no goods nor gear but was owed some sums of money (possibly for work or goods as the money was not explicitly described as 'borowit'), and Bessie Daid ('puir wedow woman in Couper') was owed 40 merks plus one boll of meal, as well as owing her rent for the last term to Jhon Baxter.[172] Equally a 'puir' cottar, Cristian Wilsone, owed 'borrowit money' when she died.[173] These people had very limited means, but their role in the economy involved small-scale credit transactions, although this may not have been representative as the debts are also likely why their testaments were registered. Some further insights into how these people survived can be gleaned from their possessions: one man in Irvine 'being ane puir fischer had nathir guidis nor geir nor debtis awand to him except his fischyne lynis and the abuilyement of his bodie estimat to iiii Lib'. He owed £5, however, in housmaill to an Irvine burgess.[174] Those who lived near the sea (or possibly rivers) might have precarious means of surviving that included fishing, and the fishing equipment would have been vital to him. Other poor testators, such as 'ane puir theikar' or cottars, only had clothing and basic furniture to their name, and their existence was clearly very precarious.[175] There is no reason why any support from their kirk sessions would be recorded in the testaments, of course, but it is clear that although supplements might be very necessary at times, relief income was not the only resource on which these individuals could draw.

Much of the evidence discussed here offers us the briefest of glimpses into enormous realms of lived experience for the poor. The relief provided by kirk sessions was the most important and extensive source of welfare, and it is therefore both the most eye-catching to historians, and the most

individuals, and a close reading of an inventory, see Dyer, 'Experience of Being Poor', pp. 23, 25.

171 NRS, CC9/7/8, pp. 196–7.

172 CC9/7/19, pp. 521–2; CC20/4/3, p. 176. See also 'ane puir creill man' Malcolm Archibald, who seems to have lent out money, although his inventory suggests less severe poverty than Dais and Lambie: CC20/4/3, p. 92.

173 CC9/7/4, p. 180.

174 CC9/7/5, p. 171.

175 CC9/7/5, pp. 35, 282–3. One recipient of kirk session relief had to consent that should he have any possessions at the time of his death 'the poore of the paroch sould be air thairto': *Dundonald*, p. 433.

central to understanding how poverty was handled by early modern Scottish society. But, if we were to look at life through the eyes of the poor, the kirk session might not appear quite so prominent. At nearest hand, we might see family and kin, whose assistance is seldom visible in the documentary record but must often have been the first port-of-call.[176] Networks of neighbours, including people of similar or not much greater means, might also have provided help, food or shelter, especially at unusually difficult times.[177] Some resources might be taken directly through means of varying legality and/or social acceptability. Beyond these immediate networks and strategies were institutions: perhaps, in some towns, the burgh council, but always, above all, the kirk session. When it came to approaching the session, poor claimants seeking relief would need to present themselves as needy but hard-working, humble and godly; even if they were successful the relief would provide assistance and supplementary income rather than resolving their problems. However, welcome or essential this may have been, it is impossible to assess how the needy felt about their benefactors (and judges) who sat on the kirk session. Even so, paying careful attention to the range of ways in which the poor survived and coped gives us a better chance of understanding the interactions between the kirk session and poverty.

Conclusion

Help was given to various groups of the impoverished and needy from numerous sources other than the church in late sixteenth- and early seventeenth-century Scotland: councils, guilds, hospitals and private individuals of varying means all contributed in their own ways (and although this leaves the least trace in the sources, poor people found casual aid and pursued their own strategies to make it through). In towns, councils and guilds tended to have their own specific (though not entirely exclusive) agenda, to care for members of their own sector of society in need, and they often displayed harsher and more punitive attitudes to non-local poor and potential vagrants. Unlike kirk sessions' relief, hospitals were sometimes geared towards a certain demographic selected by their founders and/or administrators, and only ever supported a select number of individuals. Similarly, personal gifts and contributions were sometimes, though by no means always, intended for certain types of poor person, and the extent of the most-easily measurable form of private giving, the bequest, seems to have been comparably limited. But the fact that these forms of charity were often on a smaller scale, narrower, and more socially selective than ecclesiastical relief does not lessen their significance as part of a mixed economy, where certain mechanisms for providing welfare were focused on certain people and operated on their own terms. They were complementary rather

[176] *OTP*, pp. 48–9, 61; Ben-Amos, *Culture of Giving*, chapters 1–2.
[177] Jutte, *Poverty*, pp. 83–6; Dyer, 'Experience of Being Poor', p. 22.

than competing and they did not operate in isolation from each other. They were strands in an inter-connected and overlapping network of relief, which were diverse (as was the range of people who might need to seek assistance as a result of poverty and necessity in early modern Scotland). Crucially, the kirk session was closely involved with many of these forms of relief, and closely connected both to the poor themselves and to those who might help them, as well as performing its own main role providing the most extensive and widespread direct welfare itself. If there was an eco-system of relief in early modern Scotland, the kirk session was at its heart.

Conclusion

The problem of poverty was not a new one after 1560, and the desire to improve the treatment of the deserving poor (and to exclude and control the undeserving) was not an invention of the Protestant Reformation, nor of the sixteenth century. The Scottish Protestant reformers certainly wanted to improve welfare provision. But far more important than their rhetorical statements on the issue, or those of their opponents, were the institutional mechanisms they created as part of their new church. Through the kirk session, the Reformation of 1559–60 created the possibility for a localised and routine system of poor relief that was entirely unprecedented in Scotland. In the following decades, local ministers, elders and deacons began to put that possibility into practice.

This book has introduced the key features of kirk session poor relief up until the middle of the seventeenth century. It has argued that, in contrast to the negative assumptions and statements made when mentioned in passing, and especially the narrative of the failed implementation of the Poor Law, the system was a generally strong one. Substantial and regular fundraising took place, drawing carefully on the available resources to support relief, on an ongoing and durable basis. While most funds were raised without legal compulsion, fundraising mechanisms sometimes blurred any line between voluntary and compulsory contribution. The system was effectively managed and administered on a localised basis by parish clergy and lay leaders, with local variations on specific issues and problems (and the level of detail recorded in the session minutes), but also a broad common approach to the core principles of the system. They were dedicated and sometimes innovative in operating poor relief, and those problems that did occur involved individual failings rather than any institutional lack of enthusiasm. It was also resilient: kirk session relief weathered very severe pressures surprisingly well, and achieved a degree of stability and continuity in relief at such times, while sometimes responding swiftly to urgent cases of distress elsewhere.

At parish level, a wide range of poor people received varying levels and frequency of support from the sessions, with some flexibility about the form and amount of relief granted to those deemed needy enough – and moral enough – to benefit. Women often outnumbered men amongst recipients (in contrast to burgh councils which tended to cater more for a smaller group of their respectable peers who had fallen on hard times), but not as a clear or consistent gendered policy. A reasonably balanced range of ages and abilities were generally assisted, with the aged and disabled well-represented though not dominating, apparently reflecting broad patterns of poverty. Indeed, the system was quite sensitive to the situation of the poor in their own parishes, and responsive to the specific circumstances of varied individuals, families and localities. And some, though not all, of the harshness and condemnation of official statements and policies on the poor was softened in practice by the kirk sessions.[1] All of these features of fundraising and distribution made kirk sessions highly distinctive when compared with other sources of relief in post-reformation Scotland. The kirk session was not the sole provider of relief, but it was by far the most important, and it was closely connected with other providers and forms of support, as it was the institution best equipped to encourage, co-ordinate, and co-operate with other strands of relief across lowland communities, both urban and rural.

Two very important qualifiers must be appended to this summary of the book's critique of the narrative of failed Poor Laws in early modern Scotland. First, and most importantly, this system – as with other Protestant institutions and practices after 1560 – was gradually established. Kirk sessions expanded across even urban Scotland at varying pace and sometimes took decades to develop. In rural Scotland progress was even slower, especially before the turn of the century. This relief did not simply spring into being when Protestantism became the established faith; but equally, the development of relief by kirk sessions went hand-in-hand with their other functions. It was an integral element of their work once they were up-and-running, not an afterthought, a lesser priority, nor the preserve of a few particularly committed kirk sessions. This was true of urban and rural parishes: they demonstrated some different patterns of need and fundraising, and obvious differences in size, but the overall nature of the system was common to both, and there was no sharp contrast between urban and rural approaches to and experiences of relief. Indeed the kirk session was an institution that made possible a comparable system of relief in towns and countryside. Second, the scale of the relief is difficult to quantify accurately or meaningfully on a comparative scale, but the total amount of funding could be relatively small, perhaps unsurprisingly given Scotland's economic position in Europe.[2] Collections were sometimes very substantial, and a wide variety of individuals might be helped in various and responsive ways, but often (though not always) the proportion of possible parish populations named as in receipt of relief seem to have been at or towards the lower end of ranges found elsewhere.[3] The sums paid were rarely designed

[1] McIntosh, *Poor Relief in England*, p. 295; cf. Wormald, *Court, Kirk, and Community*, p. 168.

[2] Houston and Whyte, 'Introduction', pp. 1, 13.

[3] See above pp. 91–100; see also Stewart, 'Poor Relief in Edinburgh', pp. 11, 19; McCallum, 'Charity and Conflict', p. 51. More detailed case-studies might be able to attain more precise and safer estimates, as well as shedding light on the applicability to Scotland of Slack's suggested doubling of numbers in receipt of relief to assess how many were helped

to provide full incomes, and were sometimes intermittent and small supplementary contributions, and so the system was only part of the range of survival strategies even for the poor people considered deserving. In this, the experience of the Scottish poor was akin to that of many of their counterparts in other countries.[4] And although there was resilience in providing some stable relief (if not averting mortality) during times of intense crisis, it is impossible to say how far the broader extent of relief was limited by more subtle factors such as the difficult economic climate and inflation of the late sixteenth century. Need was often great during this period, but so were pressures on the purses of potential contributors. This was a system well designed to extract as much funding as possible and provide stable support to a specific body of poor, rather than an inherently wealthy system. There is no satisfactory measure of what could be classified as 'insufficient', 'adequate', or 'generous' relief spending, (even allowing for variations in the resources of a community, or nation), especially when it is considered that the aim could not have been to eradicate poverty but to alleviate suffering and protect the health of the community. But it is important not to exaggerate the size of kirk session relief.

Taking these qualifications into account, the processes of relief uncovered by this book in filling in the gap in our knowledge of parish poor relief in the sixteenth and seventeenth centuries have several significant implications. Most importantly, the emphasis on the failure of legislation, and indeed the perceived centrality of the Poor Laws in understanding Scottish poor relief, has been seriously undermined. It was not the case that 'little or nothing' was done for the Scottish poor, and characterisations of Scottish poor relief in this period as weak, haphazard, or as mere ecclesiastical charity, have turned out to be quite misleading.[5] Even if historians prefer to emphasise the smallness of some collections or distributions, this potential weakness must be understood as a specific phenomenon, and explained in relation to the mechanisms of kirk session poor relief and the socio-economic climate of the parishes they raised funds in, not as an automatic corollary of the absence of secular, compulsory or statutory welfare. Beyond the Scottish historiography, doubts have also been raised about the conventional sense of a sharp Anglo-Scottish contrast in the nature and effectiveness of early modern poor relief: whatever else it was, this was not a failed version of the English system. It may be that the recent questioning of English exceptionalism needs to be further expanded beyond prosperous Dutch communities.[6] More generally, the sharpness of distinctions between voluntary and compulsory, centralised and local, and secular and

(Slack, *Poverty and Policy*, p. 174), but it is obvious that some more individuals must have benefitted than those named in receipt of relief.

[4] Wales, 'Poverty', p. 388; van Leeuwen, 'Giving', p. 303.

[5] Mitchison, 'Poor Relief and Health Care', p. 220; see also above pp. 3–4.

[6] Meerkerk and Teeuwen, 'Stability of Voluntarism'; Goose and Looijesteijn, 'Almshouses'.

ecclesiastical schemes has been further softened by Scotland's distinctive example of an efficient and meaningful local ecclesiastical relief system funded by a range of sources across the voluntary-compulsory spectrum.[7] More comparative research is clearly needed to develop our understanding of these themes, and it will need to encompass a wider range of territories beyond the more familiar examples, as well as placing less emphasis on straightforward or binary classifications of welfare systems. In any case, this book suggests that the creation of kirk sessions starting in 1559–60, rather than the legislation of the 1570s, should be seen as the starting place for Scotland's contribution to the series of sixteenth-century welfare reforms and schemes that form the basis for current surveys.[8] Grander schemes for raising funds through teinds and regular taxation may have failed, but the kirk sessions developed practices of poor relief that it is hard to see having been achieved through any other means.

The relief work of the kirk sessions adds an extra element to our understanding of the Protestant Reformation in Scotland, and of the centrality of the kirk in social and economic life after 1560.[9] It certainly augments Margo Todd's arguments about the role of kirk sessions in negotiating religious change at local level: part of the 'social service' remit of the kirk sessions that enhanced their popularity (or at least acceptance) was an impressive range of poor relief work.[10] That this provided valued support for many poor individuals adds to the possibility that this helped the reformation to 'bed down' in the parishes (while complementing the disciplinary agenda by providing economic incentives to avoid being seen as ungodly). The social pressure to contribute at collections means that it would be hazardous to infer theological support or positive enthusiasm about the kirk session from the generally stable regular donations, but they do seem to suggest a broad public sympathy for the session's relief work, as do the personal gifts and donations to session relief funds made individually. In any case, the evidence of regular and careful relief certainly suggests a greater degree of success for the kirk in achieving some of the initial reforming aims dating back to the *First Book of Discipline* (and beyond) than has been allowed, especially where the failure to acquire ecclesiastical revenues has been foregrounded. This was another way in which the Protestant Reformation had a substantial socio-economic impact on Scottish communities.

It has been suggested that European reformations acted as a 'catalyst', rather than root causes, of poor relief reform.[11] There certainly was an

7 Bavel and Rijpma, 'How important were formalized charity and social spending', pp. 181–2.

8 Cf. Jutte, *Poverty*, pp. 105–42.

9 Stewart, *Rethinking the Scottish Revolution*; Mutch, *Religion and National Identity*; Langley, *Worship*.

10 *COP*.

11 Olson, 'Continuity or Radical Change', p. 171.

appetite for improvements prior to 1560 amongst many, and Protestant ideology in itself was certainly not a root cause, but one amongst a wide range of overlapping (and not mutually exclusive) motivations to relieve the poor.[12] On the other hand, the label 'catalyst' fails to capture the contribution of institutional reformation in Scotland, and the importance of the creation of kirk sessions, which should be considered as the engines of poor relief. Their characteristics certainly provided the basis for key features in relief provision such as breadth of coverage, durability, predictability, and organisational skills.[13] 1560 was not a sharp dividing line, as we have seen, but it was the starting point of an institutional transformation in poor relief at parish level in Scotland.

The statement that 'more research is needed' is perhaps a tedious truism with which to conclude a book. But as this is the first book to address this kirk session poor relief as a subject in its own right, some important remaining questions need to be highlighted. Some of these obviously relate to what this book has not attempted to cover, such as the highland situation. Other forms of relief and charitable giving would benefit from greater attention, especially where there is evidence available outside the years 1560–1650.[14] The lives and experiences of the poor themselves have been only a marginal presence in this book: kirk session material on relief offers one avenue for gaining further glimpses through dedicated studies and consideration of specific groups within the poor.[15] But concerning the main subject of parochial poor relief, there are some obvious next steps. The evidence discussed in this book suggests that we would have much to learn from similarly detailed studies of regular relief practice during the years after 1650: it is possible that despite new legislation some similar experiences might be identified in later seventeenth- and eighteenth-century parishes. The strength of kirk session practices as developed by 1650 might also have implications for understanding later processes of transition towards the poor relief of the later eighteenth century and the growing relationship with (and controversies over) legislation.[16] Equally, for the seventeenth century in general, there is huge scope for more detailed local case-studies,

[12] van Leeuwen, 'Logic of Charity'; see also above, pp. 9, 13–14, 44–8, 137–9, 224–6.

[13] Meerkerk and Teeuwen, 'Stability of voluntarism'; McIntosh, *Poor Relief in England*, p. 96; Olson, 'Continuity or Radical Change?', p. 172.

[14] Medieval charitable giving might repay specialist study incorporating diverse primary source material on the fourteenth to early sixteenth centuries; other potential avenues include charity amongst other religious groupings (Scottish Catholics, and for later periods possibly other Protestant denominations), and other elements in the 'mixed economy' of relief, such as elite giving and hospitality or philanthropy, where again source material is likely to improve by the later seventeenth century.

[15] See especially Langley, *Cultures of Care* (forthcoming).

[16] *OPL*, pp. 22–4, 45–67, 114–32. More detailed studies of the later seventeenth century tend to be focused on the famine of the 1690s or attempts to introduce compulsory assessment for relief, rather than routine practice, although Edinburgh and Aberdeen have some useful surveys: see above, pp. 4n–5n.

especially where the records might permit close contextualisation with the socio-economic and demographic evidence for a parish, and perhaps longitudinal analysis. As outlined here, local variations did not amount to regionally distinct welfare systems or contrasting approaches to poor relief, but the benefits of tracing relief and its recipients in individual communities could be significant.

Other questions could no doubt be asked of the rich kirk session manuscript material. But for all future research, one thing that is apparent is that the first century or so after 1560 cannot be treated merely as the first bleak and faltering steps of Scottish poor relief. And because the kirk sessions shaped and developed their own welfare provision, and provided the energy and focus for the poor relief system, it will make little sense to start with central policy and then look outwards for implementation or its absence. The Poor Laws need not be the guiding concern. Instead, as we have done for religious belief, practice and discipline, there is a strong case for focusing our gaze on the individual parishes and churches of Scotland when trying to understand its historic experience of poverty and its relief.

APPENDIX

Equivalent Values from Wages and Prices

As the Introduction discussed, precise quantification or purely statistical comparison of the real value of relief collections or distributions is impossible, because the records do not tell us about the specific needs or situations of most individuals, and more importantly we rarely have adequate information on important variables such as the contemporary population of a parish, or local prices, rents or wages. The book's analysis therefore offers more fine-grained and contextual readings of relief efforts in each parish considered (especially in Chapters 2–4), and integrates quantitative and qualitative approaches as appropriate to each example. However there are some sixteenth- and seventeenth-century value equivalents that can provide a broad and approximate framework for conceptualising the size of relief payments. These are discussed at various points in the chapters; the purpose of this appendix is to explain and contextualise these values more fully. All wage and price comparisons in the chapters, unless stated otherwise, are based on this Appendix.

Such an enterprise is fraught with problems of evidence and interpretation, as anyone familiar with Gibson and Smout's masterly investigation, *Prices, Food and Wages in Scotland, 1550–1780*, will be all too aware. As the authors note, calculating the real value of wages and the cost of living is exceptionally difficult even for the eighteenth century, and much of the necessary evidence does not exist prior to the 1790s.[1] Their study is also naturally more concerned with fluctuations and price trends rather than individual prices. Rather than attempting to create a simple index of values, therefore, it makes more sense for our purposes to establish a rough sense of what relatively humble workers might have expected to earn, or to pay for goods, during our period and in relevant locations, although even this basic task is hindered by the patchiness of useful evidence. Many wage rates were assessments and maximums (rather than real wages paid), and tend to relate to better-paid male workers, whereas women were well-represented amongst relief recipients, as discussed in Chapter 6.[2] They are often day wage rates, but the number of days worked must have been very variable: by the early eighteenth century when an estimate can be offered, workers would be fortunate to work 220 days in a year.[3] Payment might be partly in

[1] Gibson and Smout, *Prices*, pp. 337–47.

[2] Gibson and Smout, *Prices*, pp. 265, 290.

[3] Gibson and Smout, *Prices*, p. 281.

kind and/or supplemented through provision of board. Geographical variation was very significant, and the emphasis here is necessarily on chronological rather than geographical proximity as a result of inflation.[4] All of the following figures should therefore be treated as providing only broad contextual information and a rough sense of general values, rather than direct comparison.

Wage rates for urban day labourers rose during our period: in the 1560s they were perhaps 1s 6d to 2s per day, rising (alongside intense price inflation) to 5s–6s by 1600 or 1610. By 1650 they were at 6s 8d–8s per day.[5] These are broad estimates: as late as 1593 the Aberdeen day labour rate was assessed at just 2s 8d.[6] Women would have earned less, men in more skilled trades would have earned more, while the number of days worked would have been at least as significant a factor as wage rates in determining annual earnings. Price values are also available for urban areas: a pound of wheatbread might cost approximately 3d–5d in the 1560s or 1570s, rising to more like 12d–16d by the early seventeenth century, and 16d–24d by the 1640s.[7] Oatbread was significantly cheaper though (still in the range of 9d–14d for the first half of the seventeenth century), and ale was 2d–5d around the 1560s, rising to 1s by about 1600 and 12d–16d by the 1640s.[8] Poorer people were of course less likely to buy high quality pre-baked wheatbread loaves. Still, for the purpose of establishing broad context, it is possible to estimate that in larger towns around the start of our period, a pound of bread and a pint of ale might have cost 5d–10d, then up to 20d–24d by around the turn of the century, then perhaps towards (though unlikely higher than) 40d by the end of our period.

Rural evidence is patchier. One comparatively certain statement is that rural wages, (at least by the later seventeenth century when fuller evidence for the comparison is available) were significantly lower than urban pay.[9] An early glimpse is provided by the Justices of the Peace for Fife and Perthshire who in 1611 set out the wages of rural workers, providing a useful benchmark, albeit a maximum. Inferior farm servants (plough callers, herds etc.) had wages set at £8 per year, £4 less than the £12 assigned for general farm servants, while for a female farm servant the figure was £6 per year (and just £3 for a lass-servant).[10] Monthly earnings might therefore range from 5s to 20s depending on one's place in the pecking order. Day labourers could expect 2s per day with food, or 5s without food, though of course the number of days likely to be worked is

[4] Gibson and Smout, *Prices*, p. 261.
[5] Gibson and Smout, *Prices*, pp. 278, 299
[6] Gibson and Smout, *Prices*, p. 319.
[7] Gibson and Smout, *Prices*, pp. 30, 50–1.
[8] Gibson and Smout, *Prices*, pp. 56, 60–2.
[9] Gibson and Smout, *Prices*, p. 278.
[10] Gibson and Smout, *Prices*, p. 265.

an unknown.[11] By the 1656 Midothian assessment wages seem to have risen, although this may reflect geographical as well as chronological differences: day wages were 3s with food or 6s without, and a male farm servant's annual wages were set at £26 13s 4d (an 'Able Woman' would earn half that, and boys and lasses still less).[12] Significantly though, as late as 1695, in Renfrewshire and Aberdeenshire, monthly wages might be in the ranges of 10s–40s for men, and 8s–30s for women.[13] The variation and uncertainty here are obvious, but it is possible to conclude that amongst the relatively lowly workers who might serve as the most useful points of comparison for recipients of poor relief, monthly pay was likely measured in shillings rather than pounds, and many people throughout the seventeenth century must have earned less than a pound per month. The sum of 40s might have represented a good month's pay for a male farm worker; while for a young female servant it might have been well out of reach.

In both town and country oatmeal rather than pre-baked bread or other purchased produce would be a more accessible form of sustenance for the poor, and it has been suggested that a single pensioner could perhaps live on about one peck of oatmeal per week.[14] Fife county fiars prices suggest a possible typical price for a peck of oatmeal of around 2s 6d at the start of our period in the 1560s, although perhaps fluctuating between more like 1s 4d and 4s.[15] By the early seventeenth century, some prices from Ayrshire and Forfar suggest a range of more like 5s–8s for a peck of oatmeal, and by the end of our period a wider range of locations give approximate price estimates ranging from 5s at cheapest up towards 10s or 11s when prices were higher in particularly bad years.[16] In the 1660s some Fife prices for oatmeal were still around the 5s to 8s mark, so this seems a useful estimate to keep in mind for the seventeenth century part of the book as a whole, with the exception of the particularly bad years of the 1620s and 1640s.[17] However, these estimates require greater caution even than some of the previous figures, because in addition to the lack of certainty around the original price ranges that survive, prices per peck have to be calculated from the trading prices per boll (16 pecks), and it is uncertain how much might have been paid, under varying circumstances, for smaller amounts of foodstuff in parish settings.

It is worth re-iterating the 'puzzle', noted by Gibson and Smout and quoted in this book's introduction, of how workers managed to survive.[18]

[11] Gibson and Smout, *Prices*, p. 281.

[12] Gibson and Smout, *Prices*, pp. 266, 320.

[13] Gibson and Smout, *Prices*, p. 300.

[14] *OPL*, p. 22.

[15] Gibson and Smout, *Prices*, p. 84 (prices per boll ranging from 18s to over £3, often close to £2: a straight division by 16 is applied to all peck prices in this paragraph).

[16] Gibson and Smout, *Prices*, pp. 64, 84, 94–5.

[17] Gibson and Smout, *Prices*, pp. 127–8.

[18] Gibson and Smout, *Prices*, p. 349; see above, p. 24.

A perusal of these values indicates how workers (and of course those receiving poor relief) needed to draw on various other sources and strategies to survive in a way that does not compare directly to that of a modern wage-based economy. It also emphasises how very broad and approximate all of these measures are. They are probably the best guide we have to the economic parameters within which relief operated, but they must be used with immense caution.

Bibliography

MANUSCRIPT SOURCES

Dundee City Archives

Town Council Minutes, Volume 4, 1613–53
Town Treasurer's Account Book, 1646–96

Dundee University Archives

BrMS 2/1/1/6: Charter by Thomas, Bishop of Brechin
BrMS 3/DC 46: [Transcript] Diary of Mr James Guthrie, Minister of Arbirlot

General Register Office for Scotland, Edinburgh

OPR310/1: Old Parochial Registers, Monifieth
OPR403/1: Old Parochial Registers, Anstruther Wester
OPR440/43: Old Parochial Registers, Kinglassie

National Records of Scotland, Edinburgh

B9/11/3: Burntisland Burgh Court Book, 1598–1606
B9/12/2: Burntisland Burgh Council Book, 1606–11
B21/10/1: Dysart Council Minutes 1623–45
B51/10/3: Montrose Court Book and Council Minutes, 1603–9

CC6/5: Registers of Testaments, Commissary Court of Dunblane
CC8/8: Registers of Testaments, Commissary Court of Edinburgh
CC9/7: Registers of Testaments, Commissary Court of Glasgow
CC10/5: Registers of Testaments, Commissary Court of Hamilton and Campsie
CC15/5: Register of Testaments, Commissary Court of Lauder
CC20/4: Registers of Testaments, Commissary Court of St Andrews

CH2/34/9: Bervie Kirk Session Minutes
CH2/77/1: Culross Kirk Session Minutes
CH2/100/1: Dunbarney Kirk Session Accounts
CH2/122/1, 3–4: Canongate Kirk Session Minutes
CH2/122/29: Canongate Kirk Session Accounts
CH2/122/48: Canongate Kirk Session, Distributions to the Poor
CH2/145/1, 3–7: Elgin Kirk Session Minutes

CH2/154/1: Fife Synod Minutes
CH2/147/1: Ellon Kirk Session Minutes
CH2/171/1–2: Glasgow Presbytery Records
CH2/185/1: Haddington Presbytery Records
CH2/198/2: Jedburgh Presbytery Records
CH2/212/18: Kilmadock Kirk Session Records, Book of Penalties and Payments to the Poor
CH2/224/1: Kirkcaldy Presbytery Minutes
CH2/234/1: Lanark Presbytery Minutes
CH2/242/1–2: Linlithgow Presbytery Minutes
CH2/264/1: Menmuir Kirk Session Minutes
CH2/266/1: Mid-Calder, St John's Kirk Session Minutes
CH2/296/1: Pencaitland Kirk Session Minutes
CH2/296/14: Pencaitland Kirk Session Accounts and Testificates
CH2/299/1: Perth Presbytery Records
CH2/377/1: Yester Kirk Session Minutes
CH2/390/1: Dysart Kirk Session Minutes
CH2/400/1: Falkirk Kirk Session Minutes
CH2/418/1: Kinnaird Kirk Session Minutes
CH2/424/1: Dalkeith Presbytery Minutes
CH2/448/1–2: Aberdeen, St Nicholas Kirk Session Minutes
CH2/450/1: Edinburgh, General Kirk Session Minutes
CH2/462/34: Dalziel Kirk Session Minutes
CH2/471/1: Lasswade Kirk Session Minutes and Accounts
CH2/472/1: Kinghorn Kirk Session Minutes
CH2/521/2–3, 6–7: Perth Kirk Session Minutes
CH2/523/1: Burntisland Kirk Session Minutes
CH2/548/1: Monimail Kirk Session Minutes
CH2/550/1–2: Glasgow, St Mungo's Kirk Session Minutes
CH2/562/1: Kirkoswald Kirk Session Minutes
CH2/621/1: North Leith Kirk Session Minutes
CH2/636/34: Kirkcaldy Kirk Session Minutes
CH2/699/1: Longside Kirk Session Minutes
CH2/716/1: South Leith Kirk Session Minutes
CH2/718/1–3, 60: St Cuthbert's Kirk Session Minutes and Accounts
CH2/722/4: Stirling Presbytery Minutes
CH2/751/1/2, 751/2: Ayr Kirk Session Minutes
CH2/799/1: Haddington Kirk Session Minutes
CH2/809/1: Monkton Kirk Session Minutes
CH2/943/1: Montrose Kirk Session Minutes and Accounts
CH2/948/1: Kinnoull Kirk Session Minutes
CH2/1026/1: Stirling Kirk Session Minutes
CH2/1142/1: Fraserburgh Kirk Session Minutes
CH2/1173/1: Old Kelso Kirk Session Minutes
CH2/1217/33: Old Deer Kirk Session Minutes and Accounts

CH2/1218/16: Dundee Kirk Treasurers' Accounts
CH2/1335/1: Galston Kirk Session Records, Book of Baptisms and Accounts

GD6/1223: Memorandum Concerning the Refoundation of the Hospital [of North Berwick], 1595–6
GD29/59: Copy of mortification by George Bruce of Carnock, 1639
GD79: Records of King James VI Hospital, Perth
GD172/2308: Papers of the Henderson Family of Fordell, Notes of Contributions to the Poor and other expenses

St Andrews University Library, Special Collections
B65/8/1: St Andrews Burgh Court Book

PRINTED PRIMARY SOURCES

Acts and Proceedings of the General Assemblies of the Kirk of Scotland, From the Year MDLX, 3 vols (Edinburgh, 1839–45).

Alesius, A., *Of the auctorite of the word of god agaynst the bisshop of london* (Strasbourg, 1544[?]).

Allen, A. and C. Spence (eds), *Edinburgh Housemails Taxation Book, 1634–1636* (Woodbridge: SHS, 2014).

Ancient Scottish Poems, Published from the MS. of George Bannatyne (Edinburgh, 1770).

Anderson, J. (ed.), *Calendar of the Laing Charters A.D. 854–1837 Belonging to the University of Edinburgh* (Edinburgh: James Thin, 1899).

Bain, J. (ed.), *The Poems of Sir Richard Maitland of Lethingtoun, knight* (Glasgow, 1830).

Beveridge, E. (ed.), *The Burgh Records of Dunfermline, transcribed from the original manuscript volume, courts, sasines, etc., 1488–1584* (Edinburgh, 1917).

Bucer, M., 'De Regno Christi', in W. Pauck (ed.), *Melanchthon and Bucer* (Philadelphia: Westminster Press, 1969).

Burgh Records of the City of Glasgow, MDLXXIII–MDLXXXI (Glasgow, 1832).

Burne, N., *The disputation concerning the controuersit headdis of religion* (Paris, 1581).

Calderwood, A. B. (ed.), *The Buik of the Kirk of the Canagait, 1564–1567* (Edinburgh: SRS, 1961).

Calderwood, D., *History of the Kirk of Scotland*, 8 vols (Edinburgh: Wodrow Society, 1842–49).

Calendar of State Papers: Scotland, Vol. I (Edinburgh, 1898).

Callander, J. (ed.), *Two Ancient Scottish Poems: The Gaberlunzie-Man and Christ's Kirk on the Green* (Edinburgh, 1782).

Cameron, J. K. (ed.), *The First Book of Discipline* (Edinburgh: Saint Andrew Press, 1972).

Collection of Epitaphs and Monumental Inscriptions, Chiefly in Scotland (Glasgow, 1834).

Cramond, W. (ed.), *Records of Elgin, 1234–1800, Volume Second* (Aberdeen: New Spalding Club, 1908).

Cranstoun, J. (ed.), *Satirical Poems of the Time of the Reformation*, 2 vols (Edinburgh: STS, 1891–3).

Cranstoun, J. (ed.), *The Poems of Alexander Scott* (Edinburgh: STS, 1896).

Cunningham, W. (ed.), *Sermons by the Rev. Robert Bruce, Minister of Edinburgh* (Edinburgh: Wodrow Society, 1843).

Dundonald Parish Records: The Session Book of Dundonald, 1602–1731, transcribed by Paton, H. (Edinburgh[?]: privately published, 1936).

Ecclesiastical Records: Selections from the Minutes of the Presbyteries of St Andrews and Cupar (Edinburgh: Abbotsford Club, 1837).

Ecclesiastical Records: Selections from the Registers of the Presbytery of Lanark (Edinburgh: Abbotsford Club, 1839).

Edinburgh Goldsmiths' Minutes 1525–1700, transcribed by Munro, J., ed. Fothringham, H. S. (Edinburgh: SRS, 2006).

Extracts from the Council Register of the Burgh of Aberdeen, 1398–1570 (Aberdeen: Spalding Club, 1844).

Extracts from the Council Register of the Burgh of Aberdeen, 1570–1625 (Aberdeen: Spalding Club, 1848).

Extracts from the Council Register of the Burgh of Aberdeen, 1625–42 (Edinburgh: Scottish Burgh Records Society, 1871).

Extracts from the Presbytery Book of Strathbogie (Aberdeen: Spalding Club, 1843).

Extracts from the Records of the Burgh of Edinburgh, A.D. 1589 to 1603 (Edinburgh: Scottish Burgh Records Society, 1927).

Extracts from the Records of the Burgh of Edinburgh, A.D. 1604 to 1626 (Edinburgh: Scottish Burgh Records Society, 1931).

Extracts from the Records of the Burgh of Edinburgh, A.D. 1626 to 1641 (Edinburgh: Scottish Burgh Records Society, 1936).

Extracts from the Records of the Burgh of Glasgow, A.D. 1573–1642 (Glasgow: Scottish Burgh Records Society, 1876).

Extracts from the Records of the Royal Burgh of Stirling, A.D. 1519–1666 (Glasgow: Scottish Burgh Records Society, 1887).

Extracts from the Records of the Royal Burgh of Stirling A.D. 1667–1752, with Appendix, A.D. 1471–1752 (Glasgow: Scottish Burgh Records Society, 1889).

Gau, J., *The richt vay to the kingdom of hevine*, ed. Mitchell, A. F. (Edinburgh, 1888).

Hall, F., and F. J. Furnivall (eds), *The extant poetical works of William Lauder* (London, 1870).

Hamilton, P., *Paitrikes places* (Antwerp, 1531).

Hay Fleming, D. (ed.), *Register of the Minister, Elders and Deacons of the Christian Congregation of St Andrews, 1559–1600*, 2 vols (Edinburgh: SHS, 1889–90).

Henderson, E. (ed.), *The Annals of Dunfermline and Vicinity* (Glasgow: John Tweed, 1879).

Houston, R. A. (ed.), *Records of a Scottish Village: Lasswade, 1650–1750* (Cambridge: Chadwyck-Healey, 1982).

Johnson, J., *An confortable exhortation: of oure mooste holy Christen faith and her frutes* (Antwerp: J. H. Hoochstraten, 1535).

Johnston, A., *Diary of Sir Archibald Johnston of Wariston*, ed. Paul, G. M. *et al.*, 3 vols (Edinburgh, 1911–40).

Kendrick, R. (ed.) (1997), *The Poems of Robert Henryson,* Univeristy of Rochester, <http://d.lib.rochester.edu/teams/publication/kindrick-the-poems-of-robert-henryson> (last accessed 18 November 2015).

Kirk, J. (ed.), *The Records of the Synod of Lothian and Tweeddale, 1589–1596, 1640–49* (Edinburgh: Stair Society, 1977).

Kyd, J. G. (ed.), *Scottish Population Statistics Including Webster's Analysis of Population 1755* (Edinburgh: SHS, 1952).

Laing, D. (ed.), *The Works of John Knox,* Volumes 1–4, 6 (Edinburgh: Wodrow Society, 1895).

Langley, C. R. (ed.), *The Minutes of the Synod of Lothian and Tweeddale, 1648–1659* (Woodbridge: SHS, 2016).

McGinnis, P. J. and A. H. Williamson (trans and eds), *George Buchanan: The Political Poetry* (Edinburgh: SHS, 1995).

Mackay, W. (ed.), *Records of the Presbyteries of Inverness and Dingwall, 1643–1688* (Edinburgh: SHS, 1896).

Mackay, W. and H. C. Boyd (eds), *Records of Inverness. Volume I, Burgh Court Books 1556–86* (Aberdeen: New Spalding Club, 1911).

Mackay, W. and G. S. Laing (eds), *Records of Inverness. Volume II, Burgh Court Books 1602–37; Minutes of Town Council, 1637–88* (Aberdeen: New Spalding Club, 1924).

Maidment J. (ed.), *The Chronicle of Perth* (Edinburgh, 1831).

Mears, N., A. Raffe, S. Taylor, P. Williamson and L. Bates (eds), *National Prayers: Special Worship Since the Reformation, Volume 1, Special Prayers, Fasts and Thanksgivings in the British Isles, 1533–1688* (Woodbridge: Church of England Record Society, 2013).

Melville, J., *The Autobiography and Diary of James Melville* (Edinburgh: Wodrow Society, 1842).

Mitchell, A. F. (ed.), *A compendious book of godly and spiritual songs, commonly known as 'The gude and godlie Ballatis' reprinted from the edition of 1567* (Edinburgh: STS, 1897).

Mullan, D. G. (ed.), *Religious Controversy in Scotland, 1625–39* (Edinburgh: SHS, 1998).

Mullan, D. G. (ed.), *Protestant Piety in Early Modern Scotland* (Edinburgh: SHS, 2008 for 2001).

Munro, A. (ed.), *Records of Old Aberdeen, MCLVII–MDCCCXCI, Volume I* (Aberdeen: New Spalding Club, 1899).

Paton, H. M. (ed.), 'Haddington Records: Books of the Common Good',

Transactions of the East Lothian Antiquarian and Field Naturalists Society, vii, 1958, pp. 46–80.

Patrick, D. (ed.), *Statutes of the Scottish Church, 1225–1559* (Edinburgh: SHS, 1907).

Pinkerton, J. (ed.), *Ancient Scottish poems, Volume II* (London, 1786).

Pryde, G. S. (ed.), *Ayr Burgh Accounts 1534–1624* (Edinburgh: SHS, 1937).

Records of the Burgh of Prestwick in the sheriffdom of Ayr (Glasgow, 1834).

Register of the Privy Council of Scotland, eds Burton, J. H. *et al.*, (Edinburgh, 1877–1901).

Robertson, D. (ed.), *South Leith Records* (Edinburgh, 1911).

The Scots Confession, 1560 (Edinburgh: Saint Andrew Press, 1960).

Shearer, A. (ed.), *Extracts from the Burgh Records of Dunfermline in 16th and 17th Centuries* (Dunfermline: Carnegie Dunfermline Trust, 1951).

Skeyne, G., *Ane breve descriptioun of the pest quhair in the causis, signis, and sum speciall preseruatioun and cure thairof ar contenit* (Edinburgh, 1568).

Small, J. (ed.), *The Poems of William Dunbar*, 2 vols (Edinburgh: STS, 1893).

Stavert, M. (ed.), *The Perth Guildry Book 1452–1601* (Edinburgh: SRS, 1993).

Todd, M., (ed.), *The Perth Kirk Session Books* (Woodbridge: SHS, 2012 for 2008).

Torrie, E. P. D. (ed.), *The Gild Court Book of Dunfermline, 1433–1597* (Edinburgh, SRS, 1986).

Tweedie, W. K. (ed.), *Select Biographies*, 2 vols (Edinburgh: Wodrow Society, 1845–7).

Warden, A. J. (ed.), *The Burgh Laws of Dundee* (London, 1872).

Welch, J., *Forty-Eight Select Sermons* (Glasgow, 1786).

Winzet, N., *Certain tractates*,2 vols (Edinburgh: STS, 1888–90).

Wood, M. (ed.), *Kirkcudbright Town Council Records, 1576–1604* (Edinburgh, 1939).

REFERENCE WORKS AND WEBSITES

Canmore, <http://canmore.org.uk> (last accessed 14 December 2016).

Dictionary of the Scots Language, <www.dsl.ac.uk> (last accessed 2 May 2017).

The Oxford Dictionary of National Biography (Oxford: Oxford University Press, 2004), <http://www.oxforddnb.com> (last accessed 19 May 2017).

The Records of the Parliaments of Scotland to 1707, eds K. M. Brown *et al.* (St Andrews: University of St Andrews, 2007–17) <http://www.rps.ac.uk> (last accessed 2 May 2017).

Scotland's Places, <http://www.scotlandsplaces.gov.uk> (last accessed 27 September 2016).

Scott, H., *Fasti Ecclesiae Scoticanae: the succession of ministers in the Church of Scotland from the Reformation*, 8 vols (Edinburgh: Oliver and Boyd, 1915–50).

SECONDARY SOURCES

Archer, I., 'The Charity of Early Modern Londoners', *Transactions of the Royal Historical Society*, 12, 2002, pp. 223–44.

Archer, I., 'The Charity of London Widows in the Later Sixteenth and Early Seventeenth Centuries', in Jones, N. L. and D. Woolf (eds), *Local Identities in Late Medieval and Early Modern England* (Basingstoke: Palgrave, 2007).

Bardgett, F. D., 'The Monifieth Kirk Register', *RSCHS*, 23, 1987–9, pp. 175–95.

Bardgett, F. D., *Scotland Reformed: The Reformation in Angus and the Mearns* (Edinburgh: John Donald, 1989).

van Bavel, B. and A. Rijpma, 'How important were formalized charity and social spending before the rise of the welfare state? A long-run analysis of selected western European cases, 1400–1850', *EcHR*, 69, 2016, pp. 159–87.

Beier, A. L., *Masterless Men: The Vagrancy Problem in England 1560–1640* (London: Methuen, 1985).

Ben-Amos, I. K., 'Good Works and Social Ties: Helping the Migrant Poor in Early Modern England', in McClendon, M. C, J. P. Ward and M. Macdonald (eds), *Protestant Identities* (Stanford: Stanford University Press, 1999).

Ben-Amos, I. K., 'Gifts and Favors: Informal Support in Early Modern England', *Journal of Modern History*, 72, 2000, pp. 295–338.

Ben-Amos, I. K., *The Culture of Giving: Informal Support and Gift Exchange in Early Modern England* (Cambridge: Cambridge University Press, 2008).

Bennett, J. M., 'Conviviality and Charity in Medieval and Early Modern England', *P&P*, 134, 1992, pp. 19–41.

Blaikie, A., 'Nuclear hardship or variant dependency? Households and the Scottish Poor Law', *C&C*, 17, 2002, pp. 253–80.

Blakeway, A., 'The sixteenth-century price rise: new evidence from Scotland, 1500–85', *EcHR*, 68, 2015, pp. 167–90.

Bos, S., 'A Tradition of giving and receiving: mutual aid within the guild system', in Prak M., C. Lis, J. Lucassen and H. Soly (eds), *Craft Guilds in the Early Modern Low Countries: Work, Power and Representation* (Aldershot: Ashgate, 2006).

Broomhall, S., 'The Politics of Charitable Men: Governing Poverty in Sixteenth-Century Paris', in Scott, A. (ed.), *Experiences of Poverty in Late-Medieval and Early Modern England and France* (Farnham: Ashgate, 2012).

Brown, K., 'Early Modern Scottish History – a Survey', *SHR*, 92, Supplement, 2013, pp. 5–24

Cage, R. A., *The Scottish Poor Law 1745–1845* (Edinburgh: Scottish Academic Press, 1981).

Cormack, A., *Poor Relief in Scotland* (Aberdeen: D. Wyllie, 1923).

Coulton, G. G., *Scottish Abbeys and Social Life* (Cambridge: Cambridge University Press, 1933).

Cowan, I. B., *The Scottish Reformation* (London: Weidenfeld and Nicolson, 1982).

Cowan, M., *Death, Life and Religious Change in Scottish Towns, c. 1350–1560* (Manchester: Manchester University Press, 2012).

Cowan, M., 'In the Borderlands of Periodization with "The blythnes that hes bein": The medieval/early modern boundary in Scottish History', *Journal of the Canadian Historical Association*, 23, 2012, pp. 142–75.

Cressy, D., 'Kinship and Kin Interaction in Early Modern England', *P&P*, 113, 1986, pp. 38–69.

Crossan, R.-M., *Poverty and Welfare in Guernsey, 1560–2015* (Woodbridge: Boydell and Brewer, 2015).

Cullen, K., *Famine in Scotland: The 'Ill Years' of the 1690s* (Edinburgh: Edinburgh University Press, 2010).

Daunton, M. (ed.), *Charity, Self-Interest and Welfare in the English Past* (London: St Martin's Press, 1996).

Daunton, M., 'Introduction', in Daunton, M. (ed.), *Charity, Self-Interest and Welfare in the English Past* (London: St Martin's Press, 1996).

Davis, A. J., 'Social and Religious Meanings of Charity in Medieval Europe', *History Compass*, 12, 2014, pp. 935–50.

Davis, N. Z., *Society and Culture in Early Modern France: Eight Essays* (Stanford: Stanford University Press, 1975).

Davis, N. Z., *The Gift in Sixteenth Century France* (Oxford: Oxford University Press, 2000).

Dawson, J., 'Calvinism and the Gaidhealtachd in Scotland', in Pettegree, A., A. Duke and G. Lewis (eds), *Calvinism in Europe, 1540–1620* (Cambridge: Cambridge University Press, 1994).

Dawson, J., *Scotland Re-Formed, 1488–1587* (Edinburgh: Edinburgh University Press, 2007).

Dawson, J. *John Knox* (New Haven: Yale University Press, 2015).

DesBrisay, G., 'City limits: female philanthropists and wet nurses in seventeenth-century Scottish towns', *Journal of the Canadian Historical Association*, 8, 1997, pp. 39–60.

Devine, T. M., 'Reappraising the Early Modern Economy', in Devine, T. M. and J. Wormald, J. (eds), *The Oxford Handbook of Modern Scottish History* (Oxford: Oxford University Press, 2012).

di Folco, J., 'Discipline and Welfare in the Mid-Seventeenth Century Scots Parish', *RSCHS*, 19, 1977, pp. 169–83.

Dingwall, H., *Late 17th-Century Edinburgh: A Demographic Study* (Aldershot: Scolar, 1994).

Donaldson, G., *The Scottish Reformation* (Cambridge: Cambridge University Press, 1960).

Donaldson, G., *Scotland, James V–James VII* (Edinburgh: Oliver and Boyd, 1965).

Durkan, J., 'Care of the Poor: Pre-Reformation Hospitals', in McRoberts, D. (ed.), *Essays on the Scottish Reformation, 1513–1625* (Glasgow: Burns, 1962).

Durkan, J., rev. and ed. J. Reid-Baxter, *Scottish Schools and Schoolmasters, 1560–1633* (Woodbridge: SHS, 2013 for 2006).

Dyer, C., 'The Experience of Being Poor in Late Medieval England', in Scott, A. (ed.), *Experiences of Poverty in Late-Medieval and Early Modern England and France* (Farnham: Ashgate, 2012).

Dyer, C., 'Poverty and its Relief in Late Medieval England', *P&P*, 216, August 2012, pp. 41–78.

Elliott, L. K., 'Charitable "Intent" in Late Sixteenth-Century France: The Nevers Foundation and Single Poor Catholic Girls', in Scott, A. (ed.), *Experiences of Poverty in Late-Medieval and Early Modern England and France* (Farnham: Ashgate, 2012).

Falconer, J. R., 'Surveying Scotland's Urban Past: the Pre-Modern Burgh', *History Compass*, 9, 2011, pp. 34–44.

Falconer, J. R., *Crime and Community in Reformation Scotland: Negotiating Power in a Burgh Society* (London: Pickering and Chatto, 2013).

Fehler, T., 'The Burden of Benevolence: Poor Relief and Parish Finance in Early Modern Emden', in Kumin, B. (ed.), *Reformations Old and New: Essays on the Socio-Economic Impact of Religious Change, c. 1470–1630* (Aldershot: Scolar, 1996).

Fehler, T., *Poor Relief and Protestantism: The Evolution of Social Welfare in Sixteenth-Century Emden* (Aldershot: Ashgate, 1999).

Ferguson, T., *The Dawn of Scottish Social Welfare* (Edinburgh: Thomas Nelson, 1948).

Fideler, P. A., 'Symposium: The Study of the Early Modern Poor and Poverty Relief', *Albion*, 32, 2000, pp. 381–407.

Fitch, A-B., *The Search for Salvation: Lay Faith in Scotland 1480–1560* (Edinburgh: John Donald, 2009).

Flinn, M. (ed.), *Scottish Population History from the 17th century to the 1930s* (Cambridge: Cambridge University Press, 1977).

Foggie, J., *Renaissance Religion in Urban Scotland: The Dominican Order, 1450–1560* (Leiden: Brill, 2003).

Foster, W. R., *The Church Before the Covenants: The Church of Scotland, 1596–1638* (Edinburgh: Scottish Academic Press, 1975).

Foyster E., and C. Whatley (eds), *A History of Everyday Life in Scotland, 1600 to 1800* (Edinburgh: Edinburgh University Press, 2010).

Foyster, E. and C. Whatley, 'Introduction: Recovering the Everyday in Early Modern Scotland', in Foyster and Whatley (eds), *A History of Everyday Life in Scotland, 1600 to 1800* (Edinburgh: Edinburgh University Press, 2010).

Frohman, L., *Poor Relief and Welfare in Germany from the Reformation to World War I* (Cambridge: Cambridge University Press, 2008).

Gibson, A. J. S. and T. C. Smout, *Prices, Food and Wages in Scotland, 1550-1780* (Cambridge: Cambridge University Press, 1995).

Glaze, A., 'Women and Kirk Discipline: Prosecution, Negotiation, and the Limits of Control', *Journal of Scottish Historical Studies*, 36, 2016, pp. 125–42.

Goodare, J., 'Review of *The Culture of Protestantism in Early Modern Scotland* by Margo Todd', *Albion*, 36, 2004, pp. 375–7.

Goodare, J., *The Government of Scotland, 1560–1625* (Oxford: Oxford University Press, 2004).

Goose, N., 'The English almshouse and the mixed economy of welfare: medieval to modern', *The Local Historian*, 40(1), 2010, pp. 3–19.

Goose, N. and Looijesteijn, H., 'Almshouses in England and the Dutch Republic circa 1350–1800: A Comparative Perspective', *Journal of Social History*, 45, 2012, pp. 1049–73.

Gowing, L., *Gender Relations in Early Modern England* (Abingdon: Pearson, 2012).

Graham, M. F., *The Uses of Reform: 'Godly Discipline' and Popular Behavior in Scotland and Beyond, 1560–1610* (Leiden: Brill, 1996).

Grant, I. F., *The Social and Economic Development of Scotland before 1603* (Edinburgh: Oliver and Boyd, 1930).

Gray, L., 'Hospitals and the Lives of the Chronically Sick: Coping with Illness in the Narratives of the Rural Poor in Early Modern Germany', in Henderson, J. *et al.* (eds), *The Impact of Hospitals, 300–2000* (Bern: Peter Lang, 2007).

Greaves, R., 'The Social Awareness of John Knox: The Problems of Poverty and Educational Reform', *Renaissance and Reformation*, 12, 1976, pp. 36–48.

Grell, O. P., 'The Religious Duty of Care and the Social Need for Control in Early Modern Europe', *Historical Journal*, 39, 1996, pp. 257–63.

Grell, O. P., 'The Protestant Imperative of Christian Care and Neighbourly Love', in Grell, O. P. and A. Cunningham (eds), *Health Care and Poor Relief in Protestant Europe, 1500–1700* (London: Routledge, 1997).

Grell, O. P. and A. Cunningham (eds), *Health Care and Poor Relief in Protestant Europe, 1500–1700* (London: Routledge, 1997).

Grell O. P. and A. Cunningham, 'The Reformation and changes in welfare provision in early modern Northern Europe', in Grell O. P. and A. Cunningham (eds), *Health Care and Poor Relief in Protestant Europe, 1500–1700* (London: Routledge, 1997).

Grell, O. P., A. Cunningham and J. Arrizabalaga (eds), *Health Care and Poor Relief in Counter-Reformation Europe* (London: Routledge, 1999).

Hall, D., '"Unto yone hospitall at the tounis end": the Scottish medieval hospital', *Tayside and Fife Archaeological Journal*, 12, 2006, pp. 89–105.

Hamilton, T., *Poor Relief in South Ayrshire 1700–1845* (Edinburgh: Oliver and Boyd, 1942).

Harvey, B., *Living and Dying in England, 1100–1540: The Monastic Experience* (Oxford: Clarendon, 1993).

Hay, G., 'Scottish Post-Reformation Church Furniture', *Proceedings of the Society of Antiquaries of Scotland*, 88, 1953–5, pp. 47–56.

Heal, F. *Hospitality in Early Modern England* (Oxford: Oxford University Press, 1990).

Heal, F., *The Power of Gifts: Gift Exchange in Early Modern England* (Oxford: Oxford University Press, 2014).

Healey, J., *The First Century of Welfare: Poverty and Poor Relief in Lancashire, 1620–1730* (Woodbridge: Boydell and Brewer, 2014).

Heijnsbergen, T. van 'Advice to a Princess: the literary articulation of a religious, political and cultural programme for Mary Queen of Scots', in Goodare, J. and A. A. MacDonald (eds), *Sixteenth-Century Scotland: Essays in Honour of Michael Lynch* (Leiden: Brill, 2008).

Henderson, J., 'Charity and Welfare in Early Modern Tuscany', in Grell, O. P., A. Cunningham and J. Arrizabalaga (eds), *Health Care and Poor Relief in Counter-Reformation Europe* (London: Routledge, 1999).

Henderson, J., P. Horden, and A. Pastore (eds), *The Impact of Hospitals, 300–2000* (Bern: Peter Lang, 2007).

Hindle, S., 'Exclusion Crises: Poverty, Migration and Parochial Responsibility in English Rural Communities, c. 1560–1660', *Rural History*, 7, 1996, pp. 125–49.

Hindle, S., *The State and Social Change in Early Modern England, 1550–1640* (Basingstoke: Palgrave, 2000).

Hindle, S., 'Dearth, Fasting and Alms: The campaign for general hospitality in late Elizabethan England', *P&P*, 172, 2001, pp. 44–86.

Hindle, S., *On the Parish? The Micro-Politics of Poor Relief in Rural England c. 1550–1750* (Oxford: Oxford University Press, 2004).

Hitchcock, T., P. King and P. Sharpe (eds), *Chronicling Poverty: The Voices and Strategies of the English Poor 1640–1840* (London: Palgrave Macmillan, 1997).

Hollander, M., 'The Name of the Father: Baptism and the Social Construction of Fatherhood in Early Modern Edinburgh', in Ewan, E. and J. Nugent (eds), *Finding the Family in Medieval and Early Modern Scotland* (Farnham: Ashgate, 2008).

Holmes, S. M., *Sacred Signs in Reformation Scotland: Interpreting Worship, 1488–1590* (Oxford: Oxford University Press, 2015).

Horden, P., 'Small Beer? The Parish and the Poor and Sick in Later Medieval England', in Burgess, C. and E. Duffy (eds), *The Parish in Late-Medieval England* (Donington: Harlaxton Medieval Studies, 2006).

Houston, R. A., *Social Change in the Age of the Enlightenment: Edinburgh 1660–1760* (Oxford: Oxford University Press, 1994).

Houston, R. A., *The Population History of Britain and Ireland, 1550–1750* (Cambridge: Cambridge University Press, 1995).

Houston, R. A., 'Poor Relief and the Dangerous and Criminal Insane in Scotland, c. 1740–1840', *Journal of Social History*, 40, 2006, pp. 453–76.

Houston, R. A., 'Custom in Context: Medieval and Early Modern Scotland and England', *P&P*, 211, 2011, pp. 35–76.

Houston, R. A., *Bride Ales and Penny Weddings: Recreations, Reciprocity and Regions in Britain from the Sixteenth to the Nineteenth Century* (Oxford: Oxford University Press, 2014).

Houston, R. A., 'Church Briefs in England and Wales from Elizabethan Times to 1828', *Huntington Library Quarterly*, 78, 2015, pp. 493–520.

Houston, R. A. and I. Whyte, 'Introduction: Scottish Society in Perspective', in Houston and Whyte (eds), *Scottish Society, 1500–1800* (Cambridge: Cambridge University Press, 1989).

Houston, R. A. and I. Whyte (eds), *Scottish Society, 1500–1800* (Cambridge: Cambridge University Press, 1989).

Hufton, O., *The Poor of Eighteenth Century France, 1750–1789* (Oxford: Clarendon Press, 1974).

Jillings, K., 'Preventing Plague in Post-Reformation Aberdeen', *International Review of Scottish Studies*, 30, 2005, pp. 108–34.

Jones, C., 'Some recent trends in the history of charity', in Daunton, M. (ed.), *Charity, Self-Interest and Welfare in the English Past* (London: St Martin's Press, 1996).

Jutte, R., *Poverty and Deviance in Early Modern Europe* (Cambridge: Cambridge University Press, 1994).

King, S., 'Poor Relief and English Economic Development Reappraised', *EcHR*, 50(2), 1997, pp. 360–8.

King, S., 'Welfare Regimes and Welfare Regions in Britain and Europe, c. 1750s to 1860s', *Journal of Modern European History*, 9, 2011, pp. 42–64.

Kitching, C. J., 'Fire Disasters and Fire Relief in Sixteenth-century England: the Nantwich Fire of 1583', *Bulletin of the Institute of Historical Research*, 54, 1981, pp. 171–87.

Lane, J., *Apprenticeship in England, 1600-1914* (London: UCL Press, 1996).

Langley, C. R., *Worship, Civil War, and Community, 1638–1660* (Abingdon: Routledge, 2015).

Langley, C. R., "A Sweet Love-Token betwixt Christ and his Church': Kirk, Communion and the Search for Further Reformation, 1646–1658', in McCallum J. (ed.), *Scotland's Long Reformation: New Perspectives on Scottish Religion, c. 1500–c. 1660* (Leiden: Brill, 2016).

Langley, C. R., 'Caring for soldiers, veterans and families in Scotland, 1638–1651', *History*, 102, 2017, pp. 5–23.

Langley, C. R., '"So necessarie and charitable a worke"': Welfare, identity and Scottish prisoners of war in England, 1650–1655', in Appleby D. and A. Hopper (eds), *Battle-Scarred: Mortality, Medical Care and Military Welfare in the British Civil Wars* (Manchester: Manchester University Press, 2018).

Langley, C. R., 'Sheltering under the Covenant: The National Covenant, Orthodoxy and the Irish Rebellion, 1638–44', *Scottish Historical Review*, 96, 2017, pp. 137–60.

Lee Jr, M., 'Sir Richard Maitland of Lethington: A Christian Laird in the Age of Reformation', in Rabb, T. and J. Seigel (eds), *Action and Conviction in Early Modern Europe: Essays in Honor of E. H. Harbison* (Princeton: Princeton University Press, 1969).

Lepine, D., 'Cathedrals and Charity: Almsgiving at English Secular Cathedrals in the Later Middle Ages', *English Historical Review*, 126, 2011, pp. 1066–96.

Lindberg, C., *Beyond Charity: Reformation Initiatives for the Poor* (Minneapolis: Fortress, 1993).

Lis, C. and H. Soly, *Poverty and Capitalism in Pre-Industrial Europe* (Atlantic Highlands NJ: Harvester Press, 1978).

Looijesteijn, H. and M. H. D. van Leeuwen, 'Founding Large Charities and community building in the Dutch Republic, c. 1600–1800', *Scandinavian Economic History Review*, 62, 2014, pp. 17–34.

Lynch, M., *Edinburgh and the Reformation* (Edinburgh: John Donald, 1981).

Lynch, M., 'Introduction: Scottish Towns, 1500–1700', in Lynch, M. (ed.), *The Early Modern Town in Scotland* (London: Croom Helm, 1987).

Lythe, S. G. E., *The Economy of Scotland in its European Setting, 1550–1625* (Edinburgh: Oliver and Boyd, 1960).

McCallum, J., *Reforming the Scottish Parish: The Reformation in Fife, 1560–1640* (Farnham: Ashgate, 2010).

McCallum, J., 'Charity Doesn't Begin at Home: Ecclesiastical Poor Relief Beyond the Parish, 1560–1650', *Journal of Scottish Historical Studies*, 32(2), 2012, 107–26.

McCallum, J., '"Nurseries of the Poore": Hospitals and Almshouses in Early Modern Scotland', *Journal of Social History*, 48(2), 2014, pp. 427–49.

McCallum, J., 'Charity and Conflict: Poor Relief in Mid-Seventeenth-Century Dundee', *SHR*, 95, 2016, pp. 30–56.

McCallum, J. (ed.), *Scotland's Long Reformation: New Perspectives on Scottish Religion, c. 1500–c. 1660* (Leiden: Brill, 2016).

McCallum, J., '"Fatheris and Provisioners of the Puir": Kirk Sessions and Poor Relief in Post-Reformation Scotland', in McCallum (ed.), *Scotland's Long Reformation: New Perspectives on Scottish Religion, c. 1500–c. 1660* (Leiden: Brill, 2016).

MacDonald A. R., and J. McCallum, J., 'The Evidence for Early Seventeenth-Century Climate from Scottish Ecclesiastical Records', *Environment and History*, 19, 2013, pp. 487–509.

MacDonald, I. G., 'The Church in Gaelic Scotland before the Reformation', in Ó hAnnracháin, T. and R. Armstrong (eds), *Christianities in the Early Modern Celtic World* (Basingstoke: Palgrave Macmillan, 2015).

McKee, E. A., *John Calvin on the Diaconate and Liturgical Almsgiving* (Geneva: Droz, 1984).

McPherson, J. M., *The Kirk's Care of the Poor: with special reference to the North-East of Scotland* (Aberdeen: John Avery, 1941).

McIntosh, M. K., 'Local Responses to the Poor in late Medieval and Tudor England', *C&C*, 3, 1988, pp. 209–45.

McIntosh, M. K., *Poor Relief in England, 1350–1600* (Cambridge: Cambridge University Press, 2011).

McIntosh, M. K., *Poor Relief and Community in Hadleigh, Suffolk 1547–1600* (Hatfield: University of Hertfordshire Press, 2013).

McIntosh, M. K., 'Poor relief in Elizabethan English communities: an analysis of Collectors' accounts', *EcHR*, 67(2), 2014, pp. 331–57.

Martz, L., *Poverty and Welfare in Habsburg Spain* (Cambridge: Cambridge University Press, 1983).

Matar, N., 'Introduction: England and Mediterranean Captivity, 1577–1704', in Viktus D. J. (ed.), *Piracy, Slavery, and Redemption: Barbary Captivity Narratives from Early Modern England* (New York: Columbia University Press, 2001).

Maxwell, A., *The History of Old Dundee* (Edinburgh and Dundee, 1884).

Meerkerk, E. and D. Teeuwen, 'The Stability of Voluntarism. Financing Social Care in Early Modern Dutch Towns Compared with the English Poor Law, c. 1600–1800', *European Review of Economic History*, 18, 2013, pp. 82–105.

Meikle M., *The Scottish People, 1490–1625* (Great Britain: Lulu.com, 2013).

Mitchison, R., 'The Making of the Old Scottish Poor Law', *P&P*, 63, May 1974, pp. 58–93.

Mitchison, R., 'A parish and its poor: Yester in the second half of the seventeenth century', *Transactions of the East Lothian Antiquarian & Field Naturalists' Society*, 14, 1974, pp. 15–28.

Mitchison, R., 'The Creation of the Disablement Rule in the Scottish Poor Law', in Smout, T. C. (ed.), *The Search for Wealth and Stability: Essays in Economic and Social History presented to M. W. Flinn* (London: Macmillan, 1979).

Mitchison, R., 'North and South: The Development of the Gulf in Poor Law Practice', in Houston and Whyte (eds), *Scottish Society, 1500–1800* (Cambridge: Cambridge University Press, 1989).

Mitchison, R., *Coping with Destitution: Poverty and Relief in Western Europe* (Toronto: University of Toronto Press, 1991).

Mitchison, R., 'Poor Relief and Health Care in Scotland, 1575–1710', in Grell, O. P. and A. Cunningham (eds), *Health Care and Poor Relief in Protestant Europe, 1500–1700* (London: Routledge, 1997).

Mitchison, R., *The Old Poor Law in Scotland: The Experience of Poverty, 1574–1845* (Edinburgh: Edinburgh University Press, 2000).

Mollat, M., *The Poor in the Middle Ages: An Essay in Social History* (transl. A. Goldhammer, A.) (New Haven: Yale University Press, 1978).

Murdock, G., *Beyond Calvin: The Intellectual, Political and Cultural World of Europe's Reformed Churches* (Basingstoke: Palgrave Macmillan, 2004).

Mullan, D. G., *Scottish Puritanism, 1590–1638* (Oxford: Oxford University Press, 2000).

Murdoch, S., 'The Repatriation of Capital to Scotland: A case study of seventeenth-century Dutch testaments and miscellaneous notarial instruments', in Varricchio, M. (ed.), *Back to Caledonia: Scottish homecomings from the seventeenth century to the present* (Edinburgh: John Donald, 2012).

Mutch, A., 'Data mining the archives: the emergence of separate books of account in the Church of Scotland 1608–1800', *Scottish Archives,* 18, 2012, pp. 78–94.

Mutch, A., *Religion and National Identity: Governing Scottish Presbyterianism in the Eighteenth Century* (Edinburgh: Edinburgh University Press, 2015).

Olson, J., 'Continuity or Radical Change? Care of the Poor, Medieval and Early Modern', in Muldoon, J. (ed.), *Bridging the Medieval-Modern Divide: Medieval Themes in the World of the Reformation* (Farnham: Ashgate, 2013).

Oram, R., '"It cannot be decernit quha are clean and quha are foulle" Responses to Epidemic Disease in Sixteenth and Seventeenth-Century Scotland', *Renaissance and Reformation,* 30(4), 2007, pp. 13–39.

Parker, C. H., *The Reformation of Community: Social Welfare and Calvinist Charity in Holland, 1572–1620* (Cambridge: Cambridge University Press, 1998).

Parker, C. H., 'Calvinism and Poor Relief in Reformation Holland', in Safley, M. (ed.), *The Reformation of Charity: The Secular and the Religious in Early Modern Poor Relief* (Boston: Brill, 2003).

Parker, G., 'The "Kirk by Law Established" and the Origins of the "Taming of Scotland": Saint Andrews 1559-1600', in Mentzer, R. (ed.), *Sin and the Calvinists: Morals Control and the Consistory in the Reformed Tradition* (Kirksville: Truman State University Press, 1994).

Patriquin, L, *Agrarian Capitalism and Poor Relief in England, 1500–1860: Rethinking the Origins of the Welfare State* (Basingstoke: Palgrave Macmillan, 2007).

Pollman, J., 'Off the Record: Problems in the Quantification of Calvinist Church Discipline', *Sixteenth Century Journal,* 33, 2002, pp. 423–38.

Pugh, W. J., 'Catholics, Protestants, and Testamentary Charity in Seventeenth-Century Lyon and Nîmes', *French Historical Studies,* 11, 1980, pp. 479–504.

Pullan, B. 'Catholics and the Poor in Early Modern Europe', *Transactions of the Royal Historical Society,* 5th Series, 26, 1976, pp. 15–34.

Pullan, B., 'Support and redeem: charity and poor relief in Italian cities from the fourteenth to the seventeenth century', *C&C,* 3, 1988, pp. 177–208.

Pullan, B., 'Charity and Poor Relief in Early Modern Italy', in Daunton, M. (ed.), *Charity, Self-Interest and Welfare in the English Past* (London: St Martin's Press, 1996).

Rawcliffe, C.,'"A word from our sponsor": Advertising the patron in the medieval hospital', in Henderson, J. *et al.* (eds), *The Impact of Hospitals, 300–2000* (Bern: Peter Lang, 2007).

Rhodes, E., 'Property and Piety: Donations to Holy Trinity Church, St Andrews', in McCallum, J. (ed.), *Scotland's Long Reformation: New Perspectives on Scottish Religion, c. 1500–c. 1660* (Leiden: Brill, 2016).

Roberts, P., 'Agencies Human and Divine: Fire in French Cities, 1520–1720', in Naphy, W. G. and P. Roberts (eds), *Fear in Early Modern Society* (Manchester: Manchester University Press, 1997).

Rubin, M., *Charity and Community in Medieval Cambridge* (Cambridge: Cambridge University Press, 1987).

Rushton, N., 'Monastic charitable provision in Tudor England: quantifying and qualifying poor relief in the early sixteenth century', *C&C*, 16, 2001, pp. 9–44.

Rushton, N., 'The Forms and Functions of Monastic Poor Relief in Late Medieval and Early Sixteenth Century England', in Scott, A. (ed.), *Experiences of Charity, 1250–1650* (Farnham: Ashgate, 2015).

Ryrie, A., *The Origins of the Scottish Reformation* (Manchester: Manchester University Press, 2006).

Ryrie, A., *Being Protestant in Reformation Britain* (Oxford: Oxford University Press, 2013).

Safley, T. M. (ed.), *The Reformation of Charity: The Secular and the Religious in Early Modern Poor Relief* (Boston: Brill, 2003).

Scott, A. (ed.), *Experiences of Poverty in Late-Medieval and Early Modern England and France* (Farnham: Ashgate, 2012).

Scott, A., 'Experiences of Poverty', in Scott, A. (ed.), *Experiences of Poverty in Late-Medieval and Early Modern England and France* (Farnham: Ashgate, 2012).

Scott, A. (ed.), *Experiences of Charity, 1250–1650* (Farnham: Ashgate, 2015).

Slack, P., *Poverty and Policy in Tudor and Stuart England* (London: Longman, 1988).

Smith, A. M., *The Guildry of Dundee* (Dundee: Abertay Historical Society, 2005).

Smout, T. C, *A History of the Scottish People, 1560–1830* (London: Collins, 1969).

Smout, T. C., 'Peasant and Lord in Scotland: Institutions Controlling Scottish Rural Society, 1500–1800', *Recueils de la Societe Jean Bodin*, 44, 1987, pp. 499–524.

Solar, P., 'Poor Relief and English Economic Development before the Industrial Revolution', *EcHR*, 48, 1995, pp. 1–22.

Sondergard, S. L., 'Rediscovering William Lauder's Poetic Advocacy of the Poor', *Studies in Scottish Literature*, 29, 1996, pp. 158–73.

Spence, C., *Women, Credit and Debt in Early Modern Scotland* (Manchester: Manchester University Press, 2016).

Sprunger, M. S., 'Mennonites and Sectarian Poor Relief in Golden-Age Amsterdam', in Safley, M. (ed.), *The Reformation of Charity: The Secular and the Religious in Early Modern Poor Relief* (Boston: Brill, 2003).

Steven, W., *History of George Heriot's Hospital* (Edinburgh: Bell and Bradfute, 1859).

Stevenson, D., *The Scottish Revolution, 1637–44*, 2nd edn, (Edinburgh: John Donald, 2003).

Stevenson, D., *Revolution and Counter-Revolution in Scotland, 1644–51*, 2nd edn (Edinburgh: John Donald, 2003).

Stewart, L., 'Poor Relief in Edinburgh and the Famine of 1621–24', *International Review of Scottish Studies*, 30, 2005, pp. 5–41.

Stewart, L., 'Power and Faith in Early Modern Scotland', *SHR*, 92, Supplement, 2013, pp. 25–37.

Stewart, L., *Rethinking the Scottish Revolution: Covenanted Scotland, 1637–1651* (Oxford: Oxford University Press, 2016).

Symonds, D. A., 'Death, Birth and Marriage in Early Modern Scotland', in Foyster E., and C. Whatley (eds.), *A History of Everyday Life in Scotland, 1600 to 1800* (Edinburgh: Edinburgh University Press, 2010).

Thane, P., 'Social Histories of Old Age and Aging', *Journal of Social History*, 37, 2003, pp. 93–111.

Todd, M., *The Culture of Protestantism in Early Modern Scotland* (New Haven: Yale University Press, 2002).

Tyson, R. E., 'Poverty and Poor Relief in Aberdeen, 1680–1705', *Scottish Archives*, 8, 2002, pp. 33–42.

van Leeuwen, M. H. D., 'Logic of Charity: Poor Relief in Preindustrial Europe', *Journal of Interdisciplinary History*, 24, 1994, pp. 589–613.

van Leeuwen, M. H. D., 'Giving in early modern history: philanthropy in Amsterdam in the Golden Age', *C&C*, 27(2), 2012, pp. 301–43.

van Leeuwen, M. H. D., E. Meerkerk and L. H. van Voss, 'Provisions for the elderly in north-western Europe: an international comparison of almshouses, sixteenth–twentieth centuries', *Scandinavian Economic History Review*, 62, 2014, pp. 1–16.

Verschuur, M., *Politics or Religion? The Reformation in Perth, 1540–1570* (Edinburgh: Dunedin, 2006).

Wales, T., 'Poverty, poor relief and the life-cycle: some evidence from seventeenth-century Norfolk', in Smith, R. (ed.), *Land, Kinship and Life-Cycle* (Cambridge: Cambridge University Press, 1984).

Walker, G., 'The Popular Voice in Sir David Lyndsay's Satire of the Thrie Estaitis', *Studies in Scottish Literature*, 40(1), 2014, pp. 39–54.

Wandel, L. P., *Always Among Us: Images of the Poor in Zwingli's Zurich* (Cambridge: Cambridge University Press, 1990).

Wandel, L. P., 'Social Welfare', in Hillerbrand H. (ed.), *The Oxford Encyclopedia of the Reformation* (Oxford: Oxford University Press, 1996).

Whyte, I., 'The Occupation Structure of Scottish Burghs in the Late Seventeenth Century', in Lynch (ed.), *The Early Modern Town in Scotland* (London: Croom Helm, 1987).

Whyte, I., 'Urbanization in Early Modern Scotland: A Preliminary Analysis', *Scottish Social and Economic History*, 9, 1989, pp. 21–37.

Whyte, I., *Scotland Before the Industrial Revolution* (London: Longman, 1995).

Whyte, I., *Scotland's Society and Economy in Transition,* c. *1500–*c. *1760* (Basingstoke: Palgrave Macmillan, 1997).

Whyte, I., 'Poverty or Prosperity? Rural Society in Lowland Scotland in the Late Sixteenth and Early Seventeenth Centuries', *Scottish Social and Economic History*, 19, 1998, pp. 19–32.

Whyte, I. and K. Whyte, 'Geographical Mobility in a Seventeenth-Century Scottish Rural Community', *Local Population Studies*, 32, 1984, pp. 45–53.

Whyte, I. and K. Whyte, 'Debt and Credit, Poverty and Prosperity in a Seventeenth-Century Rural Scottish Community', in Mitchison, R. and P. Roebuck (eds), *Economy and Society in Scotland and Ireland, 1500–1939* (Edinburgh: John Donald, 1988).

Wilbraham, K. and C. Lodge, 'Responses to Poverty in Ayrshire, 1574–1845', *Scottish Archives*, 8, 2002, pp. 57–70.

Wooding, L., 'Charity, Community and Reformation Propaganda', *Reformation*, 11, 2006, pp. 131–69.

Wormald, J., *Court, Kirk, and Community: Scotland, 1470–1625* (Edinburgh: Edinburgh University Press, 1981).

Wormald, J., 'Reformed and Godly Scotland?', in Devine, T. M. and J. Wormald (eds), *The Oxford Handbook of Modern Scottish History* (Oxford: Oxford University Press, 2012).

Wrightson, K., *Earthly Necessities: Economic Lives in Early Modern Britain, 1470–1750* (London: Penguin, 2002).

Wrightson, K. and D. Levine, *Poverty and Piety in an English Village: Terling, 1525–1700* (New York: Academic Press, 1979).

Young, J., 'The Covenanters and the Scottish Parliament, 1639–51: the Rule of the Godly and the second Scottish Reformation', in Boran, E. and C. Gribben (eds), *Enforcing Reformation in Ireland and Scotland, 1550–1700* (Aldershot: Ashgate, 2006).

Young, J., '"Escaping Massacre": refugees in Scotland in the aftermath of the 1641 Ulster Rebellion', in Edwards, D., P. Lenihan and C. Tait (eds), *Age of Atrocity. Violence and Political Conflict in Early Modern Ireland* (Dublin: Four Courts, 2007).

UNPUBLISHED THESES

Brown, H., 'Lay Piety in Later Medieval Lothian, *c.* 1306–*c.* 1513' (unpublished PhD thesis, University of Edinburgh, 2006).

Brown, J., 'The social, political and economic influences of the Edinburgh merchant elite, 1600–1638' (unpublished PhD thesis, University of Edinburgh, 1985).

Cornell, H., 'Gender, Sex and Social Control: East Lothian, 1610–1640' (unpublished PhD thesis, University of Edinburgh, 2012).

DesBrisay, G. 'Authority and Discipline in Aberdeen: 1650–1700' (unpublished PhD thesis, University of St Andrews, 1989).

Fitch, Audrey-Beth, 'The Search for Salvation: Lay Faith in Scotland, 1480 to 1560' (unpublished PhD thesis, University of Glasgow, 1994).

Flett, I., 'The conflict of the Reformation and democracy in the Geneva of Scotland, 1443–1610: an introduction to edited texts of documents relating to the Burgh of Dundee' (unpublished MPhil thesis, University of St Andrews, 1981).

Goodare, J., 'Parliament and Society in Scotland, 1560–1603' (unpublished PhD thesis, University of Edinburgh, 1989).

Macleod, D., 'Servants to St. Mungo: The Church in Sixteenth-Century Glasgow' (unpublished PhD thesis, University of Guelph, 2013).

Smith, M., 'The Presbytery of St Andrews 1586–1605: A Study and Annotated Edition of the Register of the Minutes of the Presbytery of St Andrews' (unpublished PhD thesis, University of St Andrews, 1985).

Tapscott, E., 'Propaganda and Persuasion in the Early Scottish Reformation, *c.* 1527–1557' (unpublished PhD thesis, University of St Andrews, 2013).

Index

CPSIA information can be obtained
at www.ICGtesting.com
Printed in the USA
BVHW061554300620
582685BV00002B/12

9 781474 474788